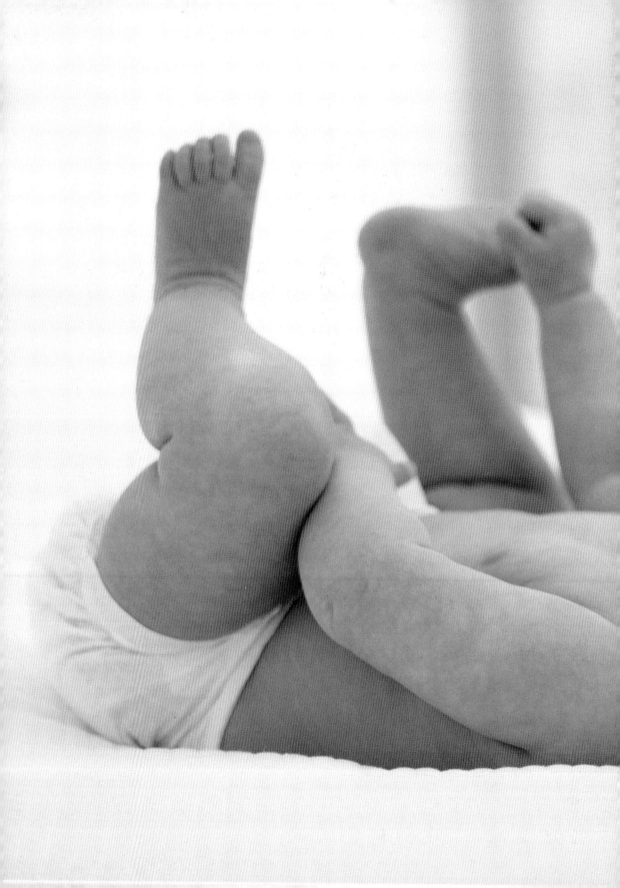

# complete baby and childcare

Dr Miriam Stoppard

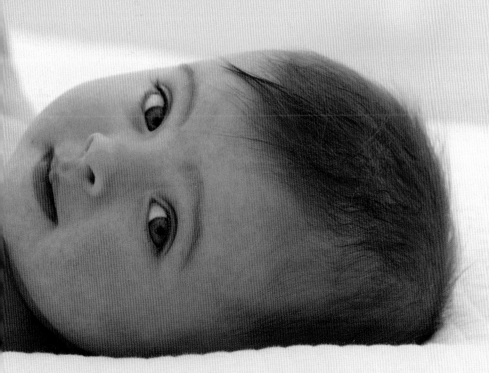

LONDON, NEW YORK,
MELBOURNE, DELHI

*For Esmé, Maggie and Evie,*
*Marley and Elia*

**Medical Consultant** Dr W John Fysh MBBS,
FRCP, FRCPCH

**Managing Editors** Penny Warren, Esther Ripley
**Managing Art Editor** Marianne Markham
**Senior Art Editor** Glenda Fisher
**Editors** Jinny Johnson, Andrea Bagg,
Diana Vowles
**Production Editors** Luca Frassinetti, Ben Marcus
**Production Controller** Mandy Inness
**Special Photography** Vanessa Davies
**Jacket Design** Smith and Gilmour
**Publisher** Peggy Vance

**Produced for Dorling Kindersley by**
**Cooling Brown**
**Creative Director** Arthur Brown
**Editor** Jemima Dunne
**Designers** Tish Jones, Peter Cooling
**Art Direction for Photography** Emma Forge

First published by Dorling Kindersley in 1995

This revised edition published in
Great Britain in 2008
by Dorling Kindersley Limited
80 Strand, London WC2R 0RL
A Penguin Company

A CIP catalogue record for this book is available
from the British Library.

ISBN 978-1-4053-2975-0

Reproduced by MDP, Bath, UK
Printed and bound in China by Sheck Wah Tong

Discover more at
**www.dk.com**

# Preface

There would hardly seem to be room for another baby book. Having worked on this subject for more than 30 years, however, I've always felt that even the best baby books have gaps. Very few, for instance, deal with three- to five-year-olds. I also feel sure that women who have children with special needs or children with chronic ailments and disabilities feel short-changed by most baby books, including mine, because their babies aren't given enough space or emphasis. Fathers continue to be a neglected group, and there's a tendency to overlook the impact of a new addition on the family as a whole. With more and more families having two working parents, choosing childcare is more important than ever.

In my previous books there was never enough space to deal with important subjects like caring for twins, to illustrate the treatment of illnesses, from glue ear to hydrocephalus, and to go fully into complicated subjects like baby first aid. Most of all I never felt that I had the freedom to talk enough about a baby's physical, mental, and social development – a subject that's crucially important to parents. For instance, close, loving maternal bonding affects how a newborn baby's brain grows. Without that bond a baby may grow up disruptive, slow to learn, difficult to quieten, and even at risk of teenage delinquency.

The scope of this book has given me the chance to plug some of those gaps and to enlarge on those two very important preschool years. Three-year-olds make huge strides in all areas of development when they're introduced to preschool classes and need a great deal of patience, understanding, and support from parents if they're going to realize their full potential – which is every child's birthright, after all. So as well as dealing with the everyday aspects of baby and childcare, this book encompasses the acquisition of skills, your role as teacher, and – something I've longed to write about – the differences between boy and girl babies, to offer parents guidance on how to treasure and nurture the best parts of being a girl and being a boy.

In 30 years of writing about childcare, my aim has always been to help parents feel independent, confident, and free to follow their instincts – which are nearly always right. In this new edition of my book, my goal remains the same and I have taken the opportunity to bring the information right up to date and include all the latest advice and research on many aspects of childcare. While this book isn't definitive, it's as near complete as I've ever hoped for.

# Contents

# Introduction

Whether you're a mother expecting your first baby, you have just given birth, or you're an expectant or new father, you may be feeling apprehensive about your new role. Don't worry: while parenting may be one of the most responsible and challenging jobs there is, it's also one of the most rewarding.

## Your new baby

You have just experienced the creation of newborn life. Your baby is probably smaller than you imagined, and she may seem very vulnerable. You may be overwhelmed by feelings of joy, but you'll also be anxious to know whether your baby is all right, and whether the sounds and movements she makes are normal. Your midwife or doctor will be able to reassure you, and you will probably be surprised at just how much your new baby can do.

## Your young baby

In the first months of life your child depends on you for everything: you will have to feed, dress, and change him, and carry him around. If he's your first child, you're bound to be nervous. You may wonder whether he's taking enough milk and putting on weight fast enough, whether he's waking too often in the night, or why he seems to cry so much. But soon your confidence will increase and you'll find you know what to do.

## Your older baby

You'll be surprised at how quickly caring for your baby becomes second nature; in fact, you will hardly believe there was once a time when you didn't know how to change a nappy! You'll be surprised, too, at how quickly your baby is growing and maturing, both socially and mentally, and how her physical skills are also developing. Soon she'll be crawling, then walking and there are all sorts of ways of helping and encouraging her development.

## Your toddler and preschooler

Sharing your child's pleasure in new skills and knowledge is one of the great joys of parenthood. It's also the most important thing you can do to promote your child's development: physically, by allowing him to explore his own capabilities in a challenging and safe environment; mentally, by taking time to talk to and play with him; and socially, by providing him with the love and security that will make him a well adjusted and happy child. In these early years, play is your child's main tool for learning. By understanding how he learns and develops you can help him to get the most from play and from his toys.

## Family life

However much getting married or deciding to live with your partner may have changed your life, the birth of your child will change it far more. You need to balance your partner's needs and the needs of your baby with your own. If you've had twins, you'll be very much in need of practical help and support. Your extended family may suddenly start to figure more largely in your life. Whether you see this as a good thing will depend on all sorts of personal factors, but your child will undoubtedly benefit from the loving interest of her relatives.

## Special needs

All parents want their children to grow up into happy, well-adjusted adults, and to live rich and fulfilling lives. If your child has special needs – and this applies to a wide variety of children, from those who are very gifted, to those born with a chronic physical condition such as cerebral palsy – then achieving this is going to require a lot of extra effort from you. If your child is ill, then at the same time you will have to cope with your own feelings of confusion, anxiety, and perhaps of guilt. Over the months that follow the diagnosis of your child's condition, however, you will learn a lot about what you can do to help your child, and you will almost certainly cope better than you had thought possible. There are many support networks available so be sure to make use of them.

## Medicine and healthcare

You are responsible for promoting your child's good health, recognizing when she's ill, and acting accordingly. Your child can't always tell you what's wrong with her, but you will become sensitive to the signs that tell you something is amiss, and you'll learn when you can look after her yourself and when you need to send for a doctor. It's your duty as a parent to learn basic first aid procedures, and it's best to attend a training course rather than try to learn from a book. (St John Ambulance, St Andrew's Ambulance, and the British Red Cross run courses; you will find your local branch in the telephone book.) Be sure to learn emergency first aid procedures by heart, and refresh your memory often.

# Your new baby

Your feelings on the birth of your new baby are likely to be pride, wonder, and exhilaration mixed with exhaustion. You may feel fiercely attached to your baby immediately, or bonding may take a little longer. You'll almost certainly be surprised at her appearance: her oddly shaped head, wrinkled face, and tiny hands and feet.

From the moment of birth your baby will exhibit reflexes and behaviour that help her survive. In such things as her sleeping patterns and crying bouts you'll see the beginnings of a personality.

The first question in every new parent's mind is "Is she all right?", and medical staff will carry out tests straight after the birth and in the first few days to reassure you. Your baby will be given all the special attention she needs. If she's premature or small for her dates, she may need to be kept in a special care unit, but you'll still be able to bond with her and take part in her care.

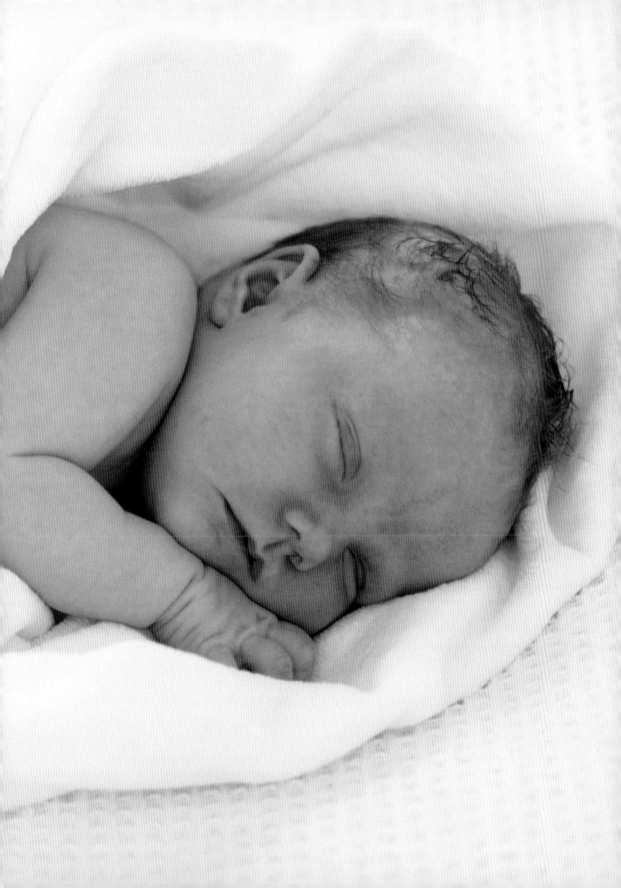

## Loving your baby

Most mothers find they establish a bond with their newborn babies within the first 72 hours, but a "bond" doesn't necessarily mean instantaneous and ecstatic love at first sight.

Taking care of your new baby's physical needs is so exhausting that it's easy to forget she also has an active emotional life. In the long term the most serious damage to a baby's health may stem from not having enough love and attention. So, in the next few weeks and months, heap as much love upon your baby as you can.

Mother love is partially hormonal, so if you don't feel it immediately it's not your fault. Mother love usually makes itself felt as your milk comes in, about 72 hours after the birth, although it may come in later and it may grow quite gradually. One of the hormones that stimulates lactation is also, in part, responsible for mother love.

Some mothers are shocked to find that don't feel a rush of maternal love when they first hold their babies. This may be due to many things, such as complications with the delivery, unrealistic expectations of childbirth, sheer exhaustion, fluctuating hormone levels, and even the mother's own experience in early childhood. Maternal "indifference" can last from an hour to a week, but rarely much longer.

# Your newborn

Whatever you had expected – bigger, smaller, quieter, less slippery – your baby will surprise and delight you. You might think your newborn is oblivious to the world about her, but babies rapidly build up a vocabulary of sensory experiences from birth. When awake, she'll be alert and listening. She can respond when spoken to, recognize you by smell, and has an intent gaze.

## Relating to your baby

At birth your baby can recognize a human face, and she will move her head in response to noise. She is born wanting to talk and will "converse" with you if you talk animatedly about 20–25cm (8–10in) from her face where she can see you clearly. She'll react to your smile by moving her mouth, nodding, sticking out her tongue, or jerking her body.

The need for physical contact throughout childhood is well documented, and this is especially true of the first weeks of life. Most newborn babies spend much of their time asleep, so it's important that you're there to hold and care for your baby when she's awake. Don't be afraid to pick her up – babies are stronger than you think and the important thing is to give her lots of cuddles. Even if your baby is in an incubator, ask to be able to stroke her and change her nappy.

## Breathing

Apart from crying, you may not hear anything more from your baby because it can be difficult to hear a newborn's light breathing. In some cases a baby may even stop breathing entirely for a few seconds, but this isn't abnormal. All babies make strange noises when they breathe – usually a noisy snuffling sound – and their breathing is often irregular.

Your baby's lungs are still weak, which means that her breathing is naturally much shallower than yours or mine. This is nothing to worry about, as her lungs will gradually get stronger each day.

## Suckling

For the first three days after your baby's birth, your breasts produce not milk, but colostrum, a thin, yellow fluid that contains water, protein, sugar, vitamins, minerals, and antibodies for protection against infectious diseases. During her first 72 hours of life, colostrum helps protect your baby against infections. To stimulate your breasts to produce milk you need to feed her frequently; your baby's sucking action stimulates hormones that, in turn, stimulate milk production. Even if you don't intend to breastfeed, it's a good idea to suckle your baby as soon as she's born, because the colostrum will be beneficial to her, and the act of suckling will help you bond with your baby.

As soon as your baby's born you can put her to your breast. She'll have a natural sucking reflex, and the sucking action will encourage your body to produce the hormone oxytocin. This hormone makes the uterus contract and expel the placenta. Touch your baby's cheek on the side nearest your nipple to stimulate her rooting reflex. Rather than just sucking on the nipple, her lips should be on the breast tissue with the whole of the nipple in her mouth.

## Sharing with your partner

It's important for father and baby to bond, too, and touch, smell, and sound are good ways to do this. He should hold his baby soon after the birth and she'll get to know his smell and the sound of his voice. In fact, if he talks to the baby while she's in the uterus, she will recognize her father's voice when she's born.

Encourage your partner to be involved in your baby's care, and this will help him build his relationship with her as he takes a share in day-to-day routines such as bathing and nappy changing. Even if you're breastfeeding, your partner can bottlefeed her sometimes using expressed breastmilk, or he can take her after feeding for winding. You can both spend time cuddling your baby against your naked skin – she'll love to feel and smell your body and hear your heart beating.

# Your baby's first breath

**In the uterus your baby's lungs are redundant – she gets all the oxygen she needs from the placenta, so the lungs are collapsed.**

The very first time your baby takes a breath her lungs expand, and the increased pressure in them shuts a valve just beyond the heart, so that the blood that used to pass to the placenta for oxygenation now goes directly to her lungs. These two crucial steps make her an independent being, able to survive without you, and they happen in an instant.

Nothing should interfere with your baby's ability to take her first breath. That's why doctors and midwives clear the baby's air passages immediately and if the first breath is delayed they resuscitate her.

Newborn babies cannot make vitamin K so your baby will be given vitamin K soon after birth.

◀ **BONDING** Your baby will be happiest next to your skin, where she can feel your warmth and hear your heartbeat.

## Spots and rashes

Most newborn babies have harmless skin irritations such as spots and rashes in the first few days. They generally clear up when the skin begins to stabilize at about three weeks old.

**Milia** These small white spots, found mainly on the bridge of the nose, but also elsewhere on the face, come from a temporary blockage of the sebaceous glands, which secrete sebum to lubricate the skin. Never squeeze them – they'll disappear of their own accord within a few days.

**Heat rash** If your baby is too warm she may get small red spots, especially on her face. Make sure that she isn't over-wrapped in clothing and/or blankets, and that the room temperature is well regulated (see p.81).

**Urticaria** This is a type of rash in which the spots have a white centre and a red halo (see p.292). It's quite common in the first week, and it may recur for a month or so. There's no need to treat it; it'll disappear quite quickly.

# Your baby's appearance

When you're given your baby to hold for the first time you'll probably be surprised by her appearance. Although your baby is undoubtedly a bundle of joy, many parents mistakenly expect a clean and placid bundle, similar to the babies who appear in advertisements for baby products. As you now suddenly discover, real life is a little bit different.

**Skin** Your baby's skin may be covered in a whitish, greasy substance called vernix, which is a natural barrier cream that prevents her skin from becoming waterlogged. It use to be wiped off meticulously, but now it is left on as it gives your baby some natural protection against minor skin irritations and helps to keep her warm; it's absorbed naturally by her skin.

Your baby's skin may look rather blotchy; this is because the tiny blood vessels are unstable. Black children are often light-skinned at birth, but the skin begins to get darker as it starts to produce melanin, its natural pigment; it will reach its permanent colour by about six months.

**Head** Your baby's skull is made up of four large plates that don't fuse, so they can move across each other, especially during labour when your baby's head is compressed by pressure from your vaginal walls. The sliding skull bones enable her to pass through the birth canal without hazard, though her head may become slightly elongated or misshapen in the process. This is entirely normal, and does not affect the brain. There may also be some bruising or swelling after the birth, but it will disappear during the first few days or weeks.

The soft spots on the top of your baby's skull where the bones are still not joined are called the fontanelles. The skull bones won't fuse completely until your baby is about two. Be careful, especially with a very young baby, not to press the fontanelles, although they are quite robust.

**Eyes** Your baby may not be able to open her eyes straight away due to puffiness caused by pressure on her head during birth. This pressure may also have broken some tiny blood vessels on your baby's eyes, causing small, red, triangular marks in the whites of the eyes. Entirely harmless, they require no treatment and will disappear within a couple of weeks. "Sticky eye", which results in a yellow discharge around the eyelids, is quite common. It's not serious, but check with your doctor if it persists for more than a day or so, as it may need treatment with antibiotics.

Your baby can see clearly up to a distance of 20–25cm (8–10in), but beyond that cannot focus both her eyes at the same time, and this may cause her to squint, or look cross-eyed. Both of these conditions will clear up as her eye muscles grow stronger (usually within a month). If your baby is still squinting (see p.95) at six months, or the squint worsens, mention it to your doctor. Most newborn babies' eyes are blue regardless of race, and your baby's eye colour is likely to change after birth because it is only then that babies acquire melanin, the body's natural pigment.

**Hair** Some babies are born with a full head of hair, while others are completely bald. The colour of your baby's hair at birth is not necessarily the permanent colour she will acquire later. The fine downy hair that many babies have on their bodies at birth is called lanugo, and this will often fall off soon after birth.

**Genitals** Many babies, both male and female, appear to have enlarged genitals shortly after birth, and babies of both genders may have enlarged "breasts" and even produce milk. This is due to the massive increase in hormone levels that you've experienced just before giving birth, some of which will have passed into your baby's bloodstream. With a baby boy this can lead to an enlarged scrotum too. This is not abnormal, and the swelling will gradually subside. A baby girl may have a swollen vulva or clitoris and a small "period" shortly after birth.

**Umbilicus** The umbilical cord, which is moist and bluish-white at birth, is clamped with forceps and then cut with scissors. Only a short length of cord remains, which dries and becomes almost black within 24 hours. The stump will shrivel up and fall off about seven days after her birth, but your baby will feel no pain.

# Umbilical hernia

**Some babies develop a small swelling near the navel, called an umbilical hernia. This is caused by weak abdominal muscles that allow the intestines to push through a little.**

Umbilical hernias are most obvious when the abdominal muscles are used for crying. These hernias are very common, and virtually always clear up within two years. If your baby has one and it enlarges or persists, check with your doctor.

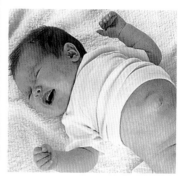

▲ SITE OF THE SWELLING A hernia may form where the umbilical cord entered your baby's abdomen because there's a gap in the abdominal muscles at that point.

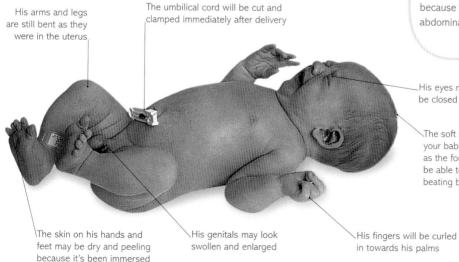

His arms and legs are still bent as they were in the uterus

The umbilical cord will be cut and clamped immediately after delivery

His eyes may look puffy and be closed most of the time

The soft spots at the top of your baby's skull are known as the fontanelles. You may be able to see a pulse beating beneath the scalp

The skin on his hands and feet may be dry and peeling because it's been immersed in liquid for so long

His genitals may look swollen and enlarged

His fingers will be curled in towards his palms

# About birthmarks

**If you haven't found a blemish anywhere on your baby's body, it's probably because you haven't looked long enough.**

Virtually every child is born with some type of birthmark, no matter how tiny. Most marks will fade and disappear on their own by the time your child is three years old, although some of them may remain and increase in size. Both my sons had stork bite, or salmon patch, birthmarks at the back of the neck just under the hairline (a very common place to find them).

Other likely places are the eyelids, the forehead, and the neck, although one might be found on any part of your baby's skin.

Superficial birthmarks are nothing to worry about. They do no harm and need no treatment.

## Measurements

Your baby's weight, length, and head circumference will be measured to give an indication of her maturity and development. These measurements can be used as a base-line for her future development. Although routine measurements are inevitably compared to "the average", don't worry about this too much. An average is just an arithmetical calculation, so the "average child" is only theoretical and doesn't exist.

**Weight** The weight range for babies born around their expected time is 2.5–4.5kg (5½–10lb). If you're tall or heavy or if you're diabetic, your baby is likely to be on the heavy side.

Women who suffer from chronic hypertension or kidney disease, or who had pre-eclampsia, or who smoked during pregnancy are likely to have lighter babies. A woman whose pregnancy is shorter than 40 weeks is also likely to have a lighter baby. Girls generally weigh slightly less than boys, and twins are each likely to weigh less than a single baby.

It's normal for your baby to lose weight in the first few days after birth as her body adjusts to new feeding requirements. She must now process her own food, and it will take a while for her to feed consistently. The usual weight loss at this time is about ten per cent of the birth weight. After a few days, when your baby settles into her feeding you can expect her weight to begin increasing again.

The significance of a baby's weight gain is what it tells us of her overall physical health. Steady weight gain indicates that her food intake is sufficient and is being absorbed, while poor or erratic weight gain or weight loss signals that food intake is insufficient or that it isn't being absorbed.

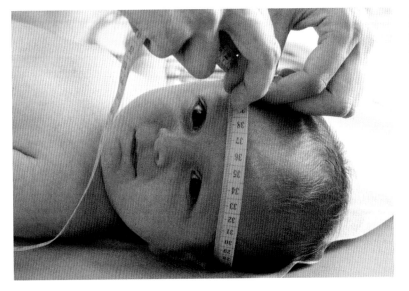

**Head circumference** Your baby's head is disproportionately large in comparison to her body size, taking up one quarter of her entire length. The younger a baby is, the larger her head is in proportion to the rest of her body. The average circumference of a newborn's head is about 35cm (14in). Measuring head circumference is an essential part of the examination of a baby

◀ **MEASUREMENTS** Your baby's head circumference and her length will be measured, and she will also be weighed.

as the growth of the head reflects the growth of the brain. An unusually large or small circumference may be an indication of an abnormality.

**Chest and abdomen** The circumference of your baby's chest will be smaller than that of her head. Her stomach might appear to be very large to you, and even distended, but given the weakness in her abdominal muscles, this is to be expected.

## The first nappies

Your baby's stools and urine may not look as you expect them to, and if you have a baby girl there may be some vaginal discharge. None of these necessarily means that something is wrong.

**Stools** Your baby's first bowel movement will consist of meconium, which is mainly digested mucus and looks blackish-green. Some of this is accumulated from swallowing amniotic fluid while inside your uterus. Your baby should pass her first meconium stool within the first 24 hours, and it's not unusual for her next bowel movement to be two days later – especially if you're breastfeeding (check, however, that your baby is wetting her nappy regularly). After the fourth day she may pass four or five motions daily.

You'll notice that the colour and composition of her stools change from dark, greenish-black sticky meconium to greenish brown, and then to a yellow semi-solid type. If you're bottlefeeding your baby, her stools might resemble scrambled eggs.

Most babies fill their nappies as soon as they've eaten, owing to a perfectly healthy gastrocolic reflex, which makes the bowel empty itself as soon as food enters the stomach. Some babies pass motions much less frequently, but as long as your baby does not have to strain too much and her motions are soft and a normal colour, there's no need for concern. If her motions are infrequent or hard, try giving her a small amount of cooled, boiled water (one tablespoon) two or three times a day.

**Urine** A newborn baby passes little urine in the first 24–48 hours because she isn't taking in much fluid. When she does, her urine will contain substances called urates that may stain her nappy dark pink or red. This is normal for a newborn.

**Vaginal discharge** Newborn baby girls sometimes produce a clear or white vaginal discharge. Occasionally you may notice a small amount of vaginal bleeding, but this is perfectly normal and will clear up naturally after a couple of days. If you're worried, check with your doctor.

# Types of birthmark

Most birthmarks are just abnormal collections of small blood vessels under the skin. They are harmless and don't cause your baby any pain. These are some common types.

**Salmon patches** Harmless and very common, these reddish marks may be on the eyelids, nose, upper lip, and nape of the neck. No treatment is needed and most fade during infancy.

**Strawberry marks** These pink discolorations of the skin usually fade with time. Very few need treatment with lasers and steroids.

**Spider birthmarks (naevi)** These small marks appear shortly after birth as a network or a cobweb of dilated vessels. They generally disappear after the first year.

**Pigmented naevi** These brownish patches can occur anywhere on the body. They are usually pale and nearly always enlarge as the child grows, but they seldom become darker.

**Port wine stains** Found anywhere on the body, these bright red or purple marks are caused by dilated capillaries in the skin. They can be removed with laser treatment, or camouflaged with special make-up.

**Mongolian spots** It's common for dark-skinned babies to have harmless, dark bluish-black discolorations of the skin, usually on the back or buttocks; these will fade naturally.

# New parents

Katharine had wanted to do everything naturally during her pregnancy. She didn't want any pain-relieving drugs during labour and the thought of a Caesarean horrified her. When she was told she had high blood pressure, she began to worry. Symptoms that virtually all pregnant women experience at some point, like faintness, headaches, or indigestion, seemed terrifying to her. Katharine's partner Adam had thought he would take the birth in his stride, but he found things more difficult than he'd expected.

## Understanding symptoms

Katharine was very concerned that she might develop eclampsia during labour, which can lead to seizures. In fact, as I explained to her, this is a rare condition that is unlikely to occur even when pre-eclampsia has been diagnosed. Because of her high blood pressure (a possible sign of pre-eclampsia) and the weight of the baby (estimated at about 4kg/9lb), Katharine agreed to being induced when she was ten days overdue.

In the event, although it was quite long (17 hours), labour went relatively smoothly for Katharine. She was induced at 9am on Monday, and at 1pm felt relaxed enough to send her husband Adam to her mother's for lunch… on the condition that he bring her back some of her homemade cake.

Katharine used a TENS machine, which stimulates the body's natural painkillers through the transmission of electrical impulses. She was put on it late, however, so she's not sure whether it helped or not. At midnight, 15 hours later, she asked for an epidural – something she had sworn not to do – and after that everything was all right. Adam, who had

found it difficult to witness Katharine's distress, felt better too because she was no longer in excessive pain. He says, "That was when I felt the most useful, because she needed someone to take her mind off what was going on. We even started planning what we were going to do once we finally got Daniel home."

At 1.45am on Tuesday Katharine had an episiotomy (which she didn't feel at all), and about ten minutes later the doctor used forceps to pull Daniel out.

## First reactions

"I got a bit of a shock when I saw him," recalls Katharine, "because his face was very red and scrunched up, his head looked slightly lopsided because of the forceps, and he seemed to be gasping for air, but not making any sound. I kept on asking the midwife 'Is he all right?! Is he all right?!' The midwife turned away for a second and I was absolutely convinced Daniel was dead. That was actually the worst moment during the whole labour, and I started to cry uncontrollably. In fact, the midwife was only doing the Apgar scores (see p.24) and, as it turned out, Daniel scored highly. About 30 seconds later we were handed a perfect little baby boy breathing normally."

"I was quite surprised that he had his eyes wide open and seemed to be looking at me and Adam in a very quizzical manner. He just sat staring for about five minutes without crying at all. Daniel is my first child, and so I wasn't prepared for the combination of sheer joy, love, and relief that flooded over me when he was placed in my arms for the first time."

"The placenta came out after only ten minutes, which I'm told is a bit unusual without the use of syntocinon, and then the midwife clamped the umbilical cord in two places, and Adam cut it."

## Looking back at the birth

The one thing Katharine regretted about the whole pregnancy was having had an episiotomy. She was sure she would have stretched enough had she been given another half hour. Although she felt no pain at the time, due to the epidural, she said the episiotomy was the only physical problem associated with the birth that didn't clear up in the first two weeks.

Three months later the episiotomy scar was still sensitive, and she said that the feeling she might tear during intercourse had put her off sex completely.

I explained to her that, although this fear of tearing is genuine, it is almost certain she would have lost her sexual appetite for a time after giving birth, with or without an episiotomy. Although the latest research indicates that tears usually heal better than episiotomies should the mother not stretch enough naturally, a forceps delivery always necessitates an episiotomy.

## Experiencing the first few days

Katharine found that despite her elation after the birth of Daniel, she soon got what are commonly known as the "baby blues", a feeling of deep depression. She found it very difficult to relate to all the people around her, including

Adam, who found this hard to cope with. She also felt guilty because she had not expected these feelings to accompany the birth of a normal, healthy baby.

## Understanding "baby blues"

I explained to Katharine that "baby blues" are caused by the huge increase in hormones in a woman's body during childbirth. It takes quite a while, sometimes weeks or months, for the body to readjust to not being pregnant, and in the meantime a new mother may have to deal with difficult bouts of depression. I suggested to Katharine that if her feelings of depression persisted or became overwhelming and difficult to deal with, she should seek advice from her doctor.

In Katharine's case, things improved when she arrived home from the hospital. Although she was physically exhausted, psychologically she felt much more in control once she was in her own home again. As Katharine said, "It was only when we walked through our own door with Daniel that I felt the three of us were a proper family."

■ If light shines in her face, she'll blink – usually whether she has her eyes open or not (never shine bright light into your baby's eyes).

■ She'll also blink if you tap the bridge of her nose or blow gently across her eyes, or if she's startled by a sudden noise.

■ If you lift your baby up and turn her left or right, her eyes won't normally move with her head, but stay fixed in the same position momentarily. Known as the "doll's-eye response", this usually disappears at about ten days.

# Newborn behaviour

Once your baby is born, it will take you a while to get used to what she can do. It's worth studying her reactions to various stimuli, and becoming familiar with some of the traits that will mark her personality. Young babies have far more individuality than people think, so bear this in mind as you get to know your child.

## Reflexes

One thing common to all healthy babies is a number of reflexes that can be stimulated from the very first moments after birth. These reflexes are unconscious movements that eventually, at about three months, start to be replaced by conscious movements.

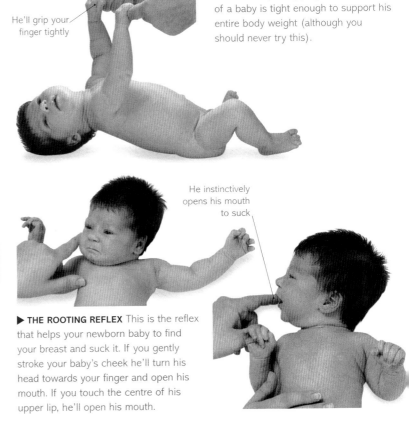

◀ **GRASP REFLEX** If you put something in the palm of your baby's hand, he will clench it surprisingly tightly. The grasp of a baby is tight enough to support his entire body weight (although you should never try this).

He'll grip your finger tightly

His fingers stretch out as he throws his arms back

He instinctively opens his mouth to suck

▲ **MORO REFLEX** Should your baby's head drop back, you might notice he throws his limbs back with fingers outstretched, then lets them fall back slowly towards his body.

▶ **THE ROOTING REFLEX** This is the reflex that helps your newborn baby to find your breast and suck it. If you gently stroke your baby's cheek he'll turn his head towards your finger and open his mouth. If you touch the centre of his upper lip, he'll open his mouth.

You might notice that your newborn baby responds in a positive way to your presence by momentarily contracting the whole of her face and body. As she learns to control her movements, you'll see that her reactions become more directed and less random. For instance, at six weeks, instead of scrunching up her whole face, she'll give you a distinct smile.

**Testing reflexes** Until your baby's physical and mental capabilities develop, it's her instinctive reflexes that show her maturity. Doctors can test these reflexes to check your baby's general health and see that her central nervous system is functioning well. More than 70 primitive reflexes have been identified, but your doctor is likely to test only a few. Premature babies don't react in the same way as full-term babies.

# Getting to know your baby

**Spend as much time as you can playing with your new baby – it's vital for her development.**

■ Watch her expressions and you'll soon start to recognize her needs. When she's content she'll look tranquil and quiet. When she's feeling miserable or uncomfortable she'll look red and flustered.

■ Play with your baby. Don't worry about looking silly – pull funny faces and use a high-pitched voice as you tell her how much you love her. She'll answer by nodding, and moving her mouth. She may stick out her tongue too and jerk her body as she responds to you.

▲ **"CRAWLING"** When you place your baby on his stomach, he will automatically assume what looks like a crawling position, with his pelvis high and his knees pulled up. When he kicks his legs he may be able to shuffle in a vague crawling manner. But this is not real crawling and will soon stop as soon as his legs uncurl and he lies flat.

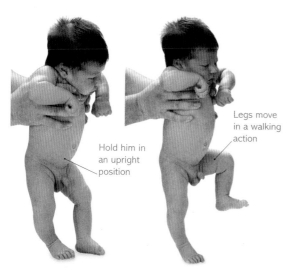

Hold him in an upright position

Legs move in a walking action

▲ **WALKING REFLEX** If you hold your baby under the shoulders so that he is in an upright position and his feet are allowed to touch a firm surface, he'll move his legs in a walking action. This reflex disappears by 11–12 weeks, and is not what helps your child learn to walk.

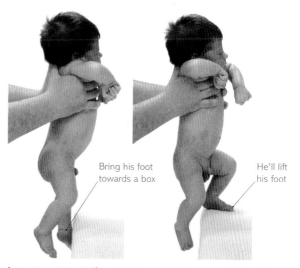

Bring his foot towards a box

He'll lift his foot

▲ **PLACING REFLEX** If you hold your baby in an upright position and bring the front of his leg into contact with the edge of a box, he'll lift his foot as if to step on to the box. The same reflex is present in the arm; if the back of your baby's forearm touches the edge of a table, for example, he will raise his arm.

# Your newborn girl

Many behavioural traits that are typical of girls can be seen in your baby as soon as she's born.

- Hearing in girls is very acute and they can be calmed down with soothing words much more readily than boys.

- A baby girl often cries longer than a boy if she hears another baby crying.

- Baby girls use their own voice to get their mother's attention earlier and more often than boys.

- Baby girls can locate the source of a sound without difficulty.

- Girls respond enthusiastically to visual stimulation from birth.

- Baby girls are interested in the unusual.

- Girls prefer the human face to almost anything else. Later in life this trait shows as intuitive reading of facial expression, regardless of cultural differences.

## Crying

Assume that your baby will cry a lot and you might be pleasantly surprised if she doesn't. If you think she won't cry and then she does, you may find yourself overwhelmed and disorientated.

Remember that there are really only three states your newborn baby can be in: asleep, awake and quiet, or awake and crying. If she's crying there are a variety of reasons for it. The most likely causes are tiredness, hunger, loneliness, and discomfort – she's too hot or too cold, is in an uncomfortable position, or needs changing. Sometimes, though, a baby will just cry for no apparent reason. This type of crying can be the most stressful for a parent.

**Responding to crying**  Leaving a child to cry on her own is never a good idea. If a baby is denied attention and friendship in her early weeks and months, she may grow up to be introverted, shy, and withdrawn. Research on newborns shows that if parents are slow to respond to their baby's crying, the result may be a baby who cries more rather than less. A recent study found that babies whose crying was ignored in their first few weeks tended to cry more frequently and persistently as they grew older.

Often people confuse spoiling a child with loving a child. In my opinion a baby cannot be "spoiled" enough. A six-month-old baby who is picked up, nursed, cuddled, and talked to soothingly and lovingly is not learning about seeking attention; she is learning about love and forming human relationships – and that is one of the most important lessons a child will ever learn in terms of her future emotional and psychological development. What we tend to call spoiling is both a natural response of a mother to a distressed child, and the natural need of the baby.

## Sleep patterns

Once you bring your newborn home, you'll have some sleepless nights unless you are very lucky. Although most newborns usually sleep when they are not feeding – typically spending at least 60 per cent of their time asleep – some will remain active and alert for surprisingly long periods during the day and night.

If you have a very wakeful baby, be consoled by the fact that as long as she isn't left bored on her own, every minute that she's awake she's learning something new – and in the long run you will be rewarded with an eager, bright child. All babies are different, and their sleep requirements depend on individual physiology. For this reason it's nonsensical to lay down rigid sleeping times that correspond to the average baby. As I've said before, the average baby doesn't exist.

# Sounds your baby makes

Babies make a variety of strange noises, including many from the gastrointestinal tract, whether asleep or awake, and this is normal. Most of the sounds she makes are due to the immaturity of her respiratory system and soon disappear.

**Snoring**  Your baby may make some grunting noises when she's asleep. This is not a true snore, and is probably caused by vibrations of the soft palate at the back of her mouth as she breathes.

**Snuffling**  Your baby may snuffle so loudly with each breath that you think she has a cold or that she has catarrh at the back of her throat, but she hasn't. In most babies these snuffling noises are harmless and occur because the bridge of the nose is low, and air is trying to get through very short, narrow nasal passages. As your baby grows bigger the bridge of her nose will get higher and the snuffling sound will gradually disappear.

**Sneezing**  You may also think your baby has a cold because she sneezes a lot, but sneezing is common in newborn babies, particularly if they open their eyes and are exposed to bright light. This sneezing can be beneficial – it helps clear out your baby's nasal passages.

**Hiccups**  Newborn babies hiccup a lot, particularly after a feed. This leads some mothers to fear that their baby has indigestion, but this is rarely so. Hiccups are due to imperfect control of the diaphragm – the sheet of muscle that separates the chest from the abdomen – and they'll disappear as your baby's nervous control of the diaphragm matures.

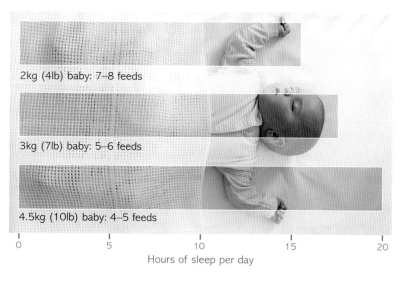

2kg (4lb) baby: 7–8 feeds

3kg (7lb) baby: 5–6 feeds

4.5kg (10lb) baby: 4–5 feeds

| | | | | |
|---|---|---|---|---|
| 0 | 5 | 10 | 15 | 20 |

Hours of sleep per day

# Your newborn boy

From the moment of birth, baby boys show characteristic male behaviour, some of which will persist throughout life.

■ Hearing in boys is less acute than in girls, so boys are more difficult to calm down.

■ If a newborn boy hears another baby cry, he'll join in, but will stop crying quite quickly.

■ Baby boys don't make sounds in answer to their mother's voice early on, but this hearing response lasts throughout life.

■ Newborn boys have difficulty in locating the source of sounds.

■ Baby boys require more visual stimulation than girls. They quickly lose interest in a picture, and lag behind girls in visual maturity up to the age of seven months.

■ Baby boys are interested in the differences between things.

■ Boys are more active, and are as interested in things as in people.

■ Boys want to taste everything, touch everything, and move things about more than girls.

◄ **NEWBORN SLEEP REQUIREMENTS**
A newborn's sleep pattern is determined by her weight and feeding needs. This means that in the first weeks, the less your baby weighs, the more often she'll need to be fed, and the less time she'll spend sleeping, and vice versa. The chart is a very rough guide to sleep requirements according to birth weights, but all babies have their own pattern.

## Apgar score

At one, five, and ten minutes after birth, your baby will be given five tests to check that she's fit and healthy. These are scored on the Apgar scale (after Dr Virginia Apgar, who devised it) to determine whether she needs immediate special attention.

Your baby is given a score of 0, 1, or 2 for each category. If she scores over 7 in total, she is in good condition. If she scores under 4, she needs help and will receive resuscitation. Most low-scoring babies score highly when tested again a few minutes later. The checks look at a newborn's activity, pulse, grimace, colour, and respiration.

**Activity** This shows the health and tone of your baby's muscles. Active movements score 2; some movements 1; limp scores 0.

**Pulse** This indicates the rate and strength of the heartbeats. 100 beats per minute scores 2; below 100 scores 1; no pulse scores 0.

**Grimace/crying** Facial expressions and responses show how alert she is to stimuli. Crying scores 2; whimpering 1; silence 0.

**Colour** This shows how well your baby's lungs are working to oxygenate her blood. Pink skin scores 2; bluish extremities 1; totally blue skin scores 0.

**Respiration** Breathing shows the health of her lungs. Regular breathing scores 2; irregular 1; none scores 0.

# Newborn health

Whether your baby is born in hospital or at home, the doctor or midwife will see to it that she's given uninterrupted expert attention until her breathing is well established. Any major problems should be identified quickly, so that if special care is required it will begin at the earliest possible moment.

Immediately after delivery the doctor or midwife will test your new baby against the Apgar scale (see left) and then examine her to assess her general condition. The sort of checks your doctor will do involve:

■ Making sure that your baby's features and body proportions are normal.
■ Turning your baby over to see that her back is normal and there is no sign of spina bifida (see p.29).
■ Examining her anus, legs, fingers, and toes.
■ Recording the number of blood vessels in the umbilical cord – normally there are two arteries and one vein.
■ Weighing your baby.
■ Measuring your baby's head and body length.
■ Checking your baby's temperature and warming her if she needs it.

This preliminary examination takes less than a minute when performed by an experienced doctor or midwife. You can then rest easy in the knowledge that your baby is healthy and normal. Once the initial checks have been carried out and you've held and suckled her for as long as you and your partner want to, your baby will be wrapped up snugly and put in her cot in order to keep warm.

## The next day

Your baby will be given a thorough medical examination 24 hours later to check that all is well. This takes place when she is warm and relaxed. Ask the hospital staff to let you know when the examination is going to take place, so that you can be there. You will have the opportunity to ask your doctor questions and to discuss any worries that you may have.

Your baby is placed on a flat surface in good light and at a convenient height for the doctor, who may be seated. You can have the examination at your bedside if you are immobile, but should you be absent, always ask for the results of the examination. Generally your doctor will start examining at the top of the head and work down to the toes.

**Head and neck** The doctor will look at the skull bones and the fontanelles, and check for any misshaping that occurred when the head passed through the birth canal during delivery. She'll look at the eyes, ears, and nose, and check the mouth for any abnormality, such as cleft palate, and for any teeth. Although it is rare, some newborn babies do have teeth. If they are loose or growing at an unusual angle, they will be removed so that there is no risk of them falling out and being swallowed. The doctor will also check your baby's neck for any cysts or swellings.

**Chest and heart** The heart and lungs are checked with a stethoscope. The lungs should be expanded and working normally. After birth, the work load of a baby's heart increases substantially when she becomes responsible for her own circulation. This may cause a heart murmur (a sound that the doctor hears with a stethoscope), but most murmurs soon disappear. Your child will be examined during the postnatal checkup to see if a heart murmur persists.

**Arms and hands** The doctor will check each arm for a pulse, and for normal movement and strength. Your baby's fingers and palm creases will also be checked. Nearly all babies have two major creases on each palm; if there's only one your doctor will look for other physical abnormalities.

**Abdomen and genitals** The doctor will press her hands gently into your baby's abdomen to check the size and shape of the liver and spleen. Both may be slightly enlarged in a newborn baby. She'll check the testes are properly descended if your baby is a boy, and that the labia are not joined and that the clitoris is a normal size for a girl. The doctor will also check the lower spine and anus for congenital abnormalities (see pp.28–9).

**Hips, legs, and feet** Your doctor will hold both thighs firmly and move each leg to see whether the head of the thigh bone is unstable or lies outside the hip joint, suggesting congenital dislocation of the hip. Testing the hips is not painful, but your baby may cry at the movement. The doctor will examine the legs and feet to make sure they are of equal size and length. If the ankle is still turned inwards as it was in the uterus, your baby may have a club foot, but this can be treated.

**Nerves and muscles** Your doctor will put your baby's arms and legs through a range of movements to make sure that they are not too stiff or floppy, and check the health of her nerves and muscles. She'll also make sure that the normal newborn reflexes, for example the grasp and Moro reflexes (see p.20), are present, and check your baby's head control.

# Jaundice

**Jaundice is not a disease and, in the majority of newborn babies, is not dangerous.**

Jaundice is likely to develop when a baby is about three days old. It is caused by the breakdown of red blood cells shortly after birth. This breakdown creates an excess in the blood of a pigment called bilirubin, causing a yellowish tinge to the baby's skin.

A newborn is unable to excrete the bilirubin sufficiently rapidly to prevent jaundice until her liver is more mature, at about one week. In most babies jaundice doesn't require treatment and clears up by itself within a week.

The level of bilirubin can be checked with a photometer "Bilicheck" first to save the baby having unnecessary skin pricks. If the level is high a blood test is then done. Some babies do need treatment for jaundice, usually with phototherapy, see below.

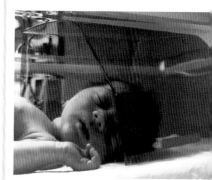

▲ **PHOTOTHERAPY** Jaundice in a newborn may be treated by exposure to ultraviolet light for about 12 hours.

## Bonding

**You should make every effort to establish bonds with your premature baby as soon as possible through your smell, your voice, and your touch.**

Much research has been done to illustrate the positive effects of physical human contact on young babies, and this applies equally to those who are premature.

If you're a new mother expecting to have your baby in your arms right after birth, it's obviously distressing to find that she's being kept behind a glass screen, and is surrounded by many machines.

Mothers who don't have early contact with their babies may start to feel cheated of motherhood. They may even blame themselves for having "failed" their babies, and these feelings of guilt are intensified because they are unable to comfort their babies, who are obviously in need of help.

It's important to realize, though, that effective bonding can take place with your baby in an incubator – indeed, it's essential that it does. No baby is so ill that you can't place your hand inside the incubator and stroke her gently. Try not to be intimidated by all the machinery; ask the hospital staff to show you what to do.

# Premature babies

One in 18 babies is premature. A premature baby is one that is born at less than 37 completed weeks and hasn't yet matured to the point when she can cope easily outside her mother's uterus. Although the chances today of a premature baby surviving and thriving are vastly improved, it's still very worrying to see your baby being taken away for special care immediately after the delivery.

Understanding why a baby needs special treatment will help lessen your anxiety. Premature babies have very weak muscle tone and don't move much. They often have calcium and iron deficiencies, as well as low blood-sugar levels. If they are very premature their eyes may still be sealed. Their heads are disproportionately large in comparison to the rest of the body, and the bones in their skull are soft. They are more than usually prone to jaundice (see p.25).

## Special needs of a premature baby

A premature baby needs to be fed more frequently than a full-term baby because she burns calories more quickly. The smaller the baby, the more often she needs to feed and the less time she spends asleep (see p.22). For premature babies the challenge of living outside the uterus is clearly an exhausting one. The lack of stimulation from being in an incubator and the inability to move very much means that, apart from frequent feeding, premature babies spend most of their time sleeping.

## Breathing problems

A premature baby may stop breathing for short periods. This is called apnoea and although it sounds frightening it's not uncommon. Most babies start breathing again after gentle stimulation, such as a tap or stroke. Other breathing problems can arise from a lack of surfactant – a substance produced in the lungs which stops the lungs collapsing inwards. If a baby's lungs don't have enough surfactant coating them, they don't expand as well as they should. This can cause the smaller air sacs to collapse inward, leading to a condition common in babies born before 28 weeks, known as hyaline membrane disease, or respiratory distress syndrome (RDS). Babies suffering from any of these complications can be given oxygen, either by way of a face mask or by a small tube inserted directly into the windpipe. Sometimes a ventilator machine is needed, which does the breathing for the baby.

Some babies may suffer from transient tachypnoea of the newborn, which means very rapid breathing due to the presence of fluid in the lungs. The problem usually clears up in a few days.

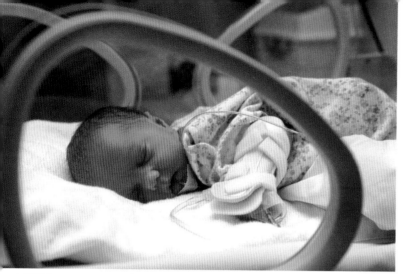

▲ **CARE IN AN INCUBATOR** A premature baby will be placed in an incubator – a closed, thermostatically controlled cabinet – to maintain her body temperature. She will be given oxygen if necessary and her temperature and breathing will be monitored.

## Tube feeding

Most premature babies don't have the strength to suck milk from a teat or bottle, and their intestines may be too weak to absorb food. There are three alternative ways of feeding:

■ Intravenous feeding is used for babies who are very ill or so premature that they can't swallow or digest food for themselves. It may continue for weeks and subsequent feeding will be through a naso-gastric tube.
■ With naso-gastric feeding a tube is passed through the baby's nose and into the stomach or intestine. The tube is very fine and soft so your baby hardly knows it's there, and it's a very comfortable way to feed.
■ When your baby is older, she'll be able to have a combination of breastfeeds or bottlefeeds and tube feeding; the baby takes as much as she can from the breast or bottle, and then tube feeding supplies the rest. Combination feeding can be used once the rooting and sucking reflexes (see p.20) are established and will continue until your baby is strong enough to feed from the breast or bottle only.

## Progress

The development of a premature baby can be slow and erratic. It is often a great shock to see just how tiny your premature baby is, but she'll have a great will to live. For a premature baby every day can be an uphill battle. Periods of improvement may well be followed by setbacks, and this constant uncertainty can make you and your partner feel anxious, moody, and restless. It is encouraging to know, however, that most babies born after 32 weeks develop normally. Of those babies born at 28 weeks, about six out of seven survive.

## Health risks

Premature babies are ill-prepared for life outside the uterus, and may have some of the problems listed below.

**Breathing** Due to the immaturity of their lungs, many premature babies experience difficulty in breathing, known as respiratory distress syndrome (RDS).

**Immune system** An under-developed immune system and a body that's too weak to defend itself properly means there's a greater risk of infection than with a full-term baby.

**Temperature regulation** A premature baby's temperature control is inefficient and she's likely to be too cold or too hot. She has less heat insulation than a full-term baby, as she lacks sufficient body fat underneath the skin.

**Reflexes** Inadequate development of her reflexes, particularly her sucking reflex, creates difficulties in feeding. Premature babies often need tube feeding.

**Digestion** A premature baby's stomach is small and sensitive, which means she's less able to hold food down, and so is more likely to vomit. The immaturity of her digestive system can make it difficult for her to digest essential proteins, so they may have to be given in a pre-digested form or by intravenous drip.

# Down's syndrome

This is by far the most common of a range of conditions called trisomies, in which one pair of chromosomes has an extra chromosome, making three.

In Down's syndrome there are three number 21 chromosomes. Affected infants characteristically have a round face, a tongue that tends to protrude, and slanting eyes with folds of skin at their inner corners. The back of the head is usually flat. They tend to be rather floppy infants and have short, wide hands with a single transverse crease across the palm. Other problems may include congenital heart disease.

Down's syndrome babies usually have learning difficulties, though the degree of difficulty varies widely; many are near normal. They are usually affectionate and happy children. With early education and careful attention they often do very well, and some manage to live independently as adults. (See p.343 for details of the Down's Syndrome Association who provide help and advice for parents of Down's children.)

# Congenital conditions

Congenital disabilities are rare. Some are genetic, while others are due to the effects on the fetus of drugs, radiation, infections, or metabolic disturbances. The fetal tissues that are most actively growing at the time when the adverse factor operates are the ones most likely to be affected. An increasing number of defects can be detected before birth and successfully treated just after birth.

**Talipes (club foot)**  Some infants – twice as many boys as girls – are born with the sole of one or both feet facing down and inwards, or up and outwards. The cause of club foot is not fully understood, but it can be inherited. The foot will be manipulated over several months, and braced or splinted in position between manipulations. If surgery is necessary, it can be carried out up to the age of nine months.

**Dislocated hip**  In about 0.4 per cent of infants, the ball at the head of the thigh bone doesn't fit snugly into its socket in the hip bone. This is also called congenital hip dysplasia. In a newborn, this is a potential rather than an actual problem. It is twice as common in girls as boys, and it's more common if there's a family history of the condition. Hip dysplasia is also more common in pregnancies in which there is an abnormally small amount of amniotic fluid in the uterus and after breech births. All breech babies should be given an ultrasound scan when they are four to six weeks old. Your doctor or midwife will check your baby's hips for excessive mobility as part of routine tests after birth (see p.24). Treatment, such as manipulation and splinting, can prevent trouble in later infancy. In severe cases, an operation may be needed.

**Hypospadias**  In a few male babies – about 0.3 per cent – the urethral opening is not at the end of the penis, but further back on its underside. In most cases it lies towards the end, but in some it is on the underside of the shaft of the penis. In severe cases, the penis is curved. Rarely, the urethral opening lies between the genitals and the anus. Surgery for this condition is usually carried out before the age of two years, allowing the normal passage of urine and, in later life, normal sexual intercourse. The condition, even in its most severe form, doesn't cause infertility.

**Congenital heart disease**  The most common form of heart disease in newborns is a hole in the ventricular septum – the thin dividing wall between the right and left ventricles (the two lower chambers of the heart). Symptoms include breathlessness, particularly during feeding, crying, and poor weight gain, but there may be no symptoms and the doctor may simply notice a murmur and pick up the condition during a routine examination. Small holes usually close spontaneously, but if they don't, surgical treatment may be necessary.

**Cleft lip and cleft palate** A cleft is a split or separation of parts. In the early part of pregnancy, separate areas of the baby's face and head develop individually, then join together. When joining doesn't take place or is incomplete, the baby can be born with a cleft upper lip on one or both sides, with or without a cleft palate. Breastfeeding is sometimes possible, perhaps using a nipple shield, or special bottles and teats are available. Some milk may return down the nose, and this should be avoided as it can possibly lead to glue ear (see p.285). Most babies with clefts need grommets inserted. A cleft lip will be surgically closed soon after birth or some weeks after. The palate will be closed from about six to nine months. Further operations may be necessary for some children.

Affected children are looked after by a cleft team who will monitor speech, hearing, and teeth, and will intervene if necessary. Support for parents is available through a national network of regional groups.

**Pyloric stenosis** In this condition, the pylorus, the passage that leads from the stomach into the small intestine, is narrow because of a thickening of the muscle. The cause is unknown and it is more common in boys than in girls. Symptoms usually first appear at two to four weeks, though they can appear earlier. The stomach contracts powerfully in an attempt to force a buildup of food through the narrow pylorus. This is impossible, however, and the contents of the stomach are vomited up so violently that they may be propelled up to 1m (3ft) – projectile vomiting. The baby may suffer from constipation, and dehydration is also a risk, so seek medical advice quickly. Ultrasound may be carried out to confirm the diagnosis. An operation to widen the pylorus can cure the condition.

**Imperforate anus** Very rarely a baby's anus is sealed at birth, either because there is a thin membrane of skin over the opening or because the anal canal, which links the rectum with the anus, hasn't developed. The baby must be referred for surgical treatment at once. This condition is checked for at every birth (see p.24), and is treated immediately if present.

**Spina bifida** Spina bifida, caused by a defect of the neural tube (the developing spine) can be detected in pregnancy by ultrasound. The introduction of folic acid to a mother's diet before conception and during pregnancy has greatly reduced the incidence of spina bifida.

# Hydrocephalus

**Also called water on the brain, this is a rare condition. It is more common in preterm babies.**

Cerebrospinal fluid (CSF) bathes the brain and spinal cord, protecting them from injury. If there is a blockage in the flow of CSF, or over-production of fluid, excess CSF builds up in the cavities of the brain. The head swells as the skull bones are still not fused, and the fontanelles (the soft spots where certain bones meet) become wide and bulging.

If hydrocephalus is suspected, frequent ultrasound checks will be made and your baby's head circumference measured every two to three days. If a child is born with hydrocephalus, a shunt may be inserted to drain the fluid. Mental development is usually affected, but some children with advanced hydrocephalus have normal intelligence.

Tip of shunt (tube)

Valve controls the rate of flow of fluid

Tube runs just beneath the skin, ending in the abdomen

▲ **SHUNT** A system of tubes with a valve runs through the body and diverts excess cerebrospinal fluid from the brain to where it can pass into the blood, usually the abdominal cavity.

# Your young baby

Looking after your baby does not require any specialist skills – just some basic knowledge, plenty of common sense, and a willingness to ask for advice. After the first few weeks your confidence and experience will increase dramatically, and you'll know the best way to change, hold, comfort, and feed your baby. You'll learn that if he needs something he'll usually find a way of communicating with you. He'll quickly learn to exchange love and friendliness with you both – the most important people in his life.

Your baby will grow rapidly in his first six months – an average baby increases his length by a quarter in this time, and doubles his weight. Watching your baby grow and develop is one of the most exciting aspects of being a parent, and you'll be astonished by how quickly your child changes. All you have to do to help his skills develop is to take your lead from your baby. Let him develop at his own pace, while at the same time providing all the encouragement and help you can.

## Safety

**When planning a nursery bear in mind that your child will be mobile before long.**

■ Make sure there are no sharp edges or corners on the furniture.

■ Choose a non-slip floor covering and fit bars and locks to windows.

■ Check that furniture can't be pulled over by your child – fix it to the wall if you are unsure.

■ Store toys at floor level so your child doesn't have to stretch to reach them.

■ Have wall-mounted lamps, or secure flexes to the wall.

■ Don't overheat the nursery; overheating is a risk factor in cot deaths (see p.80).

# Equipping your baby's room

Your baby may have a room of his own or share yours; once he's sleeping through the night, however, he should have his own space. You won't need a lot of special equipment and you can improvise with household items. For example, a sink will do as a baby bath, and a folded towel as a changing mat – but many parents really enjoy preparing their baby's room.

If this is your first child, ask friends with children which items they found most useful, and weigh up their advice against your own lifestyle. If there's anything you're unsure about, shop around and have a look through the catalogues of the major stores before making a final decision. There'll be many things that you can manage without. The only essentials are somewhere for your baby to sleep, clothes (see pp.60–1), nappies (see pp.72–3), and his feeding equipment.

You don't have to buy everything brand new; look out for secondhand items advertised on notice boards in the local clinic or on eBay or other Internet sites. As babies grow so quickly, it makes sense to borrow some items from friends if you can. If you buy secondhand equipment, always check carefully for general wear and tear, and make sure that all surfaces are smooth and free of rust for your baby's safety. Check, too, that they still comply with the latest safety regulations. Beware of painted items; old-fashioned paints may contain lead, which is poisonous. Never buy secondhand car seats, though, as they may have been in an accident.

## Basic equipment

| Sleeping | Transport | Bathing | Other |
|---|---|---|---|
| ■ Crib, or cot | ■ Pram, buggy, or | ■ Baby bath | ■ Bouncing chair |
| ■ Mattress with waterproof | pushchair | ■ Cotton wool | ■ Muslin squares |
| cover | ■ Sling | ■ Large soft towel | |
| ■ Fitted cot sheets | ■ Infant car seat | ■ Flannel or sponge | |
| ■ Cellular blankets | | ■ Baby brush | |
| ■ Swaddling shawls | | ■ Baby bath lotion | |
| (optional) | | ■ Blunt-ended scissors | |
| ■ Baby monitor | | | |

▲ **PLANNING A BABY'S ROOM** A baby's room doesn't have to be smart or filled with lots of special furniture. The essentials are a cot, a comfortable chair for you to sit in when feeding, and somewhere to change his nappy.

## Arranging a nursery

Planning your baby's room, like buying equipment, is best done before he's born: once you bring him home you'll be far too busy feeding and changing and you're likely to be tired, too.

Try to ensure that the room is as easy as possible to keep clean, with wipeable surfaces. Make sure that any painted surfaces are non-toxic and lead-free, and use flameproof fabric for bedding, upholstery, and curtains. You'll need some storage space for clothes and changing equipment and somewhere to change his nappy. Some parents like to have a special nappy-changing unit, but most are happy to use a changing mat on the floor. You'll also find it useful to have a comfortable chair near the cot where you can sit and feed your baby. The floor covering should be hard-wearing and easy to keep clean.

**Heating and light** The baby's room doesn't have to be very warm, but should be kept at a constant temperature. Around 18°C (65°F) is suitable if your baby is covered with two blankets and a sheet; if the room is warmer, he should have fewer blankets (see p.81). If your baby is tucked up snugly in his cot, all-night heating won't be necessary except during very cold weather: a thermostatically controlled room heater is the most suitable. It is a good idea to fit a dimmer switch so that you can gently bring up the lights without startling your baby. If you like, the light can be left on low as an alternative to a night light.

## Decorating the nursery

Although a newborn's vision is limited, cheerful colours and decorations will provide a stimulating environment.

■ Light, cheerful colours are the most suitable for your baby's room. White always looks fresh and clean or the colours of nature – yellow, blue, and grassy green – will be soothing to your baby. Use vivid splashes of primary colours to enliven the room.

■ A newborn baby has a very limited range of vision – only 20–25cm (8–10in) – so hang mobiles above his cot. Their colours and movement will make your baby alert to his surroundings.

■ Put an unbreakable mirror on the side of the cot so your baby can see his face; the human face is fascinating to very young babies.

■ Choose fabrics and wall coverings that are washable.

■ A folding screen may be useful to shelter the cot from bright sunshine or from cold draughts.

■ Carpet is warm and will absorb noise, but can be difficult to keep clean; good alternatives are wooden flooring, vinyl, cork, or linoleum floor coverings. If you have a rug on the floor, make sure it has a non-slip underlay.

## Safety concerns

Safety is the most important consideration when choosing equipment for your baby.

■ Make sure the cot you choose is sturdy and is finished with non-toxic paint or varnish. Check it for sharp edges and screws.

■ The gaps between the bars should be in the range of 2.5–6cm (1–2½in) so your baby can't get his head stuck between them.

■ The drop side should have safety locks at both ends so that your child can't let it down.

■ Choose a good firm mattress, preferably new, that's covered in PVC or other wipe-clean material.

■ Choose closely woven blankets that don't trap fingers.

# Sleeping

The best choice of bed for your newborn is a Moses basket or a carrycot pram; some prams convert to pushchairs for use later when he's able to support himself sitting up. Your baby will outgrow a Moses basket or a cradle quite quickly, so don't splash out on an expensive one unless you're sure you can afford it.

When your baby outgrows his Moses basket or carrycot, you'll need a full-sized cot. Choose one with bars that are set closely together – a distance of 2.5–6cm (1–2½in) is suitable – and one drop side so that you can lift your baby out easily. The mattress should fit snugly, so your baby can't get his arm or his leg, or even his head, trapped down the side. The cot will last you until your baby is big enough to clamber out, when you'll need to buy a bed – at about two or two-and-a-half years. The cot mattress should be a foam type. Some have air holes that allow your child to breathe if he turns over on to his front while asleep. Travel cots are very useful for going on holiday or taking your baby out for the evening. They have fabric sides and are collapsible so that they can easily be carried. All sleeping equipment must comply with safety standards.

▲ **YOUR BABY'S COT** When buying a cot for your baby, look for one that has two mattress heights, so you don't have to bend down too far in the early months. Make sure it has drop sides so that you can get at your baby easily.

◀ **MOSES BASKET** A Moses basket is easy to carry from room to room so makes an ideal first bed for your newborn. He'll soon outgrow it, though, so have a cot ready.

Because a young baby can't regulate his body temperature effectively, use a cotton sheet and cellular blankets for the cot so that you can easily add one or take one away. Once he is a year old, a cot duvet will be suitable. Make sure that any bedding you buy is flameproof and conforms to current safety standards. Never put a hotwater bottle or electric blanket in your baby's bed, and don't place the cot next to a radiator or heater.

**Sleeping temperatures** Research into cot death has shown that babies who get too hot are at a greater risk of cot death. While the temperature of the nursery is an important factor, the number of blankets is even more so. If the nursery is at 18°C (65°F), then a sheet and two layers of blankets will keep your baby at an ideal temperature, if he's wearing a vest, nappy, and stretch suit. If the room is warmer, you should use correspondingly fewer blankets (see p.81). In summer, your baby may only need only a sheet and a vest.

Similarly, cot bumpers and pillows can make your baby too hot. Babies lose heat through their heads, so if your baby's head is buried in a pillow or bumper, heat loss will be reduced. These days baby nests are not advised either because the baby is at risk of overheating.

# Baby listeners

**A baby listener will allow you to keep in touch with your baby, even when he's in another room.**

■ Baby listeners are available in different versions: battery- or mains-operated and rechargeable.

■ Lights indicating whether the batteries are low, or the baby unit is out of range, are useful.

▲ **KEEP IN TOUCH** The latest models allow you to talk to your baby via the monitor and even play lullabies. Some also have a screen so you can see as well as hear your baby.

## Sleeping accessories

The first requirement is a mattress that is thin and fits closely into the cot with no gaps between the edges of the mattress and the frame. You will also need sheets and covers as suggested here.

■ Cotton sheets
■ Cotton cellular blankets
■ Tie-on waterproof sheet to protect the mattress

■ Cot duvet and cover (not for babies under 12 months)

▶ **BABY'S BEDDING** It's very important for your baby not to overheat in his cot, so choose light cellular blankets that are easy to add or take away as necessary. Remember that a folded blanket counts as two blankets, not one.

## Pram or pushchair?

**A pram or pushchair will probably be one of the most expensive things you buy for your baby so choose carefully.**

■ Think about how and where you will use it most? Do you need something that's easy to get in the car? Or are you more likely to be travelling on public transport and need something that folds easily?

■ Before making your purchase, ask the salesperson to demonstrate the pushchair or pram so you are quite sure it's easy to deal with.

■ Check on what guarantee the product carries and how easy it is to get any repairs for it should you need them.

# Walking and carrying

Your baby will spend most of his time being carried, wheeled, or secured in some way, and there's a wide variety of prams and carriers available. When choosing equipment of this kind, you'll need to think carefully about safety and portability.

Slings are one of the best ways of transporting a newborn; they're light and comfortable, and allow you to carry your baby close while keeping both hands free. There are different types so try the sling with your baby before you buy it, and make sure it has a head support. Backpacks, which have supportive frames that make it easier to bear a larger baby's weight, are suitable once your baby can sit up by himself.

For longer journeys you'll need a pram or pushchair in which your baby can sit or lie down. One in which your baby can lie flat should be used for the first three months, until he has some head control. The pram you choose will depend on your budget and lifestyle. Think about where you'll keep it and whether you will need to take it on buses and trains or up stairs. Whichever pram you choose, it should have a safety harness or rings to fix one in place.

A hood shield will protect your baby from rain

The top lifts off and can be used as a carrycot

Make sure the brakes are easy to use

▶ **CARRYCOT PRAMS** For the first three months, your baby must be able to lie flat. Reclining pushchairs are available, but a carrycot pram like this one is more versatile. Many models can be converted into pushchairs later.

**▼WRAPAROUND SLING** Your baby will feel safe and secure inside a sling, and it leaves your arms free.

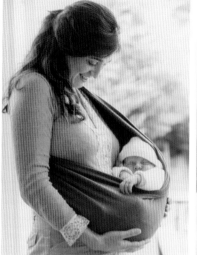

**▼BABY CARRIER** This type of sling holds your baby upright. He will enjoy the movement as you walk around.

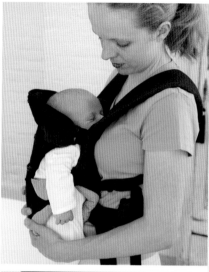

# Safety harnesses

Your young baby has no fear of falling, so wherever he sits he will have to be strapped in for his own safety.

■ A five-point harness, which has straps for the shoulders as well as the waist and crotch, is safest.

■ Your baby's pram should have a built-in harness, or fixing points so that you can attach one to it.

■ Highchairs often have a built-in crotch strap, and should also have rings to take a safety harness, which you can buy separately.

■ Many harnesses come with reins that can be attached when your baby is old enough to walk.

**▲BOUNCING CHAIR** Your baby can be propped up so that he can look around him in a purpose-made chair. Make sure he is safely strapped in. Always place the chair on the floor, never on a table in case he rocks the chair over the edge.

**▶ USING A BACKPACK** You can carry your older baby in a backpack once he becomes too heavy for a sling. Make sure that he is comfortable and is not restricted by the leg openings.

## Your baby's weight

In the first six months of life, your baby will be growing fast and will double his birth weight. See also pp.318–19.

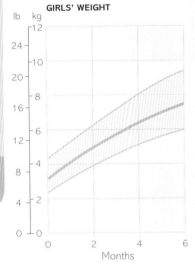

**GIRLS' WEIGHT**

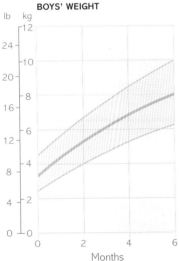

**BOYS' WEIGHT**

▲ **YOUR BABY'S WEIGHT** The middle line represents the 50th centile: 50 per cent of babies will be below this weight and 50 per cent will weigh more. Any weight within the coloured band is normal.

# Feeding your baby

Breastmilk is the ideal food for a baby, but if you do bottlefeed, rest assured that your baby will still thrive. Feeding takes a great deal of time, so it's important to choose a method that's suitable for both you and your baby. Well before delivery, decide whether you're going to breastfeed or bottlefeed and prepare for your choice.

It's quite normal for all babies, breastfed or bottlefed, not to take much colostrum (see p.40) at first, because they take a while to get the hang of feeding. Your baby will cry when he's hungry, and you should take your lead from him in setting the pattern of feeds.

Babies grow most rapidly during the first six months – most double their birth weight in four to five months. Your baby's nutritional needs reflect this tremendous growth. A healthy baby's food has to contain adequate amounts of calories, protein, fats, carbohydrates, vitamins, and minerals, and until he's at least six months old, your baby will receive all he needs from breast or formula milk (see column opposite).

## Why breast is best

Human breastmilk is the perfect food for babies. Because it doesn't look as rich and creamy as cows' milk, you may think that it isn't good enough, but don't be put off. It contains just what your baby needs. Breastmilk has many benefits for your baby. Breastfed babies tend to suffer less than bottlefed babies from such illnesses as gastroenteritis and chest infections. This is because antibodies from the colostrum and the mother's milk are absorbed into your baby's bloodstream, and protect the him against infections. In the first few days after birth, they also protect the intestine, reducing the chances of intestinal upsets.

Breastmilk has other advantages for a baby's digestion. Breastfed babies don't get constipated, since breastmilk is more easily digestible than cows' milk, although they pass few stools because the milk is so completely digested that there is little waste. They are less prone to ammoniacal nappy rash (see p.77), too. Breastfed babies usually also sleep longer, suffer less from wind, and posset – that is, regurgitate food – less, and the posset smells less unpleasant.

You may feel that one of the few drawbacks of breastfeeding is that until your milk supply is sufficiently well established for you to express and store milk for later feeding by bottle, you are the only person who can feed your baby. However, this stage doesn't last long.

▲ **BREASTFEEDING** Suckling helps to form a very strong bond between you and your new baby.

▲ **BOTTLEFEEDING** Encourage your partner to hold the baby close and talk to him while feeding.

Some women worry that breastfeeding will make their breasts sag. This is not the case. In fact, breastfeeding is good for your figure, as it helps you lose any weight gained during pregnancy. While you are breastfeeding, the hormone oxytocin (see p.40), which stimulates milk flow, also encourages the uterus to return to its pre-pregnant state. Your pelvis and waistline will also get back to normal more quickly.

Studies have shown that breast cancer is rarer in those parts of the world where breastfeeding is the norm, and it's possible that breastfeeding may provide some protection against the disease.

## Bottlefeeding

Almost every woman is capable of breastfeeding her baby, and you should try to do so. Many women feel that they must breastfeed to be a good mother, and feel guilty if they decide not to. On the other hand, some women find it emotionally or psychologically difficult to breastfeed, and others find that, however much they try, they just can't master breastfeeding. If this is the case, then you should forget about it and concentrate on bottlefeeding: he'll still thrive.

You may prefer the freedom of bottlefeeding, particularly if you intend to return to work soon after the birth, but remember that it's also possible to express enough milk so your partner or a childminder can feed your baby in your absence. That way your baby can have the benefits of your milk, and you can still have the flexibility of bottlefeeding.

One of the benefits of bottlefeeding is that your partner can be really involved with feeding the new baby. It's a good idea for him to start feeding as soon as possible after the birth, so that he can learn to handle the baby confidently, and if possible share the feeding equally with you.

## Milk is the ideal food

In the first months milk will supply all of your baby's basic nutrients, as well as necessary vitamins and minerals.

**Calories** The energy content of food is measured in calories. Babies need two and a half times more than adults.

**Protein** Vital for building body cells, a baby needs three times more protein than an adult.

**Fats** Traces of fatty acids are needed for growth and repair.

**Carbohydrates** These are a major source of calories for your baby.

**Vitamins** Formula milks contain all your baby's vitamin requirements, but paediatricians recommend vitamin A and vitamin D supplements for breastfed babies over the age of six months. Keep on taking your antenatal vitamins while breastfeeding.

**Minerals** Calcium, phosphorus, and magnesium are necessary for the growth of bone and muscle, and are contained in breastmilk and formula. Babies are born with an iron reserve that lasts about six months; after this they have to be given it in food or as supplements.

**Trace elements** Minerals like zinc, copper, and fluoride are essential to your baby's health. The first two are present in breast and formula milk, but fluoride is not. But never give fluoride supplements without checking with your midwife or doctor first.

## Ensuring a good milk supply

**Looking after yourself properly is the key to a good milk supply. If you stay relaxed, eat well, and drink enough fluids, you will have plenty of milk for your baby.**

■ Rest as much as you can, particularly during the first weeks, and try to get plenty of sleep.

■ You produce most milk in the morning when you are rested. If you become tense during the day, your supply could be poor by evening. Go through your antenatal relaxation routines and have a lie-down every day.

■ Let the housework go; do only what is absolutely necessary.

■ Eat a well-balanced diet that is fairly rich in protein. Avoid highly refined carbohydrates (cakes, biscuits, sweets, and so on).

■ Keep taking your antenatal vitamin supplements.

■ Drink about 3 litres (5pt) of fluid a day; keep a drink by you while you are feeding.

■ Express any milk your baby doesn't take in the early feeds of the day to encourage your breasts to keep producing milk.

■ The combined contraceptive pill can decrease your milk supply, so avoid while breastfeeding. The progestogen-only pill may be prescribed instead, but discuss methods of contraception with your doctor. Don't rely on breastfeeding alone.

# All about breastfeeding

Breastfeeding has to be learned, and you'll need support and advice from your family, from friends with babies, and from your midwife or health visitor. Above all you'll learn from your baby, by understanding his signals and discovering how to respond to them. No special action is needed to prepare your breasts for feeding unless you have an inverted nipple. If you do, use a breast shell to make your nipple protrude so that your baby will be able to latch on to it. If you're having your baby in hospital, make sure the nursing staff know that you intend to breastfeed, and don't be afraid to ask for help. Suckle your baby as soon as he's born to form a bond with him as early as possible and let him get used to suckling.

## Colostrum and breastmilk

During the 72 hours after delivery, the breasts produce a thin, yellow fluid called colostrum, made up of water, protein, and minerals. Colostrum contains antibodies that protect the baby against a range of intestinal and respiratory infections. In the first few days, your baby should be put regularly to the breast, both to feed on the colostrum and to get used to latching on to the breast (see p.42).

Once your breasts start to produce milk, you may be surprised by its watery appearance. When your baby sucks, the first milk that he gets – the foremilk – is thin, watery, and thirst-quenching. Then comes the hindmilk, which is richer in fat and protein.

## Feeding your baby

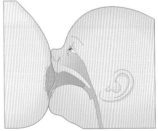

▲ **LATCHING ON** The key to successful breastfeeding is getting your baby's mouth correctly fixed or latched on to your breast, with your nipple well inside his mouth (left and above). Your baby stimulates milk to flow by pressing the tip of his tongue against your areola. Then he presses the back of his tongue up towards his palate to squeeze milk from your nipple into his throat.

# Breastfeeding positions

If you are sitting make sure you are well supported. Lying down is ideal for night feeds; when your baby is very small you may need to lay him on a pillow so that he can reach your nipple. You may find a lying position the most suitable if you have had an episiotomy and sitting is uncomfortable. If you've had a Caesarean section and your stomach is still tender, try lying with your baby's feet tucked under your arm.

▲ **LYING POSITION** Breastfeeding positions that allow you to lie down are a restful alternative, especially at night, and can keep a wriggling baby off a tender Caesarean incision.

◀ **SITTING POSITION** Make sure that your arms and back are supported and you are comfortable and relaxed. Raise your baby to the right height with a cushion.

# Nursing bras

**It really helps to wear a good supportive nursing bra when you're breastfeeding.**

A few weeks before the birth get advice from an in-store expert who will help you try some on. Look for one with front fastenings and wide straps that won't cut into your shoulders. Drop-front or zip-fastening bras are easy to undo with one hand while you hold your baby. A good bra will minimize discomfort if your breasts become sore.

# Supply and demand

**Milk is produced in glands that are deeply buried in the breast, not in the fatty tissue, so breast size is no indication of how much milk you can produce; even small breasts are perfectly adequate milk producers.**

Milk is produced according to demand – you supply what your baby needs, so don't worry that you'll run out of milk if your baby feeds very often. Your breasts are stimulated to produce milk by your baby's sucking, so the more eagerly he feeds, the more milk they will produce, and vice versa. I'm against babies being fed by the clock so I'm loth to show any kind of chart, but the following will give you some idea of what to expect in the early months.

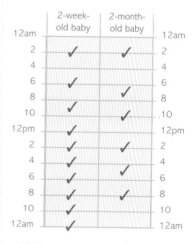

|  | 2-week-old baby | 2-month-old baby |  |
| --- | --- | --- | --- |
| 12am |  |  | 12am |
| 2 | ✓ | ✓ | 2 |
| 4 |  |  | 4 |
| 6 | ✓ | ✓ | 6 |
| 8 | ✓ |  | 8 |
| 10 | ✓ | ✓ | 10 |
| 12pm | ✓ | ✓ | 12pm |
| 2 | ✓ | ✓ | 2 |
| 4 | ✓ |  | 4 |
| 6 | ✓ | ✓ | 6 |
| 8 | ✓ | ✓ | 8 |
| 10 | ✓ |  | 10 |
| 12am | ✓ |  | 12am |

▲ **FREQUENCY OF FEEDS** This is an example of what may happen. At first your baby will feed little and often. By two months he will feed about every four hours and take more at each feed than before.

## How long on each breast?

**Keep your baby on the breast for as long as he wants to suck.**

■ If your baby continues to suck after your breasts have emptied, it may be that he's just enjoying the sensation; this is fine if it's not making your breasts sore.

■ When your baby has finished feeding from one breast, gently take him off your nipple (see below right) and put him on to the other breast. He may not suck for as long on the second breast.

■ Alternate the first breast you offer at each feed. To remind you which breast was last suckled, put a safety pin on your bra.

# Breastfeeding your baby

Breastfeeding creates a strong bond between mother and baby if feeding time is relaxed and pleasurable for both. Make sure your baby can see you, and smile and talk to him while he is suckling. He will come to associate the pleasure of feeding with the sight of your face, the sound of your voice, and the smell of your skin. Make sure you are both comfortable before you start (see pp.40–1). If your baby still seems hungry after feeding for as long as he wants from one breast, offer the other breast, winding him before changing over (see p.55).

## Possible problems

It is perfectly normal for breastfeeding not to go smoothly at first, so don't worry about minor setbacks, such as your baby refusing a feed. Remember that he too is learning and that it will take time for you to get used to each other, so persevere, and ask your midwife or health visitor for advice and suggestions.

If you do have problems, try not to get too worked up about them. Nervousness may lead to more difficulties, which will make you more discouraged, can affect your milk, and may even put you off breastfeeding. Don't let small problems lead you to hasty decisions.

# Giving a breastfeed

**1 THE ROOTING REFLEX** Prompt your baby to look for the breast by gently stroking the cheek nearest to it. Your baby will immediately turn towards your breast, open-mouthed.

**2 LATCHING ON** Your baby should take the nipple and a good proportion of the areola into his mouth. The milk is drawn out by a combination of sucking and squeezing the tongue on to the hard palate.

**3 RELEASING THE NIPPLE** To break the suction, slip your little finger into the corner of the baby's mouth. Your breast will slip out easily instead of being dragged out.

**Refusing the breast** It is quite usual for a newborn not to suck very vigorously or for very long during his first 24–36 hours. If this occurs later, however, there may be a problem that needs to be addressed. Breathing difficulties are the most likely cause of a baby's having problems taking the breast. It may be that your breast is covering his nostrils; if so, gently pull the breast back from your baby's face, just above the areola. If he seems to have a snuffly or blocked nose, consult your doctor, who may prescribe nose drops to clear the nostrils.

If there's no obvious cause for your baby's refusal to feed, he may simply be fretful. A baby who has been crying with hunger, or has been changed or fussed over when he's hungry, can become too distressed to feed. You'll need to soothe him by holding him firmly and talking or singing. There's no point in trying to feed him until he's calmed down.

If there's been some delay in starting to breastfeed, your baby may find it more difficult to take the breast, and you will have to be patient and persevere. Your midwife or health visitor will advise you if you need to give expressed milk from a special cup until your baby can take all he needs from the breast. Supplementary bottles are rarely necessary, and they may cause mothers to give up breastfeeding. Giving expressed milk is a much better alternative.

**Comfort sucking** Most babies enjoy sucking on their mothers' breasts for its own sake just as much as feeding. You will learn to tell the difference between actual feeding and comfort sucking. During a feed you may notice that your baby is sucking strongly without actually swallowing. There's no reason why your baby shouldn't suck as long as he wants, provided your nipples are not sore, although he takes most of his feed in the first few minutes.

**Sleeping through feeds** If your baby doesn't seem very interested in food during the first few days, make sure that he takes as much as he wants from one breast. If he sleeps at the breast, it means he's contented and doing well, though premature babies should be woken and fed regularly, as they tend to sleep a lot. If your baby does fall asleep at the breast, wake him gently half an hour later and offer a feed; if he's hungry he will soon perk up.

**Fretful feeding** If your baby doesn't settle down to feed, or appears not to be satisfied, he is probably sucking on the nipple alone and not getting enough milk. This may also lead to sore nipples. Check that your baby is positioned correctly on the breast. If he's had to wait for a feed and is distressed, try to calm him before feeding.

# Underfeeding

You may feel anxious that you can't see how much your baby has taken, but it's rare for a breastfed baby not to get enough milk. Remember, though, that it does take time for both mothers and babies to get the hang of breastfeeding.

■ If your baby wants to continue sucking even though he's finished feeding from both breasts, it doesn't always signify hunger; he may just enjoy sucking.

■ Thirst may cause your baby to go on sucking after he's emptied your breasts. Try giving about 30ml (1 fl oz) of cooled, boiled water from a special cup.

■ If he seems fretful and hungry, have him weighed at your baby clinic to check if he is gaining weight as quickly as expected. If you're at all worried about your baby's feeding, talk to your health visitor or doctor.

## Expressing tips

**Make expressing milk as easy on yourself as possible, and take care to store your milk correctly.**

■ Make sure the container is at a convenient height; if you have to lean over a low surface, expressing may give you backache.

■ Expressing milk should be painless. If it hurts, stop. Ask your midwife or health visitor if you are expressing correctly.

■ The more relaxed you are, the easier it will be to express. If the milk won't start to flow, place a warm flannel over your breasts to open the ducts, or try expressing in the bath.

■ If you're concerned that your baby might not go back to breastfeeding after getting used to the bottle, try feeding him milk from a specially designed cup, or spooning the expressed milk from a cup. Make sure that both spoon and cup are sterilized before use.

■ Your hands must be clean, and every piece of equipment and all containers should be sterile.

■ Milk will go off unless it is stored correctly, which could make your baby ill. Refrigerate or freeze your milk as soon as you've collected it. Refrigerated milk keeps for 24 hours; frozen milk for up to a week in the freezer compartment of a fridge or three months in a freezer.

■ Put milk into sterile, sealable containers. Sterile plastic bottle liners are ideal; don't use glass containers as they can crack.

# Expressing milk

Expressed milk can be easily stored either in the refrigerator or in the freezer. This will free you from feeling tied down by breastfeeding, and allow your baby to be fed with your milk if you're away. It also allows your partner to share in feeding your baby.

Milk can be expressed from your breasts using either your hands or a breast pump, which may be manual or electric, although some women find small battery pumps easier and more convenient.

## Expressing by hand

Before you start, you'll need a bowl, a funnel, and a container that can be sealed. All equipment must be sterilized (see p.50). Start by massaging your breast with flat hands, beginning at your ribs and working towards your areola, gradually going over the whole breast. Then roll your fingers and thumb together below and above your areola so that you press on the wider milk ducts behind the nipple.

In the first six weeks hand expressing is nearly always a bit difficult, as the breasts have not reached full production, but don't give up. Because breasts produce milk in response to demand, you may need to express milk to keep your supply going – if your baby is premature and can't yet breastfeed, for example. Even if you do want to use a pump, learn the technique of hand expressing just in case your pump doesn't work. The best time to express is in the morning when you have more milk, although once your baby drops his night feed, the evening may be the best time.

## Using a pump

Some women prefer to use a pump for expressing their milk. All pumps work on suction and comprise a funnel or shield, pump mechanism, and container. The assembly and operation of the different brands will vary, so always follow the manufacturer's instructions.

◀ **PRACTISE PUMPING** If you're planning to return to work before weaning your baby, start expressing a few weeks beforehand so you get used to the process and know how long it takes.

## Types of breast pump

A breast pump applies a rhythmical suction to the breast to remove the milk. Hand pumps are the cheapest option, but electric pumps are quicker and easier to use. The latest models even have an electronic memory that records your particular pumping rhythm.

Pump mechanism

Container doubles as feeding bottle

Pump mechanism

Funnel

Container doubles as feeding bottle

▲ **MANUAL PUMP** Start by fitting the funnel of the pump over your areola to form an airtight seal. You then operate the lever or plunger of the pump to express the milk.

▲ **ELECTRIC PUMP** This imitates a baby's natural sucking cycle more closely and is best if you're going back to work before weaning and so need to express often.

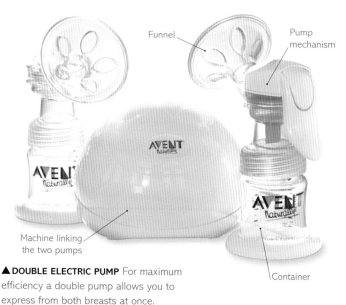

Funnel

Pump mechanism

Machine linking the two pumps

▲ **DOUBLE ELECTRIC PUMP** For maximum efficiency a double pump allows you to express from both breasts at once.

Container

## Supplementary bottles

There may be times, such as when you have a blocked duct or a very sore nipple, when it is painful to breastfeed.

Hard as it is, it's best to avoid offering formula if you possibly can. There are so many benefits to your baby being exclusively breastfed for the first six months if possible. When feeding is painful, many mothers prefer to express milk from the affected breast and give this milk in a bottle. Giving supplementary formula feeds can undermine the production of breastmilk.

A baby who has become used to the nipple may dislike plastic teats. Unfortunately, it can be difficult to tell whether your baby just dislikes the teat, or is not hungry. He'll eventually get used to the bottle if you persist, but you may then find that he doesn't want to go back to the breast. If this happens, try giving the milk from a sterilized spoon or cup, then reintroducing the breast later.

## Accessories

Breast pads and shields do help you keep your nipples clean and dry, although not everyone finds them essential.

Plastic breast shell

Fabric pads are washable and absorbent

▲ BREAST SHELLS AND PADS When you are feeding from one breast, milk may drip or even flow from the other. A plastic shell can be used to collect this excess milk, which can then be stored in the fridge for up to 24 hours or frozen. Disposable and washable fabric pads are also available, which fit inside your bra and protect your clothes from leaks of milk.

# Managing breastfeeding

For some mums breastfeeding goes smoothly right from the start, but it's also normal to be a bit clumsy at first, for the baby not to suck for very long, or for your breasts to be a bit sore. It takes time to learn, so if problems arise, do persevere until things get easier.

## Care of the breasts

The daily hygiene of your breasts and nipples is very important. Wash them every day with water (not soap, which defats the skin and can aggravate a sore or cracked nipple), and gently pat them dry. Dry them gently after feeding. Wear your bra all the time, even at night, as you'll need lots of support. Treat the sore nipple like a cracked lip and put on some ointment such as Vaseline after each feed.

Once your milk flow is established the milk may leak out quite a lot. Use breast pads or clean handkerchiefs inside your bra to soak it up and change them often. A plastic breast shell with a reservoir will help to keep your nipples dry and catch the leaks of milk. Milk can be frozen or refrigerated in a sterile bottle. Wash and sterilize the shell before reusing.

## If you are ill

You can express milk so that your partner can feed the baby if you're not feeling up to it. If you're too ill to express your milk, your baby can be given formula milk by bottle or by spoon and, although he may not like this at first, he will take the milk as he becomes hungrier.

If you have to go into hospital you can still breastfeed. Tell the nursing staff as soon as possible that this is what you want to do, so that they can make the necessary arrangements, for example someone will have to be available to lift and change your baby if you are too tired or ill to do so. If you have an operation, though, you will not be able to breastfeed afterwards because of the anaesthetic – you'll be too groggy and, more importantly, the drugs you have been given will have passed into your milk. If you know you'll be having an operation, try to express and freeze your milk so that your baby can be bottlefed until you've recovered. It will take up to ten days for your milk to return; your baby should suck as often as he wishes meanwhile.

## Drugs and breastfeeding

Drug manufacturers almost always advise you to stop breastfeeding while taking their products, but this is not always necessary. Ask your doctor for advice. Always tell your doctor that you are breastfeeding if you are already taking medications, or if you consult her for any new problems;

she may prescribe something more appropriate. If you want to use oral contraceptives, it's probably best to take the progestogen-only "mini-pill", as the oestrogen in the combined pill is thought to reduce your milk supply. Check with your doctor or family planning clinic.

## Problems

The best way to prevent problems is to keep your breasts clean and dry and make sure your baby always empties them when he feeds. You should also wear a proper nursing bra. If your nipples do become sore or cracked, take action immediately or they will get worse.

**Cracked nipple** If sore nipples are not dealt with properly, they may become cracked. If this happens, you'll feel a shooting pain as your baby suckles. Keep your nipples dry with breast pads or clean tissues, and continue feeding if you can. Go topless at home so the air can get to your breasts to help them heal. See advice (column right) and if necessary express milk by hand so it can be fed to your baby.

**Engorgement** Towards the end of the first week, before breastfeeding is fully established, your breasts may become over-full and painful and quite hard to the touch. If this happens, your baby won't be able to latch on successfully. Make sure you wear a good bra to minimize discomfort, and gently express some milk before feeding to relieve the fullness. Having warm baths also helps to relieve the discomfort by promoting milk flow.

**Blocked duct** Tight clothing or engorgement can cause a blocked milk duct, resulting in a hard red patch on the outside of the breast where the duct lies. You can prevent this by feeding often and encouraging your baby to empty your breasts, and by making sure that your bra fits properly. If you do get a blocked duct, feed often and offer the affected breast first.

**Mastitis** If a blocked duct is not treated, it can lead to an acute infection known as mastitis. The breast will be inflamed and a red patch will appear on the outside, as with a blocked duct. You should continue to breastfeed because you need to empty the breast. Your doctor may prescribe antibiotics to clear up the infection.

**Breast abscess** An untreated blocked duct or mastitis can result in a breast abscess. You may feel feverish, and you may have a very tender shiny red patch on your breast. Your doctor should prescribe antibiotics; if the abscess does not clear up, it will have to be drained surgically, but you may be able to continue feeding – ask your doctor for advice.

# Preventing sore nipples

Suckling your baby can cause soreness around the nipples, especially if you're fair-skinned. There are a few things that might help you avoid problems.

■ Always make sure that your baby has the nipple and areola well into his mouth.

■ Always take your baby off the breast gently (see p.42).

■ Keep your nipples as dry as possible between feeds.

■ Make sure your nipples are dry before putting your bra back on after a feed.

If one of your nipples does become sore, it may be due to poor positioning or your baby not latching on properly. Ask your health visitor's advice on correct positioning and see pp.40–3. To prevent the nipple from becoming cracked, you can apply a camomile or calendula cream two or three times a day.

▲ **NIPPLE SHIELD** This is made of soft silicone and can protect a sore nipple; the baby sucks through a small teat on the front. Sterilize before use.

# Miriam's casebook

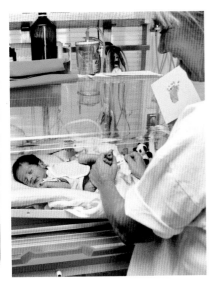

# Pre-term baby

Cathy and Dave's first baby, Sam, was born prematurely at 28 weeks. Cathy's pregnancy had been normal and she did everything she could to ensure her own and her baby's good health. But at 28 weeks she experienced strong contractions. She went straight to hospital, where Sam was born. He weighed only 1.3kg (2lb 13oz) and was put in an incubator in a special care baby unit.

## First days

It's a huge shock for any mother to have a premature baby – in this case a full three months before the due date. Of course, Cathy and Dave were desperately worried and concerned for their tiny baby. They found it so hard to sit by and watch him in the incubator, unable to cuddle and hold him. Most of all Cathy longed to breastfeed him, something she had always planned to do.

I explained to Cathy that although no feeding is straightforward for premature babies, breastmilk is especially beneficial to them, as it provides protection against infections in the first few risky weeks of life. Sam had to be fed intravenously for several days and then through a stomach tube because he had not had time to develop the rooting and sucking reflexes. Cathy expressed her milk from day one and stored it so that it could be used to feed Sam when the stomach tube was in place.

## Keeping up supplies

Cathy was adamant that she wanted to breastfeed Sam when she could eventually take him home, and as soon as he could be released from the incubator for short periods, the nurses encouraged Cathy to put him on the breast. I

reminded her that breastmilk is produced in response to demand. If it's not removed by a nursing infant, then it must be expressed or production stops. This meant Cathy had to express milk to keep up production until Sam was able to breastfeed regularly.

## Feeding a pre-term baby

Expressing milk for a premature baby is difficult because all the natural cues for the milk let-down reflex are missing: the baby's hungry cry, lifting him up, putting his mouth to the breast. It can help to express while sitting beside the baby or with pictures of him on view. In order to master the technique of expressing milk (see pp.44–5), Cathy needed lots of support from Dave; many times she felt like giving up. Her breasts became engorged on day three and she could hardly bear to massage them. She explained her problems to the staff nurse on the unit, who arranged for a rota of nurses to help and encourage her to take off milk every two hours (as a very small baby would) and store it hygienically. Cathy continued to express milk and by the second week she'd become quite expert, and was even asked to teach other mothers how to express.

## Loving contact

One of Cathy's main worries was that Sam wouldn't bond with her and Dave because he couldn't hear their voices properly, and couldn't smell their skin or enjoy cuddles. The hospital staff showed them how they could put a clean hand into the incubator to stroke and caress Sam gently. Within a week, Sam was showing signs of loving this contact and responded by wriggling when touched. Cathy and Dave talked to Sam as he did this, and during the second week saw him flick his eyes in recognition at the sound of their voices. They thought of this as their first conversation with their baby and continued to chat to him happily during their time together. The nurses also suggested Cathy and Dave record themselves reading stories and nursery rhymes so these could be played to Sam when they weren't there.

## Taking time out

The hospital staff encouraged both parents to spend as much time as possible with Sam, and to help feed and change him as their confidence grew. But two and a half weeks after Sam's birth, Cathy had a crisis. The shock of the premature birth, the anxiety of the first few days, and the loss of sleep because of expressing at night were all having their effect, and she felt that she had no emotional resources left to carry her through. She was physically and mentally exhausted by the whole experience. In addition, she was constantly anxious about Sam and especially worried about how he would cope once he was out of his incubator and the special care baby unit.

When one of the nurses found her sobbing, she realized that Cathy herself needed some tender loving care. She suggested that Cathy talk to Dave about her feelings. Dave had thought that Cathy was totally absorbed with Sam, but he was only too happy to spend time with Cathy each day for cuddles, and to share the care of Sam. Cathy also started to take some time for herself and to spoil herself now and then with nutritious treats like strawberries out of season. She made sure she drank lots of mineral water to keep herself healthy and well hydrated for breastfeeding.

There are many things you can do to help your pre-term baby in the first days and weeks of his life in the special care baby unit.

- If at all possible, express breastmilk for your pre-term baby.

- Do everything you can to stay in touch with your baby while he is in an incubator. Ask the nurses to let you help change him, and make sure you stroke and caress him whenever you can.

- Keep talking to your baby. The sound of your voice will comfort him.

- Don't forget to look after yourself too. You'll need all your strength to care for your baby when he's ready to come home.

*Miriam Stoppard*

## Going home

Before Sam was ready to leave hospital, the staff got him used to breastmilk from a bottle so that he learned to suck well before he was put on to the breast. In the last week before he was due to go home, he was taking five meals out of eight from Cathy's breast, so she got over the tricky stage of getting Sam used to the breast in the reassuring environment of the unit and with expert midwife advice and help at hand.

When Sam was 38 weeks, and 2.5kg (5lb 8oz) in weight – ten weeks after he was born – Cathy and Dave took him home and felt like a real family for the first time.

A week later Sam weighed in at 2.6kg (5lb 12oz) and was thriving. Cathy and Dave were delighted by his progress. However, I explained to Cathy that she must age Sam as if he were still in her womb: he wasn't two months old, but 39 weeks, and so she shouldn't expect him to catch up completely with full-term babies of his age until he was about two years old.

## Milk formulas

A variety of milk formulas is available, all carefully formulated to make them as close as possible to breastmilk.

Most formulas are based on cows' milk. Some formulas are available both in powder and ready-mixed forms. There are soya-based formulas available, but never give these to your baby without the advice of your doctor or midwife.

■ Ready-mixed milk comes in cartons or ready-to-feed bottles and is ultra-heat-treated (UHT), which means it is sterile and will keep in a cool place until the "best before" date. Once the carton has been opened, the milk will keep for 24 hours in a refrigerator. Ready-mixed milk is more expensive than powdered formula, but it is very convenient, and you may like to use it when you are travelling.

■ If you use powdered formula it is essential that you make it up precisely according to the manufacturer's instructions. Some parents are tempted to add extra powder to make the milk "more nourishing", but this will lead to your baby getting too much protein and fat, and not enough water. This can cause constipation.

■ If you add too little powder as you make up the feed, your baby will not be getting the nutrients he needs for healthy growth.

# Bottles and milk

Once you make the decision to bottlefeed, stick to it, and don't feel guilty about it. The majority of babies will have a bottle at some stage – if not continuously right from the start, then often after weaning or with supplementary bottles. New infant formulas, bottles, and teats appear on the market regularly, all with the aim of making bottlefeeding as convenient and as similar to breastfeeding as possible. Just make sure that your baby has the same attention and closeness at feeding times as he would have if you were breastfeeding. Mother's milk is important to your baby, but it is not as important as your love.

The one thing you can't give your baby if you bottlefeed from the start is colostrum. This contains antibodies that protect your baby against a range of infections (see p.40), so even if you're not intending to breastfeed your baby, you will be giving him a good start if you put him to the breast in the first few days. If you decide not to do this, the hospital staff or your partner can take care of your baby's first feeds.

One of the good things about bottlefeeding is that the new father can be just as involved as mum at feeding times. Make sure that your partner feeds your baby as soon as possible after the birth. This way he can get used to the technique and won't be afraid to handle the baby. The sooner he learns to do all the things that your baby needs, the better. Encourage your partner to open his shirt when giving a bottle so that the baby nestles up to his skin as he feeds and bonds with his father's smell.

## Bottles and teats

There's a wide range of different feeding bottles and teats now available. You may need to try a few to find out what suits your baby best. Below are some examples.

◄ BOTTLES (LEFT TO RIGHT)
Tapered bottle, Waisted bottle, Easy-grip bottle, Disposable bottle.

▲ CLEANING IN A DISHWASHER Once your baby is over 12 months you can wash feeding equipment in a dishwasher on the normal cycle. Clean teats before they go in (see column, right).

▲ BOILING To sterilize your baby's bottles and teats by boiling, you need to boil them for at least ten minutes. Then remove them from the water and allow them to cool down before using.

# Take care

To reduce the risk of your baby contracting any kind of gastro-intestinal infection, make sure that everything that comes in contact with your baby's food is thoroughly cleaned or sterilized before use.

Always make sure that you wash your hands before handling any formula or feeding equipment. Your baby's dummies and teething rings should also be thoroughly cleaned each time they are used.

You should always make up your baby's bottle when you need it, and never in advance. Making up formula feeds in advance then reheating a bottle when your baby needs a feed increases the risk of him becoming ill as they are prime sources of infection. Also if your baby doesn't finish a bottle throw the milk away.

## Buying feeding equipment

If you know you are going to bottlefeed, buy your feeding equipment well in advance of having your baby so that you can practise with it before the birth. Large department stores and chemists sell bottlefeeding packs that contain all the essential equipment. Buy unbreakable bottles with a wide neck as they're easier to fill and to clean; the 250ml (10floz) size is the most suitable. The teat should ideally be one shaped to fit the baby's mouth. Disposable bottles are useful when travelling, and for when you run out of sterilized bottles.

## Sterilizing feeding equipment

Young babies are very vulnerable to infections so every bit of feeding equipment needs to be carefully cleaned after use. It is not enough just to wash equipment – it must also be sterilized and there are several ways of doing this. Popular methods include boiling or using a cold-water sterilizing unit or a steam sterilizer. Whatever type you use, always read the manufacturer's instructions carefully and follow them exactly.

With cold-water sterilizing units, bottles can be left in the solution until needed. Before using a bottle, shake off any excess solution from both the bottle and the teat or rinse with cooled, boiled water from the kettle. If using a steam sterilizer, equipment should be re-sterilized before you use it if not used straight after sterilizing.

You can also sterilize your equipment in the microwave using a specially designed steam unit, as long as the feeding equipment is suitable for microwave use.

▲ WASHING BOTTLES AND TEATS All equipment should be washed in hot, soapy water. Scrub the insides of the bottles with a bottle brush and rub the teats to remove any traces of milk. Rinse everything under warm, running water to remove soap, then sterilize.

## Ready-mixed formula

Using a ready-made formula is more straightforward than mixing your own, but strict rules of hygiene should still be observed.

■ Use a clean brush to scrub the top of the carton before opening, particularly the cutting line.

■ Cut the corner off the carton with clean scissors. Avoid touching the cut edges, as you could contaminate the milk.

■ Don't store milk that your baby has left in the bottle; it will have been contaminated with saliva.

# Bottlefeeding your baby

When you're bottlefeeding, there are a couple of essential points to bear in mind. The formula should be properly made up so that your baby gets correct amounts of both nutrients and water, and your baby should be able to draw milk at a comfortable rate. Make up one bottle at a time, mixing it in the bottle according to the manufacturer's instructions. Never add an extra scoop of formula or sugar. Always make sure your hands and the work surface you're using are scrupulously clean.

## Giving a bottlefeed

When you're giving your baby a bottle, imitate the closeness of breastfeeding. Make sure you're comfortable and your arms are well supported. Hold your baby half-sitting with his head in the crook of your elbow and his back along your forearm; this will allow him to swallow safely and easily. Keep your face close to his and chat to him all the time.

If you prefer, there are other positions that are suitable for bottlefeeding. For example, you could try lying down with your baby tucked under your arm – this position is especially comfortable for

# Making up formula

1 **WASHING EQUIPMENT** Always wash your baby's bottles as soon as possible after a feed. Wash all of the equipment in hot, soapy water. Scrub the insides of bottles with a bottle brush and rub teats thoroughly to remove milk. Rinse everything well in warm, running water then sterilize them.

2 **MEASURING OUT FORMULA** Wash your hands well. Fill a feeding bottle with the correct amount of cooled boiled water. Using the scoop provided, measure out the required amount of formula and add to the bottle. Use a knife to level off each scoopful; don't pack the formula down into the scoop.

3 **MIXING FORMULA** Put the cap and teat on the bottle. Shake it until you're sure that there are no lumps or residue and the mixture is smooth. Never add extra formula to a bottle or the milk will be too concentrated and could be dangerous for your baby; it can also cause constipation.

night feeds. Try several different feeding positions until you decide which one suits you and your baby best (see p.41).

Before you begin, test the heat of the milk (see right); you should already have tested the flow (see below). If necessary, slightly loosen the cap of the bottle so that air can get in. If your baby is having difficulty drawing the milk, gently remove the bottle from his mouth so that air can enter the bottle, then continue as before. Hold the bottle at an angle so that your baby doesn't swallow air with the milk.

## The flow of milk

The hole in a teat should be large enough to let the milk flow in a stream of several drops per second when the bottle is inverted. If the hole is too large, your baby will get too much milk too fast and splutter; if it's too small, your baby will get tired from sucking before he's satisfied. You can buy teats with different-sized holes. Alternatively, to make the hole in a teat bigger, insert a fine, red-hot needle gently through the hole to melt the rubber (stick one end of the needle into a cork so you can hold it over a flame to heat it). Sculpted teats, which are shaped to fit the baby's palate and allow him more control over the flow, are best.

## Checking the temperature

Always feed your baby freshly made formula milk. Making feeds in advance and storing them increases the risk of contamination, which could make your baby ill. Check the milk is at the correct temperature before you begin.

■ **Testing milk temperature** Try a few drops on your wrist: it should be neither hot nor cold to the touch.

■ **Cooling the milk** Place the bottle in a jug or bowl of cold water for a few minutes. You could also run it under the cold tap, shaking it all the time.

# Bottlefeeding

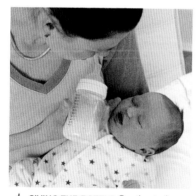

1 **GIVING THE BOTTLE** Gently stroke your baby's nearest cheek to elicit his sucking reflex. Insert the teat carefully into his mouth. If you push the teat too far back he may gag on it.

2 **DURING THE FEED** Chat to your baby as you feed. Let him pause mid-feed if he likes. Change him on to the other arm at this stage to give him a new view, and your arm a rest.

3 **REMOVING THE BOTTLE** If you want your baby to release the bottle, gently slide your little finger into the corner of his mouth. This will break the suction on the teat.

# Tips on bottlefeeding

Bottlefeeding is simple and straightforward, but you'll need to make sure that your baby can swallow properly, and that he's not taking in air with the milk.

■ Never leave your baby with the bottle propped up on a pillow or cushion; it can be dangerous. He could become very uncomfortable if he swallows a lot of air with the feed, and he could choke. Moreover, he'll miss the cuddling and affection that he should enjoy while he feeds.

■ Tilt your baby on your arm. It's very difficult for your baby to swallow when he's lying flat so don't feed him in this position; he may gag or even be sick.

■ If your baby has a blocked nose he can't swallow and breathe at the same time. Your doctor can give you nose drops to be used before each feed.

■ Don't change your milk formula without first consulting your midwife or health visitor, even if you think your baby doesn't like it. It's very unusual for a brand of milk to be responsible for a baby not feeding well; very rarely cows' milk causes allergies in babies, but never change to a substitute formula without medical advice.

■ Your baby knows when he's had enough, so don't try to force him to finish the bottle after he's stopped sucking.

# Bottlefeeding routines

Bottlefed babies tend to be fed less frequently than breastfed ones. This is because formula milk contains slightly different proteins and takes longer to digest than breast milk. A four-hourly regime of six feeds a day seems to suit most bottlefed babies after the first two or three days, whereas breastfed babies will probably take seven feeds a day. When first born, your baby will probably not take much over 60ml (2floz) at each feed, but as he grows he'll take fewer and larger feeds.

Never feed your baby according to the clock; let him determine when he is to be fed. He'll let you know quite clearly with cries when he's hungry. Your baby's appetite will vary, so if he seems satisfied, allow him to leave what he doesn't want. Don't feel that your baby has to finish the bottle at each feed. He'll get too full and posset it back (see opposite); or worse, become overfed and fat. But if your baby is still hungry, give him some extra from another bottle. If this happens regularly, start to make more milk for every feed.

## Night feeds

Your baby will need feeding at least once during the night, and this break in your sleep on top of all the other things that you have to do may make you extremely tired and tense. The problem isn't so much the sleep that you lose, but more the way in which your sleep patterns are broken over long periods. For this reason, try to get adequate rest, day and night, and share the jobs with your partner.

## Reducing night feeds

At first your baby won't be able to sleep for more than five hours at a time without waking with hunger. Once he reaches a weight of about 5kg (11lb), you can try to stretch the time between feeds until you're getting about six hours of undisturbed sleep at night. Although your baby will have his own routine, try to time his last feed to coincide with your own bedtime, which should be as late as possible. You may find that he still wakes up for the early morning feed, but you'll just have to be patient until he no longer needs it.

## Overfeeding

Obese babies are nine times more likely to be obese adults, with all the attendant dangers to health. Unfortunately, it's easy to overfeed a bottlefed baby, for two reasons. First, it's tempting to put extra formula into the bottle, so always follow the instructions precisely (see p.52), otherwise you'll be giving your baby unwanted calories. Second, in your anxiety to feed him "properly" you'll want to see your baby finish the last drop of his feed, but you should always let him decide when he's finished. Introducing solids too early and giving sweet, syrupy drinks also cause overfeeding.

## Underfeeding

This is rare in bottlefed babies, but if your child consistently seems fretful after he drains each bottle, he may well be hungry. Offer him an extra 60ml (2floz) of formula. If he takes it, then he needs it.

If your baby demands frequent feeds but doesn't take much, the teat hole may be too small (see p.52) so that he is having difficulty sucking the milk and is tired before he gets enough.

## Winding

Winding releases air that's swallowed during feeding. It's unlikely that wind causes your baby discomfort, and many babies are not noticeably happier or more contented for having been winded. Swallowing air is more common in bottlefed babies, but you can prevent it to some extent by tilting the bottle more as your baby empties it so that the teat is full of milk and not air, or by using disposable bottles. Whether you breast- or bottlefeed, winding your baby makes you pause, slow down, hold him gently, and stroke or pat him, and this is good for you both.

## Possetting

If your baby tends to bring food straight back up (and some babies never do), you may wonder if he's keeping enough down. My youngest son had a tendency to posset, and I worried that he wasn't getting enough to eat. I simply followed my own instinct, which was to offer him more food. If he didn't take it, I assumed that he had possetted an excess that he didn't need. The most common cause of possetting in very young babies is overfeeding, and this is another reason why you should never insist that your baby finishes his bottle.

Forcible vomiting, especially if it occurs after several feeds, should be reported immediately to your doctor; vomiting is always very serious in a small baby as it can quickly lead to dehydration (see Pyloric stenosis, p.29).

◀ **WINDING YOUR BABY** Hold your baby close to you and stroke or pat him gently to help him bring up air bubbles.

## Putting your baby down

**You should always lay your baby down on his back to sleep.**

Research has shown that babies who sleep on their fronts are at greater risk from cot death than those placed on their backs, and publicity in the UK about this finding has resulted in a significant drop in cot deaths. But it is important to be sure your baby moves his head from side to side to avoid the back of his skull becoming flattened.

# Holding and handling

A young baby is more robust than you think, but when you handle your baby keep your movements as slow, gentle, and quiet as possible. You'll find that you instinctively hold your baby close, look into his eyes, and talk soothingly to him. For your baby's comfort, and your own peace of mind, it's important to feel at ease when you handle him; you need to hold your baby confidently in order to bathe, dress, and feed him successfully.

## Handling your baby

Babies love physical contact. Premature babies, for example, gain more weight when they are laid on fleecy sheets that give them the sensation of being touched, than when they are laid on smooth ones. Your newborn baby will find comfort in any kind of skin-to-skin contact, but the best way to give him this is for both of you to lie naked in bed. Here he can get to know the smell and feel your skin and hear your heart beating.

## How to pick up your baby

1 **PICKING UP** To lift your baby, slide one hand under his bottom and cradle his head with your other hand. His head must always be well supported. Talk to him all the time so he feels safe and comforted.

2 **SMOOTH AND STEADY** Lift your baby gently but firmly towards you, keeping your movements smooth and steady so he isn't startled or feels as though he is going to fall. Look into his eyes and keep talking to him.

3 **HOLD HIM CLOSE** Turn his body round so that he's resting against your chest and his back and arms are cradled by your arms. All babies love to be held where they can hear the familiar sound of your heartbeat.

## Picking up your baby

Whenever you pick your baby up and put him down, do it in a way that supports his head; until he is about four weeks old he'll have little control over it. If his head flops back, he will think that he is going to fall, his body will jerk, and he'll stretch out both arms and legs in the Moro, or "startle", reflex (see p.20).

Put your baby down and pick him up with your whole arm supporting his spine, neck, and head. You may like to try swaddling your baby: wrap him firmly in a shawl or blanket so that his head is supported and his arms held close against his body. Once he lies down in the cot, you can gently unwrap him. Swaddling your baby tightly makes him feel secure, so it's a useful way of comforting and calming a distressed baby, especially during colicky time in the evening.

## Carrying your baby

One way to carry your baby in your arms is to cradle his head in the crook of either arm, which is slightly inclined. The rest of his body will rest on the lower part of your arm, encircled by your wrist and hand, which support his back and bottom. Your other arm will provide additional support to his bottom and legs, and your baby can see your face as you talk to him and smile at him.

The second way to carry your baby is to hold him against the upper part of your chest with his head on your shoulder. Place your forearm across his back and support his resting head with your hand, leaving your other hand free. Use this hand to support your baby's bottom, or to help you balance as you get used to carrying your new baby.

◀ **SUPPORTING AND CRADLING** Hold your baby's head and support the length of his body when carrying him. Holding him close will make your baby feel secure and relaxed, especially if he can see your face.

## Baby carriers

**Young babies are best carried in slings worn on your chest, where they feel close to you and secure.**

■ Make sure your sling is easy to put on and comfortable to wear. Try it out with your baby before you buy it.

■ Your sling should support your baby's head and neck, and keep him secure; he must not be able to slip out of the sides.

■ The shoulder straps must be wide enough to support your growing baby's weight. Wide shoulder straps make carrying more comfortable.

■ It has been said that a baby shouldn't be carried in a sling until he can support his own head. This is not true. Use a sling as soon as you and your baby are happy about it.

▲ **USING A SLING** Carrying a baby in a lightweight fabric sling is comfortable for you and your young baby.

## Benefits for parents

Massage is a delightful and valuable activity that has advantages for you and your partner as well as your baby.

■ Massaging your newborn helps to enhance the bonding process between you and your child.

■ If you are anxious or have had little experience with children, massage allows you to get used to handling your new baby.

■ Massage is an ideal way to soothe an unsettled baby and can also help to calm your nerves with its relaxing effects.

■ You'll find that massaging your baby's soft, smooth skin is a sensual experience for both of you.

# Baby massage

Massage can have all the benefits for a baby that it has for an adult: it is soothing and can calm a fretful baby, and it's a marvellous way of showing love. If you massage your baby every day he will learn to recognize the routine and will show pleasure as you begin. You can continue to massage your baby as he gets older; a massage is often the ideal way to calm an excited toddler.

## Preparing for the massage

Provide a relaxed atmosphere before you start. As this will be a new experience for you both, any distractions can spoil the mood and upset your baby, so choose a time when there is no one else around and unplug the phone. Make sure the room is nice and warm and lay your baby on a warm towel or sheepskin, or on your lap. Make sure your hands are warm too. Use baby oil if you like, but don't use aromatherapy oils or nut-based oils such as almond. Stop massaging if your baby seems upset or appears not to be enjoying being massaged.

Make eye contact with your baby throughout the massage and talk quietly and lovingly to him. Start by lightly massaging the crown of your baby's head using a circular motion. Work from his head down using light, even strokes, and massage both sides of his body symmetrically.

# Giving a massage

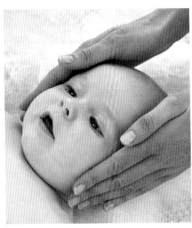

1 **HEAD** Stroke down the sides of your baby's face. Gently massage his forehead, working from the centre out, and moving over the eyebrows and cheeks to finish around his ears.

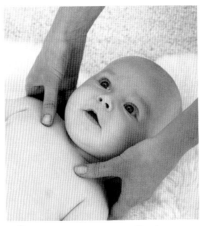

2 **NECK AND SHOULDERS** Gently massage your baby's neck from his ears to his shoulders and from his chin to his chest. Then stroke his shoulders from his neck outward.

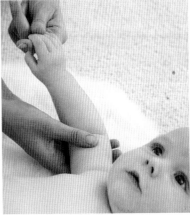

3 **ARMS** Stroke down his arms from his shoulders to his fingertips. Then using your fingers and thumb, gently squeeze all along his arm, working from his shoulder toward his wrist and hand.

**4 CHEST AND ABDOMEN** Gently stroke down your baby's chest, following the delicate curves of his ribs. Rub his abdomen in a circular motion, working outward from the navel.

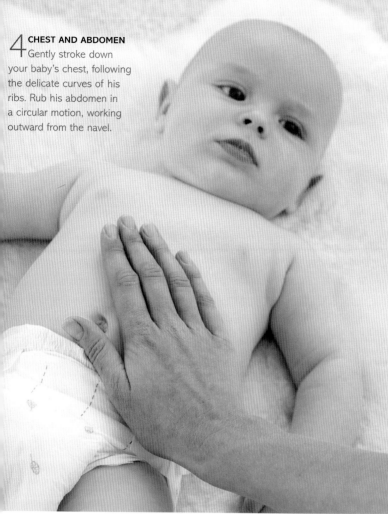

# Benefits for baby

**Your baby can only gain from the pleasures and sensations of a loving massage.**

■ Your baby loves being with you and the intimate contact of massage enhances this. He will recognize it as a clear sign of your love.

■ If he's unsettled your baby will be calmed by the soothing strokes of your hands, which will make him feel secure and relieve anxiety.

■ Massage can often ease minor digestive upsets, such as wind, which may well be making your baby fretful.

■ Babies need touch. Research has shown that they would rather be stroked than fed.

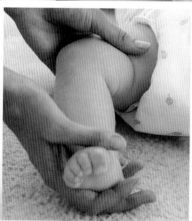

**5 LEGS** Now massage your baby's legs, working from his thighs down to his knees. Stroke down the shins, and move around to his calves and ankles. Then gently squeeze all the way down.

**6 FEET AND TOES** Rub your baby's ankles and feet, stroking from heel to toe, and massaging each toe. End with some long, light strokes running the whole length of your baby's front.

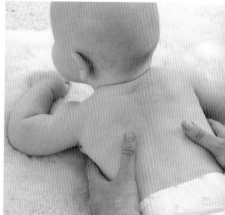

**7 BACK** Once you have massaged your baby's front, turn him over and work on his back. Massage from his shoulders downward. Continue to speak gently to your baby as you massage.

## Girls' clothes

Unisex stretch suits and rompers are ideal for everyday wear, but you may prefer more feminine clothes for special occasions.

■ Make sure all clothes are machine washable as they won't stay clean for long.

■ Avoid very fluffy or lacy cardigans. Fluffy ones will irritate your baby's skin, and tiny fingers catch in lacy ones.

■ Hats can be both practical and pretty. Choose one with ties or elastic and a wide brim for sun protection in summer.

▲ **DRESSING UP** Practical clothes are great for every day, but for special occasions it's fun to put your baby girl in a pretty dress.

# Dressing

Everyone loves dressing a baby. Your friends and family will all want to buy clothes for your baby. You are bound to take great pride in his appearance, and might like to buy some dressy clothes for special occasions, but there's no need to spend a lot of money – he will grow out of clothes very quickly. You might be able to buy some items secondhand from friends or relatives.

Remember that as far as your baby is concerned anything goes as long as it's soft and comfortable to wear, and can be put on and taken off without too much disturbance.

Your baby will posset and dribble on his clothes, and there are bound to be accidents and leaks from nappies, so buy only machine-washable, colour-fast clothing, and avoid white – it quickly gets dirty, and frequent washing makes it drab. Look for soft and comfortable clothes with no hard seams or rough stitching. Towelling, cotton, or pure wool clothes will feel nicer on your baby's skin. If you do buy clothes made of synthetic fibres, check that they feel soft.

Always choose clothes that are non-flammable, and avoid open-weave shawls and cardigans,

A chunky cardigan is a good alternative to a coat on cool days

◀ **CHOOSING CLOTHES**
Easy-fitting clothes will give your baby the most comfort and warmth. Pay special attention to the cuffs, ankles, and neck where fastenings could cause discomfort.

Dungarees are snug and comfy for babies

Loose-fitting shoes with soft soles allow movement

▲**BABY SLEEPING BAG** A baby sleeping bag is a good alternative to blankets. It can't be kicked off so keeps your baby warm and snug all night long.

▲**ALL IN ONE** Suits like this allow easy access for night-time changes. The type without feet may be best in summer so your baby doesn't get too hot

because your baby's fingers could easily get caught in the holes. Check the fastenings, too: poppers in the crotch allow easy access to the nappy area, and poppers at the neck mean your baby won't grow out of something quickly just because his head is too big for the neck opening. Babies hate having their faces covered, so look for wide, envelope necks or clothes that fasten down the front. Front-fastening clothes also allow you to dress (or undress) your baby without having to turn him over. This will make dressing more comfortable for him and easier for you.

Make a note of your baby's measurements and bring this with you when you go shopping for baby clothes. Babies of the same age vary a great deal in size, so look at the height and weight given on the label rather than the age. If in doubt, buy the larger size: loose-fitting clothes are warmer and much more comfortable than clothes that are too small and your baby will soon grow into them.

## Basic layette

- 6 wide-necked cotton vests or T-shirts
- 1 hat
- 1 shawl for swaddling
- 8 all-in-one stretch suits
- 2 woollen jackets or cardigans (4 in winter)

- 2 nightdresses with drawstring ends
- 2 pairs of socks and padders
- 2 pairs of mittens (for winter)
- 1 padded or fleecy all-in-one pram suit

# Boys' clothes

Look for clothes that are practical as well as smart to dress your baby boy.

- Strong primary colours look good on both sexes.

- A dungaree and T-shirt set is comfortable and looks smart. Look for dungarees with poppers at the crotch so that you can get at your baby's nappy easily.

- Hats with tie-down ear flaps are cosy in winter.

- Don't think tights are just for girls; babies lose socks and bootees very easily, so tights are practical as well as warm.

- Tracksuits are very comfortable and allow easy access to the nappy.

▲**SMART CLOTHES** You'll want some special clothes for your little boy to wear when you take him out. Soft corduroy trousers and a smart jumper look good and are practical too.

# Keeping your baby warm

You may worry that your new baby isn't warm enough, but a few common-sense precautions will keep him comfortable and safe. Remember that babies can easily become too hot; this could lead to heat rash, and is also a factor in cot death.

■ A great deal of body heat is lost through a bare head; make sure your baby always wears a hat when you take him outdoors.

■ Very young babies are unable to conserve body heat, and should be undressed only in a well-heated room and out of draughts.

■ Your baby's room should be at a constant temperature and the number of blankets he needs will depend on this temperature (see p.81).

■ If your baby is cold, you may need to warm him up. Adding a layer of clothes is not enough in itself; you need to put him in a warmer place first so that he can regain his normal body temperature, or hold him close to share your body heat.

■ Never leave your baby to sleep in the sun, or close to a source of direct heat such as a radiator.

■ Wrap your baby up if you take him outdoors, but remove outdoor clothes once you bring him inside again, otherwise he won't be able to cool down efficiently.

# Dressing your baby

At first you may be nervous about dressing and undressing your baby, but it will become easier with practice, so just be gentle and patient.

Always dress and undress a young baby on a non-slip flat surface, as this allows you to keep both hands free – a changing mat is ideal at first. Your baby is very likely to cry as you take off his clothes. This is because young babies hate the feel of the air on their naked bodies; they like to feel snug and secure. It's not because you're hurting him, so don't get flustered by him if he does cry.

## How to dress your baby

1 **PUT VEST OVER HEAD** Lay your baby on a flat, non-slip surface and check her nappy is clean. Roll the vest up and pull the neck apart. Put it over her head so that it doesn't touch her face, raising her head slightly as you do so.

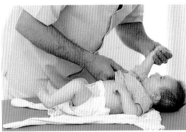

2 **VEST ARMHOLES** Widen the left sleeve or armhole and gently guide your baby's arm through it. Repeat with the other arm. Pull the vest down.

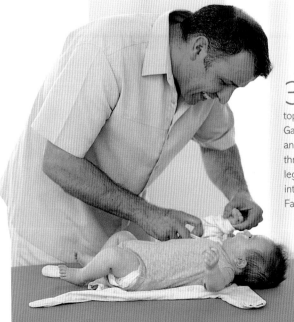

3 **STRETCH SUIT** Lay your baby on top of the open suit. Gather up each sleeve and guide her fists through. Open up each leg and guide her feet into the stretch suit. Fasten the suit.

# How to undress your baby

## Dressing on your lap

When your baby is three or four months old, he'll have enough muscle control to sit on your lap while you dress and undress him.

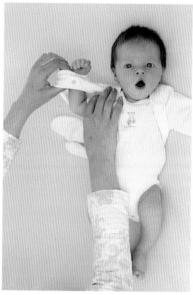

▲ **SIT WITH YOUR LEGS CROSSED** Your baby will fit neatly in the hollow of your legs. Cradle her with your arm, as her back will still need some support. You may find it easier to deal with her bottom half while she's lying flat.

1 **UNDOING THE SUIT** Put your baby on a flat, non-slip surface and unfasten his stretch suit. If his nappy needs changing, gently pull both legs out of the suit so that his top remains covered while you change him.

2 **REMOVING THE TOP** Grasp each sleeve by the cuff and gently slide your baby's hand out. If he's wearing a vest, roll it up towards the neck and gently pull his arms from the sleeves, holding him by each elbow as you do so.

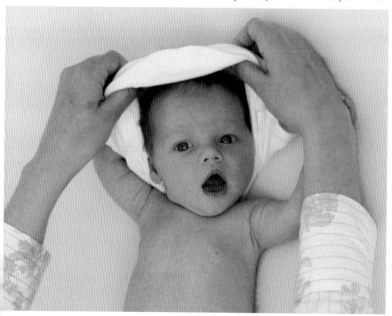

3 **TAKING OFF THE VEST** Stretch the neck of the vest as wide as you can and lift it over your baby's head, keeping the fabric off his face.

4

## Washing a girl

When you are washing your baby girl wipe from front to back – that is, towards the anus – when you clean the nappy area.

This will avoid soiling the vulva, and minimize the risk of spreading bacteria from the bowels to the bladder or vagina, which could cause infection.

If any faeces should get into the vagina, gently part the labia and clean by squeezing a large ball of cotton wool moistened with warm water from front to back on the outside of the vagina.

# Bathing and hygiene

Part of your daily routine will be to keep your baby clean. Many new parents worry about handling a very small baby in the baby bath, but you'll soon get used to bath times and look forward to them as a chance to have fun and play with your baby. Instead of feeling apprehensive, set aside half an hour and have everything you need around you. Relax, and you will enjoy it.

A young baby doesn't need bathing very often because only his bottom, face and neck, and skin creases get dirty. You only have to bathe him every two or three days, and even then you can top and tail him instead of putting him in the bath (see below). This allows you to wash the parts of your baby that really need washing with the minimum of disturbance and distress to him. Use cooled boiled water for a newborn, but when your baby is a little older you can use warm water straight from the tap. Do wash your baby's hair frequently to prevent cradle cap forming (see p.69). There is no need to use soap for a newborn; from about six weeks you can use bath lotion, soap, or other baby toiletries.

Many young babies don't like having their skin exposed to the air, so don't leave your baby undressed for any longer than you have to at bath time. Warm a big, fluffy towel on a radiator (not too hot) while you are

## Topping and tailing

1 **FACE AND EARS** Using cooled boiled water, moisten a piece of cotton wool and gently wipe your baby's face. Wipe the eyes from the bridge of the nose outwards. Clean the outer ear, then clean behind the ear.

2 **HANDS AND FEET** Clean with new pieces of cotton wool. Dry hands and feet thoroughly with a towel. For an older baby you can use a facecloth.

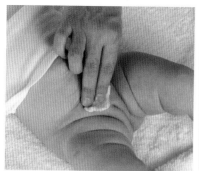

▲ **WET NAPPY** Remove her nappy. If it's just wet, wipe the nappy area with cotton wool dampened with water or some baby lotion.

▲ **SOILED NAPPY** If her nappy is soiled, remove as much of the faeces as you can with the nappy. Clean the nappy area with moist cotton wool (see p.74).

bathing him and have it ready to wrap your baby in as soon as you are finished. Then sit him on your knee while you dry him gently.

## Body care

Once you have taken care of your baby's nappy area, and made sure that his skin is free from any traces of food or dirt that might cause irritation, the rest will take care of itself.

**Eyes, nose, and ears** Wash your baby's eyes with cotton wool and some cooled boiled water. Work from the inner part of the eye to the outer, and use a different piece of cotton wool for each eye to avoid spreading any infection that may be present.

Don't poke around inside your baby's nose and ears; they are self-cleaning so don't use nose or ear drops, except on your doctor's advice. Just clean ears using moist cotton wool. If you see wax in your baby's ears, don't try to scrape it out; it is a natural secretion of the canal of the outer ear, is antiseptic, and protects the eardrum from dust and grit. Removing it will only cause the ear to produce more. If you are concerned, consult your doctor.

**Nails** Your newborn baby's nails should be kept short; otherwise he may scratch his skin. The best time to trim your baby's nails is after a bath, when they are soft; use a pair of small, blunt-ended scissors or file them gently with a soft emery board. Don't bite them.

**Navel** During the few days after birth, the umbilical stump (see p.15) dries and shrivels, and then it drops off. You can bathe your baby before the stump has healed, as long as you dry the area thoroughly afterwards. Allow the area to stay open to the air as much as you can to help speed up the shrinking and healing process.

## Washing a boy

Never pull your baby boy's foreskin back for cleaning; it's quite tight and could get stuck. Wash the whole of the nappy area and dry carefully, particularly the skin creases. By the time your baby is three or four years of age, the foreskin will be loose and can retract without force.

**Circumcision** If your baby has just been circumcised, you should watch carefully for any signs of bleeding. A few drops of blood are quite normal; so is swelling and slight inflammation, but this will settle down. If bleeding persists, however, or if there is any sign of infection, consult your doctor. Make sure that you get advice about bathing your baby and special care of the penis, and what to do about the dressing if one has been applied.

## Bathing tips

**Make bath times as pleasant as possible for you and your baby.**

■ Before you start, check you have everything that you need to hand.

■ Always put cold water into the bath first. Test the final temperature with your elbow or the inner side of your wrist.

■ Keep the bath shallow. About 5–8cm (2–3in) is deep enough.

■ Keep the time that your baby is undressed to a minimum; small babies quickly become cold.

■ Wear a waterproof apron to protect your clothing; a plastic-backed towelling one will feel nice against your baby's skin.

■ Warm a towel on a radiator, but don't let it get too hot.

■ Baby bath lotion added to the bath water is better to use than soap as it is less dehydrating.

# Giving a bath

You can bathe your baby in any room that is warm, has no draughts, and has enough space to lay out all that you need. If necessary you can fill the baby's bath in the kitchen or bathroom and then carry it to the chosen room, provided it's not too heavy.

A small baby can be washed in a specially designed plastic baby bath with a non-slip surface. Place the bath on a worktop or table of a convenient height, usually about hip-height, so that you don't have to bend too much. This will protect your back from unnecessary strain. Some baby baths come with their own stands, or are designed to straddle the bath tub, which makes bathing your baby a far more comfortable task.

## Giving your baby a bath

**2 BEFORE THE BATH** Undress your baby, clean his nappy area (see pp.74–5), and wrap him in a towel. Clean his face and ears gently with moistened cotton wool (see p.64).

**1 TEST THE WATER** Use your elbow or the inner side of your wrist to test the temperature of the water. It should feel neither very hot nor very cold. Until you get the feel of the right temperature, use a bath thermometer, which should register 29.4°C (85°F).

3 **WASHING HIS HEAD** Holding your baby in a football carry, as shown, lean over the bath, and wash his head. Rinse well and pat dry. A gentle brushing is good for cradle cap.

4 **PUTTING HIM IN THE BATH** Support your baby's shoulders with one hand, tucking your fingers under his armpit, and support his legs or bottom with the other. Keep smiling and talking to him as you place him in the bath.

# Fear of bathing

Some babies are terrified of having a bath. Should your baby be frightened, don't force him to remain in the water; try again after a couple of days, using only a little water in the bath. You can give sponge baths or top and tail in the meantime.

If your baby continues to be frightened of water, introduce it in a play context. Fill a large bowl and place it in a warm room (not the bathroom) and put some toys into the bowl. Undress your baby and encourage him to play with the toys. If he seems happy, encourage him to paddle in the water, keeping a firm grip on him.

After you have done this a couple of times, swap the bowl for a baby bath and continue to let your baby play. When he tries to get into the water with the toys, you'll know he's lost his fear of water, but be patient; let him do this a couple of times before you wash him in the bath as well as letting him play.

5 **WASHING** Keep one hand under your baby's shoulders so that his head and shoulders are kept out of the water, and use your free hand to wash him.

6 **LIFTING HIM OUT** When your baby is clean and well rinsed, lift him gently on to the towel, supporting him as before.

7 **DRYING** Wrap your baby in the towel and dry him thoroughly. Don't use talcum powder on the nappy area; it could cause irritation.

## Toiletries

A newborn's skin is delicate.
Avoid using soap or wipes until
your baby is at least six weeks
old as it will remove the natural
oils from his skin and leave it dry
and uncomfortable. Special baby
toiletries are mild and won't
irritate your baby's skin – many
are hypo-allergenic.

■ A little baby oil or olive oil in
your baby's bath water is a
good moisturizer for very dry
skin Adding oil makes your baby
slippery, so take special care
when using oils at bath time.

■ For delicate skin, like the nappy
area, baby lotion is an ideal
cleanser and moisturizer.

■ Baby powder can be drying to
your baby's skin and has very little
benefit. Most parents find it best
to use an ointment instead.

■ Zinc and castor oil cream or
petroleum jelly are waterproof
and will protect your baby's skin
from urine. Medicated nappy
creams containing titanium salts
are good if your baby has nappy
rash (see p.77).

# Giving a sponge bath

If your baby really hates being undressed, or if you're a bit daunted by
giving him a bath, give him a sponge bath instead. Hold your baby securely
on your lap while removing the minimum amount of clothing at any time.
If you find it difficult to manoeuvre your baby while he's on your lap, put
him on a changing mat and follow the same sponge bath method.

## How to give a sponge bath

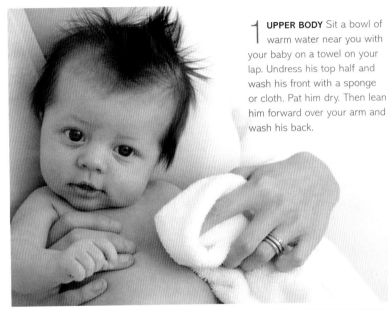

1 **UPPER BODY** Sit a bowl of
warm water near you with
your baby on a towel on your
lap. Undress his top half and
wash his front with a sponge
or cloth. Pat him dry. Then lean
him forward over your arm and
wash his back.

2 **NAPPY AREA** Either wash your
baby's hair at this stage, or remove
his lower clothing and nappy. Clean the
nappy area (see p.75); put a vest on
him if he doesn't like being undressed.

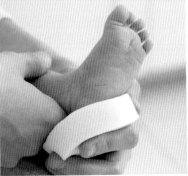

3 **LOWER BODY** Using the sponge or
cloth, wash your baby's legs and
feet. Gently pat his skin dry, put on
barrier cream (if you use it) and a
clean nappy, and dress him.

# Care of the hair

From birth you can wash your baby's hair every day if you choose, with bath lotion dissolved in water. After about 12 to 16 weeks, wash his hair once or twice a week with baby shampoo. A non-sting variety of baby shampoo is best, but still take care to avoid his eyes. You can use a "football carry" (see picture, right) for a small baby, or you can sit on the edge of the bath with your baby across your legs, facing you. (He will feel secure this way.) Don't be nervous about the fontanelles (see p.14); the membrane that covers them is very tough, and there's no

▲ HAIR WASHING Tuck the legs under your armpit in a "football carry". Support the back and cradle the head.

need to scrub the hair, so you can do no harm as long as you're gentle. Apply the shampoo or bath lotion to your baby's hair and gradually work it in until a lather forms. Wait about 15 seconds before rinsing it off; there's no need to apply it a second time. To rinse the hair, just use a flannel dipped in warm water to wipe the suds away. Try to remove every trace of soap. When drying your baby's hair, try not to cover his face as he may panic and start to cry.

## Dislike of hair washing

Many babies hate having their hair washed, even if they enjoy having a bath. If this is the case with your baby, it may be best to keep hair washing separate from bath time; if your child associates the two he may start to fuss about taking baths as well. The main reason for dislike of hair washing is that babies hate water and soap in their eyes. Shields are available that fit around the hairline and prevent water and suds running down your baby's face. He'll be less distressed if you hold him in your lap while you wash his hair, and use a flannel to wet and rinse his hair rather than pouring water over his head.

Never try to force the issue, and never forcibly hold your baby still while you wash his hair. If hair washing is very distressing for him, give up for two or three weeks before trying again. Keep his hair reasonably clean by sponging it to remove any dirt, or brushing it out with a soft, damp brush. The hair will probably become greasy, but this won't do any harm.

# Cradle cap

Occasionally, pale, scaly patches may appear on your baby's scalp. Cradle cap is extremely common, and isn't caused by a lack of hygiene, or by any shampoo you're using. It usually disappears after a few weeks.

Prevent cradle cap from forming by gently washing your newborn baby's scalp every day with a very soft bristle brush and a little baby shampoo dissolved in warm water. Comb through the hair, even if he has very little, to stop scales from forming. If cradle cap does appear, smear a little olive oil on his scalp at night to soften and loosen the scales, making them easy to wash away. Don't be tempted to pick them off with your fingernail as that only encourages more scales to form. If the condition persists or spreads, consult your health visitor or pharmacist, who may recommend a special shampoo.

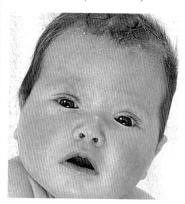

▲ CRADLE CAP Scaly patches on a baby's scalp are very common. They're harmless, and usually clear up after a few weeks without any need for special treatment.

## Kidneys and bladder

Once food has been absorbed into the bloodstream, waste has to be removed from the blood by the kidneys and eliminated as urine from the bladder.

**Urine production** Waste chemicals in the blood are removed and dissolved in water by the kidneys. The urine then passes down the ureters and into the bladder.

**Voiding** Urine is temporarily stored in the bladder, which is periodically emptied through the urethra. Your baby will not even be aware of passing urine until he's about 15–18 months (see pp.126–27). The sensation of wanting to pass urine doesn't come until several months later, because the infant bladder can only hold urine for a few minutes.

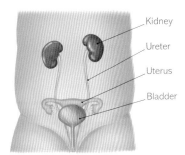

Kidney
Ureter
Uterus
Bladder

▲ **KIDNEYS AND BLADDER** The urinary and reproductive systems are closely linked; a girl's bladder is in front of the uterus.

# Bowel and bladder

A newborn baby can need up to ten nappy changes a day and, although the frequency of changes will decrease, most babies don't achieve a degree of bowel and bladder control until the second year. Although you can't speed up this process, your help and support will be very important to your child.

## Passing urine

A young baby's bladder will empty itself automatically and frequently both day and night. As soon as it contains a little urine, the bladder wall stretches and the emptying action is stimulated. This is absolutely normal, and your baby cannot be expected to behave differently, at least until the bladder has developed sufficiently to hold urine for longer periods.

## Bowel movements

When your baby was in the womb, his intestines were filled with a sticky, black substance called meconium. Meconium is passed in the first 24 hours after delivery, and once this has happened normal motions will take over. Once your baby settles into a regular routine, his stools will become firmer and paler.

The number of stools a baby passes varies greatly, and initially most bottlefed babies pass a stool for every feed. On the other hand, a breastfed baby may pass only one stool a day or less because there is little waste. The frequency of bowel motions gradually decreases as your baby gets older. It may be that, at the beginning, your baby passes five or six a day, but after three or four weeks he may have only two movements a day. This is quite normal and should cause you no worry. Similarly, the odd loose, unformed stool or totally green stool is no cause for concern unless looseness persists beyond 24 hours; then seek your doctor's advice.

## Changes in bowel movements

Don't worry if your baby's stools change in appearance from one day to the next. It's normal for a stool to turn green or brown when left exposed to the air. If you are worried, ask your midwife or doctor, who will be able to advise and reassure you. As a rule, loose stools are not an indication of an infection. Watery stools, however, if accompanied by a sudden change in colour or smell, or in frequency of passing stools, should be mentioned to your doctor, especially if your baby is "off colour" (see p.276).

Blood-streaked stools are never normal. The cause may be quite minor – a tiny crack in the skin around the anus, perhaps – but you must consult your doctor. Larger amounts of blood, or the appearance of pus or mucus, may indicate an intestinal infection, so call your doctor at once.

**The breastfed baby** By the third to fifth day, the light yellow stools typical of the breastfed baby will appear. The stools are rarely hard or smelly and may be no thicker than cream soup. The food you eat affects your baby and anything very spicy or acidic could upset his digestion.

**The bottlefed baby** A baby fed on formula has a tendency to more frequent stools, which are firmer, browner, and smellier than those of a breastfed baby. The most common tendency is for the stools to be rather hard. The easiest way to put this right is to give your baby a little cooled, boiled water to drink in between feeds.

## Diarrhoea

Diarrhoea – loose, frequent, and watery stools – is a sign of irritation of the intestines. In young babies diarrhoea is always potentially serious because of the risk of dehydration, which can develop very quickly. If your baby refuses food or has any of the following symptoms, you must contact your doctor immediately.

- Repeated watery stools.
- Repeated green and smelly stools.
- A fever of 38°C (100°F) or more.
- Pus or blood in his stools.
- Listlessness and dark-ringed eyes.

If you think your baby is dehydrated, look at his fontanelles. If they are depressed, your baby is dehydrated: contact your doctor immediately. If it is treated early, diarrhoea can be cured quickly.

You can start treating your baby immediately yourself if his diarrhoea is mild, and he has no other symptoms. Continue to nurse your baby if you are breastfeeding; diarrhoea usually clears up well on breastmilk. If you're bottlefeeding, giving half-strength formula may help. Make the bottle up with half the regular formula to the usual amount of water. He may feed for less time than usual, and be hungry more often. If mild diarrhoea doesn't improve within two days, check with your doctor.

Drinks of mineral replacement salts formulated specially for infants may be helpful at this stage. If all goes well, you can return to feeding your baby as usual.

## Bowel function

Food passes through the stomach into the small intestine, and from there to the large intestine. The waste products of food are stored in the rectum before finally being eliminated as faeces.

**Digestion** The food is broken down by enzymes. Digestion starts in the mouth, then continues in the stomach and the upper part of the small intestine.

**Absorption** Once the food has been reduced to simple molecules, it is absorbed into the bloodstream as it continues its path through the small intestine. It then passes through the large intestine, where any water is absorbed by the body. The waste products pass on to the rectum as faeces.

**Elimination** Faeces are stored in the rectum and expelled through the anus. A baby can't control the reflex that causes the rectum to empty – even for a second. Young babies generally have bowel movements with each feed.

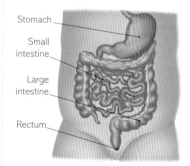

Stomach

Small intestine

Large intestine

Rectum

▲ **THE BOWEL SYSTEM** After food has been digested in the stomach and small intestine, the waste is passed out of the body as faeces.

## Girls' nappies

**A girl will tend to wet her nappy at the centre, or towards the back if she's lying down.**

Disposable day- and night-time nappies are designed differently to take this into account, with the padding at its thickest where it's needed most.

▼ **SPECIAL OCCASIONS** You may like to buy decorative or frilly pants to cover fabric nappies; these look pretty under a dress for a special occasion.

# Nappies

Your first choice in nappies will be between reusable and disposable types. Most parents prefer to use disposables, though an increasing consciousness of environmental issues and concerns over the length of time it takes for the chemicals in disposable nappies to decompose has led many parents to reconsider the virtues of fabric nappies. Yet the issue is not clear cut: the detergents required to clean fabric nappies can be viewed as pollutants to the water supply, and the energy required to wash them might also be regarded as wasteful. While fabric nappies are cheaper than disposables in the long run, you need to consider the increased electricity bills for frequent washing-machine and tumble-dryer runs, and the cost in your time.

## Disposable nappies

There's no doubt disposables make nappy changing as simple as it can be. They are easy to put on and can be discarded when they are wet or dirty. They are convenient when you're travelling as you don't have to carry wet, smelly nappies home with you to be washed. You'll need a constant supply so, to avoid carrying huge loads with your shopping, ask your local store to deliver to you or buy online in large batches. Never flush disposable nappies down the lavatory as they inevitably get stuck at the S-bend. Instead, put the soiled nappy in a strong plastic bag tied firmly at the neck and place in the bin. You may wish to consider buying a nappy bin which compresses, seals, and stores several days' worth of dirty nappies hygienically and without smell and which you can empty into your outdoor dustbin every few days.

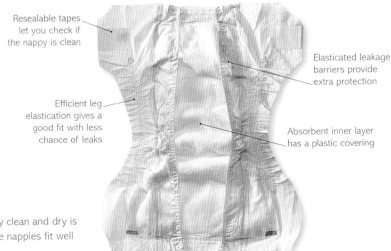

Resealable tapes let you check if the nappy is clean

Elasticated leakage barriers provide extra protection

Efficient leg elastication gives a good fit with less chance of leaks

Absorbent inner layer has a plastic covering

▶ **DISPOSABLE NAPPIES** Keeping your baby clean and dry is key to his health and wellbeing. Disposable nappies fit well and are extremely simple to use.

# Reusable nappies

Although resuable nappies are more expensive than disposables at first, they can work out cheaper in the long run. But fabric nappies involve much more work than disposables because they have to be rinsed, sterilized, washed, and dried after use, although nappy laundry services are now available in many areas. You'll need a minimum of 24 nappies to ensure that you always have enough clean ones, but the more nappies you can buy the less often you'll have to do the washing. When buying fabric nappies, choose the best that you can afford. They'll last longer; they'll also be more absorbent, and therefore more comfortable for your baby.

Towelling squares can be folded in various ways, depending on your baby's size and needs. They're very absorbent – more so than most disposables – so they are good at night. If you use these you'll also need at least 12 nappy pins and six pairs of plastic pants.

Shaped fabric nappies are T-shaped, made of a softer, finer towelling than squares, and have a triple-layered central panel for added absorbency. They are more straightforward to put on than squares, and fit more neatly. Many shaped fabric nappies offer all the features of a disposable, but are produced using fewer chemicals, are made of cotton, and don't contain dye, latex, or perfume. They are machine washable, can be brightly coloured, have Velcro closing tabs and elasticated legs, and are made of several layers of absorbent fabric with an anti-leak outer layer, so you don't need plastic pants either. Your baby's faeces are collected in liners and the used nappy can be stored in a nappy bucket until you have sufficient used nappies to make up a load for your washing machine.

**Nappy liners** With reusable nappies you'll need nappy liners. Choose the "one-way" variety that lets urine pass through, but remains dry next to the baby's skin, minimizing the risk of a sore bottom. Liners prevent the nappy from getting badly soiled; they can be lifted out with any faeces and flushed away if biodegradable, or if made of fabric, washed with the nappies.

# Boys' nappies

**Boys tend to wet the front of the nappy, and boys' disposables are designed to cope with this, with extra padding towards the front.**

■ Fold fabric nappies in such a way that more of the fabric is at the front, particularly at night.

■ Boys often urinate when they are being changed, so cover the penis with a spare, clean nappy as you take the soiled one off.

■ Always tuck your baby boy's penis down when putting on a clean nappy to avoid urine escaping from the top of the nappy.

7

▼**FABRIC NAPPIES AND ACCESSORIES** If you're using fabric nappies, you'll need to stock up on nappy liners to put inside them. For non-shaped nappies you'll need plastic pants and either safety pins or clip closures.

Plastic pants

Fabric nappy with velcro fastener

Fabric nappy liner

Liners and safety pins with locking heads

## Cleaning a girl

Always wipe your baby girl from front to back, and don't clean inside the lips of the vulva.

▲ **REMOVE URINE** Use wipes or moistened cotton wool to clean the genitals and the surrounding skin.

▲ **CLEAN BOTTOM** Lift up her legs as shown, and wipe from front to back. Dry thoroughly.

# Changing a nappy

Often parents decide upon disposable nappies, and one of the main reasons for this is how straightforward they are to change once you select the appropriate size. Reusable, fabric nappies allow you to choose the fold that suits you. Triple absorbent folds with a square base are ideal for

## Changing a disposable nappy

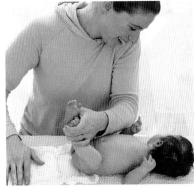

1 **POSITIONING YOUR BABY** Lay the nappy flat, with the tabs at the back. Slide the nappy under your baby so that the top aligns with her waist.

2 **FASTENING THE FRONT** Bring the front up between the legs and tuck it around the tummy. Unpeel the tabs.

3 **A COMFORTABLE FIT** Pull the tabs firmly over the front flap and fasten the nappy. It should fit snugly.

newborns, while parallel or kite folds based on a diamond shape suit a larger baby. Some reusable nappies are shaped like disposables, so they fit around your baby without being folded and fasten with Velcro tabs.

Your baby's nappy needs changing whenever it's wet or soiled; in a newborn this will be very often. It's likely you'll have to change him when he wakes, before he sleeps at night, and straight after each feed. So it's important to ensure that you have everything to hand in your changing area. You will need a changing mat; these mats are padded with raised edges and a wipe-clean surface. You will also need baby wipes, tissues, cotton wool, baby lotion (a good alternative to water alone for cleaning), and barrier cream. It's important to clean your baby's bottom thoroughly at every nappy change to avoid soreness and irritation. Wash your hands first. Lay your baby on the mat and undo his clothing; undo his nappy and open it out. If he's wearing a reusable nappy, wipe off as much faeces as possible with a clean corner. For a disposable nappy, wipe off most of the faeces with tissues. Fold the nappy down under him as you lift his legs. Proceed with cleaning (see columns, left and right). Dispose of the soiled nappy and put on a clean one.

# Cleaning a boy

Boys often pass urine when released from their nappy. A tissue laid over the penis will minimize the mess.

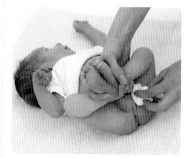

▲ **REMOVE URINE** Using either wipes or moistened cotton wool, work from the leg creases in towards the penis. Never pull the foreskin back.

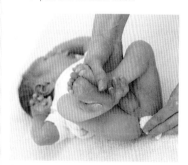

▲ **CLEAN BOTTOM** Lift his legs to clean his bottom by holding both ankles as shown. Dry thoroughly.

# Changing a shaped reusable nappy

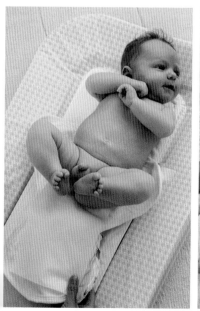

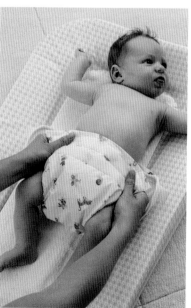

1 **POSITIONING THE NAPPY** Begin by sliding the nappy under your baby so his waist aligns with the top edge of the nappy.

2 **MAKING IT FIT SNUGLY** Bring the nappy up between his legs and hold it in place while you fold the sides in to the centre and fasten with Velcro tabs.

## Making washing easy

If you use fabric nappies washing them will take up quite a lot of your time, so make life easy for yourself by being as organized as you can. These tips are designed to make your washing routine easier on you.

■ Use plastic tongs or gloves for lifting nappies out of the sterilizing bucket; keep them nearby.

■ When you change a nappy at night, keep the dirty nappy in a separate bucket or a plastic bag, and add it to the new sterilizing solution the following morning.

■ If you use a powder sterilant, always put the water in the bucket first; otherwise you run the risk of inhaling the powder.

■ Drying nappies on radiators makes the fabric hard and uncomfortable. Use a tumble dryer, an outside line, or a rack that can be placed over the bath.

■ You may like to use an air freshener in the nappy bucket.

▲ DRYING FABRIC NAPPIES Hang fabric nappies to dry outside if you can; the sun bleaches out any stains.

# Nappy hygiene

It's very important to wash reusable nappies thoroughly; any traces of ammonia from urine will irritate your baby's skin, and faecal bacteria could cause infection. Strong detergents and biological powders can also irritate your baby's skin, so always use pure soap flakes or powders. You might even like to consider using a nappy laundering service, available nationwide, except in very isolated areas, for a weekly fee. You store dirty nappies in a deodorized bin that has a biodegradable liner and the nappy laundering service takes away your dirty nappies and replaces them with fresh nappies. You may need more nappies though.

## Washing routine for reusables

Establishing a routine will make life easier, especially if you aim to wash the nappies in large loads. You'll need a large supply of nappies – at least 24 – and a similar number of liners if using fabric ones. You'll need two plastic sterilizing bins with lids and strong handles: one for soiled nappies and the liners, and one for wet ones. Any good-sized bucket with a lid will do. They should be big enough to hold at least six nappies, with lots of room for solution, but not so large that you can't carry them when full.

Fill the bins with sterilizing solution each morning. Rinse each nappy before adding it to the bucket. Wet nappies should be rinsed in cold water, wrung out, and added to the solution. With soiled nappies, remove as much faeces as possible down the lavatory and hold the nappy under the lavatory spray as you flush it. Squeeze out the excess moisture and put the nappy in the "soiled" bucket. When the nappies have been soaking for the required time, wring them out. The urine-soaked ones should be rinsed thoroughly in hot water and then dried; the soiled ones will need to be washed on the hot programme, then rinsed, and dried. Sterilize, wash, and dry fabric liners with the nappies.

Plastic pants will become hard and unusable if you wash them in water that is either too hot or too cold. Wash them in warm water with a little washing-up liquid, then pat them dry and leave them to air. If they do become hard, you can soften them in a tumble dryer with towels.

## Nappy rash

If urine is left too long in a nappy or on the skin, it is broken down to ammonia by bacteria from your baby's stools. The ammonia then irritates and burns the skin and this is the most common cause of nappy rash. A mild nappy rash will appear as small red dots on your baby's bottom, but if it becomes more serious, you'll see an inflamed area of broken skin and possibly pus-filled spots. The bacteria that produce ammonia dermatitis (nappy rash) thrive in an alkaline medium. Breastfed babies are less prone to nappy rash than bottlefed babies. If you follow the guidelines given (right), you'll minimize the possibility of nappy rash. If your baby does develop a sore bottom, check the chart below to see if he needs treatment. If not, continue your preventive measures (except for the use of barrier cream), as well as the following:

■ Change your baby's nappy more often.
■ Use a disposable pad inside a towelling nappy for extra absorbency at night, especially if your baby sleeps through the night.
■ Once your baby has nappy rash, it is important that his skin be aired between nappy changes for, say, 15–20 minutes.

Not all skin conditions occurring in the nappy area are true nappy rash (see chart below). It is important that you identify a rash correctly so that you can take appropriate action.

# Identifying nappy rashes

| APPEARANCE OF RASH | CAUSE AND TREATMENT |
|---|---|
| General redness that starts around the genitals rather than the anus. You will notice a strong smell of ammonia. In severe cases it may spread to the bottom, groin, and thighs, and can lead to ulceration if not attended to. | Ammonia dermatitis, caused by irritation from ammonia. If the treatment outlined above and right doesn't work, check with your doctor. |
| Small blisters all over the baby's nappy area in addition to a rash elsewhere on the body. | Heat rash. Stop using plastic pants, and leave your baby's nappy off at every opportunity. Cool your baby down by using fewer clothes. |
| Redness and broken skin in the leg folds. | Inadequate drying. Dry your baby meticulously and don't use talcum powder. |
| Brownish-red, scaly rash on the genitals and skin creases, especially the groin, and anywhere the skin is greasy – the scalp, for instance. | Seborrhoeic eczema (see p.290). Your doctor will prescribe an ointment for the rash, and lotion for an affected scalp. Rare in babies. |
| Spotty rash that starts around the anus and spreads to the buttocks and thighs. You may also notice white patches inside your baby's mouth. | Thrush (see p.288), caused by a yeast infection. Check with your doctor. She'll probably give you anti-fungal treatments. |

# Preventing nappy rash

**The essentials are to keep your baby's skin dry and well aired, and to make sure that nappies are always thoroughly washed and well rinsed.**

■ Start using a nappy rash cream at the first sign of broken skin. Ones that include titanium salts are especially good. Stop using plastic pants, too, if you are using them, as they will prevent the urine evaporating.

■ Don't wash your baby's bottom with soap and water, as they both defat the skin.

■ Use one-way nappy liners, or disposables with a one-way lining, to keep your baby's skin dry.

■ Use a fairly thick barrier cream, applied generously. Don't use this with one-way liners or disposables, however, as it will clog the one-way fabric.

■ Make sure all traces of ammonia are removed from the nappy by thorough washing and rinsing.

■ Never leave your baby lying in a wet nappy.

■ Leave your baby's bottom open to the air whenever you can.

## Evenings out

**Because young babies are easy to carry and they sleep a lot, they're very portable, so you can still enjoy going out by taking your baby with you.**

In the early weeks it's a good thing for new parents, especially mothers, to get out of the house and relax with friends. It's easier to do this while your baby is young because he'll sleep anywhere. A car seat that doubles as a free-standing chair is ideal for this; it can be safely strapped in place in the car, then carried indoors when you reach your destination, while your baby sleeps.

Take advantage of this flexibility while you can; once your baby starts sleeping through the night you'll need to stick to a regular bedtime routine.

▲ **SLEEPING** Ensure your baby is warm and covered, but not too warm (see p.81). A picture of a face will hold his attention if he's awake.

# Sleep and wakefulness

A newborn baby needs a lot of sleep and unless he's hungry, cold, or uncomfortable, he's likely to spend at least 60 per cent of his time asleep.

Your baby may fall asleep immediately after – and sometimes during – a feed. He'll probably be indifferent to noises such as doors shutting or the radio – in fact, he may find droning noises soothing. Babies' sleeping patterns do vary, though, so if your baby is wakeful after a feed, don't insist that he stays in his cot. Your baby needs to learn to tell day from night. When it becomes dark outside, close the curtains and turn the lights very low. Make sure that he's warm and covered and, when he wakes during the night, feed him quickly and quietly without turning the lights up, and don't play with him. In time he'll learn the difference between a day- and a night-time feed.

## Where should your baby sleep?

It's probably easiest to let your baby sleep in something that makes him portable, such as a Moses basket, but later on he'll need a proper cot. He can also take naps in his pram or pushchair.

**Sleeping with you** It's lovely to cuddle and feed your baby in bed, but the safest place for him to sleep is in his own cot beside your bed. It's best not to have him sleep with you, but if you do need to for some reason, let him lie between you and your partner so that he can't fall out of bed. Never sleep with your baby if you have been drinking or have taken drugs that make you sleep heavily because of the increased risk of cot death.

**Your baby's bedroom** Pay careful attention to the temperature of your baby's room. Babies cannot regulate their body temperatures as well as adults and to maintain the right level of warmth they need a constant temperature and enough blankets to keep them warm – but not too warm (see p.81). A night-light or dimmer switch will mean that you can check your baby during the night without waking him.

**Clothing** Your baby should wear something that gives you easy access to his nappy at night. An all-in-one stretch suit or a nightdress – one with a drawstring at the end so it doesn't ride up his back – is best.

It's important that your baby doesn't get too hot or too cold. In warm weather a nappy and a vest will be enough. In winter, check that your baby is warm enough by touching the back of his neck with your hand. His skin should feel about the same temperature as yours. If he feels too hot and clammy, you should take a blanket off and let him cool down.

**Sleeping outdoors** Except when it's chilly your baby will sleep quite happily outside in a pram or pushchair, but make sure he's wrapped up and visible at all times, and never place him in direct sunlight; choose a shady area or protect him with a canopy. Put a cat net over the pram.

## Wakeful babies

If your baby wakes you frequently during the night or he cries when you try to go back to bed, you'll be short of sleep and you'll find it difficult to cope. It is essential that you get enough rest and you should share the responsibility of night feeds with your partner – even if you are breastfeeding, your partner could give your baby expressed milk on some nights. Alternatively, ask your partner to bring you the baby to feed and then he can change his nappy. If you're exhausted, get help from a friend or relative, relax your routine, get up late, and take daytime naps.

Encourage your baby to sleep at night by tiring him out in the day with plenty of stimulation: talk to him, pick him up, and give him lots of different things to look at. If he wakes up a lot in the night because he is wet, use double nappies or nappy liners, and if he cries when you leave him, don't immediately return and pick him up. Rocking his cot, removing a blanket, or changing his position may be sufficient to soothe him back to sleep. Early on, swaddling, or wrapping, your baby in a shawl or blanket may help him to sleep; the sensation of being tightly enclosed can give a baby a great feeling of security (although not all babies like it).

**Swaddling a baby** To swaddle your baby, you need a shawl or small light blanket. Fold the shawl in half to form a triangle and lay your baby on it, aligning his head with the longest edge. Then fold one point of the shawl across your baby and tuck it firmly behind his back. Do the same with the other point. Tuck the bottom of the shawl back underneath your baby's feet to keep them covered – always make sure his head is uncovered, then put him in his bed on his back. The close wrapping holds your baby's arms in a comfortable position that feels safe and secure. Swaddling is also a useful way of calming a distressed baby.

It's safe to swaddle your baby in cold weather, but keep a careful check on his temperature by touching his skin. Unwrap him right away if he feels or looks too hot.

# Settling your baby

Here are several things you can do to ensure that your baby settles down to sleep.

■ In the first month or so, wrap or swaddle your baby before you put him down.

■ Give your baby a comfort suck from breast or bottle.

■ Darken the room at night.

■ In cold weather put a hotwater bottle in the cot for a short time before you put your baby down – but never leave it in the cot.

■ Hang a musical mobile over the cot to soothe your baby.

■ If he doesn't seem to be settling down, rock him gently or stroke his back or limbs to soothe him.

■ If your baby won't settle in his cot, try carrying him around in a sling and jogging him up and down. Your closeness and the sound of your heartbeat will help him to settle down.

## Safety measures

By following these guidelines you will significantly reduce your baby's risk of cot death.

■ Always place your baby on his back to sleep.

■ Don't smoke and don't allow anyone in your house to smoke.

■ Breastfeed – the cot death rate is lower in breastfed babies.

■ Don't let your baby get too hot. Avoid tucking in bedclothes so your baby can kick them off if hot.

■ When covering your baby, allow for room temperature – the higher the temperature, the fewer bedclothes your baby needs, and vice versa (see chart opposite).

■ If you think your baby is unwell, contact your doctor without delay.

■ If your baby has a fever, don't increase the wrapping – reduce it so he can lose heat.

# Reducing the risk of cot death

Sudden Infant Death Syndrome (SIDS), known colloquially as "cot death", is the sudden and unexpected death of a baby for no obvious reason. The present rate for cot deaths in the UK is one per 2,000 live births. Since the start of the Reduce the Risk campaign in 1991, the number of cot deaths has fallen by 75 per cent.

The causes of cot death are unknown, and there's nothing that can guarantee its prevention. There are, however, ways in which parents can vastly reduce the risk. Recent surveys have proved that immunization reduces the risk, as does keeping your baby in your room with you at night for the first six months. Falling asleep with your baby on the sofa greatly increases the risk of cot death. Interestingly, the use of dummies has also recently been shown to reduce the risk.

## Your baby's sleeping position

One of the most crucial risk factors is the position in which you put your baby down to sleep. In most countries, babies have traditionally slept on their backs. In the UK as well, most babies slept on their backs until the 1960s, and the number of cot deaths was low. In 1970, however, special care baby units started to lay pre-term babies face down because it seemed this position improved breathing and reduced vomiting, and eventually the practice was extended to full-term babies.

The significance of sleeping position in relation to SIDS was looked at in 1965, but the evidence was not convincing, and it wasn't until 1986, when SIDS rates in different communities were compared, that it became clear that SIDS was less common where babies slept on their backs. The safest sleeping position for your baby, therefore, is on his back. Some people will tell you that this position may allow inhalation of posset, but there is no evidence to support this.

◄ FEET TO FOOT Lay your baby on his back with his feet touching the foot of the cot, even if it means his head is halfway down the mattress.

## Controlling the temperature

Keep a thermometer in your baby's room so that you can see how many blankets he needs. At 18°C (65°F), a sheet and two blankets is adequate.

| TEMPERATURE | BEDDING |
| --- | --- |
| 14°C (57°F) | sheet and three or four blankets |
| 16°C (60°F) | sheet and three blankets |
| 18°C (65°F) | sheet and two blankets |
| 20°C (68°F) | sheet and one blanket |
| 24°C (75°F) | sheet only |

## Smoking

A mother who smokes during pregnancy increases the risk of SIDS. (She also increases the risk of a premature or low-birthweight baby.) What's more, the risk increases with the number of cigarettes smoked. The risk of SIDS in babies born to smokers is twice that for babies born to non-smokers, and with every ten cigarettes a day the risk increases threefold. Even more cot deaths could be avoided if parents stopped smoking.

## Temperature

There's no doubt that overheating from too many night clothes, too many blankets, and too high a room temperature is a contributory factor, as SIDS is much more common in overheated babies. Many parents increase the amount of bedding when a baby is unwell, but this is not what your baby needs. High temperature plus infection in babies over ten weeks old greatly increases the risk of cot death. If heat loss is prevented, the body temperature of a restless baby with an infection will rise by at least 1°C per hour. A baby loses most heat from his head, chest, and abdomen, so lying on his back allows body temperature to be better controlled.

If you do have a heater in the nursery, use a thermostatically controlled one that will switch off if the room gets too warm, and switch back on again as it cools down.

## Continuing research

Although risk factors have been identified, the causes of cot death are still not understood. Current areas of research include the development of a baby's temperature control mechanisms and respiratory system in the first six months, and the recent discovery that an inherited enzyme deficiency may be responsible for a small number – about one per cent – of cot deaths. Two-thirds of cot deaths occur in winter.

## Getting help

The unexpected death of a baby is a particularly painful bereavement. Support is available to help parents cope with their feelings of grief and bewilderment (see Useful addresses, p.342).

■ Many parents seek help immediately after the death – sometimes within hours – and telephone support lines are available that can provide parents with information and a sympathetic listener.

■ In the longer term, parents may seek professional help. The continued support of a health visitor, social worker, or religious adviser can be invaluable, so don't be afraid to ask.

■ Parents may be helped by being able to talk to someone who has been through a similar experience, either in support groups or on a one-to-one basis.

■ Befriending schemes exist in some areas that continue long after professional help may have ceased, and these can be invaluable at times of particular grief such as the anniversaries of the baby's birth and death.

■ Parents who have lost one baby through cot death are extremely anxious when another baby is born. Support schemes exist that involve the parents, midwife, doctor, and health visitor in making sure the new baby gets the best possible care.

## Crying girls

The amount of crying, and reasons for crying, are different in boys and girls.

■ Baby girls are less vulnerable to stress at the time of birth than male babies and less likely to cry.

■ An American study has shown that girls are less irritable than boys at the age of three weeks, and therefore cry less.

■ Girls are less likely than boys to cry in new situations.

■ Mothers tend to give extra attention to girls who cry a lot.

# Crying and comforting

Be prepared for your baby to cry. There will be times when the reason is obvious: he's hungry, too hot, too cold, bored, uncomfortable because of a dirty nappy, or he might simply want your closeness. Another reason that we often fail to recognize is the desire for sleep. I remember trying to console my newborn son in all kinds of ways before I realized he just wanted to go to sleep.

Very young babies cry when they are disturbed, when they are roughly handled, such as at bath times, or when they get a shock, perhaps from feeling that they are going to be dropped, from a loud noise, or from a bright light. A two-week-old baby always responds to the security of being firmly wrapped in a shawl or held in strong, confident arms. Once you've investigated your baby's crying, don't worry too much about it – crying is practically his only way of communicating.

**Recognizing different cries** Within a few weeks, you can tell between the different cries that mean your baby is hungry, is niggling because he's bored, wants to be put down to sleep, or wants a cuddle. Of course your baby is learning about you, too, and how to communicate with you. He cries out of need and you respond by giving him what he wants.

## Responding to your baby

I believe you should respond quite quickly to your baby's cry. If you don't respond, then your baby feels as you would if you were ignored in a conversation. There's quite a lot of research to show that your baby is affected by how you respond to crying. For instance, mothers who respond quickly to crying tend to have children with more advanced communication skills, including speaking and outgoing behaviour. Babies who are ignored tend to cry more often and for longer in the first year than babies who are attended to quickly. It seems that mothers cause their babies to settle into a pattern of crying often and persistently because they fail to respond. A vicious circle is set up in which the baby cries, the mother fails to respond, the baby cries more, and the mother is even less inclined to act. A sensitive response from you now will help promote self-confidence and self-esteem in later life.

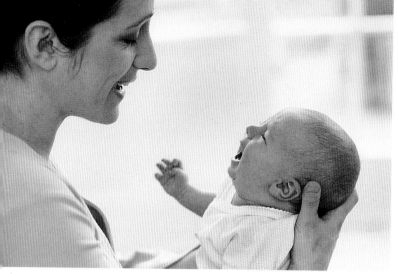

▲ **COMFORT YOUR BABY** Always respond to your baby's needs. There's no way you can spoil a baby by giving him attention in his first year.

## Crying spells

Most babies have crying spells. Often crying occurs in the late afternoon or early evening, when your baby may cry for as long as half an hour. If your baby has colic (see p.85), evening crying spells can last up to two hours. Always try to console your baby during a crying spell.

Once your child establishes a pattern of crying spells they may go on for several weeks. It's your baby's way of becoming adjusted to being in a very different world from that experienced inside your uterus. The more sensitively you respond and take your lead from him, the more rapidly he'll become acclimatized to his new lifestyle; the sooner you accommodate his likes and dislikes, the sooner crying spells will stop.

**Night-time crying** There's no doubt that every parent finds crying spells difficult to cope with, especially if they occur at night. During the night, crying will almost certainly make you feel impatient at the least, and at the worst, that you will do anything to stop your baby crying. These feelings are normal, so try not to become frightened and tense, otherwise the crying will simply get worse. Swaddling may help your baby settle.

## Why does my baby cry so much?

There's research that shows that your child may cry despite your efforts to console him, regardless of whether or not he feels any discomfort. For instance, babies who've been delivered by forceps tend to cry more in the first weeks of life. Similarly, babies born after a long labour are likely to sleep in short bursts, and to cry quite a lot in between. There's no question that a mother communicates her mood to her baby, so if you are tense, irritable, and impatient your baby will feel it, and cry. Some babies cry more than others even if they're given the same care and attention.

## Crying boys

**Boys differ from girls in their reasons for crying, and in the way they respond to attempts to soothe them.**

■ Baby boys tend to benefit from a regular routine early on, and if the routine is disturbed they quite often resort to crying.

■ Boys tend to take longer to adapt to new situations, and may cry if pushed.

■ More boys than girls tend to be labelled as difficult, but studies show that "difficult" baby boys are no more difficult than any other boys by the age of two years, especially if their parents work hard to console them and make them happy.

■ Boys seem to need responsiveness from their parents more than girls in order to be happy, and cry readily if parental attention and love are not forthcoming.

■ Some mothers of boys think that they shouldn't give their sons extra attention and cuddles when they're crying because they mistakenly want them to be tough. This is quite wrong – baby boys need cuddles just as much as girls.

## Dummies

Babies are born with a sucking reflex. Without it they wouldn't suckle and wouldn't nourish themselves. I feel it's important that babies are allowed to indulge their desire to suck.

Some babies are more "sucky" than others; I certainly had one who wanted to suck all the time, whether he was hungry or not. With all my sons, I used to put their thumbs into their mouths gently so that they could suck to soothe themselves. But at the same time I see nothing wrong with using a dummy as a comforter.

Dummies for a young baby should be sterilized in exactly the same way as you sterilize feeding bottles and teats. Once your baby is being weaned, however, and starts to use his fingers for feeding himself, it is pointless to sterilize dummies. Careful washing and rinsing is all that's needed. Better still, this may be the time to encourage your baby to give up the dummy.

# Soothing your baby

There are lots of remedies you can try to soothe and console your baby if he's crying. As a general rule, most babies respond to movement and sound: hence the effectiveness of taking them out in the car, where the motion of the vehicle and the steady humming sound of the engine will usually quieten them. Your baby will probably find any of the following movements or sounds soothing:

- A movement that rocks him, whether it's you, a swing, a rocking cradle, or a rocking chair.
- Walking or dancing with an emphasis on rhythm, since it reminds him of the time when he was being jogged inside your uterus.
- Bouncing him in your arms or in the cot.
- Putting him in a sling.
- Any form of music as long as it isn't too loud but is rhythmic – specially recorded sleeping tapes are available.
- A noisy toy that your baby can shake or rattle.
- A steady household noise such as the washing machine.
- Your own singing voice, especially if you sing a lullaby.

## Understanding the cause

Learn to read your baby's signals and gain insight into his needs and desires. Once you recognize your baby's cry you have to respond to it, otherwise he's bound to scream even louder. Always be sensitive to your baby's needs. Look, listen, and try to interpret what he's trying to say to you through his behaviour. As you get to know your baby, you will learn to understand what he really wants. If you know, for example, that he's

hungry, don't delay his feed by deciding to give him a bath first, simply as a matter of sticking to your routine. Responding to your baby's crying is more important.

There are all sorts of signs of small discomforts to which you must be alert. When your baby has a cold, for instance, his nose may become blocked, making it impossible for him to breathe and feed at the same time, so he'll become angry and frustrated and almost certainly cry.

▶ **UNDRESSING** Some very young babies cry when they are having a bath, because they hate the feeling of their skin being exposed to the air. Other babies are soothed by the water.

# What to do when your baby cries

| CAUSE OF CRYING | WAYS OF COMFORTING |
|---|---|
| **Hunger** A hungry cry is nearly always the first cry that a parent recognizes and it is the most common reason that young babies cry. They rarely cry after feeding. Babies love the sensation of a full stomach, more than being held or sucking. | Feed on demand. If you have a baby who wants to suck all the time you don't need to feed; just give him a drink of boiled water. Use a dummy, holding it in his mouth if necessary, so that he can suck on it. |
| **Tiredness** Until they're used to their new world, babies cry when they are tired and it takes an observant parent to realize this and to put a baby down. | Lay your baby down where he is quiet and warm. Wrapping or swaddling him before you put him down to sleep helps, too. |
| **Lack of contact** Some babies will stop crying as soon as you pick them up, because they want a cuddle. Babies brought up in cultures where they are constantly in a sling or swaddled rarely cry. | Give your baby lots of body contact. Carry him around in a shawl or a sling. Lay your baby tummy down across your lap and gently massage his back. |
| **Being startled** A jerky movement, a sudden noise, or a bright light can upset your baby. If physical games are too rough, he'll cry. | Hold your baby close, rock him gently, and sing to him. Avoid sudden jerky movements, noises, and bright lights. |
| **Undressing** Most babies dislike being undressed as it puts their bodies through movements that are neither familiar nor comforting and they hate the feel of air on their skin. Being jerked suddenly while being undressed makes them fearful. | Undress your baby as little as possible in the first few weeks, and keep him wrapped or covered with a towel as you remove layers of clothing. Keep up a running commentary of reassuring talk as you undress him. |
| **Temperature** Babies tend to cry if they become too hot or too cold. They may cry if a wet or soiled nappy gets cold or if they are suffering from nappy rash. | Keep your baby's room at 16–20°C (61–68°F) with the number of blankets suggested on p.81. Remove covers and clothing if your baby is too hot; add another layer of clothing and a blanket if he's too cold. Change his nappy if necessary. |
| **Pain** An ear infection or some other source of pain may cause your baby to cry. If his ear hurts, he may hit it with his fist; if it's colic, his legs may be drawn up to his abdomen. | Hold your baby close, cuddle him, and talk soothingly. If you can find the source of pain, such as a nappy pin, remove it immediately. If your baby seems ill, seek medical advice. |

# Colic

**This describes bouts of unexplained crying that usually happen in the late afternoon or evening, but can be at any time. The crying is not generally pacified by the usual remedies. The baby's face becomes very red, the legs are drawn up to the abdomen, and the fists clenched.**

Colic generally stops by the age of three or four months. It is not known why it happens, but it usually starts in the first three weeks of a baby's life.

The gastro-colic reflex can cause bowel spasm in babies and this is thought to be one of the reasons for colic. Other causes could be overfeeding, underfeeding, wind in the bowel, being picked up too much or too little, indigestion, and tension. Gastro-oesophageal reflux is also a possibility, so check with your doctor if symptoms are severe.

It has always struck me that tension probably contributes to the problem. You're preoccupied in the evening with bath time and bedtime for the baby as well as getting your evening meal. It is likely that your baby picks up on your tension and feels it too.

As your baby is likely to cry every night for 12 weeks, I'm against using medicine to forestall the crying. Of course you should try to soothe your baby, but don't expect him to respond readily. Try to take comfort from the fact that this phase won't last long.

## Your baby at 2–4 months

Here are some ways of encouraging the development of your baby at this stage.

■ Introduce him to small toys with different textures and say out loud how they feel.

■ Act out nursery rhymes and play pat-a-cake.

■ Play lots of physical games, such as gentle jerks, knee bends, arm pulls, and tickling feet.

■ Take him into the bath with you and encourage him to do plenty of kicking and splashing. Make him aware of his hands by splashing them in the water.

■ Gently pull him up when he's lying on his back.

■ Put objects on a string over his cot so that he can look at them. One day he'll reach out and knock one of them.

▲ YOUR BABY GIRL Even as babies, girls tend to be more sociable than boys and are more interested in people than things.

# Your baby's development

Development is continuous, although at times your baby's progress may seem very slow. The speed and ease of acquiring skills, however, is entirely individual so don't worry if your baby is slower to develop in some areas than other babies of the same age.

Although you can influence the pace of your child's development by giving him the right stimulation at the right time, the stages of development occur in a strictly unchangeable sequence.

## Physical development

There are a few general principles that apply to physical development in all babies. The stages, or "milestones", always follow the same order, as each one depends on the previous stages. To give an obvious example, your child can't walk until he can stand.

Often a previously learned skill may appear to be forgotten while your baby is concentrating on learning a new one, but will reappear when the new one is successfully learned. Sometimes a generalized activity makes way for a specific one: at six months your baby may make rather random leg movements that resemble walking, but they are quite different from the ones he will make when he actually starts to walk at about one year.

One important physical milestone will be when your baby's teeth start to come through. Although this might not seem like a developmental step, teeth are essential to your baby's learning to chew solid food and to being able to speak properly.

**Learning to walk** It may come as something of a surprise to learn that all locomotion – that is, walking and running – begins with the acquisition of head control. Your child can't sit up, stand up, crawl, or walk without first being able to control the position of his head. Development of any kind proceeds from head to toe, so head control is the essential first phase of learning to walk.

At first your baby's movements seem random and jerky; a newborn infant may move his arms, legs, head, hands, and feet when all he wants to do is smile. Gradually over the next three years his movements are refined, becoming increasingly specific to match the task in hand.

**Manipulation** The primitive grasp reflex in newborns (see p.20) must fade before your baby can grasp an object purposefully. At first, he uses his mouth as the main organ for touch; the fingertips take over only as he learns how to use his hands. He'll refine his ability to grasp things, at first grasping them in his palm and eventually learning to use his finger and thumb. He'll learn how to release as well as grasp an object.

**Hearing and vision** Your child's hearing is essential to his development of speech, and there are clues you can look for very early on that indicate normal hearing: does he turn towards the direction of a sound, or respond to your voice by turning or smiling, for instance? Although a newborn baby can't see things at a distance, he may be able to focus on your face, provided it's only 20–25cm (8–10in) from his. A baby's vision improves rapidly but variably in the months after birth.

## Intellectual development

Your baby's brain doubles in weight in the first year due not to the growth in the number of brain cells, but to the connections between them. These connections only begin to form when your baby has to think about something. Contact with new sights, sounds, smells, tastes, and textures makes your baby think, and that's why stimulation is essential from birth.

In order for your baby to understand what is going on around him, he must use his senses, his intellect, and his body to form mental connections so that he understands cause and effect. In order to pick up a favourite toy, for example, he must be able to see it, remember that he likes it, reach for it, and then pick it up. Your baby's mental skills will advance with stimulation and teaching, so your involvement is crucial all the time, particularly when the brain goes through growth spurts in the first and third years. You are your child's first and most important teacher.

## Sociability and personality

Babies become social by imitating us and will respond to a human voice from birth, so talk to your baby from the day that he's born. Your child's personality and social skills can affect his achievement of developmental milestones. An independent and determined child will tend to try new movements earlier than a more timid child, and a sociable child will seek social contact and communication with others and develop speech earlier than other children.

Your child's personality has three main components: sociability, activity, and emotion. If any one of these traits is more pronounced in your child try to be accommodating, at the same time encouraging the development of the other two qualities.

Here are some ways of encouraging the development of your baby at this stage.

■ Play rocking games while he's sitting on your lap.

■ Encourage him to open his fingers by playing giving and taking-away games. Always give him the object when he reaches out for it.

■ You can play weight-bearing games that help to strengthen him. Hold him on your lap or on the floor, and gently bounce him up and down; you'll feel him push off with his feet.

■ Reward him for holding out his arms by playing lifting games – squeal with delight as you lift him and swing him round.

■ Show him cause and effect. Push a ball to him while he's sitting up and say "the ball is rolling".

▲ **YOUR BABY BOY** Give your baby boy lots of physical contact and comfort. Never expect him to suppress his feelings "because he's a boy".

## Head control

Proportionately, a newborn's head is very large and heavy for his body, which means that before he can begin to control the rest of his body, he must gain control of his head.

Once your baby can raise his head from the mattress he'll begin to increase his strength, which will encourage him to further movement skills. Holding your baby in the air in a face-down position will encourage him to raise his head, and he'll try it for himself when lying on his stomach.

As he becomes stronger, your baby's head control is steadier, and his spine will gradually take more of the weight of his torso. This is the first stage in his learning to sit, crawl, and then walk.

# On the move

The first few months of your baby's development are a very exciting time for you as a parent as you watch him first see the world, then move to become involved in it.

As your baby's coordination and strength increase, his body control will quickly improve. The gradual refinement of his movements and his growing curiosity are excellent stimulation for all his development. The stages he goes through now are all geared toward learning to walk. Every child develops at his own pace, so the ages given here are only rough guidelines.

▶ **NEWBORN** Your baby will flex his limbs towards his body, which will remain curled up for several weeks as he gradually straightens out of the fetal position. His head will be very floppy at first, but you will notice that he turns it to his preferred side when lying down.

▲ **1 MONTH** By now your baby will be able to lift his head up slightly for a few seconds and will have lost his newborn appearance. If you raise your baby from the mattress, he may be able to keep his head up in line with his body for a

second or two. His knees and hips are growing stronger and his body begins to straighten even more. Supervised "tummy time" – playtime on his tummy – can start from the first week and helps the development of head control.

▲ **2 MONTHS** Your baby can hold his head up for longer now if you hold him in sitting position. When lying down, he'll hold his head in line with his body and will quickly progress to raising his face from the mattress to an angle of 45°.

▼ **3 MONTHS** Your baby can now lie quite flat and take the weight of her shoulders and head on outstretched arms when she lies on her tummy. There is little head lag when she's held in a sitting or standing position.

# Your baby's posture

Although your baby's posture will mature as his muscles strengthen naturally, you may both enjoy doing some gentle bending and stretching exercises.

Changing time is a good opportunity to do this; your baby will come to associate the pleasure of being clean and dry with movement. Take your baby's feet gently by the ankles and bend and straighten his legs a few times. Take it slowly, and stop if your baby doesn't seem comfortable with these movements.

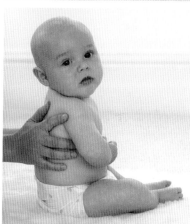

▲ **4 MONTHS** Your baby is learning to sit up unsupported. His head control is increasing and he turns to the left and right when his attention is caught. He can support his chest and head on his outstretched arms when lying prone.

▲ **5 MONTHS** Your baby has full head control even when pulled into a sitting position. She may be able to take the full weight of her head, shoulders, and chest on outstretched hands. She'll enjoy playing rocking games with you.

▲ **6 MONTHS** As your baby's limbs get stronger, he can take a lot of his weight on his arms. He'll sit with his hands forward for support, and reach up to you when he wants to be lifted. He may even sit alone for a few seconds.

## Shuffling

Before he can crawl your baby may work out his own highly individual way of moving around using the coordination he has mastered.

Some babies shuffle along on their bottoms, others use crab-like, sideways movements, and others devise their own unique methods. It is not important which manoeuvre your baby works out: he's managed a great personal achievement in being able to move independently for the first time and that is all that matters.

Never discourage your baby from his first attempts at being mobile. They are his tools for learning to control his body and it's important that he's allowed to discover the limits of this control. Give his curiosity and spirit of adventure free rein.

# Encouraging movement

Although your baby may appear to make crawling movements in his first weeks (see p.21), he'll stop this as his body straightens out. Before he can really begin to crawl, he must uncurl his body, control his head, lift his chest clear of the floor, and develop strength in his arms and legs.

## How you can help

Your encouragement and praise will make this an exciting and pleasurable time for both of you. As your baby gains head control, for instance, you can encourage him to lift his head by holding a brightly coloured toy above him. As his back and shoulder muscles gain strength, help him by occasionally pulling him into a sitting position when he's lying on his back. Once he can sit up, you can play games that make him swivel in this position; call "peek-a-boo" from his side so that he has to turn to look at you. By about five months, when your baby has full head control, rocking and swinging games help him practise keeping his head stable.

**Propping** From as early as six weeks, include your baby in daily life by propping him in an upright position with pillows. As he can focus better by now, this allows him to see what's going on. Once this stimulation begins, your baby will find the desire for involvement irresistible.

## Preparing to crawl

Your baby has to be strong enough to hold his head and chest off the floor before he can crawl. By the time he's about six months old, he'll be able to push his chest clear of the floor and hold this position with his knees under him, but he'll be around eight months before he can pull himself forward along the floor.

It's impossible to pinpoint exactly when your baby will crawl, if at all. Some babies leave out crawling altogether, but go on to learn to walk perfectly. You can encourage your baby to crawl in a number of ways, the best being to use yourself as an enticement. Praise any efforts he makes in order to divert him from feeling frustrated by unsuccessful attempts. Your support is far more useful to him than attempts to "teach" him to crawl by moving his arms and legs in a crawling movement.

## Preparing to stand

Before your baby can stand he must have strength and balance. Although he's unlikely to have strong leg muscles or control over them before he's ten or 11 months old, one of the most enjoyable games for a young baby is to be bounced up and down on your knee. Hold your baby facing you with his feet touching your knees and raise and lower him – make sure that his neck is supported. Your baby will really enjoy the sensation of taking his own weight, and it will strengthen his leg muscles in preparation for walking. From about six months, he'll try to bend and straighten his legs in a jumping movement whenever he is held in a standing position. These movements are your baby's earliest attempts at walking.

## Exercises

You can encourage your baby's physical development from an early age by playing simple exercise games. Dress him comfortably, but if he's in a warm room with no draughts, his nappy will be all that he needs.

▼**ARM STRETCH** Lie your baby on her back and let her grasp your thumbs. Stretch one arm above her head, then as you lower it, raise the other arm.

▼**CROSSOVERS** Sit your baby comfortably against you. Holding your baby's hands, stretch her arms out to the side then back across her chest. Repeat.

◀**FLIER** Lie on your back with your knees drawn up and balance your baby on her stomach, on your shins and knees. Stretch her arms out to the side – this should make her raise her head – and then bring her arms back to the original position and begin again.

# Safety

From the moment your baby becomes mobile, it is vital that your home is "childproof" (see pp.306–11) to prevent accidents.

■ Never leave your baby unattended. Even before he's mobile your baby will need to be with you for reassurance and safety.

■ Once your baby learns to roll, never leave him lying anywhere except on the floor. Keep the area clear of sharp or hard objects.

■ Even when he has mastered control over his head, continue to put pillows around your baby's bottom and lower spine.

■ Keep all poisonous substances out of your baby's reach.

■ Securely guard all fires, cupboards, banisters, and stairways.

## Your baby's hands

At first your baby has little interest in his hands, but as he becomes more aware of his body they'll begin to fascinate him more and more.

When he waves his arms around, his hand will accidentally touch his face and he'll put it in his mouth to suck. At two to three months, he finds the movements of his fingers fascinating and will watch them for ages. By about four months, he'll grab hold of objects to "test" them in his mouth. At six months, he refines his manual skills and feels with his fingers as much as his mouth.

# Using hands

Your baby was born with the reflex to grasp anything that's placed in his palm – such as your finger – and not let go; his grip is so strong he can support his own weight (although you should not actually let him do so).

When he's not holding something his hands will be tightly closed in a fist, although they'll probably open and close when he cries, and he'll open them instinctively when he's startled (see p.20). The early reflex grasp must be lost if he's to learn to select an object, and reach out and pick it up with his thumb and forefinger – the basic skill of manual dexterity. Most babies will develop a mature "pincer" grip by one year of age.

▼ **NEWBORN** From birth your baby has the ability to grasp an object and hold on to it firmly. This grasping reflex is very strong initially.

▼ **TWO MONTHS** Your baby is becoming more aware of his hands and his reflex grasping action has almost gone. His hands are much more open now, too.

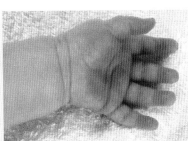

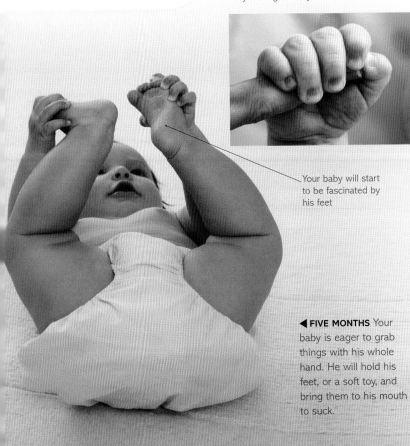

Your baby will start to be fascinated by his feet

◀ **FIVE MONTHS** Your baby is eager to grab things with his whole hand. He will hold his feet, or a soft toy, and bring them to his mouth to suck.

▲ **SIX MONTHS** Your baby can hold his bottle, and he'll be able to hold an object that is given to him between two hands.

## Encouraging skills

Even the most simple activities can add to your baby's feelings of confidence and achievement. He needs to feel that his hard work is noticed and appreciated by you, and that you're as pleased as he is about his cleverness and growing independence.

**Up to six weeks** Your baby must ignore his instinctive grasp reflex before he can manipulate objects. Test this reflex by letting him grasp your fingers and seeing how far you can pull him up off the mattress. Encourage him to open his fingers by gently unfolding them one at a time as you play games like "this little piggy". Stroke the back of his hand and his wrist and fingers will open.

**Six weeks** Your baby's hands are opening and he's becoming aware of them. Help him to take an interest in his hands by tickling his palms and fingertips with materials of different textures: soft, furry, smooth, or ridged – corduroy, for example. A gentle hand massage or rubbing of his palms will encourage him to open his hands.

**Two months** Your baby's hands are more open now, so continue to provide plenty of tactile stimulation by giving him objects of different textures to hold. Lay each object across his palm, following the horizontal creases, so that he can wrap his hand around it.

**Three months** Your baby uses a wide-open hand to grasp and reaches for things inaccurately. Encourage a mature grasp by giving him things to hold. Place a rattle in his hand and shake it a few times – he'll be fascinated by both its feel and the sound. Put a mobile above his cot to give him something to look at, and string toys across his pram to swipe at – make sure they are secure.

**Four months** As your baby starts to get his hand and arm movements under control, he'll reach out for things with increasing accuracy. Encourage him by presenting interesting objects while he's sitting propped up or lying down. He'll still tend to overshoot when he reaches for something, so you'll need to give him some help.

**Five months** Your baby will be grabbing everything within reach and he'll love crumpling paper, so give him tissue paper to play with. He will love you to play with his feet where he can see them, so play "this little piggy" with his toes. Play giving and taking-away games to encourage him to open his fingers and let go. He'll reach for a bottle to try to feed himself.

## Hand–eye coordination

**From six months your baby's coordination and manipulation skills will develop rapidly.**

His finger movements are becoming more precise all the time. You can let him hold his own bottle in two hands and teach him how to pass an object from one hand to the other. As soon as this is mastered, he'll love to practise his letting-go skill and throw everything on the floor.

Once he starts on solid foods, he'll be able to pick up and hold finger foods such as rusks.

▲ **SELF-FEEDING** Your baby will like to have a try at picking up finger foods and feeding himself, although he may not be very accurate yet at getting the food into his mouth. This also helps his development.

## Helping your baby

The development of normal vision requires two properly functioning eyes and plenty of visual stimulation. Try the following ideas.

■ From the day he's born, put a photo of a face – yours or one cut from a magazine – on the side of the cot for your baby to look at.

■ A simple mobile over the cot will give your baby something interesting to look at. Babies enjoy looking at black and white as well as coloured objects at this age.

■ Your baby is never too young to go sightseeing. If he's in a pushchair he'll be able to look all around himself.

▲ **STIMULATING TOYS** Give your baby plenty of toys to keep him entertained while you're changing his nappy.

# Vision

At birth your baby can see, but focuses on objects at a fixed distance of 20–25cm (8–10in), which allows him to see your face when you're holding him. From the moment he's born, he needs lots of stimulation in order to develop his eyesight fully. He can see as well as you or I can by about six to eight months.

**Your newborn** Although your baby's eyesight is limited, his eyes are very sensitive to the human face and anything that moves. If you bring your face within his field of vision, he'll see you and you'll notice his eyes move in recognition and his expression change. A newborn baby's vision is more limited than an older child's, so you'll have to fit his visual world into a range that he can perceive. The colour-sensitive cells in his eyes aren't yet fully developed so he'll see things in muted shades.

**Increasing recognition** At two weeks, a baby will automatically raise a hand to protect himself from something that's moving quickly towards him. At three weeks his whole body may react with excited jerking movements when your face comes into focus. By eight weeks he'll recognize your face and respond to it with smiles and waving arms. He's also more conscious of other objects but, because he can only focus on nearby objects, the world appears rather flat and distant details are lost to him.

**Depth of vision** By three to four months, your baby can take in details and is able to build up a three-dimensional picture of the world – a necessary step before he becomes mobile, as he probably won't start crawling until his vision allows him to understand depth as well as height and width. He can tell the difference between pictures with two and three items, and can recognize patterns and primary colours. This eye for detail improves until, by five to six months, he can discriminate between different facial expressions, such as sadness, fear, and joy, and he'll respond to them with his own expression. He will show excitement when he sees you getting ready to feed him.

**A sense of permanence** From six months, he can identify objects and can adjust his position to see those that most interest him. From now on the biggest development in your baby's visual skill is the way his brain interprets the information he sees.

# Testing vision

There are many clues that will warn parents if a child has a sight defect. If you're in any doubt about your baby's vision, or if your child's eyes water a lot and bright lights cause him discomfort, consult your doctor. The following eye conditions may show up even in a very young baby. Although you should not try to diagnose them yourself, here are some things you might observe; if you do, check with your doctor. If there is a history of sight problems in your family, talk to your doctor about them.

**Squint (strabismus)**  It's common (and normal) for newborn babies to squint sometimes, particularly if they're tired. If this continues once your baby is over six to eight months old, or if it worsens at any stage before that, tell your doctor. If you notice that only one of your baby's eyes is focused on an object of interest and the other is pointing too far in or too far out, he may be suffering from strabismus. He may tilt his head or hold it in an unusual position to get his vision in line. To check, find an object, such as a toy, and, keeping your child's head still (you may need another adult to help you), move the toy to spell the letter H in the air. Check that both eyes follow the toy in unison. (See also Squint, p.287.)

**Lazy eye**  If your child suffers from weak eye muscles around one eye he may turn his head so that the eye with better sight can more easily follow the action around him. Check that both eyelids are level when your baby is concentrating on a moving object. If he obviously favours one eye over the other, check with your doctor.

**Colour blindness**  This often runs in families. The most common form is the inability to distinguish between red and green (mostly, but not exclusively, found in boys). Use colourful sweets, such as jelly beans, and and ask him to pick out the same colours as you. When he is older and knows his colours, ask your child to pick out certain colours for you.

**Peripheral vision test**  To assess whether your child has a normal field of vision, choose a favourite toy and, with your child staring directly ahead, slowly move it from the outside to in front of his face until he sees it. His field of vision should extend about 45 degrees on either side.

**Visual accuracy**  You can test the accuracy of an older baby's vision with the following game. Stand about 6m (20ft) away from him and hold up some fingers. Get him to hold up the same number as you. If he fails, it's probably best to check with your doctor.

## The visually impaired child

**Some problems are difficult to assess in a young baby. If your child's vision is poor, he'll need regular checkups with a specialist.**

■ A visually impaired child needs stimulation by touch, noise, and smell, so choose toys that have interesting textures and make different noises. Puzzles are particularly important; those with large, colourful pieces are best.

■ Long-sighted children will need six-monthly checkups to see if their prescription for spectacles needs changing. A child who's long-sighted or has astigmatism may need to wear glasses only for two or three years until his eyesight develops normally.

■ The earlier a child starts to wear glasses, the more likely he is to accept them. At first he may take them off and play with them, but he'll soon show a preference for seeing the world clearly.

## Helping your baby

By explaining sounds and playing appropriate games with your baby, you can help him to listen in a discerning way to the confusion of sounds that he hears around him.

■ Be theatrical when you describe sounds. For example, put your finger to your lips and say "Sssh, let's be quiet as mice" to explain the idea of quietness.

■ Describe sounds and music with appropriate adjectives such as "loud" or "soft".

■ Teach the concept of high and low notes by singing songs.

■ Help him understand rhythm with rhymes and clapping songs – this will also help your child's speech.

■ Name new sounds, such as the cat purring, and imitate them.

By the time he's four months old, your baby should be able to discriminate between certain sounds. For example, when he hears your voice he will quieten or smile, and he'll turn his head and eyes towards your sound, even if he can't see where you are.

# Hearing

Your baby needs to be able to hear if he's to be able to talk correctly. Only when your child shows that he can hear, and later that he can imitate sounds, and eventually that he can use different sounds to form speech, can you be sure that he can discriminate between different sounds across the full normal range of hearing.

Your newborn baby reacts to noises without really understanding them. If he's startled by a sudden loud noise, such as a hand clap or a door slamming, he may throw out his arms and legs in a "startle" reflex action, as though to save himself from falling. A little later, sudden sounds will make him blink or open his eyes wide in surprise. By four weeks he'll begin to notice sudden prolonged noises, like the sound of a vacuum cleaner.

Parents with profoundly deaf children usually become aware that there is a problem fairly quickly. It's more difficult to identify those with partial hearing loss, as their symptoms can be mistaken for inattentiveness, slow learning, or shyness. If you are worried about your child's hearing, you should have him examined by your doctor as soon as possible so that he can be given appropriate help.

## Newborn hearing screening test

Your baby's first hearing test will probably be in the maternity unit shortly after birth. A screening test is carried out on every new baby a day or two after birth, which is much more reliable than the distraction tests that used to be carried out on older babies. One or two babies in every 1,000 born in the UK every year have hearing difficulties, and screening is vitally important as the sooner any problems are detected the better the prospects for a child's development. If deafness is not diagnosed until a child is two or three years old, he will have missed out on a critical stage of development in language skills.

**How it works** The test is called an oto-acoustic emission test. It is quick and easy to do and doesn't hurt your baby; your baby doesn't even have to be awake. You'll be asked to hold your baby while the person doing the test puts a small probe just inside his ear. The probe makes a small sound, then measures the echo produced by the inner ear in response to the sound. Both ears are checked and you'll have the results immediately. If the test does not detect an echo, this does not mean your baby is deaf, but he will need further tests.

# Speech and language

Babies need and want to communicate from the very earliest days, and even before they can talk they'll listen to and try to imitate sounds. The basics of language are built into babies' brains and a deaf infant starts to babble at the same age as a child with normal hearing. Some theorists say we have a "language-acquisition device" somewhere in the brain that makes language inevitable.

Before your baby is six weeks old, he'll have learned that if he smiles or makes sounds, you'll respond. What is remarkable is that even at this early stage he realizes that he can call the shots: he smiles, you are pleased and so talk to him more, and he can keep a two-way "conversation" going. By smiling and talking to your baby and showing your pleasure when he responds, you're giving him his very first lesson in communication.

**Newborn** Your baby may respond to human voices from the moment of birth, and he will try to imitate gestures and expressions. He will sense when you are talking to him and he'll respond with sounds and by moving his entire body. Help your baby by talking non-stop and be very theatrical with your conversations and gestures.

**Four to six weeks** He can already recognize your voice. He'll respond to your smiles and speech by gurgling, and wait for you to reply. Keep your face close to his when you talk to him so that he can see you, and reward his sounds with more smiles and talking. Show affection in your tone of voice, which will forge close emotional links between you and your baby and provide him with lots of encouragement.

**Four months** Your baby now has a range of sounds, including squeals and blowing between his lips. He communicates with you through laughter, so laugh and giggle a lot when you talk to him.

**Six months** There are many signs that your baby is beginning to understand what you say. He babbles and strings sounds together. Singing to him, repeating rhymes, and speaking rhythmically will all help him to understand language and encourage early speaking. He'll be making consonant sounds – "m", "p", and "b" – and so may say "ma" or "pa" very early on, although he'll attach no meaning to these sounds.

## First ways of communicating

**Your baby first starts to communicate with you at birth, but without sounds.**

Within half an hour of birth your baby may move his eyes at your voice, and when you're 25cm (10in) away from his face he may smile and mouth in imitation and recognition of hearing speech. He's born to talk!

Crying becomes the major way of saying he's discontented; burbles of contentment don't appear for another six weeks.

Social smiling at six weeks marks his desire to converse with you, and a few weeks later he'll start to make vowel sounds, such as "eh", "ah", "uh", "oh".

▼ **TALKING TO YOUR BABY** Your earliest conversations with your baby will involve smiles rather than sounds.

## The female brain

When a baby girl is born, her brain is already sexed – that is, programmed for femaleness. Brain structure is responsible for many developmental differences between boys and girls.

■ In the womb, the cortex, which determines intellect, develops sooner in girls than in boys.

■ The left half of the cortex, that which controls thinking, develops earlier in girls than in boys.

■ The corpus callosum, the part of the brain that connects the right lobe to the left, is better developed in girls than in boys.

■ The earlier development of the left side of the brain in girls gives them greater language-related skills.

■ The right and left sides of the brain "talk" to each other earlier and better in girls, and this gives them an advantage in reading skills, which draw on both sides.

■ Girls show earlier and greater fear of separation than boys because their nervous connections mature earlier. This leads to faster message transmission than in boys, and so girls recognize earlier what's going on around them.

# Your baby's mind

Your baby is born with a finite number of brain cells, yet his brain doubles in weight in the first year. The increase in weight is due to the growth of connections between the cells used in thinking. For example, when your baby sees a toy, points to it, reaches for it, and puts it in his mouth to explore, he's built up four brain connections and slotted them all into his memory.

## Predicting intelligence

Although it's difficult to say what "normal" intelligence is, many experts in the field of development can define the sequence and rate of mental development in the average baby and use this to predict intelligence. Remember that the average baby doesn't exist: an average is theoretical, so you should never apply it to your own baby, nor should you compare him with other babies of his age.

There are major variations in the rate of development from baby to baby, and there is no correct age when any milestones should be reached. Most babies have growth spurts and pauses. Some show a temporary developmental pause and then go on to develop normally; others appear advanced in infancy but turn out to be average in later years. Then there is the well-known "slow starter", the child who is slightly behind as a baby yet later does very well. The conclusion is that you shouldn't try to predict your baby's intelligence unless there is a very good reason to do so.

The great majority of babies turn out to be perfectly normal children. Sadly, a very small number lag seriously behind in all fields of development and, unless the lag is due to a serious physical difficulty, can grow up to be educationally under par. Throughout the first three years the mentally impaired child shows below-average concentration and interest in his surroundings. He's late in aspects of development such as head control, sitting up, and grasping his toes, and in outgrowing his primitive birth reflexes, which may persist long after the usual age.

While there are clear indicators that a child is mentally slow, it is more difficult to spot the baby with above-average abilities. A particularly intelligent baby may reach some developmental milestones earlier than average, but the real indicators of his superior intelligence are more subtle: for example, he'll display a greater variety of behaviour, a greater interest in his surroundings, and more interaction with his environment than the average baby.

## The parent's role

Very few babies are developmentally delayed, and equally few are especially gifted, so the chances are that your baby falls within the normal range of intelligence. Your task as a parent is to accept his abilities and to help him develop his strengths by careful teaching. But this is not teaching in the formal sense; there are no rules or targets that your baby has to reach.

▲ **EAGER TO LEARN** Your baby wants to learn. She is keen to meet new sights, sounds, tastes, and textures.

The best way to "teach" your baby is to make the world interesting for him and introduce him to a wide range of experiences. Explain everything that you see and, above all, join in with every activity so that you and your baby learn together. Give encouragement at all times, give praise when even something small is achieved, and provide constant support. Without your support your baby won't gain the confidence he needs.

Never push your baby: accept him for who he is; give him every opportunity to develop his talents; show him and let him know that you love and respect him just as he is.

## Read to your baby

Babies love books and your baby will respond from a surprisingly early age if you look at books with him and read to him. Reading books together will teach your child about colours and names for simple objects.

Your baby's never too young to be read to – your voice will be soothing to him, and you'll soon find that reading a book at bedtime is a useful and pacifying part of your evening routine. The bonus you may not expect is that once you have introduced your baby to books, he'll want to read them by himself later. You'll have done him a great service because you'll not only have introduced him to the idea of entertaining himself, but also to a pleasure that will last him for the rest of his life – reading and learning from books.

## Creativity

There is a whole range of skills and mental processes that you can encourage in your baby to stimulate his creative abilities: point out the things happening around him; show him patterns, colours, flowers, animals, and smells; and act out empathy for other people.

## The male brain

Even while your baby is in the womb, his brain is programmed for maleness. Differences in brain structure and function between boys and girls affect the way they develop.

■ A boy's brain weight and volume are greater than a girl's by about ten to 15 per cent.

■ When the right side of the brain is ready to send connections to the left, the appropriate cells don't yet exist in boys. As a result the fibres go back into the right side. This enriches connections within the right lobe and could explain why boys have greater spatial awareness than girls.

■ Boys show less fear of separation than girls because they have slower message transmission than girls until the brain matures. From as young as nine or ten months, they bring the fear under control by activities such as playing with a toy or crawling so as to distract themselves. This mode of behaviour continues into adulthood.

# Your baby's smile

**The first time your baby smiles at you is an exciting milestone in your relationship together; it's also an important sign that he's developing mentally.**

When your baby begins to smile, he's demonstrating that he can recognize you. It also shows that he wants to engage with you in an exchange – he's already starting to be sociable. He'll begin to respond to your talking to him with smiles, because he's learned that this pleases you and makes you talk to him more – these are in fact his first attempts at "conversation" with you (see p.105).

Smiling is also an important indicator of a baby's maturity and of his desire for interaction with other people.

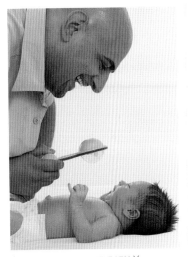

▲ **STIMULATING YOUR BABY** You can encourage your young baby to focus on objects by rattling and shaking toys in her line of vision.

## Milestones

In the early weeks your baby is busy sorting out the most important things in his world: your face and voice will be among the first he recognizes. He demonstrates his good memory and his hearing by quietening if you play a recording of the human heartbeat – something that's comforted him for nine months.

**Newborn** Within half an hour of birth your baby will flicker his eyes when spoken to. After one week he knows your voice, and after two he'll show that he recognizes you. If you speak to your baby from 20–25cm (8–10in) away, where he can see your face, he will open and close his mouth in response.

**One month** He'll respond to the tone of your voice, becoming calm if you speak soothingly, and distressed in response to rough tones. He gets very excited and his whole body jerks when he attempts to "speak". He follows a moving object with his eyes.

**Two months** He smiles in response to your face and voice. He looks around in response to sounds, and stares at objects with intense interest.

**Three months** Your baby is becoming more aware of his body, and will look at his hands and move them. He responds to conversation with a variety of nods, smiles, mouth movements, noises, squeaks, and other expressions of delight. He'll also make excited movements of his body.

**Four months** Your baby's curiosity is obvious. He's interested in new toys, new sounds, new places, new people, and new sensations. He likes to sit propped against cushions so he can look around. He now recognizes familiar objects and remembers routines; he'll get excited at the sight of a breast or bottle, and he's beginning to reveal a sense of humour. He plays with his feet when lying on his back.

**Five months** Your baby now spends longer examining things, showing that his concentration is developing. He turns to unseen sounds, and moves his arms and legs to attract your attention. He loves games, including splashing in the bath.

**Six months** Your baby makes sounds to attract your attention, gets excited when he hears someone coming, and puts out his arms to be picked up. He "speaks" and smiles to his reflection in a mirror. He may start to show shyness with strangers.

# How you can help

Talk and sing to your baby from the earliest days. His movements and sounds are his earliest attempts at speaking, so answer them to encourage him; make sure he can see your face clearly and make eye contact with him at all times, smile a lot, and exaggerate your mouth movements.

**Feed his curiosity** Everything is new and interesting to your baby, so show him objects and give him a chance to hold them. By the time he is two months old, he'll like to sit propped up so that he can look around himself more easily; put lots of small, soft toys within his reach where he can see and touch them. Talk to him constantly.

**Encourage awareness of himself** Your baby's discovery of his own body is a gradual process. When he's about eight weeks old, you can start showing him his hands, and play simple physical games. Hold him in front of a mirror, so he can see himself in it.

# Perception

Your baby experiences things through his senses just as you do, but he has to learn to single out what's important and what is not. Help him to connect the information given by his different senses: show him a rattle, allow him to touch it, then shake it and draw his attention to the sound. Touch is one of the main ways that your baby explores his environment, so introduce him to lots of different textures.

▲ **USING A MIRROR** Point at your baby's reflection and say his name, so he starts to gain a sense of himself. Use his name often to bolster his sense of identity.

# Testing perception

From an early stage, your baby can make basic distinctions between big and small. He'll also show interest in new sights and sounds, as the following test, which can be carried out from four months, demonstrates.

■ First show your baby the card with a small diamond above a large diamond.

■ Next, show him a card with a small circle above a large circle drawn on it. He's already starting to see the relationship between the small and large shapes.

■ Now show him a card with a small triangle above a large one. Because this fits the pattern set by the first two, he will probably show no interest in it.

■ If you show him a card with a large triangle above a small one, he will probably show renewed interest because the pattern of small above large has changed.

▲ **TEST CARDS** Your baby will be able to make quite sophisticated distinctions involving pattern and shape.

## The right toys

**As they develop, babies need different stimuli so bear this in mind when you choose toys.**

It's very important that the toys you give your baby are right for his age. If a toy is too advanced for your baby he won't know how to play with it in the proper way and won't get much fun from it. But if the toy is too primitive, he'll get bored quickly.

Suitable toys for a baby under one year are those that give experience of colours, textures, materials, and interesting and varied shapes and sounds, so choose toys that provide a variety of these things. Toys that make noises and react to actions, such as rattles, give a sense of control and encourage the development of manipulation skills and coordination.

▲ **LOOK AND LEARN** Colour, shape, and noise are all interesting to your baby, so choose toys that give a variety of these things.

# Learning through play

Babies and children learn through play, and play is a very serious business! Everything is a learning experience for your baby, and anything new is fun, so learning and playing are indistinguishable. If you are aware of the skills he's developing in his first six months, you can choose games and toys that interest him and help to encourage his abilities. At this age, toys that stimulate his senses will be most interesting to him.

**Simple games**  Because your baby is fascinated by your face, "peek-a-boo" is one of the best games you can play with him. Hide your face in your hands or with a scarf or towel, then peek out at him, saying "peek-a-boo" as you do it. Babies develop a sense of humour quite early, and this is a game that they find endlessly amusing. When he's old enough to sit up without support, roll a large, soft ball gently towards him; he'll eventually try to push it back to you. Then you've got a real game going and he's acquiring early ball sense.

**Rhymes and songs**  Your baby will love listening to rhymes even when he's very young because he likes to be talked to, and rhythmic sounds are easier for him to listen to than normal speech. He'll love being sung to, as well, whether it's a soothing lullaby or a more lively tune sung while you bounce him on your knee. Rhyming, rhythmic songs and games encourage early speech.

**Physical fun**  Even a very young baby loves to play bouncing, swinging, and rocking games with you. They make him aware of his own body and improve his movement skills such as crawling and walking as well as balance and coordination.

**Feed his senses**  Your baby explores the world through his senses, and he will find anything new interesting (see Testing perception, p.101). Allow him to spend as much time as possible propped up in a sitting position so that he can see what's going on around him, and leave small toys within his reach so he can handle them – toys that make noises or are made of differently textured materials are best. When he's older and able to grasp objects, you can give him stacking beakers or rings – ones with large pieces are suitable while his grasp is still quite primitive. The kitchen is a good source of interesting toys for your child: wooden spoons, spatulas, small pans with lids, colanders and sieves, funnels, a set of measuring spoons, plastic cups, ice cube trays, or egg cartons. Let your baby create his own uses for them.

▲ **FUN WITH FACES** Your baby loves to look at your face so play "peek-a-boo" and point out the parts of your face, then his face. Show him pictures of faces, too.

## Choosing toys

Many parents and relatives find it hard to choose toys for a new baby. A young baby won't be able to interact with his toys much at first, so they should be soft, simple, sturdy, and attractive to look at and touch.

**Soft toys**  Your baby will like soft toys that he can squeeze and that are nice to touch. Make sure they're washable and colourfast, because he'll keep putting them in his mouth.

**Mobiles**  For a newborn, a mobile hung 25cm (10in) above a cot or pram provides visual stimulation, but make sure it's out of his reach. Change the parts around every few days to hold his interest.

**Noisy toys**  Rattles, soft toys that squeak, and musical toys are all fun for a young baby. By six months, he loves to play with a music box that he can operate perhaps by pressing a button or pulling a string.

**Books**  Your baby is never too young to be read to, so start as soon as he's born. Choose books with large, brightly coloured pictures; point to common objects and name them while you're looking at them together.

# Toy safety

Be very careful when choosing toys. With a young baby bear in mind that he is likely to put everything in his mouth.

■ Toys such as rattles should be lightweight in case your baby hits himself with them.

■ Avoid toys with small holes that could trap your baby's fingers.

■ Long strings on toys could be swallowed or get wrapped around your baby's neck.

■ Soft toys should be made of flame-retardant material and should also be colourfast; otherwise your baby could suck the dye off and become ill.

■ Small parts that could choke your baby, such as eyes on soft toys, should be firmly attached.

■ Check seams on soft toys. The filling could choke a baby if swallowed.

■ Don't let your young baby play with small objects such as coins, buttons, or beads that he could swallow and choke on.

■ Check rattles and other toys for sharp edges, points, or splinters.

## Girls' behaviour

Girls tend to develop social skills and enjoy the company of other people far earlier than boys do. While not all children conform to a stereotype, in general girls:

- are more sociable than boys, and form closer friendships from an earlier age

- are more compliant with adult requests than boys tend to be in early childhood

- show fewer competitive traits and are less socially aggressive and dominant than boys

- cope far more easily with physical, emotional, and intellectual stress than boys.

# Social behaviour

Many features of your child's personality will affect his development as well as his future prospects in life. Helpful traits include the ability to get on well with people, to concentrate, to learn from mistakes, a willingness to work hard, good powers of observation, thoroughness, creativity, an enquiring mind, and determination.

Less helpful traits are slowness of thought, a child's difficulty in expressing himself, overactivity, and diminished concentration, which may occur even in a highly intelligent child.

Your young baby needs to interact socially, especially with you, his parents. He's learning to be sociable by imitating you, first with facial expressions, then with gestures and movements, and finally with complete patterns of behaviour. In this way the relationship between parent and child forms the blueprint for all subsequent relationships, so it's your responsibility to be more aware of your behaviour and responses than ever before. From the moment you first talked to your baby, he began to develop into a social being because he longs to converse with you.

Like all other development, social development has its own well-defined stages. Your young baby will still rely very much on you, his parents, to help him control his responses and behaviour. Sometimes his feelings will be overwhelming and he needs you to help him contain and understand them. Although at times you'll believe that this phase will go on forever, remember it's simply a stage in his social development.

## Predicting personality

It would be marvellous if we could predict the future personality of a child when he was still an infant. Certainly we can do so with intelligence. Personality and character, however, derive partly from heredity and partly from environment, so there always remains the possibility that, as the result of a bad environment or the lack of secure, loving relationships, a child may not have the opportunities necessary to grow up as a loving and lovable adult.

In view of the profound effect of environment and family on character, predictions during infancy are doomed to failure. However, observant parents with several children can detect differences in their personalities from the outset. Perhaps it's a good thing that personality prediction is so difficult. From the point of view of adoption it would be a pity if such predictions were possible. Adoptive parents may wish to be able to assess the intelligence of the child whom they are thinking of adopting, but they can't know what his personality will be like. Watching your child's personality emerge as he grows up is part of the adventure you enter into when you become a parent.

## Individuality

Your young baby's individuality will gradually become more and more apparent as he grows and learns. As loving parents, you'll treasure your baby's individuality and nurture his growth and strength.

The gradual insight you gain into your baby's personality is like watching a thrilling film in slow motion. All his preferences, the things that make him laugh and cry, the foods he likes, his favourite toys, come together to create his unique personality.

**Baby types**  There's much evidence now that within a week or so of birth infants show a primitive form of all the traits they'll show as they grow up and probably later in life. Undeniably, environment has a profound effect on character formation, but much of a child's basic character is inherited from his parents, so it's fair to say that each baby will show basic personality traits that don't change much with age.

The traits that are easily recognizable by any parent are the amount of energy your child has, how well he can control his body (as opposed to being floppy), self-reliance, social responsiveness, family attachment, communicativeness, adaptability to various situations, exploitation of the environment, sense of humour, emotional expressiveness, reaction to success, reaction to restriction, readiness of smiling, and readiness of crying. Your baby will probably fall into one of three personality types:

He may be quite "good" or "easy", eating and sleeping well and seldom getting over-enthusiastic in his responses.

He may be what is sometimes referred to as a high-keyed "sparkler", becoming as demanding in his bids for companionship as he first was for food and comfort; the zest for living keeps him growing in self-play.

He may be an "in-betweener", having up-days and hours and down-days and hours, and asking only that you respond in kind.

While some personality traits may be apparent very early on, it's in the first few months that each new baby starts to become more distinctly himself. You might notice some of the following traits developing in your young baby: easy-going, placid, and prone to day-dreaming; cross and irritable, with signs of being a leader; sociable and tending to follow the lead of others; serious and determined; independent and often perverse; imaginative and sometimes difficult to handle.

# Boys' behaviour

Boys tend to be slower to develop social skills than girls. While not all boys will show these traits to a marked degree, in general boys:

▓ tend to be slower to develop social skills than girls

▓ are more socially aggressive

▓ have more friendships than girls, but they tend to be superficial and short-lived

▓ are more emotionally vulnerable than girls

▓ tend to have more behavioural problems, particularly when around authority figures.

▲ **FIRST CONVERSATIONS** Your young baby will love to respond to your words with his own babbling and gurgling. He's learning how to have a conversation.

## Bonding

The relationship between you and your baby begins from the moment you give birth and every aspect of your being becomes a comfort and joy to your baby.

He'll respond to your smell, the sound of your voice, the touch of your skin, and the sight of your face. This bond is so complete, your baby will be able to single you out from others in an astoundingly short time. It will be the same for your partner when he spends time alone with your baby.

Make every effort to ensure that the contact you and your partner have with your baby is pleasant, calm, and loving, even if at times this seems difficult. Cuddle him and give him skin-to-skin contact whenever possible. It'll make him feel really loved and secure.

▲ AN EARLY START By developing a close, loving relationship with your baby from birth, you're laying the foundations of a good relationship in future years.

# Early communication

Your baby's first six months are a crucial time for his social development. It's during these early weeks that your baby comes to understand the pleasure of social interaction and the importance of communication.

Your baby grows beyond the basic requirements of warmth and feeding as he begins to enjoy the social aspects of being alive. Because you and your partner mean comfort, pleasure, and security for your baby, you're naturally the best people to teach him loving relationships, the basics of which are learned through the initial skin contact that he loves so much during the first few weeks.

**Newborn** From the very beginning, your baby will want to be close to you. He'll appeal to you through head nodding, mouth and tongue movements, and jerks of his body. These are his earliest conversations; he's talking to you, so answer with noises, laughter, and bobbing head movements. He'll soon learn that he can make you respond.

**Three months** Your baby's conversational gestures are far more controlled. He'll turn towards the sound of your voice and wriggle with pleasure on seeing you. He understands that a smile is a happy greeting – his earliest "hello". Your baby will learn that being friendly is rewarding if you respond with interest, love, cuddles, comfort, and soothing noises. A child who's smiled at, smiles back, and smiles in greeting. When you feed him, make this a time of physical intimacy. Hold him close, look into his eyes, and talk to him gently.

**Four months** By now your baby is such a social being he'll cry soon after being left alone, even if he has many toys around him. He'll stop crying if you go to him and he'll wriggle his body in anticipation. He'll be happy to respond to people who acknowledge him, but will have a special response for you and the rest of the family. Make eye contact as often as possible and exaggerate all facial expressions and gestures.

**Five months** At this age your baby has four main methods of communication: sounds, gestures, facial expressions, and crying, and unless he is asleep, he'll make the most of all four. Imitate all your baby's sounds with changes in pitch and loudness. Interest him in subtle sounds. Play soft music, crunch up tissue paper, and ring small bells. He can also tell the difference between an angry voice and a friendly one now, and will react to each differently. He now shows a certain shyness with strangers, but will smile at a familiar face.

**Six months** Your baby's social advances are far more physical now, even aggressive, but they may be offset by a growing fear of strangers, and a possessiveness over you. He'll explore much more with his hands, patting and touching your face and hands rather than just searching your face with his eyes. Help your baby by giving him lots of physical affection.

## Responding to your baby

Any response you make to your baby's attempts at conversation will help his understanding of communication, so do try to be as positive as you can all the time. If a baby's gurgling is met with silence, he'll soon grow tired of such an unrewarding game and may well give up on all but the most basic communication. Always encourage a "two-way" conversation, either by imitating your baby's gestures and noises in an overt way, or by chatting to him in order to elicit a response. Be theatrical with your voice and gestures. The broader your gestures, the more he understands, the more fun he has, and the closer the bond between you becomes.

A young baby is sensitive to sudden noises, so bear in mind that, although a wide variety of noises are tranquillizing for him, harsh or very loud noises will frighten and upset him.

Encourage your baby to cope with meeting new faces by introducing him to friends who come to see you. This will allow him to get used to strangers in the security of your home. The more your baby enjoys the company, the more likely he is to enjoy socializing as he grows older. Songs and rhythmic games will also encourage him to equate joyful times with mixing with other people.

## Difficult babies

A demanding baby, one who cries constantly and can't be comforted, can be difficult to cope with. It's vital that you share the responsibility with your partner and try very hard to control your temper. There are many causes of, and solutions to, a crying baby, and constant tears is a phase that's fortunately short-lived. If your baby is difficult, it's important to understand why he's crying, keeping you awake, or ignoring you. Whatever his particular problem, your calm, loving, and understanding approach will have a far more positive effect on him than being chastised or ignored. Your health visitor can offer support and advice on whether medical assessment is necessary.

If you have an antisocial baby, for example one who is discontented when hungry, but never enjoys feeding or being held, you may feel rejected by him, or responsible for his unhappiness. Try to keep these negative thoughts at bay. Some babies are less social than others, but no matter how much he rejects you, keep trying to engage his interest.

# One of the family

**Your baby is longing to be part of the family with all its routines, rules, and customs.**

To become interested he needs to learn how to fit in. For this reason, include him in all your family activities, outings, shopping, daily chores, and visits to friends, from as early as possible. Talk to your child about all the members of the family and show him photos.

The family group will be the basis of your baby's learning about the workings of groups in general. His behaviour with family members will teach him about his expected behaviour with strangers, and will introduce him to the social customs of his society.

Your baby learns chiefly through imitation, so by copying your behaviour he learns how to be friendly and loving with others.

▲ **INVOLVE YOUR BABY** Try to include your baby in your activities, even if they don't directly involve him. He'll enjoy watching you and hearing you talk about what you're doing.

# Your older baby

By six months or so life will have settled down somewhat. Your baby may be sleeping longer at night and have started on some solid food. Caring for her and changing her nappies will be second nature, and you'll have learned to recognize her cries and what they mean.

Over the next 12 months your baby will continue to mature socially and mentally, and she'll also become more skilled physically. Sitting up gives her a new exciting view of the world. Next she'll learn to crawl and later to walk, and she will develop fine manipulation skills. All these things will open up new areas of experience for her.

The moment when your child begins to speak is enormously exciting. It's a tool with which she can learn and she no longer has to rely on crying to communicate with you.

## Girls' weight

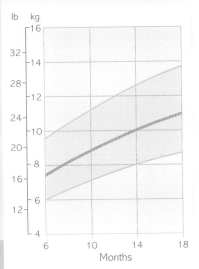

lb   kg

Months

▲ **YOUR BABY'S WEIGHT** The rapid weight gain of the first few months slows down, but your baby is still putting on weight steadily. Any weight within the coloured band is normal. (For a full explanation of this chart, see Your baby's weight, p.38.)

# Feeding and nutrition

During your baby's first year you'll start weaning her on to solid foods, although not before she's six months old. Before this, your baby's digestive tract is incapable of digesting and absorbing more complex foods.

Breastmilk (or its formula equivalent) is the only food that your baby needs in the early months, and if a baby is introduced to solids too young it can lessen her desire to suck. In addition solids that are introduced too early will pass through largely undigested, and will put an increased strain on your baby's immature kidneys. Breastfed babies will take less milk from your breasts, and you'll respond by producing less milk. Either way your baby will end up having an unsatisfactory diet for her needs.

## When to wean

As your baby grows, she'll need to drink more and more milk to maintain this growth. But your baby's stomach can only hold a certain amount of milk at each feed; eventually, she'll reach a point when she's drinking to full capacity at each feed, but still doesn't have enough calories for her needs. Your baby will let you know that she needs more to eat by a change in her feeding habits. She may start to demand more milk and appear very unsatisfied after each feed, or she may start demanding a sixth feed, having previously been content on five. A classic case is a baby

## Examples of weaning stages

| FEEDS | 1ST WEEK | 3RD WEEK |
|---|---|---|
| 1st feed | Breast- or bottlefeed | Breast- or bottlefeed |
| 2nd feed | Half breast- or bottlefeed Try one or two teaspoons of purée or cereal then give remainder of milk feed | Half breast- or bottlefeed Two teaspoons of cereal Remainder of milk feed |
| 3rd feed | Breast- or bottlefeed | Half breast- or bottlefeed Two teaspoons of vegetable or fruit purée Remainder of milk feed |
| 4th feed | Breast- or bottlefeed | Breast- or bottlefeed |
| 5th feed | Breast- or bottlefeed | Breast- or bottlefeed |

who's been sleeping through the night starting to wake for a night-time feed. This is the time to introduce solids. Many babies do this at around six months, when their intense desire to suck lessens, although it can be later. Tune in to the signs that your baby gives you, and follow her lead for the introduction of solids – some people think the first tooth definitely indicates a need for solids. Talk to your health visitor if you're unsure.

## Giving the first solids

Have a small amount of prepared food to hand and then settle in your normal position to feed your baby. Although your baby is ready for the calories that solids provide, she'll prefer what she knows is satisfying – milk. Start by feeding her from one breast or giving half the usual bottle. Then give her one or two teaspoons of food. The midday meal is ideal because your baby won't be ravenous, but will be awake and cooperative.

Never force your baby to take more food than she wants. When she's taken the solid food, give her the rest of the milk. Once she becomes used to solids, she may prefer to take them first. As soon as your baby is having any quantity of solid food, she'll need water as well as milk to drink. Start her off with 15ml (½floz) of water between and after feeds, and whenever she's thirsty during the day. Avoid syrups, cordials, and any sweetened drinks, as these will damage your baby's teeth. Give no more than 120ml (4floz) water a day; milk is still your baby's main source of fluid and nutrition. Dentists recommend you avoid fruit juice for a few months yet.

## Weaning tips

Your baby may be reluctant to try new foods, so give her time to get used to each new food and don't persist if she seems to dislike a particular food.

■ Give one new food at a time. Try it once and wait for several days before giving it again to see if there's an adverse reaction.

■ Use dry infant cereals rather than ready-mixed ones as they are more nutritious.

■ Don't give foods containing gluten, nuts, dairy products (for example, cheese or yogurts), or eggs before six months, to avoid developing allergies later.

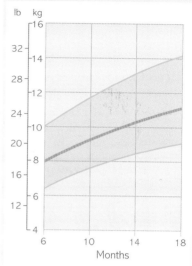

Months

**▲ YOUR BABY'S WEIGHT** The rapid weight gain of the first few months has past, but your little boy is still getting steadily heavier. Any weight that falls within the coloured band is normal. (For a full explanation of this chart, see Your baby's weight, p.38.)

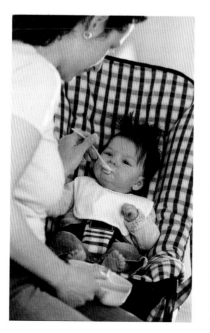

**◄ GIVING THE FOOD** Halfway through her normal breast- or bottle feed, scoop up some food on a small spoon and insert it gently between her lips. Don't push the spoon in too far or your baby may gag. She may take a month or so to get used to using a spoon. Your baby may push more food out than she takes in. Gently scrape the excess on to her lips; she will turn away once she's had enough.

FEEDING AND NUTRITION

11

## Introducing cups

Some breastfed babies never accept a bottle and go straight to a cup for water. You can introduce your baby to drinking from a cup when she's about four months old. Aim for your baby to give up bottles by 12 months.

■ Beakers with spouts are best as your baby will have to half suck and half drink to get anything. Soft spouts are the easiest to use.

■ As your baby progresses, she may prefer to move on to a two-handled cup that she can grasp more easily. Those with specially slanted lips are excellent because the contents come out with very little tipping.

▲ **TRAINER CUPS** Lunchtime and late afternoon feeds are probably the best times to use the trainer cup; these are times when your baby will be more likely to eat solids.

# Introducing solids and self-feeding

During the second half of her first year, your baby will move on from mere "tastes" of solid foods with her milk feeds to three meals a day, with drinks of water, diluted fruit juice, or milk.

Once your baby is happy with a couple of different solids, it's important to introduce a variety of tastes and textures. Not only will she be able to deal with foods that have been puréed, mashed, or chopped, she'll also learn to enjoy chewing and sucking on larger chunks of food (see Finger foods, opposite), but it's important to remember that every baby has different requirements and appetites. If you're in any doubt, just feed your baby as much as she'll take happily. The amount of milk she requires will lessen as the number of solid meals she takes increases, but she should still be drinking 300–600ml (10–20floz) of milk a day at 12 months. Since she'll be getting most of her calories from solids rather than from milk, your baby will become thirsty. When she does, give her plain water or diluted fruit juice to drink, rather than milk. Never give your baby commercial drinks containing sugar and colourings.

## Feeding your child

You will probably begin by feeding your baby in an infant chair or on your lap, but once she's used to the idea, you may like to use a highchair or feeding table. With a feeding table you'll have to bend down to feed your baby and at first you may have to prop her up with cushions, so a highchair is probably better; make sure your baby is properly strapped in.

Your child should always be supervised while she's eating. Almost all children gag on some food at some stage and it is essential that you react quickly. A new texture, taken for the first time, may make her gag out of surprise. If she does, pat her firmly on the back and encourage her to cough until the food is dislodged. Talk soothingly and gently rub her back and she'll be more able to swallow the new food. If your baby's choking is severe, and especially if she loses consciousness, you must know how to give her first aid (see p.326).

## Self-feeding

Your baby will soon look forward to meal times as an opportunity to play as well as to eat, so feeding will be messier. Keep your baby's highchair away from the walls and put newspapers on the floor in case she starts throwing food. Within a month or so of starting solids, your baby will be able to take food from the spoon. Learning to feed herself is a huge step

◄ **SELF-FEEDING** Allow your child to feed himself if he wants to. He'll enjoy it and it helps his manual dexterity.

in your baby's physical and intellectual development so encourage all her efforts. Her manual dexterity and hand–eye coordination will greatly improve with self-feeding, so let her experiment if she shows an interest and don't worry about the mess. Food gives your baby the perfect motivation for speeding up muscle coordination and balance. It may be several months before your baby becomes proficient at feeding herself. You can help by giving her non-runny foods that stick to the spoon, such as porridge, scrambled eggs, or thick vegetable purées. If she finds trying to use a spoon very frustrating, let her try finger foods. Food will be a plaything – much of it will land on the floor rather than in your baby's stomach – but there's no cause for concern; at the time when a baby starts to self-feed, the initial growth spurt is beginning to slacken off, so she needs less food anyway.

The best way to make sure that your baby gets at least some food is for both of you to have a spoon. Use two spoons of the same colour and type so that you can swap your full spoon for her empty one when she has difficulty scooping up the food.

# Finger foods

If your baby has difficulty using a spoon, she'll find finger foods easier to handle; even if the food is hard, she will suck it.

When your baby is teething she'll like to chew and suck to soothe her gums. Never leave her alone with food as she could choke.

▲ **SAFETY** Give your child large pieces of raw or cooked vegetables or fruit to chew on.

# Foods for self-feeding

| FRUIT AND VEGETABLES | CEREALS | PROTEIN |
|---|---|---|
| Any fresh fruit that is easy to hold, like bananas, cut into slices with the skin or pips removed | Small pieces of dried, sugar-free cereal | Wholemeal bread |
| | Boiled rice | Pieces of soft cheese |
| Vegetables, particularly carrots, cut into a stick or shape that is easy to grasp. Don't cut vegetables too small | Wholemeal bread or rusks (without the complete grains) | Toast fingers with cheese |
| | | Small pieces of white meat in easily held pieces |
| Mashed potato, cooked broccoli "trees" | Pasta shapes | Low-fat cheese |
| | | Filleted fish in firm chunks |
| | | Sliced hard-boiled egg yolk |

# Your baby's needs

Your baby will always take enough food to satisfy her needs. If she doesn't want to eat, then she doesn't need to. This means that there will be days when she will eat hardly anything, but these will be followed by periods when she'll eat a lot.

## Balanced diet is important

To eat a balanced diet, your baby should take in foods from each of the food groups in the correct proportions (see below). This doesn't have to be on a daily basis, though. So when you're considering whether she's eating well, think in the long term: look at what she has eaten in the last week, not just today. Viewed like this, a binge of eating nothing but bread for two days is nothing to worry about, as your baby will probably eat enough fruit and vegetables during the week to balance this out. What is important is that she should be given a wide variety of foods to choose from: she can't eat the foods she requires if they're not available to her.

Your baby will gradually come to eat many of the same foods as you, prepared in a form that she can manage. It would be wrong, however, to suppose that her needs are the same as yours, or that a diet that is recommended as healthy for you will be good for her. You may aim to reduce your fat intake by using low-fat dairy products, for example, but your child needs whole milk until she is two years old; after that you

▶ **THE FOOD PYRAMID** This table shows the proportions in which the main food groups should be eaten in order for your baby to take in the right balance of nutrients. The two most important groups are carbohydrates and fruit and vegetables, followed by protein-rich foods like meat, pulses, and dairy products. Sugars, fats, and oils should form the smallest part of your baby's diet – in fact, the amounts of these that occur naturally in other foods will be more than enough. By following these guidelines for your baby, you will be helping her form good habits for life.

Fats, oils, and sugars

Protein: Meat, fish, eggs, dairy foods, and pulses

Fruit and vegetables

Carbohydrates: Bread, cereal, rice, and pasta

# Suggested menus: eight to ten months

| DAY 1 | DAY 2 | DAY 3 |
|---|---|---|
| **Breakfast**<br>Rice cakes<br>Hard-boiled egg yolk<br>Milk | **Breakfast**<br>Mashed banana<br>Wholemeal toast fingers<br>Milk | **Breakfast**<br>Cottage cheese or yogurt<br>Wholemeal toast fingers<br>Milk |
| **Lunch**<br>Strained vegetable<br>  and chicken<br>Stewed apple<br>Diluted fruit juice | **Lunch**<br>Mashed potato and<br>  cheese<br>Pear slices<br>Diluted fruit juice | **Lunch**<br>Strained lentils and mixed<br>  vegetables<br>Banana and fromage frais<br>Diluted fruit juice |
| **Snack**<br>Wholemeal toast<br>  fingers<br>Orange segments<br>Milk | **Snack**<br>Rice cakes<br>Apple pieces<br>Milk | **Snack**<br>Homemade rusks<br>Fresh fruit<br>Milk |
| **Supper**<br>Cauliflower cheese<br>Semolina and fruit<br>  purée<br>Diluted fruit juice | **Supper**<br>Pasta and tomato sauce<br>Yogurt with fruit purée<br>Diluted fruit juice | **Supper**<br>Tuna and mashed potato<br>  with steamed courgettes<br>Rice pudding<br>Diluted fruit juice |

can introduce semi-skimmed milk. The health benefits of limiting sugar intake, though, apply as much to babies as to adults. Never add any salt to your baby's meals; her kidneys are too immature to cope with salty foods.

## Keep a flexible attitude

The sample menus shown above are intended as a guide to your baby's main meals. Remember, a baby's stomach can't hold very much, and she'll need to eat more often than an adult; so don't insist she finishes her meals, and be prepared to give snacks in between meal times. Of course you should encourage your baby to have regular feeding times, but if you try to make her eat at meal times only, they will become battlegrounds, and she may end up not getting the food she needs when she needs it. If she shows that she's had enough, don't try to make her eat more.

Of course it's frustrating if you've spent a lot of time preparing a meal and your baby refuses it, or it ends up on the floor. The answer is to make feeding times as easy on yourself as possible: don't spend a lot of time preparing complicated dishes, and take precautions to protect the walls and the floor from thrown food.

## Kitchen hygiene

Scares about food poisoning in recent years have made parents much more aware of the dangers of poor food hygiene. Follow these common-sense safety measures to protect your baby.

■ Always wash your hands with soap before handling food, especially after using the toilet or changing a nappy, and after playing with pets. Make sure your family does the same.

■ Wash your hands, utensils, and chopping boards after handling raw meat.

■ Be scrupulous about keeping the kitchen clean, especially work surfaces, chopping boards, and utensils used in food preparation.

■ Always use a clean tea-towel or paper towels to dry dishes, or let them dry in a rack after rinsing them with hot water.

■ Keep the kitchen bin covered. Empty it often, and rinse it out with hot water and a little disinfectant each time you empty it.

■ Cover any food that is left out of the cupboard.

■ Any leftover food in your baby's dish should be thrown away.

■ Keep separate cloths for dirty tasks and for washing your child's highchair. Change cloths every week at least or wash them on the hot cycle of the washing machine.

# Food preparation

Once your baby is on solids, you don't need to sterilize all feeding utensils, although bottles and teats used for milk should still be sterilized until your baby is about a year old. Cups, bowls, and cutlery can be washed in hot, soapy water and rinsed with hot water, or put in a dishwasher. However, you need to take precautions to protect your child from the effects of harmful bacteria – salmonella and listeria poisoning, for example.

## Buying and storing

The most important thing to look for when buying food is freshness. Shop often, and use food as quickly as possible. Bruised or damaged fruit and vegetables deteriorate quickly, so don't buy them. Always wash fruit if the skin is to be eaten, as there may be a residue of insecticides or other chemicals. Check the "sell by", "best before", or "use by" dates on packaged foods and make sure that there are no signs of damage.

Store food in the fridge in clean, covered containers. Store cooked and raw foods on separate shelves, and put raw meat and fish on a plate so that the juices can't drip on to food below. Always defrost frozen foods thoroughly, and never refreeze food once it has been defrosted.

## Cooking and reheating

Always cook your baby's food thoroughly; this applies especially to meat, poultry, and eggs. Never give raw or soft-cooked eggs, liver pâté, soft cheeses, or nut products to your baby. It's also best not to give your baby

▲ PREPARE IN ADVANCE Save time by preparing puréed vegetables and freezing them in plastic containers – ice cube trays are ideal for very small amounts. This makes it easy to have a nutritious meal ready for your baby in very little time.

reheated leftovers, chilled, or frozen foods. If you're preparing food in bulk quantities, don't leave it to cool before putting it into the fridge, as this will just give the bacteria a chance to multiply; put it in a cold dish, cover it, and put it straight into the fridge or freezer.

## Preparation

At first you'll have to purée all your baby's food, but this stage won't last very long, so if you don't have a blender or liquidizer you can use a cheap hand-operated food mill. A hand-held blender is also inexpensive and convenient. As your baby gets older, you can feed her coarser mashed or minced foods. By the time she's nine to 12 months she'll enjoy soft pieces of food and finger foods.

You can use a variety of liquids to thin down home-prepared foods: the water you've used to steam fruit or vegetables is ideal as it contains minerals from the foods. To thicken foods, you can use ground, wholegrain cereals, cottage cheese, yogurt, or mashed potato. If you feel you need to sweeten your baby's food, use naturally sweet fruit juice, not sugar.

## Preparation tips

| DO | DON'T |
| --- | --- |
| Use fruit and vegetables as soon as possible after buying. | Buy bruised or wrinkled fruit and vegetables. |
| Peel tough-skinned fruit and vegetables if the skin is likely to cause your baby problems. | Prepare vegetables a long time in advance or soak them in water, as this destroys the vitamins. |
| Cook soft-skinned fruit and vegetables in their skins; this helps to retain the vitamins and provides additional fibre. | Crush or bruise fruit and vegetables; this destroys vitamin C. |
| | Give red meat more than twice a week as it has a high saturated fat content. |
| Cook fruit and vegetables in a steamer or tightly covered pan with as little water as possible. This helps to retain the vitamins normally lost in cooking. | Overcook tinned foods, as this destroys the vitamins. |
| | Add salt or sugar to your child's food; her immature kidneys can't handle a lot of salt, and giving her sweet foods will encourage a sweet tooth. |
| Give your baby cooked and puréed meat or fish; a purée can be thinned with vegetable water or soup. | |
| Use sunflower or corn oil. Never cook with butter or saturated fats. | Leave prepared food to cool at room temperature; refrigerate it straight away. |

## Using packaged foods

Packaged foods are more expensive than homemade ones, but they are convenient when you're in a hurry or you're travelling. Always follow these guidelines when using them.

■ Check the ingredients listed on the tin or jar. They are listed in order of quantity, so anything that has water near the top of the list will not be very nutritious.

■ Avoid foods with added sugar or modified starch. It is illegal for baby foods to contain added salt or monosodium glutamate (MSG).

■ Make sure that the seal is intact; if it's damaged, the food could be contaminated.

■ Don't heat the food up in the jar – the glass might crack.

■ Don't feed your baby from the jar if you intend to keep some of the food, as the leftovers will become contaminated with saliva.

■ Don't keep opened jars in the fridge for longer than two days, and never keep them beyond the "best before" date.

■ Never store baby food in an opened tin; put it in a dish, cover, and refrigerate.

■ Check the ingredients lists carefully if you are introducing food types gradually – many contain eggs, gluten, and dairy products. Some even contain nuts.

■ Buy organic brands of baby food whenever possible.

# Miriam's casebook

# Vegetarian weaning

Penny and David have been vegetarian for three years. They know that a vegetarian diet that excludes meat, poultry, and fish, but contains eggs and milk can provide all the nutrients for health and vitality as long as a proper balance of the different food groups is maintained. They want their son Sam to be vegetarian also but to be certain that his diet is nutritionally balanced and healthy for a growing baby.

## Balancing nutritional needs

Penny was nervous about not giving Sam a really balanced diet with enough protein, vitamins D and $B_{12}$, calcium, and iron, even though she knew many vegetarian foods were fortified with extra $B_{12}$ and protein. I told her that a growing baby can get all the nourishment he needs from a carefully planned diet, although if she wished to bring up Sam as a vegan (no animal foods whatsoever, no dairy produce, and no eggs) she would need to see a paediatric nutritionist.

When Sam was six months old, Penny started to wean him gradually by replacing breastfeeds with solid foods so that Sam would end up on three meals a day. Penny and I planned a schedule whereby she would introduce one food at a time, withdrawing it if it didn't suit Sam and trying it again ten days later. Sam's diet had to include foods from each of the major food groups (see p.114).

## Sources of good nutrition

Sam would get protein, essential for growth in a young baby, from egg yolks, pulses, cheese, and milk as well as sunflower seed spread, soya yogurt, and grains. I pointed out to Penny that she shouldn't replace cows' milk with sheep's or goats' milk before Sam was 12–18 months old and that egg whites

shouldn't be given until Sam was nine to ten months old. Foods made from cereals and grains provide carbohydrates to give Sam the energy to grow and develop, while fruit and vegetables supply essential vitamins and minerals. I told Penny that vegetarian diets tend to be bulky and lower in calories than a diet including meat. This can be hard for a baby because Sam could feel full before he's taken all the food that he needs for good nutrition, so Penny should give him a wide variety of foods that are low in fibre. I advised Penny not to overcook vegetables and to peel and stone fruit. We then drew up a menu plan (see opposite) for Sam.

## Successful weaning

I was delighted to see that Sam sailed through his weaning. He really seemed to enjoy foods without salt and sugar, foods Penny thought he would find too bland. Penny found that Sam adored pease pudding made from lentils, a food she introduced when Sam was seven months old. He also relished the yolk of an egg finely chopped and then mashed with soya yogurt. The more solid food he ate, the more fluid Sam wanted to drink, and a little unsweetened orange juice diluted half and half with water became his standard drink.

# Miriam's top tips

In hot weather Penny found that Sam could easily drink 280ml (10floz) of this favourite drink every day. Penny was of course keen to introduce Sam to new flavours. She asked if there were any foods she shouldn't give, and I advised her to introduce strongly flavoured vegetables such as broccoli, onions, or peppers gradually, and not to give wholegrain bread or unpeeled fruit until Sam is a year old and his digestive system is more mature.

## Healthy growth and development

Sam is now nine months old and very much one of the family, eating more and more family food, which only needs sieving or mashing to suit him. He loves gravies and sauces, and Penny has found that these help him to take almost any new food. Ice cream has become such a favourite that Penny has to limit this treat to once or twice a week so that Sam isn't getting too much sugar and fat. He's gaining weight steadily, but he's not fat.

Choose a time when your baby is hungry, but not very hungry, such as the middle of the day, to try the first solids.

■ First foods should be smooth in texture and mild in taste. Baby rice, cooked puréed fruit such as apples and pears, or vegetables such as carrots or potatoes (with no added salt) are ideal.

■ Avoid adding seasoning or sugar.

■ Adding a spoonful of your baby's usual milk to the food helps him take to a new taste more readily.

# Vegetarian menu for an eight-month-old baby

Your baby's main source of calories at this stage is still breastmilk or formula, so offer this at each feed, but you should also give him drinks of cooled boiled water, preferably in a cup.

| | | | |
|---|---|---|---|
| **Breakfast** | ■ Breast- or bottlefeed<br>■ Baby yogurt dessert | ■ Breast- or bottlefeed<br>■ Breakfast cereal with milk | ■ Breast- or bottlefeed<br>■ Baby rice |
| **Lunch** | ■ Diluted unsweetened fruit juice or cooled boiled water<br>■ Cooked puréed lentils with vegetables<br>■ Puréed fruit | ■ Diluted unsweetened fruit juice or cooled boiled water<br>■ Hard-boiled egg and spinach with bread fingers<br>■ Puréed fruit | ■ Diluted unsweetened fruit juice or cooled boiled water<br>■ Cheese with vegetable purée<br>■ Mashed banana and yogurt |
| **Tea** | ■ Breast- or bottlefeed | ■ Breast- or bottlefeed | ■ Breast- or bottlefeed |
| **Evening** | ■ Mashed potato with grated cheese and broccoli<br>■ Soaked dried fruit, mashed banana | ■ Thick lentil soup<br>■ Baked apple with rice or wheatgerm | ■ Puréed cabbage with tofu and pitta bread |

# Holding and handling

By now you should be quite relaxed about carrying your baby. You will probably settle on a couple of favourite ways of carrying her, depending on whether she wants to be cuddled or to look at what is going on all around her. She is much heavier now, so make sure that you adopt a method of lifting her that won't strain your back.

## Picking up and carrying your baby

Your baby can now control her head, so there is no longer any need to support it as you did when she was newborn. Now you can pick her up simply by putting your hands under her armpits and lifting her forward towards you. This is also a very good way of putting her into a highchair: her legs will dangle and she can be slipped into the chair. Alternatively, you can lift her with one hand curled diagonally around her back, and the other supporting her bottom.

You can carry your baby in the crook of your arm, against your shoulder so that she faces you, or with your arm stretched diagonally across her back and holding her thigh as she sits astride one hip. You might like to carry her in a sling when you go out, although for longer journeys a backpack will give you more support.

▶ **ON ONE HIP** Your baby can now support herself well enough to sit astride your hip. This allows her to look all around.

▲ **FACING FORWARDS** Hold your baby securely around her middle, so that she can look around her. Use your other hand to support her too, or keep it free.

# Swinging and bouncing games

All babies love to be bounced and swung, but just how much they enjoy it will depend on how they're feeling. Being swung up in the air is exciting for your baby, as she can look at her surroundings – and see your face – from a whole new perspective. Always give your baby a chance to relax after boisterous games by cuddling her quietly for a few minutes.

▼ **ROCKING** You can turn this activity into a boisterous game by swinging your baby quite high, or just doing it very gently to soothe her.

▼ **BOUNCING** Lift your baby up and down on your knees rhythmically. You should always support her body so that she doesn't slip backwards.

◀ **SWINGING** Raise your baby up high then swoop her down between your legs. She will love looking down at your face from a height.

# How we handle boys

Experiments have shown that we handle baby boys differently from baby girls, and that we persist in this stereotyping even if we are merely fooled by, say, their wearing pink or blue clothes. When handling boys, we:

■ speak, laugh, even shout out loudly, and grasp them firmly

■ swing them about so that they get used to lots of action and physical movement

■ encourage them to splash and kick in the bath

■ give them tough, hard toys and praise adventurousness, even naughtiness, with encouraging words or phrases

■ are efficient rather than tender when a boy grazes his knee, discouraging shows of emotion and applauding independence.

If you want your son to be more in touch with his gentler side, adjust your behaviour so you treat him more like a girl (see opposite page).

## Make clothes last longer

Babies grow quickly, so keep your child's latest measurements jotted down and check them regularly. There are several ways to make clothes last longer.

■ Make summer shorts from long trousers that are too short or have become worn at the knees.

■ Cut out the sleeves from a jacket that your child has outgrown so she can wear it as a waistcoat.

■ Reinforce the knees on the inside of new jeans with the extra fabric you trim from the bottoms of the legs, or use iron-on patches.

■ When sleep suits get too short for comfort, cut off the feet for an extra few months' wear.

▶ **CLOTHES FOR CRAWLING (RIGHT)**
Ensure your baby's knees are protected if she is crawling. Long trousers such as tracksuits or dungarees are good at this stage; skirts or dresses get in the way.

▶ **FIRST SHOES (FAR RIGHT)** Choose sturdy shoes that give enough support, and get them fitted professionally. When your baby has his first pair of shoes, cover the soles with a piece of adhesive tape so that he won't slide on a slippery floor; or score the soles with scissors so they grip more effectively.

# Dressing

Once your baby has learned to crawl, she'll want to be on the go all the time and she'll be far less willing to sit or lie still while you get her dressed. On the other hand, she's now better able to help you as you put on her clothes. For example, an 11-month-old baby can make a fist or stretch out an arm, if you ask her to, or hold her arm still while you pull her sleeve into place.

If your baby is very restless, you can sing a song to her or distract her with a toy, or involve her in the whole process by naming each item of clothing as you put it on or take it off, and getting her to repeat the names after you, for example. You could also turn dressing into a peek-a-boo game: "Where's your foot? Oh, look, here it is!" Here are some other tips.

■ Stand her between your legs while you pull up her trousers or tights.
■ Sit her in her high chair so that you can put on her shoes.
■ You can make a game out of her putting on her shoes by placing them at the bottom of the stairs and getting her to step down into them carefully while you steady her.

## Choosing clothes

Now that your baby is more active, you will need to look for clothes that allow easy movement. She will be awake for longer, and moving around, so her clothes are more likely to get dirty and you'll need more of them. You'll also have to consider whether they are tough enough for the wear and tear that your child will give them: look for sturdy fabrics that last, and strong fastenings that won't break or fall off.

When you're buying clothes, check the label to see what sort of material they are made from. Natural fibres are both strong and comfortable, so look for pure cotton or a fabric with a high cotton content. Towelling, denim, and corduroy are all strong and hard-wearing. Look, too, for clothes that can be easily pulled on and off (especially when she wants to help you dress her). Avoid zip fasteners or fiddly fastenings; elasticated waists are by far the easiest to manage.

## Choosing socks and shoes

Until she's walking, socks or fabric bootees are all your baby needs, even when she's crawling. Fabric bootees with elasticated ankles stay on better. Ensure there's plenty of room for movement; the bones in your baby's feet are so soft and pliable that even tightly fitting socks could misshape the toes if worn regularly.

**Her first shoes**  Once your baby begins to walk, she'll need shoes. Always go to a reputable shop where the staff have been trained to measure and fit children's shoes properly. The assistant should measure the length and the width of your child's foot before trying any shoes. Once your child tries on a pair of shoes, the assistant should press the joints of the foot to make sure that it is not restricted in any way, and check that the fastenings hold the shoe firmly in place and don't let your child's foot slip about. Make sure your child stands up and walks about in the shoes to check that the toe doesn't pinch and hurt when she's walking and to double-check that the shoes don't slip off at the back.

It's still better to let your child go without shoes as much as possible in the early days of walking. At first she'll only need shoes for going outside. A sturdy, well-made pair of leather shoes is most suitable for general outdoor wear, especially once she is running about. You should, however, get a pair of wellington boots for wet or muddy conditions. Although leather shoes and sandals are solid and sensible and last well, there is nothing wrong with inexpensive canvas shoes as long as you make sure that they fit properly. If your child suddenly becomes less steady on her feet, it may be a sign that she is outgrowing her shoes. Well-fitting shoes are essential to ensure that your child has good feet in adult life.

## Outdoor clothes for babies

Your child is becoming more active now so look for outdoor clothes that are comfortable and won't restrict her movements.

■ Buy outdoor clothes on the large side. This leaves room for extra layers underneath, and allows your child to grow into them.

■ Avoid man-made fabrics – they don't "breathe" like natural fibres and could make your child uncomfortably hot, especially in the summer.

▲ **WARM HEAD** When it's cold outside always make sure your baby's head and feet are warm. More heat is lost through the head than from any other part of the body.

## Safety checklist

Be very careful when bathing your child – there are several points to remember.

■ Place a non-slip bath mat in the bottom of the bath.

■ Always check the temperature of the water before putting your baby in the bath. Even older babies need the water to be considerably cooler than do most adults.

■ Turn the taps off tightly before putting your baby in the bath. Never add more hot water while your baby is in the bath.

■ Cover the taps with a flannel so that your baby doesn't scald or hurt herself on the metal.

■ Don't let your baby stand or jump in the water unsupported. A fall, even if she isn't injured, could put her off future bathing.

■ If your child likes toys in the bath, choose light plastic ones with no sharp edges.

■ Don't remove the plug while your baby is still in the bath. Many babies find the noise and the sensation of the water disappearing rather frightening.

■ When you lift your baby out of the bath, make sure that you are standing steadily. Take the strain with your legs, not your back.

■ Make sure you dry your baby well after a bath. Giving her a cuddle wrapped in a warm towel can provide a comforting end to bath time, even for older children.

# Bathing and hygiene

Your baby will quickly grow too big for a baby bath, so you will have to start using the bathtub. To make the transition easier for your baby, first place the baby bath inside the bathtub so that she gets used to this larger bath. Once she gets used to it, she'll probably spend many happy hours there enjoying her favourite toys.

## Bath-time routine

Once your baby is mobile, she'll get much dirtier than before and baths will become a regular feature of your day. Washing a baby is more awkward in the bathtub than in the baby bath. Spare your back by kneeling next to the bath and make sure that you have everything that you need to hand. Keep the water shallow – no deeper than 10–13cm (4–5in) and use a plastic suction mat on the bottom of the bath to prevent your baby sliding about or use one of the wide range of baby bath supports. Keep a close watch on her; it takes only a moment for a baby to slip under the water, so you should never leave her alone, or turn away from her.

By about six months, your baby will feel quite secure in the water and will no longer be scared of being undressed. Try to make bath times fun and as trouble-free as possible.

## Fear of the bathtub

If your child finds the bathtub frightening, you'll have to be patient and let her get used to it gradually. You could try filling the baby bath with water and put a few toys in; then place it inside the bathtub and put a non-slip bath mat next to it. Put your baby in the bathtub where she can play with the toys and climb into the baby bath if she likes. Once she has got used to this, you could also add a small amount of water to the bathtub. Your child can then climb in and out of the baby bath

◀ THE "BIG BATH" Use a non-slip mat in the bathtub to prevent your baby from slipping or sliding about.

▲ **BATH-TIME PLAY** Your baby will love playing with simple floating toys at bath time. But however happy and secure your baby may seem playing with her toys, no baby of this age should be left in the bath unwatched, even for the shortest period of time.

and get used to sitting in the shallow water in the bathtub. You can gradually increase the amount of water that you put in the bathtub; after a while you will probably find that your child doesn't notice whether the baby bath is there or not. If you feel she still needs reassurance, get into the bath with her and play water games with her on your lap.

## Bath-time play

Once your baby is able to sit up, you can give her some extra time in the bath after she's been washed, and let her enjoy splashing and playing with toys. You don't have to provide special toys; sponges, bowls, and mugs will keep her entertained. If you have two small children, you could try bathing them together. It will save time for you, and your older child will be able to share games with the baby. Suds are always a great favourite, so you could add lots of bubble bath to the water (take care, as bubble bath can irritate the vulval area in little girls). Every now and then, get into the bath with your baby and have fun together.

## Bath toys

Your baby will love playing with everyday household objects. Make sure that any bath toys you use are clean and waterproof, without sharp edges, and reasonably light. If you give your baby plastic bottles – for example, old shampoo bottles – make sure that they have been thoroughly washed to remove all traces of their previous contents and remove the lids; your baby will put all these "toys" into her mouth.

Many toys, particularly those made of hard plastic, such as rattles and beakers, are also fun to play with in the bath. If you want to buy special bath toys, there are lots to choose from. Boats and ducks are always great favourites, but you can also get waterproof books for the older baby, or activity centres that work when water is poured through them.

# Early dental care

**As early as possible encourage your baby to form good habits with a toothbrushing game.**

Let your baby see you brush your teeth so that she can see how it should be done, then offer her a soft toothbrush to play with. She'll try to imitate you by putting the brush in her mouth and moving it about. You don't need to see that she's doing it properly; at this stage it's a game to introduce her to the idea that toothbrushing is something she likes.

When you really want to clean your baby's teeth, wet a handkerchief and smear on a pea-sized helping of toothpaste, then gently rub it across the gums and any teeth that she has. Even if she has no teeth at all yet, cleaning her gums helps her get used to the idea of cleaning her teeth and makes brushing easier later on.

## Development in girls

Bowel and bladder control usually start earlier and are complete more quickly in girls.

**Early stages: 12–18 months**
The first sign that the bladder is maturing is when she gestures or makes a sound to indicate she's aware of passing urine. There's usually no sign of bowel control at this stage.

**Middle stages: 18 months to two years**
One day, between 15 and 18 months, she'll bring the potty to you and you may catch her in time.

By 18 months to two years you may find a stool in the potty after a meal. She'll tell you she needs the potty and can wait for it. Once she can wait five minutes or so, try trainer pants during the day.

**Later stages: Two to three-and-a-half years**
She's clean and dry all day. She may also be dry at night apart from the odd accident. Try trainer pants at night.

▲ **POTTIES** Specially moulded potties provide support and are suitable for both boys and girls.

# Bowel and bladder

Once your baby starts taking solids, you'll find that she soils her nappy less often. You'll continue to see changes in her bowel movements as her digestive system matures, right up to the age of five or six years. After she's taken solids for a few months, you may feel it's time she used the potty, but don't rush this.

## Changes in bowel movements

In general, you can expect your baby's stools to become firmer and less frequent with age. There are pretty standard changes at some ages; I give them only to reassure you, not so that you will obsessively examine your child's stools. All dates are approximate.

**Up to six months** The stools may be almost as frequent as the feeds, and are very soft. They go through colour changes: first greenish-black (meconium, see p.104), then yellow, then light brown.

**Six to 12 months** After your baby starts on solids, the stools become drier, darker in colour, and less frequent, say three times a day. Lots of drinks will keep the stools soft.

**One to three years** As soon as your child is on the family diet, she will probably pass only two stools a day.

**Three to five years** The stools are identical to adult stools, except in size, and your child will rarely pass more than one a day.

## The case against "training"

Babies who are allowed to achieve bowel and bladder control at their own pace learn to use the potty quickly. It's only when parents interfere with their child's steady progress by enforcing timetables or expecting too much too soon that things go awry. Babies are born wanting to be clean and dry; our job is simply to allow them to achieve this milestone happily.

An over-authoritarian parent can do untold harm, even at an early stage, and may be responsible for problems in later life. Imagine the scenario: a domineering, insistent mother is bending over, telling her child that she can't get off her potty until she's performed. The child can't understand what her mother's getting at, because she's unaware of passing urine or stools – her bladder and nervous system are still too immature. Even if

# Introducing the potty

These are the ways you can help your baby to become dry and clean, but only after she indicates to you by sound or gesture that she knows she's passed urine or had a bowel movement. Allow her to find her own pace, without any pressure from you.

**Step 1** Give her her own "potty" chair, which is like your lavatory. Let her see you or her daddy using the toilet and show her the results if she asks.

**Step 2** Let her sit on the potty chair fully clothed while you read her a story.

**Step 3** Gradually let her get used to sitting without a nappy.

**Step 4** When she soils or wets her nappy, sit her gently on the chair after you've cleaned her while you collect fresh things.

**Step 5** Once she's interested, let her sit two or three times a day.

she did understand, she has no "control", as you think of it. She can't figure out why something so natural to her is so important to her mother. And so she has no idea how to please her normally very loving mother. When she gets up to leave the mother is unusually rough, the child can't cope, so she cries. And if things go on like this she's certainly going to use her mother's obsession with training as a weapon against her later – she sees her stools as something her mother wants and so she'll withhold them when she is pitting her will against her mother's.

The answer is to be flexible. At no point pressure or scold. Praise every success. Let little boys see their fathers passing urine. Children who are pressured into early training tend to be bedwetters, and engage more in pica (eating stools or other non-food substances) and soiling than those children who develop at their own speed.

## Toddler diarrhoea

Some toddlers who are healthy and eat well often have diarrhoea that contains undigested food. The exact cause of toddler diarrhoea is not known, but it may be linked to drinking too much fluid, particularly fruit juice, not eating enough fat, or eating too quickly. If your child is healthy and there's no underlying illness, changes in her diet usually help.

■ Give your child water or milk to drink instead of fruit juice. Clear apple juice seems to be a particular culprit.

■ Slightly increase your child's fat intake. Give her whole milk, add butter to her meals, and don't give her low-fat foods.

■ Encourage her to eat plenty of fruit and vegetables, but don't give her excessive amounts of fibre.

# Development in boys

Boys are generally later than girls in developing bowel and bladder control and bedwetting is more frequent in boys. The age ranges given are just a rough guide.

### Early stages: 18 months to two-and-a-half years
■ At this stage your little boy has no "control". His bladder is still immature and can't hold on to urine for a single second.

■ He still can't wait for you to get the potty after signalling that he's letting go of his urine.

### Middle stages: two-and-a-half to three-and-a-half years
■ Your little boy can bring the potty to you only when he has enough control to hold on to his urine for a minute or two.

■ He'll come and tell you he needs the potty, but will still have frequent accidents.

■ When he's indicated he can wait several minutes and not before, try trainer pants during the day only.

### Later stages: three-and-a-half to six years
■ He may be clean by day, with accidents, but wet at night.

■ He's clean, with accidents, day and night. When he's dry all day try trainer pants during his nap.

■ He's dry all day, but needs a nappy at night.

■ He can stay dry through the night with very few accidents.

## Causes of wakefulness

A baby may wake through the night for several reasons. Here are some things you can do:

■ Make sure that your baby is neither too hot nor too cold (see p.81).

■ Check that your baby isn't in any discomfort from a soiled nappy or nappy rash.

■ Don't keep popping into your baby's room to see if she's asleep.

■ If your child suddenly becomes sleepless, think about the possible causes, such as a change in routine, someone new staying with you, or your going out to work. Whatever the cause, she will need lots of your attention.

▲ **RESTLESSNESS** Put some interesting toys on the side of the cot to amuse your restless baby.

# Sleep and wakefulness

Babies usually establish their sleep patterns within the first few months and if you find that your baby sleeps a lot in her first year, she will probably do the same in her second. Once she starts to crawl, she'll be using up so much energy during the day that she may sleep for ten or 11 uninterrupted hours at night.

Even though your baby needs sleep, she's able to keep herself awake so that she can stay with you. She may whimper and cry, become hot and bothered, and then so tense and unhappy that sleep becomes impossible. If your baby is clingy and sleepless and appears to be insecure, the best treatment for her is you. Stay with her, hold her close to you, rock her, sing to her, soothe her, and walk up and down with her until she feels that you are not going to leave her and is reassured by your closeness. This may take half an hour, but usually she'll fall asleep in your arms after about ten or 15 minutes, and then you can put her back in her cot.

## Wakeful babies

There's no question that some babies need very little sleep. Wakeful babies, as I like to call them, are usually bright, curious, intelligent, and very affectionate. They quickly latch on to the fact that you're there all through the night and that they can attract your attention with crying or calling out to you. I firmly believe that no baby's crying should be ignored. A baby who's left to cry quickly learns that adults don't respond to her cries for help and love. She will stop asking for attention and may become solitary and withdrawn. Try not to get upset because your baby is wakeful; she's demonstrating her sociability and intelligence because she's learning all the time, and you'll find as she grows up that she's a very rewarding friend. If your baby wakes before your bedtime, try carrying her around in a sling or put her in a baby bouncer so that she can tire herself out.

**Solutions** Wakeful babies very often need diversion, so as soon as your baby can sit up, leave some favourite soft toys or soft books in the cot. Put a mirror on the side of the cot so that she can look in it and talk to herself. A mobile above the cot that makes different sounds can fascinate your baby for quite a long time, too.

I had two wakeful babies and I had to resort to extreme measures to get any sleep myself. I erected a camp bed alongside my baby's cot, and when he woke up in the middle of the night I would soothe him so that he went back to sleep without really waking up. This prevented him from getting upset with a crying bout.

If your baby only whimpers, don't get up immediately because she may go back to sleep without any soothing at all. If, however, the whimper becomes true crying then you should go and see her. The first time you go in try soothing talk while patting her on the back. If this doesn't work, you'll have to pick her up to soothe her, then put her back in her cot, and leave the room. If she continues to cry, you may decide to go back every five minutes to calm your baby down. (If you do, try to soothe your baby without lifting her up – say by rocking the cot or talking to her.)

## Bedtime routines

As your baby gets older, she'll love to have lots of your attention at bedtime, and she'll probably have settled into some routine that she needs in order to sleep, such as a story, a song, or some kind of gentle game. Do everything you can to make your baby tranquil and happy before sleep. If necessary, forgo a scolding for a minor misdemeanour; you don't want your child to face bedtime feeling tearful and upset. I've always believed in keeping the hour before bed as happy and pleasant as possible so your child goes off to sleep feeling calm and secure.

Your child may become attached to a comfort item of some sort: a doll, a small handkerchief, or a piece of torn blanket. You may also find

that habits such as rocking, sucking a dummy or her own thumb, or twisting her hair will become part of her bedtime routine. There's nothing wrong with any of these bedtime rituals. By using a comforter to help her to go to sleep, your baby is using her inner resources and becoming self-reliant. There's no particular age at which comforters should or shouldn't be used and she'll give up these habits in her own time.

◀ **COMFORT HABITS** Let your baby develop a comfort habit, such as sucking a dummy or her thumb, if she needs to.

**Some babies sleep through the night from early on, some don't. As a general rule, the more mobile your baby is and the more energy she uses, the more soundly she sleeps – sleep being divided between daytime naps and night time.**

When your baby grows, night sleep usually becomes unbroken and naps are fairly regular – one in the morning and one in the afternoon for varying lengths of time.

Later, your baby's nap times will change: she may put off her morning nap until after lunch, and then need another nap at around 3.30 or 4pm before sleeping for the night at around 7pm. Every day may be different.

Whatever time your baby is disposed to nap, take the lead from her; don't try to impose nap times on her. And try to clear your time so that you are able to take a nap with your baby; both of you will be recharged when you wake up.

## Comfort objects

When children need comfort they may become attached to an object such as a blanket or special toy, or turn to thumb-sucking as a consolation, especially when you're not around.

Nearly all children like to have some form of comfort that they control. Very often comfort objects are ones that children suck or stroke in moments of anxiety or stress, to stimulate the effect of being stroked or being comforted. Let them have their comfort objects and don't interfere.

▼ **DEALING WITH ANXIETY** Unfamiliar people and places can make your baby anxious so reassure her with lots of hugs and cuddles.

# Crying and comforting

As your baby grows older and her world becomes more complex, the causes of crying change. In an older baby the cause is nearly always some form of emotional disturbance, such as boredom, fear of mother or father leaving, insecurity, anxiety, or frustration.

## Boredom

The older she gets the longer your baby will spend being awake, so there's more scope for her getting bored. Many children cry out of sheer boredom, especially if left alone with no distractions, nothing to look at, and no one to play with. Your older baby enjoys your company more than anything else, and is constantly interested in what you are doing.

**What to do**  Always leave toys in her cot, such as board books or cloth books. Mobiles, baby gyms, or strings of interesting objects above the cot will help to amuse and distract your baby. She'll cry a great deal less from boredom if you keep her with you as much as you can.

## Fear of separation

When your baby is about six to eight months, separation from a parent becomes the greatest source of distress to her and nearly always precipitates crying. Try to get your baby accustomed to separation over several months by leaving her for longer and longer periods, say 20 minutes, then an hour, then three hours. If you go out to work, you will find your baby's fear upsetting, but this phase will pass as she gets used to seeing you go and always returning. While it lasts, be very careful about the way you take leave of your baby, and ensure that she's familiar with her surroundings and the people she's with. If she finds separation very unpleasant the first time, she's likely to respond with crying the second time. It's up to you to make separation as easy as possible.

**What to do**  Be sympathetic and supportive and never make fun of your child's fears. She will respond better to reassuring actions than words, so if you make a promise to her that you are coming back, always keep it. If you say that you're only going for five minutes, just leave the room, get on with some small job, and come back in exactly that time.

# Insecurity and anxiety

As your baby gets older, she'll become increasingly aware of strangers. Those situations that cause her most anxiety are being in a strange place with you, or being with strangers. As long as you're there she can cope, but being left in a strange place with strange people completely unnerves her. Never do it. Any source of anxiety makes your child clingy. She'll turn to you for comfort. She may even go off her food. If you become aware that your child is anxious, respond to her immediately. There's lots of research that shows the child who feels secure develops in almost every way more successfully than the child who is insecure. It's important to help your baby feel secure from the moment she's born.

**What to do** The best thing is extra reassurance, physical contact, cuddles, love, and soothing talk. Your child will grow out of this period of anxiety, but it helps never to force her to go to a stranger if she doesn't really want to. Explain to new people that she's shy and needs some time to get used to them. Your presence will help her to cope with new situations and experiences, even though she may feel fearful and uncomfortable at first. Whatever you do, always let your baby have the comforter of her choice, and always give her lots of cuddles to reassure her.

This doesn't mean to say you can't gently encourage your child to be curious and adventurous. To grow up with a feeling of self-confidence and self-worth, your child needs plenty of approval, love, and praise from you, so give these every time she shows some independence.

# Frustration

As your baby grows up, her desire to do things far outstrips her ability to do them, and so she becomes frustrated. This often results in crying. As she starts to crawl, then cruises along the furniture, then walks, you will almost certainly have to restrain her, which will result in added frustration, and crying every time you do it. By the time she gets to 18 months, your baby's spirit of adventure makes her want to do much more than she can manage in terms of balance, mobility, and coordination. She's likely to try to do things that are beyond her and she'll become very frustrated as a result. Even though you know she's frustrated, you are going to have to stop her doing some things simply to protect her.

**What to do** Make your home as childproof as possible (see pp.306–9): remove precious objects from within her reach, and fit safety plugs and guards around the house to make sure she can't injure herself. Distraction is a good ploy for frustration, so always have a favourite toy to hand or be ready with a game if she becomes upset.

# Bedtime crying

Babies tend to cry at bedtime because they're tired, irritable, and don't wish to be separated from you. You can reassure your baby by establishing happy bedtime routines (see p.129).

■ Make the hour before bedtime a really happy one. Sit your child on your lap, read or tell her a story, play a quiet game, or sing some songs to her.

■ A gentle, playful bath time will make your baby feel relaxed and slightly sleepy, as will a warm drink before being put to bed.

■ Your baby will almost certainly have a favourite game, song, or story and for a baby repetition is happiness, so if she wants the same story night after night do as she asks; it makes her feel secure and feeling secure is good for her.

▲ RELAXED BEDTIMES Spend time with your child just before bedtime in some quiet activity so she goes to bed calm and relaxed.

## Choosing toys

Your child will grow and learn very rapidly in her early years, and the right toys can help stimulate her development.

■ Simple toys are more versatile so they have a longer life and are better for imaginative play.

■ A baby will need toys that stimulate all five senses. Introduce your baby to different colours, textures, shapes, and noises.

■ Older babies enjoy games that involve building, particularly "put-in, take-out" toys, so bricks of different sizes are ideal.

■ As your child's manipulation skills develop, she will be able to manage interlocking blocks and more advanced shape-sorters.

▲ PUT-IN, TAKE-OUT GAMES Your baby will love games that involve moving things in and out of a container.

# Your baby's development

I firmly believe that the most important teacher in a baby's life is the person who most consistently looks after her health and wellbeing – in other words, you. Your role as teacher continues for many years; it's your job to make her world an interesting and exciting place in which she can grow and learn.

Your baby enjoys a unique bond with her parents, which means that you and your partner are best equipped to teach her about her world, for even as adults we learn best from people with whom we feel comfortable or have a rapport. Look for every opportunity to share in your baby's progress; much of her early development will be dependent on a secure and caring environment so make sure you give her lots of attention.

Your baby wants to do more things, explore more areas, and widen her horizons more than anyone else you know. She also wants to please you, and the combination of these qualities gives her an appetite for learning that should thrill you. But don't set her tasks that are beyond her as these will only frustrate her. Guide her but never try to force her.

## Providing the right environment

Your baby demands and deserves a rich, stimulating environment in order to experience fully as many sensations as possible because she's dependent on her senses for learning. Her intellectual and emotional development, therefore, will only be improved through the different experiences you introduce her to.

Rather than buying your child new toys all the time, encourage her to interact with existing toys in different ways – for example, by showing her how to use a cardboard box as a car or a boat. Children don't always need shop-bought toys to encourage them to play.

In order to allow your baby to achieve her full potential, set aside time to work with her, matching your efforts to your baby's stages of development. Responsible parents find the role of teacher comes effortlessly and naturally. Your baby is always eager to learn new things, so make the experience fun and mutually rewarding. Take any opportunity that presents itself – intimate moments of play or telling stories, for example, to teach colours, textures, opposites, and so on.

# The importance of play

Your child's development will centre around play, and this is the most natural way for her to learn. It is only in the last 20 years that the full value of development through play has been recognized, since playing was previously regarded as an empty activity, used to fill the time when children could not be usefully employed.

The best toys are the ones that children return to again and again because they are limitless in their appeal – usually ones that encourage inventiveness. For this reason ordinary household items such as a whisk or a sieve may give your baby more lasting pleasure than many an expensive and elaborate toy. By sharing and encouraging your baby in her play, you will strengthen the bond between you as she comes to see you as a giver of knowledge and fun.

# Learning spurts

Your baby doesn't grow, develop, and learn at a constant rate. Learning spurts are well known and every child has them. During a learning spurt, your baby will gobble up new ideas, acquire new skills, and put them into practice immediately. However, while she's going through these learning spurts some activities, and possibly certain skills that she's already learned, may appear to slip. Don't worry. They won't have gone for good. It is just that your baby is using all her concentration to learn something new, but once it is learned she'll regain all the other skills.

During a learning spurt you should try to make your child's life as interesting as possible. Of course, if your child shows that certain things are enjoyable then you should do them as often as you can, but don't hesitate to introduce your baby to new things; she is ready to learn and absorb information at a very fast rate. And don't be too discriminating about the kind of entertainment you give either. Babies simply sieve out what they prefer and understand, and let the rest go by. In the first year learning is an entirely piecemeal process, so you'll help your baby best if you provide her with as wide and interesting a range as possible. But it's not your job to decide which of these things she should find most interesting – that's up to her. In other words, having presented her with the menu, you must let her choose her own dishes.

Learning spurts are invariably followed by periods when development appears to slow down. Treat them as recovery periods during which your baby can consolidate newly learned skills and prepare herself for the next spurt. Don't get anxious about this – just let her practise the skills that she has already learned. You can help during these slower learning times by practising with her, saying something like "Let's sing that song again", or "Why don't we try to push the peg through that hole again?".

## TV and computers

**Half an hour a day in front of a television or computer screen is enough for your baby.**

More than this may prevent her from acquiring communication, imaginative, and coordination skills that could be more thoroughly developed through games and storytelling. In fact, some American doctors believe that children under two shouldn't watch any TV at all.

Monitor the amount of television your child watches and be wary of using the TV or computer as a convenient babysitting tool when you don't feel like amusing her. Used carefully, television can be a useful aid to acquiring new concepts, like telling the time.

Research shows that your child could continue to live in the fantasy world of television long after she's stopped watching, causing nightmares if she's watched anything frightening.

Researchers have shown that bringing your child back into the real world – with a story, toothbrushing, or laying out tomorrow's clothes – can banish this unpleasant effect of television.

## Stages of standing

**As your baby learns to sit unsupported for longer periods of time, her sense of balance and her desire to walk will increase.**

■ From about six or seven months your baby will begin to take her full weight on her knees and hips, but she'll need to be balanced by you. She'll test her leg strength with a sort of dancing movement; a hop from one foot to another, and as she becomes more confident she'll practise bending and stretching her legs.

■ By nine months your baby's ability to balance will be greatly improved. She may be able to take all her own weight on her legs, but she'll still need to hold on to something. Any stable piece of furniture will support her. She should never be left alone in this position; she'll find it difficult to sit from a standing position and a fall may seriously affect her confidence and pleasure in standing.

■ By about ten to 12 months your baby will be able to lift one foot while she stands, provided she's supported. She'll be able to pull herself into a standing position, but will still have trouble lowering herself down again.

# Learning to walk

During her first few months your baby achieved head control and learned to coordinate and refine her movements in stages as her muscles became stronger and her balance improved. Now she is ready to start moving around, and the next year will be an exciting one for both of you as she learns to crawl and then to walk.

It's important to remember that all babies develop at their own speed and the ages given here are the approximate times by which most babies have achieved these skills. A few babies crawl by six months; others show no interest in crawling at all, but walk perfectly later on, so don't be too concerned if your baby's development doesn't exactly match these stages.

Some babies miss out the crawling stage altogether, and go straight from shuffling along on their bottoms to walking. Other babies crawl "bear-like" on their hands and feet rather than on their hands and knees. Both of these are completely normal.

▲ **EIGHT MONTHS** Your baby will sit unsupported, briefly at first, but gradually for longer periods of time. She'll stretch for things that are held beyond her reach. She'll master leaning, both forward and to the sides, and will test her own balance by rocking back and forth in a sitting position or twisting round, though she'll probably fall over.

▲ **TEN MONTHS** He's probably mastered creeping, or even crawling, and his arms can now take some of his weight. He may be able to pull himself to his feet, but you'll still have to hold him in a standing position and help him sit down again. Your baby may be able to stand unaided (holding on to something) for up to ten minutes.

**▼ 12 MONTHS** Your baby can now turn around when sitting down and can creep or crawl. When held in a standing position she'll try stepping. She may try "cruising" – walking sideways while holding on to something.

**▼ 14 MONTHS** Your baby will perfect standing alone, and may even take her first independent step. Soon she'll be taking a few steps together between one stable support and another or while pushing a sturdy walk-along toy.

# Balance

Between seven and 12 months your baby will develop righting reflexes, which control her basic body movements.

These help her move from prone to standing positions and vice versa, to get to her hands and knees, and to sit up. They control the position and movement of her head and are responsible for the development of balance.

■ By eight months your sitting baby will lean forward and backward in order to test her balance.

■ At nine months your baby can lean forward and to the side without losing her balance. She can roll over and will try to crawl.

■ From ten months she can twist her upper body while sitting. This strengthens her lateral trunk muscles and improves her ability to balance while moving.

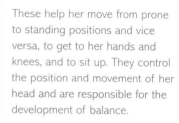

**▲ 16 MONTHS** Your baby's steps are high and unsteady, but her style will soon become more refined. She'll stand up and sit down without help.

**▶ 18 MONTHS** Your toddler can crawl or climb stairs unaided, although he needs support to keep balanced. His steps are lower and more steady.

## Stages of walking

Your baby's first attempts at walking will be unsteady and she'll hang on to objects for support, but soon she'll be moving around by herself.

■ Your baby will "cruise" before she walks – that is, haul herself up on any large item, and then sidle around it. Make sure any unsteady furniture is out of her way.

■ Next she'll start to move one hand over the other as she cruises rather than sliding them together and then moving both hands and feet at the same time. She'll develop the confidence and balance to take all her weight, briefly, on one foot.

■ Her next goal is to negotiate gaps between two supports. She'll hold on to both at once, and only let go of one support when she's holding firmly on to the other.

■ She'll progress to crossing wider gaps. Still holding on to a support with one hand, she'll move into the centre of the gap and, once she's got her balance, release one support and step towards the next, grabbing for it with both hands.

■ Finally, your baby will begin to "toddle", staggering a couple of paces to reach the second support. She'll launch herself into the open and take several unsupported steps. She may lose her balance, sitting down with a thud, but she'll usually set off for her goal and waddle towards it with her arms held high and wide.

# Encouraging skills

The transition your child makes from an uncoordinated baby to an independent toddler is a major turning point. You can help by encouraging her to stand and gently urging her on with her early attempts at walking. Praise her at every stage, but try not to push her to go faster than she feels she can – walking involves tricky techniques of balance and coordination and so is one of the most difficult skills she will ever learn.

## Helping your child stand

Let your baby take more and more of her own standing weight from the time she can control her head. Her leg muscles, hips, and knees will gradually strengthen and she'll relish taking her own weight on them. When you hold her hands, she'll bounce about and play standing and bouncing games. Hold her on your lap, on cushions, on a bed, or in the bath and encourage these active games.

**From nine months**  Your baby will take nearly her entire weight on her legs, but may still need support to do so because her muscle strength is more advanced than her balance. You can encourage her by taking her to stable pieces of furniture and getting her to grip her hands on so that she is nicely balanced. Stay close while she holds on. She'll need to develop her balance in order to stand securely, so when she is sitting, urge her to lean forward and sideways by placing toys just out of reach in front and by her sides; this will strengthen her trunk muscles. She'll find it difficult to sit down from a standing position, but you can make it easier by gently manipulating her hips and knees.

**Around ten months**  Your baby is far more mobile on her hands and knees. The muscles of her trunk are getting stronger all the time as she twists and turns while sitting or crawling. Offer your fingers to encourage her to pull herself up to sit and stand.

▲ **LEARNING TO STAND** Teach your baby the sensation of supporting his own weight by encouraging him to stand using the furniture around him.

▶ **TROLLEY TOY** A sturdy, wheeled push-along toy can encourage your baby to practise walking alone.

## Learning to walk

Your baby will learn to walk on her own, but it's fun to help her practise if you have the time. Put your baby on her hands and knees and sit a short distance away. This will encourage her to move towards you. She'll come more eagerly if you hold out your arms, call her name, or offer a favourite toy. To prompt your baby to twist, place a toy behind her back and support her as she turns around. By ten months she'll be able to stand up if supported by furniture. While she is standing and firmly supported, bend one of her knees and lift her foot; this will help her learn to step and bear her weight momentarily on one foot.

**From 11 months** Help your baby to practise walking forwards by holding her hands and guiding her. Make cruising easier by positioning stable pieces of furniture around the room, but remove unsteady items. Improve your baby's stepping skills by calling to her while she is cruising around the room. Give her the courage to launch herself by moving the pieces of furniture slightly further apart. Sit a little way from her and, while she is holding on to the furniture, hold out your arms and call her to you – but always be close enough to catch her if she stumbles.

**13–15 months** Your baby can stand alone and may take her first independent step. At 15 months your baby can kneel, lower her body without support, and stand up unaided. A chair with arms allows her to sit down without falling and will provide good bending practice for her hips and knees. Practise more leg movements with your baby, using a large soft ball that she can try to kick to you. This is also good for acquiring balance. Show her how to squat, and help her master hip and knee bends – all the more enjoyable if you do them together to music. Games that use backwards or sideways steps will help her walking and balancing skills.

There's no right age for your baby to start to walk, but she is most likely to take her first unsupported steps when she's between the ages of nine and 15 months.

## Safety

**As your baby's independence grows, safety in her environment becomes increasingly important.**

■ Keep close at hand when your baby is taking her first unsteady steps and take particular care when she walks and creeps upstairs. Make sure the floor is not slippery and don't give her shoes until she is walking outdoors.

■ Give your baby plenty of clear space for her walking attempts. Trailing flexes or small pieces of furniture might cause her to trip.

■ Special protective edges are available for sharp-cornered furniture or door handles.

■ Glass-topped items should be removed or fitted with safety film.

■ Fit safety gates at the bottom of your stairs. Gates should have vertical bars and never horizontal ones that your baby could climb. It's not a good idea to fit gates at the top of the stairs as they can be a trip hazard, especially if there is a bar across the base. Instead you can fit safety gates across bedroom doorways.

■ Keep all poisonous substances well out of reach, and out of sight, in a lockable cupboard. Even vitamin pills are dangerous.

■ Don't leave sharp or hot objects within your baby's reach.

## Right- or left-handed

Right- or left-handedness develops as one or the other side of your baby's brain becomes dominant: if the right side dominates, she will be left-handed, and vice versa.

Even as a newborn, your baby may have shown a tendency to turn her head more to the right than the left. Now she may start to favour one hand. Never try to dissuade her from being left-handed. You could cause psychological side effects such as stuttering as well as reading and writing problems by trying to alter what your baby's brain naturally wants to do.

# Using hands

By the age of six months your baby will have learned to grasp objects at will, and now she'll gradually refine her handling skills as she learns to use her hands to eat, dress, wash, and pick things up. You'll find this time both rewarding and frustrating – your baby is learning to do more things for herself, but she won't be very adept at first, so you'll have to be patient while she learns.

By the end of her first year your baby will have the mature adult grasp, which is a fine movement achieved by bringing the thumb and index finger together (opposition). She can give something to you by releasing her grip, and she will be able to roll a ball to you.

## How you can help

You can still encourage your baby's new skills with games that you can play together. Now that she's older, however, she'll be able to pursue some activities by herself; she'll also be able to apply herself to everyday tasks.

▲ **NINE MONTHS** Your baby's handling skills become more refined and she can pick up small things with her thumb and index finger. She points with her index finger when she's reaching for something. She's also eager to feed herself and enjoys finger foods.

▲ **12 MONTHS** Your baby still enjoys throwing things as he practises "ungrasping". He can build a tower of two blocks or cups and can hold on to two things in one hand. He can draw lines with a pencil. His coordination is improving so he spills less food.

▲ **18 MONTHS** Now your toddler can turn two or three pages of a book at a time, and build a tower of three blocks. She can feed herself completely with a spoon and drink from a cup without spilling anything. She enjoys finger painting and scribbling.

**Everyday activities** The business of getting food into her mouth will give your child a powerful motive to improve her hand–eye coordination. As soon as she is able – from about six months – let her hold her own bottle or cup while she drinks from it, and give her finger foods to encourage fine finger movements. Before long she'll be able to feed herself with a spoon, a skill you can encourage by preparing semi-solid foods that will stick to the spoon.

Dressing is another everyday activity that your baby will try increasingly to do for herself. She may be able to pull some of her clothes on and off, but won't be able to manage fastenings yet, though she will want to try.

▲ **WATER PLAY** Your baby will have hours of fun with a bowl of water and some simple cups and toys. And she'll be practising essential skills as she puts things in and out of the water.

**Building blocks** Once your baby is able to grasp a block, you can teach her to place one on top of another. At six or seven months she will be able to copy you. Continue to stack blocks – three or four high or side by side – for her to see and copy. As her grasp develops (see column, right), she will practise the novel skill of letting go and dropping things, and will start to throw blocks. By the time she's one year old, she'll be able to build a tower of two blocks by herself, and by 15 months she'll probably manage a tower of three.

**Games** There are all sorts of simple games your baby can play to develop her hand skills. She'll love making lots of noise by banging a wooden spoon on some pots and pans. Once she learns to let objects go, she will enjoy throwing them out of her pushchair or highchair. You can make this into a game by showing her how to put objects into a container and take them out again.

**Drawing** Your baby won't be able to manage a pencil or crayon until she's about a year old, but once she starts, she will love to scribble. Give her lots of scrap paper – wallpaper offcuts are good – and pin her pictures up where she can see them.

# Your baby's grasp

The ability to grasp small objects precisely between the thumb and finger – opposition – will be one of the major achievements of your baby's first year.

■ At about five months your baby will grasp objects in her palm on the little finger side.

■ At about eight months she'll be able to grasp an object with her fingers, perhaps pushing it against the base of the thumb.

■ At about nine months she will use her index finger to point – a step towards holding small objects with the thumb and index finger.

■ Next she learns to "ungrasp" and practises this by dropping and throwing things.

■ By the time she's one year old she'll have achieved a mature "pincer" grip, grasping objects between her thumb and her index finger.

## Help your baby

**Here are some ways you can stimulate your older baby and help her mental development.**

Play hide-and-seek with a toy. Place a toy in front of your baby and let her reach for it several times, then put a piece of paper in front to hide it. Your baby will move the paper to find the toy.

Choose soft baby books with large colourful illustrations, and set aside time each day to read. Try naming several items on a page, and then take your baby's hand and point to them. Name the items again.

By the age of one year your baby will begin to understand cause and effect if you describe your actions while, for example, putting her coat on her and taking it off, or dressing and undressing a doll.

Describe what's happening when she plays. For instance, if she knocks over her bricks, say "All fall down".

Give an older baby, of around 15 months, simple tasks to do, such as tidying up and putting things away in the right place or fetching something for you, to stimulate her sense of achievement and to encourage her feelings of pride.

Help her to string words together to make simple sentences. Introduce the concept of possession, particularly with her own things: "That's Jessica's ball, this is your ball."

# Your baby's mind

Your baby is developing new mental abilities at an amazing rate, mostly through play, and you can help by giving her lots of interesting new experiences. Be guided by her and respond to her needs. She will develop much faster if you let her learn what she wants to, rather than what you think is best.

**Seven months** Your baby is beginning to know the meaning of words and understands "no". She shows signs of determination by going for toys that are out of reach. Your baby takes a keen interest in games, and concentrates deeply on her toys. She will look around for a toy she has dropped, demonstrating a developing memory.

**Eight months** Your baby's memory takes a leap forward at eight months. She recognizes familiar games and rhymes, and turns her head when she hears her name. She can anticipate movement and will hold out her hands to be washed, but will turn her face away from a flannel.

**Nine months** Your baby is learning routines, such as waving bye-bye and putting out her foot so you can put on her sock. She also knows "pat-a-cake" all the way through. Your baby knows what a doll or teddy is and will pat it, and she'll look around corners for a toy, and for Daddy, if you say "Where's Daddy?". This is a very important perceptual step: she's learned that things are still there even if she can't see them. When an object is hidden under a cloth, she'll lift the cloth to see the object.

**Ten months** Your baby may point out things in a book by the time she is ten months but she won't concentrate for long. She will be constantly dropping toys out of

▲**LETTING GO** Now he can release his grip your baby will love to drop toys from his highchair and watch them fall. He'll want you to pick them up again.

her pram and wanting them picked up because she's learned the "letting go" skill. She may say one word with meaning. She is also starting to understand simple words and the concepts of "here" and "there", "in" and "out", and "up" and "down".

**11 months**  Your baby loves jokes now and will repeat anything that makes you laugh. Her interest in books is growing and she likes to have items pointed out; then she points them out if you ask her. She'll repeat her name and shake her head for "no". She'll enjoy simple games like "peek and boo". She'll become very noisy and will want to shake and bang anything that makes a noise.

**12 months**  She'll say two or three words with meaning. She'll pick up a toy and hand it to you, and may point to an object that she recognizes in a picture spontaneously. She starts to understand simple questions. She'll enjoy looking at books with you and help you undress her by lifting up her arms when you take off her clothes.

**15 months**  She'll love to help with household chores, like dusting. Even though she doesn't understand all the individual words, she can understand quite complex sentences.

## Styles of perception

From about the age of six months, a child will be developing her own "style of perception" – that is, the time and care she takes to look at a situation before making a decision. Broadly speaking, most people fall into one of two styles: they are reflective or impulsive. A reflective baby will look at something with fixed concentration, and remain very still, whereas an impulsive baby will become excited, and then look away again after only a short period of examination.

When your baby is 18 months old, you can tell which style most closely describes her by trying a simple test: show your baby a card on which there is a picture, and below variations of this picture. Ask her to select the picture that exactly matches the picture at the top. A reflective child will look at all the options carefully before making a choice, and is usually right. An impulsive child is more likely to look at all the pictures quickly and then make a snap decision, which is often the wrong one. Reflective children often do slightly better at school, especially in learning to read. An impulsive child may therefore need more help with schooling. Reflectiveness, however, isn't always best. There are occasions when your child has to think fast, such as when playing games, and an impulsive child may be better able to make a good decision in the short time available.

143

# Memory

**Now that your baby is older, her developing memory becomes more apparent. There are many things you can do to help.**

■ Repeat a short rhyme to your child over and over again, until she learns how to say it herself.

■ Sing a brief song to your baby, accentuating the rhythm with hand claps, head nods, and gestures of your body.

■ Reading aloud to your baby is by far the best way to develop memory. If a story is repeated several times, she will anticipate events and say them before you get there. If you hesitate dramatically in mid-sentence, she will supply the missing word, such as duck, tree, baby, or kitten.

■ Reciting sequences of numbers will stimulate her memory, as will parroting the alphabet, especially if you give it a definite rhythm or rhyming pattern.

## Homemade toys

A baby under one year doesn't need shop-bought toys. Use colourful, noisy, household items to stimulate and fascinate her.

■ Anything that rolls: cotton reels or the cardboard tube inside kitchen rolls and toilet rolls.

■ Interesting textures: pieces of felt, a string of beads, thick strands of wool, or bean bags.

■ Interesting shapes: plastic ice cube trays, whisks, egg cartons, colanders, and sieves, or plastic bottles of all shapes and sizes.

■ Anything that's noisy: wooden spoons, small saucepans and lids, cake tins, or plastic cups.

■ Anything that rattles: plastic jars with seeds, beads, or paper clips inside (but make sure the lid is on really tight).

▲ NOISY TOYS A baby will love playing with pots, pans, and saucepan lids. The more noise she can make, the more fun she'll have.

# Learning through play

Your baby learns through play, and to develop fully she needs all her senses in use: sight, hearing, smell, touch, and taste. To provide the necessary stimulation, her toys and games should be full of variety so that they'll appeal to all these senses. While obviously it's important for you to play with your baby as much as possible, she also needs to learn to play on her own so that her sense of exploration and imagination is given full rein and allowed to develop.

At seven months your baby's mouth is still an important sense organ and she'll want interesting objects that she can investigate safely. Her toys should be bright, colourful, and have an interesting shape to stimulate her perception of form and space as well as her sense of colour. Primary colours are most appealing for babies of this age. Always name the colour of an object she plays with.

## Toys she'll love

Stimulate your child's hearing with toys that make ringing or rattling sounds when she shakes them. Musical boxes provide endless fascination for young children, particularly ones with a string that your baby can pull. As your baby's hand skills improve, she'll become absorbed by touch as well as sound. She'll love toys that make a noise when she squeezes them. Activity centres, which have a series of knobs and buttons that your baby can push or turn to make noises, can be attached to a cot or a bath. As well as stimulating both her hearing and sense of touch, they will help her understand the link between cause and effect. Rubber balls of all sizes are always a favourite.

Any fairly small objects that are interesting to touch, with holes or handles into which your baby can poke her fingers or wrap them around, are ideal. Look for objects that are brightly coloured and, if possible, make a noise, like rings with bells on them. She'll love a large, specially designed baby mirror placed in her cot for her to stare into. Never put one of your own mirrors in the cot as it could easily break.

## Encouraging her new skills

When she is ten months to one year old, your baby will pick up small objects like pencils, crayons, and, eventually, paint brushes. She'll be starting to become more mobile now and will enjoy being able to push or pull toys like trains, cars, or trolleys.

From one year to 18 months, having achieved some measure of dexterity, your baby will enjoy toys that challenge her hand skills, such as puzzles. Nesting and stacking toys that can be built up or fitted together

▲ **FUN AND LEARNING** Your older baby needs a range of toys that are fun but will also help her develop her hand skills and challenge her imagination.

# Playing together

Your baby will love playing games with you. To help her make the most of new toys, show her how they can be used and encourage her to be imaginative with them.

■ Roll a ball to her and encourage her to roll it back to you; her hand–eye coordination will develop.

■ Show her how to build a more complicated structure with blocks, such as a bridge; she'll improve her delicate hand skills.

■ Fill a container with water or sand and show her how to fill up measuring cups and containers; she'll experience the movement of different substances.

▲ **WATER PLAY** All babies enjoy splashing in water or floating a boat in a bowl. Provide her with unbreakable containers to pour and fill.

will encourage dexterity and spatial visualization. Now that she speaks and understands some words and ideas, she'll love hearing stories and looking at books with you. Those with brightly coloured illustrations and different textures are best.

As your baby grows, her developing skills and mental abilities will be reflected in toys that capture her imagination. Free-standing rattles that she can swipe at while feeding, for example, will keep her amused at first. Large soft blocks are ideal for a six-month-old baby because they can be used for building and throwing, but an older baby will prefer hard blocks of wood or plastic, stable enough to create more complicated structures.

Puzzles and games that challenge your baby, such as simple jigsaws, are important for her development. The puzzles should have knobs to make the pieces easier to pick up, or a very few large pieces that are simple to put together.

## The hearing-impaired child

Children must be able to hear in order to speak, and must speak to learn, read, and write, so it is essential to pick up any hearing impairment early and seek professional help for your child as soon as possible (see p.96).

Children with incurable hearing loss can function quite well with a hearing aid, and many doctors now fit them at infancy rather than at four or five years. In profoundly deaf children, however, comprehension of sound and language is significantly impaired.

There are many ways to approach communication for profoundly deaf children, and they are often used in combination. Among them are: cochlear implants, one of several signing languages, lip-reading, and oral language.

# Beginning to talk

For your baby to talk, she must first understand what you say, and her understanding will increase rapidly towards the end of the first year. From six months onwards, she'll understand when you say "no" firmly, and at nine months she can follow simple orders such as waving bye-bye. You can help her by making meanings clear with theatrical emphasis and gestures: read to her, show her pictures and repeat the names of the things she can see, and give her a clear, slow running commentary about everyday actions.

Children who are sung to, read to, have nursery rhymes repeated to them, are spoken to in a rhythmical way, and are involved in singing, rhyming, and clapping games, speak earlier and better than children who don't. Try to do all these things from your child's earliest days. As soon as your child says her first word, or what you think might be a word, repeat it to her. Tell her she's a clever girl and how pleased you are.

**Seven months** By now you will be able to discern clear syllables in your baby's sounds, such as "ba" or "ka". She'll probably use a special sound to attract your attention, such as a cough or a squeal, and will have started to play games with her tongue and lips.

**Eight to ten months** Your baby's range of sounds is increasing, and she has added the consonants "t", "d", and "w" to her repertoire. She'll start to imitate real speech sounds, and by ten months may use one word with meaning. She pays close attention to adult conversations.

**11 months** By now your baby is almost certainly using one word with meaning, and can understand a few simple words, such as bath, drink, and dinner. Praise her for every new word, and repeat it; she'll say it over and over when she sees your approval. You are your child's first model of good speech, so speak clearly and slowly when you're talking to her.

**15 months** Your baby is breaking gradually into jargon – that is, strings of sounds with the odd recognizable word and with the phrasing and inflections of real speech. This is a sign that she is just about to start talking. She may start to use some favourite phrase of yours, such as "oh dear", in appropriate situations.

**18 months** Your baby may be able to use about ten words with meaning. Her understanding is increasing all the time, and she can point out many objects in her picture books or in the world around her if you ask her to.

# Teeth

People used to think a child's first teeth weren't very important because the adult teeth would come in later. But they are vital as they guide in the adult teeth so they grow in the correct position. And if the first teeth are lost through decay, this can spread to the bone beneath and erode the support needed by the adult teeth.

**Cutting time**  There is no standard time for your baby to cut her first tooth. Some babies are born with one tooth, while others still have none at 12 months of age. (If a baby is born with a tooth this is sometimes removed if, for instance, it's crooked or badly positioned, or if it's loose and there is a risk of its falling out and causing the baby to choke.) As a general rule, though, teething starts at around six months to cope with solid food and a changing diet, after which many teeth appear up to the end of her first year. Your baby will be teething for most of the second year, and the canine teeth, which usually come through at 15–18 months, are often the most painful.

**Signs of teething**  When your baby is cutting a tooth she'll be irritable. The gum will be red and swollen, and you may be able to feel the tooth through the gum. Your baby's cheeks may be red, and she may dribble. Giving your baby something to chew on can help. Symptoms such as a high temperature, vomiting, or diarrhoea are never caused by teething, so you should not dismiss them – check with your doctor.

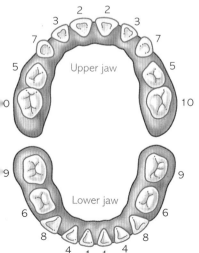

◀ **HOW THE TEETH COME IN** The numbers indicate usual order in which the teeth arrive. The first to erupt are usually the lower front two teeth, then the upper two front teeth. Upper side teeth come next, followed by the lower side teeth. After this, the first upper molars erupt and then come the first lower molars. The upper canines come in next, one each side, followed by the lower canines. The second molars erupt first in the lower jaw, and then they appear in the upper jaw.

## Using her teeth

**A raw carrot or a rusk will give your baby something firm to chew on when she is teething. This principle continues to hold good once she has all her teeth.**

Chewy foods, and particularly fresh fruit and raw vegetables, encourage the development of strong jaw muscles. They also strengthen the teeth and have a cleansing effect as the fibres within them are shredded during the chewing process. Your baby's diet should contain calcium and vitamin D (from dairy foods – after she's one – and fatty fish such as herring) to ensure the healthy formation of the permanent teeth that are growing in the jawbones.

▲ **EXERCISE FOR TEETH** Chewing on firm-textured foods helps strengthen your baby's teeth and jaw muscles.

# A will of her own

From six months onwards your baby will show her assertiveness in her demands and preferences. Your older baby is:

■ very keen to show how grown up she is becoming

■ determined to be independent and to manage without help

■ demonstrating likes and dislikes with certainty and assertion, if not consistency

■ unable to consider consequences and gets very angry when she has to wait, often showing this with violent noises and actions

■ aware that she is a separate being from you and, as such, is determined to have her own way

■ often confused and unhappy at the conflict between wanting to please you and her desire to be independent

■ seemingly infatuated with saying the word "no".

▲ EMOTIONS Your older baby may be extreme in her emotions, from great happiness to temper tantrums.

# Social behaviour

Your baby is becoming more socially adept by now, and enjoys meeting and being with other people. She's learning to understand certain words and phrases, and uses the communication skills she has learned in order to mix with others in the world around her.

Touching, smiling, and all the contact of general company are vital to your baby's happiness at this stage, as she gradually learns to refine her conversational gestures and cries into recognizable signs of communication with other people.

**Six to eight months** Closeness to another baby will be a delight. She'll reach out and touch new friends and enjoys social games like "peek-a-boo". She'll try to communicate with a series of shrieks, grunts, raspberries, and coughs, and mimics facial expressions and conversational gestures. Always "answer" her in order to stimulate these "conversations" and impress upon her that social interaction is a two-way activity.

**Eight to 12 months** She will respond to her own name now, and will understand that a firm "no" means that she should stop whatever she is doing. She is affectionate and will demand closeness with you, particularly big hugs and intimate smiles. Certain social rituals are common to her now – like saying "bye-bye" – which she'll imitate with little prompting. She'll no longer calmly allow a toy to be taken away and she'll even show anger if this happens.

**12 to 15 months** Her sociability is constantly expanding and she enjoys being in groups, especially when she can follow conversations and join in whenever there's a lull. Despite her outgoing attitude, she will still need to be close to you for reassurance and security, and will often look to you when meeting new people – just holding hands will give her the confidence she needs. She can say a few words, ask for things, and show thanks when things are done for her in an obvious way. She likes to be helpful, and enjoys sharing tasks with you.

**15 to 18 months** By now your baby is even more helpful with daily chores, and loves the independence of dressing and undressing herself. She's very affectionate, and shows love for her family, pets, and favourite toys. She tries to imitate adult behaviour and is fascinated by adult interaction and conversation. Although she's becoming more socially aware, she'll tend to play alone and, although she will enjoy playing near another child, she won't usually play with her.

## How to help

The concept of sharing is particularly difficult for your baby to grasp. It's unrealistic to expect your baby to give a toy to another baby if she's still playing with it. It is equally unfair to expect your baby to understand that she can't take another baby's toy simply because she wants it. Show her that if she takes another baby's toy, she must replace it with one of her own so that they can both play. Your baby is wholly capable of unselfishness and generosity, but any such act must be seen to be a pleasure for both parties.

Always include your baby in social gatherings. Introduce her to lots of new faces and teach her the basic pleasantries from as early as possible. It will help her to feel secure when she is away from you or her usual carer, although this shouldn't happen too frequently, or for long periods of time.

## When to say no

Smacking, threats, and withdrawal of pleasures have no place with small children. If you are too severe, too tolerant, or you are inconsistent, your baby can become insecure. Before she is three, your child can't respond to reason, and she still can't grasp the connection between cause and effect. However, she'll understand that she's done wrong, or that you're angry, although it will take her some time to remember to connect a particular action with a particular outcome. For this reason, it's vital that you point out a mistake to your child immediately so that she learns to link the action with the punishment. Bear in mind that your baby's memory is very short, so if you brood over your anger and act later, she won't understand and won't learn from your attempts at correction.

During a baby's first year there are very few reasons for saying "no". I kept the rules for my children to a minimum. I had only one unbreakable rule in their first year: when they were doing something that was unsafe for themselves or others, I would say "no" firmly while removing an object or stopping my child doing something dangerous. I didn't wait for my child to stop. As I was trying to teach what was unsafe, I always explained why I was stopping him.

Your baby will be receptive to justice and fair play, and to their opposites. She immediately recognizes inconsistency, and so gently applied and consistent guidance will help your child to develop self-control and a conscience, which will help her in her decision-making in later life. It will also give her a sense of responsibility towards others.

# Fear of strangers

It's not uncommon for a normally talkative and sociable child to become withdrawn, even tearful, when introduced to strangers or taken to a strange place. This is quite normal and should never be ridiculed or made into an issue.

Don't insist that she joins in immediately with the group. A gentle introduction from you is by far the best. Your baby will soon forget her nerves and find her place within the social gathering.

Even a very shy child, if gently encouraged, will join in with new friends after an hour or so, but rushing her may make her more insecure. Having a favourite toy or comforter with her will bolster her confidence, so don't take this security away. Once she feels relaxed, she'll play happily with her new playmates.

# Your toddler and preschooler

During these years your child will consolidate all the physical skills he learned in his first 18 months and he'll continue to master one of the most difficult intellectual ones – speech. Your child will be struggling to express his thoughts and desires through speech, and with his increasingly able brain he'll now see himself as a separate entity to you: he'll be aware of "self". He'll probably be quite frustrated at times and you may notice more tantrums. But his parents are still the centre of his world and he'll need a lot of affection, encouragement, and support.

Play has a vital role in your child's development. Your child is now entering into what I call the proper "toy" stage, and using his imagination to breathe life into his toys and games. Playing with other children will help him discover friendship and how to get on with people.

## Girls' weight

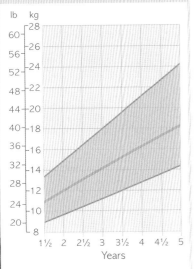

lb kg

60 — 28
56 — 26
52 — 24
48 — 22
44 — 20
40 — 18
36 — 16
32 — 14
28 — 12
24 — 10
20 — 8

1½  2  2½  3  3½  4  4½  5
Years

▲ YOUR TODDLER'S WEIGHT Weight
gain may be irregular during spurts
of growth, but any weight within the
coloured band is normal. (See also
Your baby's weight, p.38.)

▲ A BALANCED DIET Variety is the key to
a good diet. Choose foods from each of
the groups in the chart (see right).

# Food for your child

As your child grows his nutritional needs increase;
greater quantities are needed during growth spurts,
and when he's learning to walk. Your child needs protein,
carbohydrates, fats, vitamins, and minerals, and he'll get
all of these as long as you provide a wide variety of
foods. Because he's growing, he still needs more protein
and calories for his body weight than an adult.

Although, broadly speaking, a variety of foods from three of the four food
groups (see p.114) – carbohydrates, fruit and vegetables (fibre), and protein-
rich foods – will fulfil your child's needs, some foods within the groups
have particular nutritional value (see chart below).

## Sources of good nutrition

| FOOD GROUPS | NUTRIENTS |
|---|---|
| **Breads and cereals** Wholemeal bread, noodles, pasta, rice | Protein, carbohydrates, B vitamins, iron, and calcium |
| **Citrus fruits** Oranges, grapefruits, lemons, limes | Vitamins A and C |
| **Fats** Butter, margarine, vegetable oils, fish oils | Vitamins A and D, essential fatty acids |
| **Green and yellow vegetables** Cabbage, sprouts, spinach, kale, green beans, squash, lettuce, celery, courgettes | Minerals, including calcium, chlorine, fluorine, chromium, cobalt, copper, zinc, manganese, potassium, sodium, and magnesium |
| **High protein** Chicken, fish, lamb, beef, pork, offal, eggs, cheese, legumes | Protein, fat, iron, vitamins A and D, B vitamins, especially $B_{12}$ (naturally present in animal proteins only) |
| **Milk and dairy products** Milk, cream, yogurt, fromage frais, ice cream, cheese | Protein, fat, calcium, vitamins A and D, B vitamins |
| **Other vegetables and fruits** Potatoes, beetroot, corn, carrots, cauliflower, pineapples, apricots, nectarines, strawberries, plums, apples, bananas | Carbohydrates, vitamins A and C and B vitamins |

# Snacks

Until the age of four or five your child will prefer to eat frequently throughout the day. His stomach still can't cope with three adult-sized meals a day, so he's not ready to adopt an adult eating pattern. He may want to eat between three and 14 times a day, but the typical range is five to seven times. What he eats is more important than how often he eats. As a rule, the more meals your child has, the smaller they'll be.

You may be accustomed to thinking of snacks as "extras", but they're an integral part of any child's diet so should not be refused. As long as the snacks do not reduce your child's daily nutrition, and are not being used as substitutes for "meals", snacks can be wonderfully useful for introducing new foods gradually without disrupting his eating patterns. Avoid giving your child highly refined and processed foods like biscuits, sweets, cakes, and ice cream, which contain a lot of calories and sugar and very few nutrients. Fresh fruits and vegetables, cubes of cheese, and cheese sandwiches made with wholemeal bread or white bread with added vitamins, and diluted fruit juice all make good, nutritious snacks.

**Planning snacks**  Snack foods should contribute to the whole day's nutrition, so don't leave them to chance; plan them carefully, and coordinate meals and snacks so that you serve different foods in the snacks and in the meals.

■ Milk and milk-based drinks make very good snacks, and contain protein, calcium, and many of the B vitamins. You should use whole milk until your child is at least two years old; then you can use semi-skimmed (but not skimmed milk unless your child is overweight). Raw fruit juice drinks are also very nutritious, and contain a lot of vitamin C. If you buy fruit juices, avoid those with added sugar.
■ Your child may become bored with certain kinds of food, so try to give him plenty of variety, and make snacks amusing if you can: you could use biscuit cutters to cut cheese or bread into interesting shapes, or make a smiling face by arranging pieces of fruit on a slice of bread.
■ A food that your child rejects in one form may be acceptable in another: yogurt can be frozen so that it becomes more like ice cream, and a child who rejects cheese sandwiches might enjoy eating pieces of cheese and tomato out of an ice cream cone.
■ You can also increase your child's interest in food by involving him in planning or even preparing part of a snack. He will take great pride in eating a sandwich if he has helped you choose the filling or wash and tear the lettuce leaves into smaller pieces, for example, and if you allow him to assemble the bread and filling himself.

## Boys' weight

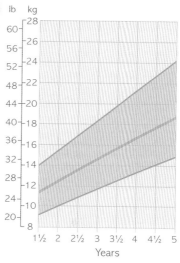

▲ **YOUR TODDLER'S WEIGHT** Your child may have spurts of growth balanced out with periods of slower weight gain. Any weight within the coloured band is normal. (See Your baby's weight, p.38, for an explanation.)

▼ **LITTLE AND OFTEN** Your child will need regular nutritious snacks as she can't yet eat large meals.

15

## Portable chairs

Your child can eat at the table in his usual highchair, but there are other types of seat available that are more portable and will give him greater independence.

**Booster seat** Help your child reach table height with a booster seat, suitable for children over 18 months. More stable than a cushion, it can be strapped to a chair.

**Clip-on chairs** These light collapsible chairs are suitable for babies over six months of age. Some grip the table when your toddler sits in the chair; others are attached to the table by clamps. These are not suitable for all tables, so be sure to check the manufacturer's recommendations.

▲ **CLIP-ON CHAIR** This chair is much more adaptable than a highchair. Check that it's properly fixed in place before putting your baby in it.

# Feeding your toddler

By the age of 18 months, your baby will already be eating more or less the same foods as you, and he'll probably take about one-third to half an adult portion at meals. Try to ensure that he has at least one protein food at each meal, and four servings of fruit and vegetables a day, but don't worry too much if he doesn't. Aim for a balanced diet over several days, with a good mixture of foods from the groups listed in the chart on p.150.

Don't give your child highly seasoned or sugary foods – fresh fruit or yogurt are much better for him than sweet puddings. Also be careful to avoid giving any small, hard pieces of food that your child could choke on, like whole nuts or popcorn, fruits with stones or pips, or very small pieces of raw fruit or vegetables.

## Family eating

Now that your toddler is feeding himself, he'll enjoy sitting at the table during family meal times. Although he's eating the same food as everyone else, you may need to mash or chop it so that he can eat it without much help. A very messy eater can be fed before the family, then allowed to sit at the table with some finger foods. Difficult eaters often feel encouraged to eat more at family meals.

It will be some time, however, before your child is ready to sit still during meal times. If he wants to get down from the table, let him go, and don't try to make him come back to finish his food if he's obviously lost interest in it; he will make up for it by eating more at the next meal.

## Messy eaters

Your child may regard meal times as just another game, and will see nothing wrong in getting food everywhere. It's just a phase, and his coordination will improve eventually. Make meal times easier on yourself by surrounding the highchair with newspaper that can be gathered up after each meal. Being tidy can be made into a game: draw a circle on the tray of the highchair to show your toddler where his mug should go; if he keeps it there, reward him.

▲ **KEEPING CLEAN** Bibs and easy-to-wash plastic equipment help to keep messy meal times manageable.

# Menu planning

The menus below assume that your toddler will eat three meals a day and several snacks. If you find in practice that he eats fewer meals and more snacks, just make sure you choose snack foods that you would have served at meal times. Always make sure that a meal contains at least one food you know your child likes and keep foods simple. Serve small amounts and allow second helpings rather than piling up the plate, which can be off-putting for a young child. If your child dislikes, or even rejects, fruit and vegetables, find a couple that he will eat and stick to those until he shows that he wants a change.

## Suggested menus at 18 months

| DAY 1 | DAY 2 | DAY 3 |
|---|---|---|
| **Breakfast**<br>½ slice wholemeal toast<br>1 chopped hard-boiled egg<br>1 cup diluted fruit juice | **Breakfast**<br>30g (1oz) cereal plus ½ cup milk<br>1 cup diluted fruit juice<br>1 sliced pear, without skin<br>½ slice wholemeal toast | **Breakfast**<br>1 cup diluted fruit juice<br>1 tablespoon baby muesli with 50ml (2floz) milk<br>½ mashed banana<br>small tub of fruit yogurt |
| **Lunch**<br>50g (2oz) white fish<br>50g (2oz) brown rice (dry weight)<br>1 tablespoon sweetcorn<br>1 cup diluted fruit juice | **Lunch**<br>1 beefburger in a wholemeal roll<br>30g (1oz) steamed broccoli<br>1 medium tomato<br>1 cup diluted fruit juice | **Lunch**<br>1 cheese sandwich with wholemeal bread<br>pieces of raw carrot<br>1 sliced apple, without skin<br>1 cup milk |
| **Snack**<br>1 cup water<br>1 small yogurt<br>1 banana<br>1 wholemeal roll | **Snack**<br>1 cup milk<br>1 wholemeal biscuit<br>1 cup water<br>1 rice cake | **Snack**<br>1 orange in pieces<br>1 fromage frais<br>1 cup diluted fruit juice<br>1 packet unsalted crisps |
| **Supper**<br>50–75g (2–3oz) cauliflower with 50g (2oz) cheese<br>50g (2oz) beans<br>50g (2oz) chicken pieces, without skin<br>½ banana blended with 1 cup milk<br>1 wholemeal roll | **Supper**<br>½ wholemeal roll<br>50g (2oz) broad beans<br>50g (2oz) chopped liver<br>50g (2oz) wholemeal pasta (dry weight)<br>1 cup water | **Supper**<br>2 sardines (not in oil)<br>50g (2oz) baked beans<br>1 medium tomato<br>1 cup milk |

# Making food fun

Making meal times exciting for your toddler will encourage him to try new foods. Fun foods don't have to be difficult; a little imagination is all it takes.

Be flexible about food – for example, give your child his meal on a toy plate occasionally or make his food into an amusing shape. Fill an ice cream cone with cheese and tomato or tuna salad for a snack on the move.

▲ **POTATO MICE** Turn baked potatoes into colourful mice. Use radishes for ears, tomatoes for a nose, raisins for eyes, and a few chives for whiskers.

▲ **COLOURFUL KEBABS** Courgettes and sweet peppers become much more fun to eat if they're made into chunky kebabs with little pieces of meat.

## Overweight

Obesity is one of the most common nutritional problems among children in prosperous Western societies.

If you think your child is overweight – that is, markedly fatter than his friends – check with your doctor who'll be able to tell you if your child's weight is above the normal range for his height.

Common causes of being overweight are a poor diet and lack of exercise. The best way to help the child is often for the whole family to adopt a healthier diet and take more exercise together. Aim to help your child keep his weight stable while he grows in height. The following guidelines may help.

■ Bake, grill, and boil foods rather than roasting or frying.

■ Give water or diluted fruit juice when your child is thirsty. Never give sweetened drinks.

■ Give wholemeal bread, raw vegetables, and fruit as snacks.

■ Wholemeal bread and pasta and brown rice are digested more slowly than their refined equivalents, so appear more filling.

■ Encourage your child to be active by playing lively games.

■ No child needs more than 500ml (18floz) milk a day. Skimmed or semi-skimmed cows' milk can be used for overweight children over the age of two years if vitamin supplements are also given.

# Feeding problems

Some young children are "difficult eaters", but in many cases the real difficulty is with a parent who expects their child to conform to an eating pattern that doesn't suit him. If you approach feeding problems with sympathy and a flexible attitude, they will usually just disappear. If there's a genuine problem, such as an intolerance of, or very rarely an allergy to, certain foodstuffs, check with your doctor. Never try to isolate a food allergy yourself; always seek medical advice.

## Food preferences

In his second year your child will start to show likes and dislikes for certain foods. It is very common for children to go through phases of eating only one kind of food and refusing everything else. For example, he may go for a week eating only yogurt and fruit, then suddenly go right off yogurt and start eating nothing but cheese and mashed potato. Don't get cross with your child about this, and don't insist that he eats certain foods. No one food is essential, and there is always a nutritious substitute for any food he refuses. As long as you offer your child a wide variety of foods, he will get a balanced diet, and it is far better for him to eat something that he likes – even if it's something you disapprove of – than to eat nothing at all. The one thing you must watch out for is your toddler refusing to eat any food from a particular group – refusing any kind of fruit or vegetables, for example. If he does, his diet will become unbalanced, so you'll have to think of ways of tempting him to eat fruit and vegetables, perhaps by cooking the food in a different way or presenting it imaginatively (see p.153). If you spend time cooking food that you know your toddler doesn't want, you'll feel annoyed and resentful when he doesn't eat it, so give yourself and him a break by cooking food that you know he'll enjoy.

Don't try to camouflage a disliked food by mixing it with something else, or bargain with your child by offering a favourite food if he eats the disliked one; he may well end up refusing other foods as well. If you're trying to introduce a new food, make sure your child is hungry; that way, he's more likely to take it. Never try to force him to eat if something he doesn't want to; if he thinks it's important to you, he may use food to manipulate you. Instead congratulate him on what he does eat.

## Refusal to eat

Not eating can be an early indication that your child may be unwell, so have a careful look at him. If he looks pale, and seems fretful and more clumsy than usual, check his temperature (see p.278), and then speak to your doctor if you're worried.

Occasionally your child may have eaten a lot of snacks or had milk before his meal, and he won't have his usual appetite. As long as the snacks are nutritious, this is OK. If he refuses to eat for no reason that you can see, don't let yourself worry. Your child will always eat as much food as he really needs, and if you insist on him eating, meal times may become a battle that you will always lose.

## Food intolerance

The inability to digest certain foods fully has to be distinguished from a true food allergy, which is quite different and very rare. Intolerance occurs when the digestive system fails to produce essential enzymes that break down food inside the body. One of the most common forms of food intolerance in children is lactose intolerance – the inability to digest the sugars in milk. The enzyme, in this case lactase, may be absent from birth, or its production may be disrupted by an intestinal disorder, such as gastroenteritis. Pale-coloured, bulky, smelly stools are characteristic of the disorder. Sometimes food intolerance occurs for reasons that are not known. If your child habitually has symptoms such as diarrhoea, nausea, or pain after eating a particular food, intolerance may be the cause. The best remedy is to avoid the food concerned, but don't try to identify it yourself; you'll need medical advice.

## Food allergy

Most cases of suspected food allergy turn out to be food intolerance, or the combination of a fussy child and a fussy mother. A true food allergy is quite rare, and happens when the body's immune system undergoes an exaggerated reaction to a protein or chemical it interprets as "foreign". It is a protective mechanism and symptoms can include a headache, nausea, profuse vomiting, a rash, widespread red blotches on the skin, and swelling of the mouth, tongue, face, and eyes. At first the allergen – the substance that causes the reaction – may produce only mild symptoms, but these may become more severe if the child keeps on having the food concerned. Some foods that commonly cause allergic reactions are wheat, shellfish, strawberries, chocolate, eggs, and cows' milk. Never attempt to isolate a food allergy on your own without medical advice.

Food allergies have sometimes been blamed for behavioural disturbances in children, including hyperactivity. In some cases it has been proved that food was responsible, but in many more, bad behaviour is a way of seeking love and attention from neglectful parents. I feel very strongly that too many parents blame foods for behavioural problems rather than look to their own attitudes as a cause. Meanwhile, many children have been needlessly deprived of nutritious foods.

Loss of appetite is often one of the first signs of illness in a child, but this need not be a worry if the illness is short.

■ Encourage your child to drink plenty of fluid, especially if he has been vomiting or had diarrhoea.

■ Most doctors recommend that your child shouldn't have drinks containing milk if he's suffering from gastroenteritis.

■ There's no need for a special invalid diet, though it's sensible not to give your child rich or heavy foods if he has an upset stomach.

■ Offer some of his favourite foods to cheer him up, and give smaller portions than usual.

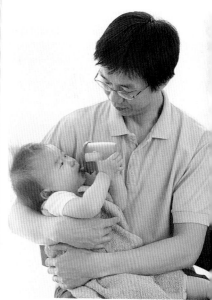

▲ GIVING DRINKS Your child's appetite may be poor when she is ill, but make sure she takes plenty of fluids by offering her favourite drink.

## Treats and rewards

Every parent knows that there are times when it's important either to reward good behaviour or to offer a bribe in return for some form of cooperation.

Sweets might seem like the most suitable reward, as they are always appreciated by children. However, you may feel that to give sweets routinely as a reward undermines the consistency of your approach to sweet-eating in general. There's no hard and fast rule on this, and there's no reason why you shouldn't occasionally reward your child with sweets as long as you make it clear that it's a one-off gift.

It's worth making an effort, though, to devise other forms of reward: a favourite yogurt flavour, a small toy, or a new box of crayons, or a specially extended bath time or bedtime story.

I don't believe in placing a total ban on sweets, because this can encourage children to be secretive and dishonest.

I do believe in rationing sweets, though, and this always worked with my own children. If you let your child have one sweet after lunch and one after supper, and encourage him to brush his teeth afterwards, you'll be encouraging self-control, good eating habits, and good oral hygiene.

# Social eating

Your preschooler will eat much the same as you – taking care of his needs may even encourage you to improve your own diet. As well as making sure he is eating well, you'll probably want to start teaching him adult behaviour and manners at meal times. This is a good time to teach him table manners that will last into adulthood.

## Family and social eating

For many families, meal times are about much more than making sure everyone has enough to eat; they are social occasions when all the members of the family sit down together, exchange news, and enjoy each other's company. For a small child these times form an important part of his learning process; he can appreciate this social aspect of meal times and will learn most of his behaviour at the table from his early experience of family eating rather than from any number of lectures at a later age.

Every family has its own accepted standards of behaviour and I'm not going to lay down rules about what these should be. What is important, however, is that your child learns to fit in so that the family can enjoy their meal times together without repeated disruptions caused by bad manners and arguments about behaviour.

As soon as your child first sat in his highchair at the family dining table he will have been watching and learning. He'll want at least to try the foods that you are eating and will often join in the conversation. Try to include your child in family meals as often as possible. Encourage him when he attempts to follow your (good) example. Give praise, for instance, when he asks for something to be passed to him instead of attempting to grab it from the other side of the table.

There will be occasions when you want your child to behave especially well at meal times – usually because you are having visitors. Allow him to join in the excitement of a special meal by letting him help with the preparations beforehand, such as laying the table with extra care. If he understands that some occasions demand an extra effort from everyone, he'll find it easier to understand why you want him to be particularly well behaved and will react better to your wishes.

## Keeping meal times relaxed

It's important to prevent meals from becoming a battleground for more generalized family conflict. The connections between food and love can be very close, and arguments about food and eating can be associated with tensions over other issues. In such cases, food and eating behaviour – for example, refusal to eat – can become a weapon that the child uses

▲ **MEALS OUT** Eating out is fun for all the family and children are often encouraged to try new foods when they see their friends eating them.

either to gain attention or to express anger or distress. It's best, therefore, to be fairly easy-going about table etiquette with your child and keep meal times as relaxed as possible. Insist only on the aspects of table manners that you consider essential; refinements can come later.

## Eating away from home

A young baby can eat only what you give him, but an older child will have pronounced preferences about what he wants to eat, and the opportunity to follow them. There are likely to be more occasions when your child is eating outside the home, and while you obviously can't account for every mouthful he eats, you should try to ensure that the good habits he's learned at home are not undermined once he starts to eat elsewhere.

If your child goes to playgroup, preschool, or "proper" school, try to make sure he has a good breakfast before he leaves home. If he doesn't, he'll be hungry again long before lunchtime, and both his temper and his concentration will be affected. A healthy mid-morning snack like a piece of fruit or a cereal bar will also help tide him over until lunchtime. If food is going to be provided for him, try to find out what will be on offer; if you are not satisfied, or if there are no arrangements to feed your child, then provide him with a nutritious packed lunch instead.

**Fast foods** Try not to resort to fast food restaurants too often when you are out with your child and he wants something to eat. Most of the foods available in these restaurants – chips, hamburgers, sausages, and sugary drinks – are high in salt, fats, or sugar, and low in nutrients. If you can, bring a supply of healthy snack foods with you, or choose somewhere that offers more healthy foods, such as sandwiches and salads. My family used to eat at a hamburger restaurant once a week, for Saturday lunch. This satisfied everyone and wasn't so frequent as to damage good health.

## Eating out

There will be many occasions when you'll take your child out to eat. Being prepared will make the experience more enjoyable.

■ Try to find out beforehand what facilities will be available at the restaurant you choose: if you are booking a table, mention that you will be bringing young children, and find out whether there will be room for your child's pushchair, and whether a highchair can be provided if you need one.

■ Many children's menus are very limited and offer just hamburgers, sausages, or fish fingers – all with chips. If you don't want your child to have these foods, ask whether you can order a small portion of a suitable dish from the main menu, and whether you will be charged full price for it.

■ Most children will enjoy the experience of eating out, and you should involve your child fully, allowing him to choose his own meal and to give his own order to the waiter if he isn't too shy.

■ Bring along your child's booster seat if he normally uses one. If you think he will have difficulty drinking from a glass, you could also bring along his trainer cup.

■ Many restaurants positively encourage children, and will be happy to provide straws for drinks, bibs and highchairs for young babies, and even gifts such as paper hats or pictures to colour in.

## Lifting your toddler

Once you have a baby you'll need to know how to handle heavy weights in a way that won't strain your back.

Your child will need constant lifting and carrying, and prams, pushchairs, and other equipment must be shifted. It's important that you learn to lift without injury and strain on your back. Keep your back straight, bend your knees, and, using the powerful thigh muscles to do all the work, lift. Never lift with your legs straight and your back curved forward.

▼ **SAFE LIFTING** Even young children can be surprisingly heavy. Always kneel down to pick up your toddler so that you don't strain your back.

# Holding and handling

Never refuse your toddler or preschooler a cuddle; although he'll need less holding than when he was a young baby, he'll want to be carried, especially when he's generally tired and cranky. He's likely to be clingy if he feels pain or discomfort, when a tooth is coming through, or if he is feeling off-colour. Respond to his signals and don't hesitate to give him a hug if he wants one.

The desire for physical affection remains with us always. Parents should never scoff at their children's needs, and always respond. When my children were growing up, they loved a cuddle, especially when they were tired, or had had a telling-off from a teacher at school, if they were fearful about my departure or absence, or if the world simply didn't feel right. Children who are given love and cuddles when they need and ask for them usually grow into independent and self-confident individuals.

## "Clingy" children

Older children will still occasionally want to sit on your lap. When they feel ill at ease in strange circumstances, they may even want to eat sitting on your knee, particularly if there are strangers present and they feel that they're being watched. Let your child do so if it's convenient; you'll probably find that just a few moments of intimacy will give him the confidence to handle any situation.

Bedtimes are particularly important times for showing affection. In my opinion, a child should never have to go to bed without some cuddling. A cuddle provides a sense of security and the conviction that you really do care. The rule is that you should always be there with a comforting arm and a kind word when your child is hurt, worried, puzzled, or frightened.

## The unresponsive child

From a very early age some children stiffen their bodies and cry when you hold them and usually grow up to be children who avoid physical contact – who turn away if you try to kiss them, for example, and make no physical advances themselves. Such children may never enjoy physical affection comfortably, and a parent may find this hard to cope with because it seems like rejection. If your child behaves in this way, don't insist on cuddles that he clearly doesn't want. Give your physical affection only when he shows you that he wants it.

# Showing affection

By the age of three or four years, your child will be much more independent, and you may assume that he needs fewer overt displays of affection. While this may be true, it's a mistake to think that he wants to go without any physical affection at all. Pay special attention to boys, who are often expected to give up cuddles and kisses at a very young age because it's not considered to be proper "masculine" behaviour.

It's all too easy to lose the habit of showing affection, so hold and touch your child as often as you can every day, whether it's letting him sit on your knee or putting an arm around him when you look at the paper, or giving him a cuddle when you put him to bed. I made it a rule to tell my children every day that I loved them.

Older children often become self-conscious about being kissed or cuddled in public, so be sensitive to this. Choose private moments when they can enjoy your care, attention, and love.

## Dividing your attention

It can be difficult to divide your time and attention evenly between several young children. A friend of mine, who had twins, adopted a pragmatic approach to this problem: rather than trying to give each twin an equal share of her attention at all times, she decided to attend to whichever twin needed her at any one time, and assumed that it would even out over the years. Her example is a good one to follow; for much of the time you will give your children equal attention, so if one of them demands more, you should feel free to give it.

## Comfort and encouragement

With any luck your child won't be averse to a cuddle even when he's an adult, but cuddles do change and get more grown-up, and you have to give the kind of cuddles that your child needs rather than the ones you want to give. So adapt your style of cuddling to what gives him comfort.

Preschool children need plenty of cuddles, especially congratulatory ones, for example when they've mastered something like getting their shoes on the correct feet. Comfort is essential at the first sign of tears. A child responds much better to a cuddle than a reprimand. Therapeutic cuddles reduce the pain of a knock or a cut (even a big one) in seconds.

As your child gets older, cuddles are transformed into other actions, but they have the same bolstering, encouraging effect. A hand on the shoulder, a small caress, or just taking your child's hand is a sign of love and his confidence will soar. Your child craves your love and approval; never leave him in any doubt that he has both in full measure.

## Giving and receiving love

As a parent, you have a responsibility to give your child the will and ability to form loving, open relationships with others as he grows up.

Babies are born into the world able to both give and receive love from the outset. As parents, we must both answer their demands for love and affection and be aware of their need for it when they don't ask.

▲ **GIVING COMFORT** Many of your child's troubles can be solved with a loving hug and a few sympathetic words from you.

# Dressing

## Dressing a girl

Your little girl will try to dress herself now, so choose clothes that she can manage easily. She's growing fast, too, so don't spend a lot of money on clothes that she'll quickly outgrow.

■ Buy dresses with fastenings at the front; ones that fasten at the back are too difficult for your little girl to manage.

■ Show her how to get her tights the right way round, and how to roll them up before she tries to put them on.

■ Avoid very fitted clothes; they don't leave much room for growth or freedom of movement.

As your child grows older, he'll develop the coordination required to dress successfully. Always encourage him in his attempts at dressing or undressing, however slow or awkward – they're a sign of growing independence and maturity. Learning to manage by himself will improve a child's coordination and increase his confidence, so be patient with his first clumsy efforts.

Lay out your child's clothes in such a way that he can put them on easily. For instance, you could drape a cardigan on the back of a chair so that he just has to sit down and slide his arms into the sleeves. Let him do as much as he is capable of, and try not to step in to help unless it's really necessary, though you'll probably have to deal with most of the fastenings yourself until your child is old enough to manage them.

At 18 months, he will be trying to manage fastenings, and by two-and-a-half he will be able to close a button in a loose buttonhole, and put on his own pants, T-shirt, and sweatshirt. By the age of four, he will probably be able to dress and undress himself completely and will have enough dexterity to put his clothes away tidily. There are several things you can do to make getting dressed easier for your child.

■ Teach him how to fasten buttons from the bottom upwards.
■ Sew large buttons on to a toddler's clothes so that he can handle them easily and fit them into the buttonholes.
■ Velcro fastenings will be easy for him to manage, but don't use them where they might chafe his skin.
■ Buy trousers with elasticated waists to avoid zip fasteners.
■ Children often find it difficult to put sweaters on the right way round, so explain to him that the label always goes at the back.

## Choosing clothes

As your child becomes more involved in dressing himself, he will become more conscious of the clothes themselves. Babies are largely unaware of what they are wearing as long as it feels comfortable and doesn't impede their activities, but toddlers gradually begin to notice the colours and type of clothing they put on, and your child may develop preferences. Clothes that seem similar to those worn by mummy or daddy might seem especially attractive to him. The feel of a garment will also be important to him –

**▼DRESSING HERSELF** By the age of three your toddler may be able to dress herself completely, though it'll take her quite a long time. Allow her some independence, and only step in to help if and when you're really needed.

**▼CHOOSING CLOTHES** As your child gets older, he will start to express a preference for certain types of clothes. When you can, let him experiment with different clothing and begin to express himself in the way he dresses.

# Dressing a boy

Help your little boy to dress himself by making sure his clothes don't have tricky fastenings.

■ Look for adjustable straps on dungarees, or add a button so the straps can be lengthened.

■ Trousers with elasticated waists are easiest but, if he has trousers that have zip fasteners, show him how to hold the zip away from his body as he pulls it up to prevent it from catching.

■ Show your little boy how to sit down to put his feet into his trouser legs, then stand up to pull them up.

■ Boys are usually slower than girls at learning to use the potty, so it is particularly important to avoid awkward fastenings on your little boy's trousers.

**◀CHOOSING FASTENINGS** Until your child has enough dexterity to manage fiddly buttons and zips, it's best to choose clothes and shoes with manageable fastenings.

▶ **MAKING CHOICES (RIGHT)** When asking your child what she'd like to wear, limit the options to two or three different outfits. That way she gets to exercise her preferences without becoming confused by too many choices.

▶ **PUTTING ON SOCKS (FAR RIGHT)** Suggest to your child that he sits down on the floor or on a chair, to put his socks on. You can make it easier for him by stretching the socks out slightly first as they may shrink a little after washing.

whether, for example, it is soft or itchy, tight or stretchy. If he takes a dislike to a garment, it may be because it doesn't fit properly and is therefore uncomfortable to wear, so it's a good idea to take notice of these preferences and, within reason, act on them.

**Involve your child** Do take your child's concerns seriously when you're buying him clothing. Forcing the issue will only lead to unnecessary unhappiness for both of you. Once your main requirements, which are usually practical ones – suitability, warmth, durability, washability, and cost – are met, there's no reason why you shouldn't indulge him a little; the image of a favourite cartoon character or a particular colour may, for him, be the deciding factor in choosing a T-shirt. Allowing him to choose which clothes to wear each day is also important and allows him self-expression, gives him confidence, and permits him to exercise choice in a safe and limited way. You may want him to dress up warmly and wear trousers on a cold day, but let him choose which pair. That way, both of you have your requirements met without any fuss.

He may develop seemingly irrational likes or dislikes for certain items of clothing – insisting on wearing a particular T-shirt every day, for example, or refusing to wear the hand-knitted pullover that granny gave him for his birthday. In instances such as these, the easiest policy is to go along with any preferences as far as practicable, though occasionally bribery, or at least negotiation, may be in order: you could offer a treat in return for wearing that pullover on the day that granny comes to tea.

# Choosing shoes

Once your child begins to walk, he'll need shoes. Always go to a reputable shop where the staff have been trained to measure and fit children's shoes. Aim to go shoe shopping at a time of day when the shop is quiet and your child isn't tired or hungry. Shoe shops can be particularly busy at the weekend or just before local children go back to school, so it's best to avoid these times if you can. The shop assistant will then be able to devote herself to you and measure the length and the width of your child's foot before trying any shoes. Once your child tries on a pair of shoes, the assistant should press the joints of each foot to make sure that the feet are not restricted in any way, that the fastenings hold the shoe firmly in place, but don't pinch his foot, and that your child's feet don't slip about. Make sure your child stands up and walks about in the shoes to check that the toes don't pinch and hurt and to double-check that his feet don't slip out of the shoes as he walks and runs about in them.

A sturdy, well-made pair of leather shoes is most suitable for general outdoor wear, especially once your child is running about and playing. It's a good idea, however, to purchase a pair of wellington boots for wet or muddy conditions. Although leather shoes and sandals are solid and sensible and last well, there's nothing wrong with inexpensive canvas shoes or sneakers as long as you make sure that they fit properly.

If your child suddenly becomes less steady on his feet, it may be a sign that he's outgrowing his shoes. Well-fitting shoes are essential to ensure that your child has good feet in adult life. Children's shoes can be expensive, but never try to save money by buying secondhand shoes; they'll have moulded themselves to the previous owner's feet and won't provide adequate support for your own child's feet.

► **STURDY SHOES** It's worth investing in well-made shoes for your child. Have his feet measured on a regular basis – children grow fast and shoe sizes can change from month to month.

## Shoes for healthy feet

New shoes need to feel comfortable on your child from the moment he tries them on. Don't allow for a "breaking in" period or expect new shoes to get more comfortable over time – they need to fit him well and feel good from the start.

■ Surfaces should be easy to clean or polish.

■ Adjustable fastenings hold the foot firmly in the shoe. Buckles and Velcro are easier for young children to manage than laces.

■ The heel should be no higher than 4cm (1½in) from the sole.

■ There should be space between your child's big toe and the end of the shoe – at least 6mm (¼in), but no more than 1.25cm (½in).

■ Shoes with wide toes allow your child's toes to fan out. Make sure the box on the toe is high enough so that it doesn't put pressure on the toenails.

■ The sole should be light and flexible, with a non-slip surface.

## Bath-time safety

Always stay with your child at bath time as he's still at risk from slipping and falling under the water. And you still need to check the water temperature to make sure it's not too hot before putting your child in the bath.

Toddlers are generally keen to do things for themselves – washing their own face, for example – so there's the added risk that your child may turn on the hot tap or grab the soap or shampoo and get it in his eyes. Covering the taps with a towel is a good way to soften any falls or bangs, and place a non-slip mat in the bath.

A child who has previously been happy in the bath may take against it, especially if he gets a fright while bathing. Providing plenty of amusements in the bath, and perhaps getting him to share the bath with a sibling, can help reduce this problem. Allowing him to share a bath with you will resolve most difficulties.

# Bathing and hygiene

Bath time is play time for a toddler and you can make a game of teaching him to wash himself. Give him his own sponge and show him how to wash his face, then his arms and legs, and so on; then have fun rinsing all the suds off. He won't be able to make a very good job of it yet, so you'll probably have to go over the same areas yourself afterwards with a facecloth.

## Washing routines

A child is often hungry when he wakes up, so it's best to leave washing until after breakfast, when he'll be more willing to stand still to have his face and hands washed, teeth brushed (see opposite), and hair combed. From the age of about 18 months, he can start learning to rinse his own hands under running water and, later on, he'll learn to soap them, though he may make quite a mess with the soap and water at first.

## Clean hands

The younger you start teaching hygiene the better, and the best way of teaching is by example. Wash your hands with your child: get your hands soapy together and wash each other's hands, then inspect each other's hands to see whose are the cleanest. Make it clear that hands should always be washed after using the lavatory. You should start this at the potty stage (see p.170) and do it with your child every single time. Encourage him to do this for himself. Similarly, make sure your child washes his hands before meals or after handling pets.

## Nail trimming

Keep your child's fingernails and toenails cut short; it's more hygienic and helps to prevent him scratching himself (or others) accidentally. Long toenails may also make his shoes feel uncomfortable. It's easiest to cut his nails when they are soft after a bath, and, as

▶ **WASHING HER OWN HANDS** Put a step in the bathroom so your child can reach the sink and make sure she knows which is the hot tap and which is the cold.

children's nails grow quickly, it's a good idea to include a nail-cutting session at bath time once a week. Use blunt-ended scissors, designed to be safe for children, or nail clippers. Follow the line of his fingernails and don't cut too close to the quick. Cut toenails straight across.

## Hair care

Your child will probably have a thick head of hair by now, and this will need regular washing. Few children enjoy this process, but you can make washing as easy as possible for your child by using the following tips to help to reduce the likelihood of problems.

■ Keep your child's hair short; it'll be easier to brush, too.
■ If your child really hates hair washing, try allowing him some control over it, for example choosing whether he holds his head back or forwards for washing, or let him hold the shower hose and wet his own hair.
■ Use a non-sting baby shampoo and get a special halo-like shield, which will keep the water and suds away from his eyes.
■ Offer a special game once hair washing is done, or even get in the bath yourself and let your child "wash" your hair in return for your doing his.

## Looking after his teeth

You'll have been brushing your baby's teeth from the time that they first appeared (see p.125), and you should continue to do so at least twice a day. Always brush his teeth after the evening meal so that food particles are not left in the mouth overnight. As your child gets older, he'll probably want to hold the toothbrush and do it himself. Encourage this, but remember that he won't be able to clean his own teeth very well, so always follow up his efforts yourself with a thorough brushing.

When brushing your child's teeth, use a small, soft-bristled brush and a toothpaste containing fluoride. Use only a pea-sized amount of toothpaste, as too much fluoride while your child's teeth are growing can cause fluorosis (discoloration or mottling of the enamel). There are many "fun" flavours of toothpaste available that may give your child an incentive to brush his teeth. Never use toothpaste containing sugar, though, so check the ingredients before you buy it. Sit your child on your knee, holding him securely with one arm, and gently brush the teeth up and down. If he won't keep his head still, try gently holding his forehead.

With any luck, it will be years before your toddler will need any form of dental treatment. Nonetheless, it is important to get him used to the idea of going to the dentist so take him with you when you go for a checkup. Most dentists are happy for your child to sit in the "magic" chair and to ask him to open his mouth so that his teeth can be counted.

# Pets and hygiene

If you have pets, you may worry about the possible health risks to your toddler. Follow a few simple rules of hygiene and there should be no cause for concern. The rewards to your child having a pet will be well worth the effort.

■ Ringworm (see p.167) is a contagious skin condition, which can be caught from pets, and it often affects children. If you suspect ringworm, check with your doctor straight away.

■ Always try to stop your child from kissing his pet, especially near its nose and mouth.

■ Encourage your child to wash his hands after playing with his pet – especially before touching or eating food.

■ Both fleas and worms are easily avoided by regular use of preventive treatments on your pets.

■ If your pet does have an infestation, treat it promptly and keep your child away from the animal until you know that the treatment has worked.

## Cleanliness in girls

**Most girls are naturally fastidious, and you can take advantage of this as you teach your child to keep herself clean.**

■ Encourage good habits in your little girl from an early age by showing her how to wash herself and clean her teeth.

■ Let her brush her own hair; she will prefer it, and it means she can choose her own hairstyle, ribbons, slides, or hairband.

■ Let her have her own special facecloth, soap dish, and towel; she'll be proud of her own things.

■ Allow her to rub baby lotion into her skin after bathing.

■ Teach her to change her underwear and socks daily.

■ Provide her own laundry basket so that she can discard her own dirty clothes.

# Hygiene for preschoolers

By the time a child has reached the age of three, he'll want increasing control over his daily routine. He may not want to cooperate with mundane tasks, such as bath time and hairbrushing, which seem like unwelcome interruptions to more exciting forms of play. The best way to avoid arguments is to turn washing and brushing into a game, or incorporate a fun element into the task.

Allowing your child to take increasing responsibility for carrying out a task, supervised if necessary, or giving him some choice – choosing which comb or which shampoo to use, for example, can make it more interesting and encourage cooperation. The following hints will make the daily routine easier and more enjoyable for both of you:

■ Try not to rush your child to complete a task he's trying to manage by himself, even if he's being very slow. It leads to tension, and may make him less willing to help next time.
■ Don't leave bath time until last thing before bedtime, or your child may be too tired to enjoy it.
■ Encourage interest in toothbrushing by using disclosing tablets once a week. The need to brush away the colour is a great way to ensure that your child cleans his teeth really well.
■ Make hair washing fun by letting your child see in a mirror all the silly hairstyles he can create from shampoo lather, or let him wash a doll's hair first.
■ Offer the bribe of the use of some grown-up toiletries, such as bubble bath, or special toys in return for his cooperation with hair washing or bath time – I believe in bribes for young children.

**Understanding hygiene** By the age of three, your child is capable of understanding, reasoning, and comprehending why something is important. If you give him a reason why he shouldn't do something

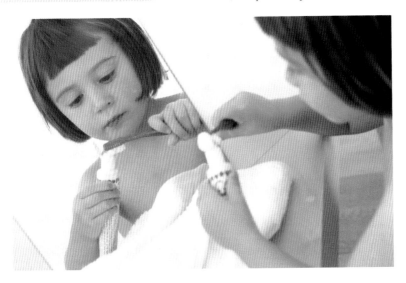

◀ **GET INTO A ROUTINE** Get your child into a regular toothbrushing routine, which should include always cleaning her teeth in the morning and before going to sleep at night.

rather than simply pulling rank, he's likely to desist and you'll gain his cooperation more readily if you present arguments in favour of certain actions. Explain to your child that if his hands are dirty they're covered in germs that could make him ill; or that if he's eaten a sweet it could give him toothache.

Once your child begins to understand the reasons for washing and toothbrushing, you must be consistent. Children are very logical, and if you've persuaded your child that it's essential to wash his hands before meals, and brush his teeth afterwards, he'll probably question you if you overlook it. At the same time, try not to be over-fussy about cleanliness because a certain amount of dirt boosts immunity.

## Conditions passed between children

As soon as your child starts to socialize with other children, he's at risk from a variety of minor disorders that are commonly passed between children. Don't be unduly upset; they are not necessarily a result of poor hygiene, and can all be easily treated. (For more information, see p.296.)

**Ringworm**  A fungal infection affecting the scalp (tinea capitis) or the body (tinea corporis), ringworm appears as small bald areas on the scalp, or round, reddish or grey, scaly patches on the skin. These are usually oval in shape and the edges of the patch remain scaly while the centre clears, leaving rings. Check with your doctor, as the condition is both irritating and contagious.

**Molluscum contagiosum**  This is a warty viral infection that may be transmitted from one child to another when sharing a bath or in a swimming pool. It generally clears up without treatment.

**Nits (head lice)**  The insects themselves are hard to see. The first sign may be that your child is scratching his head. Most people first notice the pale, oval-shaped eggs (nits) that become firmly attached to the hair. Your pharmacist can recommend a special shampoo and/or conditioner, to treat the problem. Wash your child's hair, cover with conditioner and comb with a nit comb. Repeat this treatment every two or three days for at least two weeks or until clear.

**Threadworms and roundworms**  Threadworms are the most common form of intestinal worm in the UK. They live in the bowel and lay eggs around the anus, which causes night-time anal itching. Roundworms are quite rare and infestation is only likely to occur if you've been abroad. Your doctor can prescribe a drug to treat either condition.

## Cleanliness in boys

**Boys are usually quite resistant to washing, and you'll have to spend a lot of time reminding yours to wash and brush.**

■ Make bath times as much fun as possible, with toys, games, and lots of suds.

■ Spend some time showing him how to wash, and do this several times if necessary.

■ Try not to be over-fussy about cleanliness; if he's in the middle of a game, let handwashing wait until he's ready.

■ Let him wash himself as soon as he can make an attempt, then clean him thoroughly yourself at the last moment.

■ Encourage a daily change of underpants and socks.

■ Give him his own laundry basket and encourage him to fill it.

## Eating for healthy teeth

Taking care that your child is eating the right foods is the most important contribution you can make to his dental health.

■ Never give your child a bottle of undiluted or sweetened juice to drink ad lib, as it means your child's teeth are bathed continuously in sugar and can result in "bottle mouth" – a mouth of rotten teeth – as early as three years old.

■ Giving sweet foods between meals increases the number of times the teeth are exposed to harmful acids, so give them at the end of a meal instead.

■ If you give sweets, don't choose sticky toffees, as these remain on the teeth for longer.

■ Giving cheese at the end of a meal makes saliva alkaline, and helps counteract the acid that erodes teeth.

■ It's better to give a piece of cake that can be eaten in a few minutes than a packet of sweets, which will be eaten all afternoon.

■ Give fruit or sugar-free yogurt as treats to avoid encouraging a sweet tooth in your child.

# Dental care

By the time your child reaches the age of three years, the basic routine of taking care of his teeth should be well established (see p.166). You'll need to supervise morning and evening toothbrushing sessions very carefully, even though a child of this age will probably be keen to carry out brushing himself. Six-monthly visits to the dentist, to check that his teeth are coming through normally, are also important. These "tooth-counting" sessions are a good way of letting your child get used to visits to the dentist so he's not scared.

Most people are now aware of the damage caused to teeth by sugar in the diet. Sugary foods produce acids in the mouth that damage the enamel coating of the teeth by removing calcium. Once this has happened, the underlying tooth is open to decay and cavities start to form. While fillings can repair cavities, the tooth is inevitably weakened and, if severely affected by decay, may need to be removed, which endangers the positioning of second teeth.

## Preventing cavities

A baby eats only those foods offered by parents and carers. As he gets older and gains in independence, he'll begin to express his own food preferences more vigorously and will have more opportunities for choosing foods for himself – and sweet foods are often favourites. For this reason, good eating habits can't be started too soon. Above all, try to control your child's intake of sweets. No child needs sugar or sweets, and you can easily find less damaging treats in the form of fruit and savoury snacks. Explain to your friends and family that you would prefer them not to give sweets to your child.

In the real world, of course, children do receive and eat a certain amount of sugary foods. You can limit the damage these do to your child's teeth by making sure they're eaten at meal times. Sugary snacks eaten between meals are the most damaging. If your child has eaten something particularly sweet, make sure he brushes his teeth as soon afterwards as possible.

Giving undiluted fruit juice is another common cause of tooth decay even among children who eat few sweets. So always dilute fruit juice with water for your child and give it at meal times not between meals. Eating, or drinking, anything other than water at night after the teeth have been brushed can also cause problems. The acids that cause tooth decay will remain in the mouth, allowing the enamel-damaging process to continue for many hours. If your child is greatly attached to having a bottle at night, give it to him before he goes to sleep, then remove it.

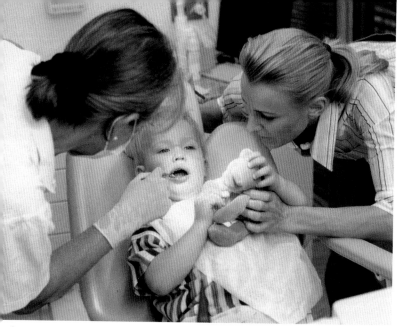

▲ **VISITING THE DENTIST** Always stay with your child during any dental treatment, or even a checkup; the reassurance of your presence is vital.

# First fillings

With luck and good brushing, your child will need little or no dental treatment throughout childhood. Your dentist will notice any signs of decay at your regular six-monthly visits, but make an extra appointment if you notice any unusual tooth discoloration or if your child complains of tooth pain. In cases of slight decay in first teeth, the dentist may decide not to fill the tooth in order to avoid unnecessary upset for your child. Tooth enamel has in fact been shown to be capable of recalcification if the cavity isn't too large.

A dentist who is used to treating children will usually have developed techniques for minimizing any fear. If treatment is needed, great care will be taken to prevent pain with the use of local anaesthetic sprays and extra-fine needles for injections, as appropriate.

# Accidents involving teeth

The need for dental treatment other than for cavities in children under five is rare. An injury to a tooth that damages the nerve can cause it to "die", even if it isn't dislodged. In this case, the tooth will become discoloured, but no other ill effects will follow and it can be safely left in place until it's replaced by the adult tooth. If a child's tooth is chipped, ask your dentist's advice. If one of the milk teeth is knocked out altogether, you'll need to get immediate dental help; take your child to the nearest emergency dental clinic, bringing the tooth with you. If you act quickly enough, the tooth can be replaced in the jaw in some cases, depending on the child's age and the position of the tooth.

# Fluoride

Fluoride is a mineral that's been shown to reduce tooth decay by strengthening the tooth enamel. It is added to many kinds of toothpaste and, in some areas, to the water supply.

■ Fluoride can also be taken by mouth in the form of drops or tablets. Dentists recommend toothpastes containing fluoride for both adults and children.

■ Many dentists would argue that fluoride toothpaste alone doesn't provide sufficient protection against dental decay.

■ If the water in your area is less than 0.7 parts fluoride per million (you can find this out from your local water authority), your child may benefit from fluoride supplements in tablet form.

■ Always consult your dentist or doctor before giving supplements, and follow his advice carefully.

■ It is important to avoid giving excessive fluoride. This can cause a condition known as fluorosis, in which the adult teeth that are developing become mottled.

## Helping a girl

Teach your little girl good habits of hygiene, like washing her hands and tidying the bathroom after herself. You'll probably find that she responds well to this.

Girls are generally neater than boys, and will enjoy turning a cleanliness routine into a game: "Now we flush the loo… Now we wash the potty… Now we wash our hands."

▲ **TOILET HYGIENE** Girls are generally more receptive than boys to being taught good habits of hygiene.

# Bowel and bladder

Once your child shows signs of being ready to use the potty, your aim should be to help and encourage him. If you do this, he's likely to achieve control without much trouble, and will remain happy and confident throughout. If you insist on him using the potty before he's ready, or try to force him, he'll be unhappy at first at not being able to please you, and then guilty and resentful.

## Bowel control

Although a baby is aware first of his bladder emptying, he'll probably achieve bowel control first as it's much easier to "hold on" with a full rectum than with a full bladder. It's a good idea to help him use the potty for bowel movements first; this is easier, in any case, because bowel movements are more predictable and take longer than passing urine. When your child indicates that he wants to pass a stool, suggest that he use the potty.

When he's finished, wipe his bottom (front-to-back for girls) then flush the toilet paper and the contents of the potty down the lavatory. Clean off any trace of faeces and rinse out the potty, using disinfectant. Wash your hands and encourage your child to do the same. If he doesn't want to use the potty, forget it for the moment and try again a few days later.

## Bladder control

The first sign that your child's bladder control is developing is when he becomes aware of the passage of urine, and he may try to attract your attention and point to his nappy. As his bladder matures and is able to contain urine for longer, you may find that his nappy is dry after a nap. Once this is happening regularly, you can leave off the nappy during the nap and encourage him to empty his bladder beforehand. When he can do this and can let you know when he wants to use the potty, you can start leaving off nappies completely during the day, provided he is able to wait for a few minutes while you take down his clothes to let him use the potty. When you are out, you might find it useful to carry a portable potty; these come with disposable liners.

At this stage your child can't hold on to a full bladder for any length of time, and accidents are inevitable, so try to take them in your stride and never scold your toddler for them. Just clean up, change his clothing, and say: "Never mind. Better luck next time."

# Achieving night-time control

Control of the bladder during the night is the last to come, as a child of two or three can't hold on to urine for much more than four to five hours. Once your child wakes up regularly with a dry nappy, you can leave off the night-time nappy, but encourage him to empty his bladder before he goes to sleep. It is a good idea to keep a potty beside the bed for your child to use if necessary, but make sure that his nightclothes are easy for him to take down and that you leave a night-light on so that he can see what he's doing. Be patient if he comes and asks for your help; it's not easy for him to take responsibility for the potty himself. Try this for a week, but if your child has several wet nights, offer him his nappy back for a while – otherwise he'll become very tired from disturbed sleep. If he does show signs of becoming more self-reliant, encourage him and boost his confidence. He'll still have accidents, so it's a good idea to protect the mattress with a rubber sheet, putting the usual sheet on top.

# Using the lavatory

When your child starts to use the potty regularly in the day, encourage him to sit on the lavatory; this will save you having to take a potty with you when you leave the house. Many children are nervous of sitting on the lavatory seat because they feel they'll fall off or even fall in. To make your child more secure on the large lavatory seat, use one of the specially designed child-size seats available that fit inside the lavatory rim. Suggest that he holds on to the sides so that he feels balanced. You should also stay nearby until you are quite sure that he is comfortable on the seat. To help him to get up easily, put a small step or box in front of the lavatory.

# Helping a boy

**Boys are often messier than girls in using the potty or the toilet, but there are some things that you can do to help.**

Boys are more likely than girls to play with their faeces. If this happens, don't show disgust; just wash your child's hands calmly, as you would if they were dirty with mud or paint.

Show your little boy how to stand in front of the lavatory and teach him to aim at the bowl before he passes any urine. You could put a piece of toilet paper in the bowl for him to aim at. Let him see his father passing urine so that he can imitate him.

# Tips for helping your toddler

| DO | DON'T |
| --- | --- |
| Praise your child and encourage him to regard control as an accomplishment. | Insist that your child sit on the potty, ever. |
| Let your child set the pace. You can help your child along, but you can't speed up the process. | Show any disgust for your child's faeces. He will regard using the potty as an achievement and will be proud of them, so tell him you are too. |
| Suggest that your child sit on the potty, but let him decide. | Ask your child to wait once he has asked for the potty, even for a moment – he can only "hold on" for a very short time. |
| Let your child be as independent as he likes, either by going to the lavatory or by using the potty, and praise his independence. | |
| | Scold mistakes and accidents. |
| Use trainer pants to give your child a sense of independence. | |

# Trainer pants

Before your child's bladder control is fully developed you may like to use trainer pants.

■ Disposable trainer pants have easily tearable side seams so that they can be quickly removed in the event of an accident.

■ Both non-disposable and disposable trainer pants can be left on at night. They are bulky, however, so some children find them uncomfortable.

▲ **TRAINER PANTS** Your child will probably prefer wearing trainer pants to nappies because they seem more grown-up.

## Accidents can happen

By three years of age, most children have fairly reliable bladder and bowel control, but accidents will still be common. During the day accidents are most likely to happen when your child ignores the signals of a full bladder because he's engrossed in play or because he's reluctant to use the lavatory in an unfamiliar place. You can help by reminding your child to go to the lavatory at regular intervals and by making a point of accompanying him to the lavatory when you visit new surroundings. Encourage your child to go independently in familiar places as soon as possible, but never insist on his going to a strange lavatory alone.

When your child does wet himself, remember that however badly you may feel about the inconvenience, it's likely that his embarrassment is much worse. Reassure him that you understand it was an accident and that he hasn't failed you. Being prepared for accidents will reduce anxiety for both of you; always carry spare underwear and trousers on outings.

## Late developers

Some children achieve bowel and bladder control later because brain–bladder connections have taken longer than average to form, so it's wrong and cruel to blame your child. Lateness in acquiring control is often hereditary; ask your parents and parents-in-law about this. If a doctor suspects there may be an underlying cause – including psychological causes – this will be investigated if appropriate. Otherwise no action is generally taken until after the age of three or four for daytime wetting or seven for bedwetting.

## Bedwetting

This can happen to a child of any age, boys being especially prone. Ten per cent of five-year-olds and five per cent of ten-year-olds still wet the bed at night. Most children grow out of it after this age without any special help. Minimize your child's embarrassment by keeping him in nappies at night until you are confident that he's reached the point where he can stay dry all night. Once you let him go without nappies be prepared for the occasional accident. Don't let your child see your concern about bedwetting; it only increases his anxiety. Encourage him instead by giving special praise if he has a dry night. (See also p.213.)

## Constipation

Should your child's stools become infrequent – that is, less often than once every three or four days – and hard enough to cause discomfort or pain, then he's constipated. Constipation without any other signs of illness is nothing to worry about, but if it causes your child discomfort, speak to your doctor. Most doctors don't recommend using laxatives or purgatives for a young child. (Constipation is rare in very young babies and can nearly always be corrected by giving your baby drinks of water.) You should never try to treat constipation yourself with oral laxatives, suppositories, or enemas without consulting your doctor.

Once your child is on a varied diet, he shouldn't suffer from constipation if you are giving him enough fluids, fresh fruit, vegetables, and wholemeal breads; if he does, just give more of these. The complex carbohydrates in root and green vegetables contain cellulose, which holds water in the stools and makes them more bulky and soft, as do oat cereals like porridge. A few stewed prunes or dried figs can help, too, often producing a soft stool within 24 hours.

A child can become chronically constipated for several reasons: if you are an over-fussy parent and obsessive about the frequency of his bowel motions, your child may withhold them as a means of getting attention; if he has experienced pain and discomfort when trying to pass a motion, he may hold on to the stools to prevent the pain recurring; or if he dislikes school or other strange lavatories he may be unwilling to use them.

Chronic constipation can also cause a condition called encopresis. Hard stools become impacted in the intestine, and loose, watery motions leak out past the blockage, sometimes causing the condition to be mistaken for diarrhoea.

Illness with a high temperature may be followed by a few days of constipation, partly because your child has eaten very little, so there are no waste products to pass, and partly because he has lost water through sweating with the fever. This kind of constipation will correct itself when your child goes back on to a normal diet.

# Regression

**If a child who has been reliably dry for some time regresses to night- or daytime wetting, it is usually a sign of anxiety.**

The arrival of a new baby is a typical reason for your child's regressing to an earlier stage as a way of winning back your attention, but any sort of upset such as a move to a new home or school can cause it. Occasionally regression can be caused by a urinary-tract infection; check with your doctor to rule this out. Take a sample of his urine for testing.

Bowel control, once developed, is usually much more reliable than urinary control. If bowel accidents do happen frequently, particularly after control has been reliable for some time, this may indicate an underlying problem such as retention of stool or some form of emotional tension. See your doctor.

## Tips for helping your preschooler

| DO | DON'T |
|---|---|
| Remind your child to go to the lavatory at regular intervals. | Draw attention to any form of accident your child has or scold him for accidents. |
| Take a spare set of clothes with you when you go out. | |
| Accompany your child to the lavatory in unfamiliar places. | Withhold fluids from a child in the evening. |
| Be sympathetic and make light of any accidents. | Compare your child with others of the same age who may have better control. |
| Offer praise when your child has a dry night. | Make an issue out of any accident in front of friends. |
| If wetting or soiling occurs after a long period of reliable control, look for the cause within the family first. If it persists, consult your doctor. | Be unsympathetic if your child needs to use the lavatory at an inconvenient moment. |

# Dethronement

Anita and Chris have a son, Will, now five years old. When Anita started to grow big with her second baby, Will couldn't understand what was going on. Anita did everything she could to reassure him, showing him pictures of babies inside their mother's tummies, letting him feel the baby kick, and involving him in all the preparations. A month before the baby was due, Will started having disturbed sleep, when he would babble about the baby, but he did not remember anything the next morning.

## A new family member

Anita's baby Jasmine was born at home. Will sat outside his mother's bedroom transfixed by all the activity, but refused to go in and see his new sister. He disowned her right from the start. Chris was very angry with Will for not showing more interest in his new baby sister Jasmine, scolded him, and sent him straight to bed. That night, because of all the upheaval in the house, Will didn't get his usual bedtime story and in the morning the bed was wet, something that hadn't happened for a full year. Chris, who was preoccupied with preparing breakfast for everyone, lost his temper with Will, who stood in the kitchen and wet himself again. "I don't know what we'll do with you", were Chris's last words to Will as he left for work.

## Late developer

Anita had expected Will to be a bit late in mastering bowel and bladder control, as she knew boys were often later than girls in accomplishing this stage of development. She'd also read that the fathers of late developers have often been late in gaining full bladder control too and knew that this had been the case with Chris. She therefore remained very calm and cool when Will was developing bladder and bowel control, and had never pushed him. Will for his part had been very cooperative and eager to please his mother, and was dry and clean by the age of three-and-a-half. So Anita realized immediately that when Will started to wet himself, something must be wrong.

## Feeling rejected

When the midwife arrived in the morning to find Will crying in the kitchen, she immediately saw what the problem was. She explained to Anita that Will was probably suffering from dethronement. Having been the apple of Anita's eye for five years, he felt knocked off his throne by the arrival of the new baby Jasmine, and Anita would have to make him feel loved and secure again. The midwife advised Anita that the doctor should test Will's urine just to make sure an infection wasn't the cause of the bedwetting – the test was negative.

## Seeking advice

Anita decided to have a heart-to-heart with her mother, who reminded her of a family rule – dad always carried the new baby so that mum had her arms free for the other children. She pointed out that Will wouldn't have felt left out if Chris had held the new baby so that Anita's arms were empty for him. Then he'd have known that Anita still had time for him and that she loved him. She reminded Anita of a tradition in her own family that the younger children always got a present from the new baby, so that they knew they were loved by her too. She also suggested that on the first night Will should have been allowed to sleep on the couch in Anita's room, so that he felt special and included.

## Understanding regression

By now Anita felt very guilty that she had taken none of these steps to make Will feel important and secure, and she went to her midwife for advice on how to give her son his self-confidence back. The midwife explained that a child who gets upset, for whatever reason, be it a new baby or starting preschool, can sometimes regress to an earlier phase of development, exactly as Will had done. She pointed out that Will had no control over this and that, far from punishing Will for future accidents, the whole family should try to relax and play them down, saying things like "It doesn't matter, Will. Let me clean you up, then we can play a game if you like."

By this stage Will was feeling far too insecure for a quick recovery, and the following morning he regressed even further and refused to feed himself: he demanded to be fed.

## Rebuilding confidence

Anita and Chris decided to take immediate positive action and, on the advice of their midwife, started changing their behaviour towards Will in order to rebuild his confidence. They told Will's teacher about the difficulties at home, and asked all the staff to be sympathetic and give Will lots of praise. Chris spent half an hour with Will when he came home each evening, giving Will his full attention and lots

It's important to make sure existing children are not overlooked when a new sibling arrives. A little careful planning can prevent any hurt feelings.

■ Set aside time each day to give older siblings your undivided attention.

■ Plan a special treat each week such as a trip to the park, or a visit to the local library for story time.

■ Eat together as a family while the baby sleeps – meal times are great opportunities for talking and catching up on the day.

of cuddles. Anita also gave Will half an hour of her time when he got home from school, with lots of cuddles and expressions of love, and took a deep interest in his school activities. Anita also had regular sit-down breakfasts with Will, putting Jasmine out of sight, if possible in her cradle. She never brought Jasmine into the room at these special times unless Will suggested it.

Will had his own private bath time, and Anita and Chris took turns to read him a bedtime story each night. Anita and Chris also alternated taking Will out for a treat on his own each week, to make sure that he had special time with each of his parents. Anita pointed out to Will all the things that he had mastered that Jasmine, a tiny baby, couldn't yet do, and suggested that perhaps Will could teach Jasmine, even protect her.

Within three days Will was feeding himself happily. Two weeks later he asked to show Jasmine his teddy bear, although he wouldn't let her touch him. He had no more daytime accidents after two weeks, and four weeks later he was sleeping dry through the night again. Reassured by his parents' loving, caring attention, Will became more accepting of Jasmine – in fact, three months later Will said that he'd marry Jasmine if he couldn't marry Anita.

# Away from home

It's quite reasonable for your child to be scared or refuse to get into a strange bed – when he goes to stay with friends or granny, for instance, and when you go away on holiday.

■ Make the new bed into a playground: put lots of toys on the bed, and let your child have drinks and food on the bed, so that he associates it with pleasant experiences.

■ Show your child that you're in easy reach. Get him to call out and then answer him back so that he knows you're close by.

■ If he gets scared and refuses to use the bed, don't ridicule him, don't force him into bed, don't leave him alone, and don't lock the door. That will only make him feel much worse.

■ Try telling him that because he's being so grown-up and sleeping in a new bed he can have a treat, such as a new bedtime story or ten minutes sitting on your knee watching television.

# Sleep and wakefulness

Many two-year-olds periodically wake up during the night. If your child is one of them, this may be distressing for you and your partner, but it's both usual and normal, and you should never deny your child love and comfort.

There may be some obvious problem, but often you won't be able to find a reason for your child's waking up. It could just be that he's a bit afraid of the dark, but he can't explain to you what's wrong, nor can you reassure him with words. You have to comfort with actions, so give lots of kisses and cuddles to show your child that he's loved.

**Daytime napping** As your child gets older you'll find that he doesn't necessarily want to sleep at nap time, but he does need a rest. Try to make a routine out of nap time whether your child sleeps or not by, say, playing some music or reading. You may find your child goes to sleep at nap time if you allow him to sleep in your bed as a special treat or if you give him some idea of how long the nap time will be; one way of doing this could be to put on his favourite CD and say that nap time isn't over until the CD is finished.

## Moving from cot to bed

When your child is strong enough and well coordinated enough to climb out of his cot, it's time for him to start using a bed. Most children will be pleased and excited with their new bed, but if your child seems nervous, there are plenty of things you can do to help. The simplest is to let him take naps in the bed until he is ready to sleep in it at night. If you're worried that your child might fall out of the bed, get a low bed, fit a bed guard to one side, or put cushions on the floor beside the bed.

## Pleasant bedtimes

From the age of three onwards, your child may well use delaying tactics in order to put off going to bed. The way you handle this situation really depends on how much energy you have at the end of the day, and what your previous bedtime routine has been.

If you've been looking after your child and managing the household tasks all day, you'll be in need of private time and may feel you can insist on him going to bed. On the other hand, if you have been out at work all

▲ **NAPS** During the day watch your child for signs of bad temper or fretfulness and ensure that she has a rest. If she really can't sleep she could play a quiet game.

## Privacy

You can teach your child to stay within his own space when he's as young as two years old, but certainly by the age of three when he's open to reason. He'll learn that it's his responsibility not to disturb you thoughtlessly just because he feels like it.

Teaching him to respect your privacy is far better than shutting him out of your room – which you should never do. You can encourage mature behaviour by providing him with his own private space, which is his alone, in which his belongings reside and where he can find his favourite things. Children respond very quickly to the idea of privacy, particularly if they are given a private space of their own that they can tidy up, be proud of, and go to if they want to be quiet and play on their own.

You can affirm this sense of privacy by always pointing out to your child that certain things belong to him: this is his book, his toy, his trousers, and they all have a proper place. In this way he will become familiar with his belongings and where he can find them. By about the age of four he'll be mature enough to realize that if he has his things, you have yours, and that just as he doesn't like his possessions being disturbed, neither do you.

day you'll want to see your child, so you may feel very sympathetic to his pleas for your attention. If you've always had quite a strict bedtime routine and your child suddenly departs from this, then it's probably best for both of you if you firmly reinstate the bedtime with loving fairness. If, however, you've been flexible about bedtimes then it's probably as well for your child's happiness and your serenity to let him stay with you and make himself comfortable. He will be asleep in a few minutes if he has the reassurance of your presence in the room.

I'm convinced that bedtimes should be happy times and with my own children I was always prepared to make concessions to this guiding principle. I would do anything to prevent my children going to bed unhappy. I'd do my utmost to prevent any crying, and whereas during the day I might punish a small misdemeanour, it would go unmarked at night time to make sure that my child didn't go to sleep with the sound of an angry parent's voice in his ears. If you have more than one child, let them enjoy their bedtimes in the same bedroom. The company is reassuring.

## Fear of the dark

As your child gets older and his imagination becomes more fertile, it's very easy to imagine frightening things in the shadows. A fear of the dark is entirely normal – even adults retain it. Leave a night light on in the room or leave a light on outside with a dimmer switch so that your child can see his way to the bathroom if he needs it, or to your room. (If you use a night light, make sure it doesn't cast frightening shadows.) Never insist on his bedroom being completely dark, and never ridicule his fear; it's really a sign that your child is growing up and learning about the world around him. Tell him that if he wakes up and he's frightened he can always come to you for a cuddle.

## Injuries

**Toddlers tend to cry at even the most minor injury such as a small scratch or scrape or a tiny bruise.**

In our house, I always had "the magic cream" (a mild antiseptic cream) on hand, and my children responded almost immediately to attention, reassurance, and a thin smear of the magic cream.

Sometimes I had to sit down with them, hold them close, give them a big cuddle, and make very sympathetic sounds to show them that I knew how much it was hurting or how frightened they were – many young children are terrified by the sight of blood. Comfort and the magic cream nearly always had a calming effect.

Whenever your child comes to you in distress, crying over a small injury, be sympathetic. Say you know how much it's hurting and don't try to make him be brave. In a few moments he'll skip off your knee and return to his play after a kiss to make it better, a cuddle, and a favourite drink or snack.

If necessary, put some interesting idea into your child's mind to distract him from the injury, such as a treat for tea, a special game with dad, a picnic, or an outing to a favourite place.

# Crying and comforting

As your child's thinking becomes more sophisticated, his reasons for crying become more complicated. He's starting to understand what you say, not only in terms of facts, but also of your answers, and he's beginning to respond to reasoned argument. He's becoming very aware of himself and other people. He'll be developing fears that relate to everyday activities, and can feel guilt, shame, jealousy, and dislike, which can make him cry.

## Common fears

The most common fears in this age group are of the dark and of thunder. Fear of the dark is so common as to be almost universal. It has no explanation, and reasoning with your child won't help. It's cruel to make fun of his fear and you should never do that. Give your child an exciting night light – perhaps one with a coloured bulb.

Fear of thunder and lightning is also very common, and the best way to deal with it is to distract your child. Play loud music, turn on the television set, or read him a story. When he's old enough, try to explain how things work: for instance, that lightning is just like a giant spark.

## Talking it through

His fears now relate to what he does during the daytime and any upset that arises from these events. So one of the best ways to dispel fears is to talk about them, and get your child to be open and frank about what frightens him. Give him your full attention and help him to explain by supplying a few examples, and confess that you have similar fears too. Never scold or ridicule your child about his fears. Do something simple and reassuring, like demonstrating to your child that it is fun in the swimming pool and the water is nothing to fear. Your child will trust you and his fear will gradually diminish.

If your child is afraid of going to a friend's house, talk him through it step by step: "First I'll drive you to Simon's house, and then you can play with him…" Nearly all children have some irrational fears, such as fear of monsters, ghosts, or dragons. Remember, to your child a fear is serious, so you shouldn't try to tell him that his fears are unreal.

# Fear of separation

Even when your child is three years old, he'll still have fears about losing you. When he was younger, he worried about losing sight of you; now, he is fearful that you will not come back, that you will die while you are away from him, and he'll be deprived of you forever. Again, a good way to reassure your child is to go step by step through what's going to happen when you leave him. The more details you give, and the more you can confirm the details, the better. What you might say is, "When Daddy comes home, we're both going to get ready to go out to visit Auntie Sarah. Then we'll put you to bed and we'll have our usual song, story, and game. I'll lie on your bed and cuddle you while we talk about your day. I won't leave you until you're fast asleep, and the next thing you'll know is that it's morning and Mummy will be there."

# A sibling on the way

Your child is bound to feel pretty distressed at the thought of a new baby brother or sister and the "dethronement" that he thinks will follow. Take all the precautions you can to make him feel good about the baby. Refer to the baby as his new sister or brother, and let him feel your tummy as the baby grows and kicks. Show him where the baby is going to sleep, and teach him all kinds of helpful things he can do to look after her. If you are having the baby in hospital, make sure your child is at ease with the person who is going to look after him while you're there.

When you come home from hospital, have someone else carry the baby; it's important for you to have your arms free to scoop your child up and give him a big cuddle. Don't turn to the new baby until he asks to see her. Make sure that you bring home a present from the baby for him. If you have to stay in hospital, let him visit you as often as you like, and when he does, make sure that the baby is not in your arms, but is lying in a cot at your side so you're free to hold your child.

# Over-tiredness

A child of this age very often becomes over-excited and over-tired towards bedtime. He'll try to put off his bedtime for as long as possible, and become more distressed. Your child might become so fragile that any small discomfort or frustration will make him start to cry inconsolably.

If you're expecting your child to have a late evening, or a special treat such as a party or a school play, make sure he has a nap during the day so that his energy will last. If he does become over-excited and over-tired, it's especially important that you remain calm and quiet. Talk to him gently, give him lots of cuddles, be infinitely patient, and take him gently to his bedroom. Sing him a song or read a story until he has quietened down.

# Tantrums

**Young children usually have tantrums out of frustration or because they are pitting their will against that of others.**

Older children have tantrums because they can think of no other way of showing their determination. In the privacy of your own home the best way to deal with a tantrum is simply to ignore it and leave the room.

It's slightly more difficult, however, in public, but don't fuss, shout, or get flustered. Take your child calmly into a quiet place and attempt to calm him down. If you're in a shop take him out into the street, or into your car, or out of the restaurant into the toilet.

▲ **AFTER THE TANTRUM** Once your toddler has calmed down, talk to him and give him a reassuring cuddle.

## Fears

**Three years is a highly anxious age, but by four years your child's fears are more clearly defined.**

He'll be easily frightened by sounds, for example, especially loud sounds outside, such as a fire engine. He may fear people of a different culture or appearance from himself, old people, "bogey men", the dark, animals, and your leaving him – especially at night. Children of this age may enjoy being mildly frightened by an adult in play, as long as it's clearly pretend.

By five years your child will probably have more concrete, down-to-earth fears, like bodily harm, falling, dogs, sounds, thunder, lightning, rain, storms (especially at night), and that his mother will not return home or be at home when he gets there.

Just as dislike of certain foods is suggested by chance remarks made by adults, fear of animals, cars, and thunder are suggested in a similar way. Gruesome tales and stories about ghosts, devils, and suchlike may terrify a young child and lead to serious sleep disturbance. For this reason, you should choose bedtime stories carefully, don't let your child watch scary television programmes just before bedtime, and never deliberately frighten him with stories of "bogey men" to make him behave.

# Crying in a preschooler

By the age of three or four, children cry a great deal and may whinge if their wants are not met and/or there's nothing interesting to play with. A five-year-old child cries much less, although he may cry if he's cross, tired, or can't have his own way. Crying doesn't usually last as long now, and your child may be able to control it and hold his tears back. He is rarely moody and may be as right as rain as soon as the crying is over. He may whine occasionally, although a lot less than he did at four years. This phase may pass, however, and give way to temper tantrums with loud, angry crying and banging about. There may be a return of moodiness, whining, and expressions of resentment, but you can often get your child to laugh when he's crying by joking with him. Your child may become astonishingly brave about real injuries yet still cry at small hurts.

## Bad dreams and nightmares

Between the ages of three and five years, children quite often have bad dreams. Your child may walk or talk in his sleep, or have night terrors. This is normal because while his understanding of the world is growing, he can't entirely make sense of it, and so he goes to sleep with unresolved questions. He's also getting more in touch with his feelings and he knows what it is to be afraid or feel something isn't quite right. These feelings come out at night.

Often a child can't explain his dreams and has difficulty in going back to sleep. Animals may chase your child during a nightmare, or he may dream of strange, bad, or odd-looking people, fires, and deep water. Only if your child wakes up should you try to console him. If he remains asleep, don't wake him; simply stay by him. If he's sleepwalking periodically you must put a gate across the stairs.

**Night terrors** Sometimes you'll find your child in bed, apparently awake, terrified, and possibly thrashing and screaming. He may be angry or desperately upset. This is a night terror rather than a nightmare, and it can be alarming. You'll feel anguished at your child's fear and pain, but all you can do is stay close and wait for the terror to pass. You can't reassure your child specifically, because he's beyond reason. Don't leave or scold him; that would simply make it worse.

## Preschool nerves

A child who goes to preschool without a backward glance, says goodbye to his mother, and gets straight into play is rather unusual. Most children harbour fears of a strange place with strange people and separation from you. You have to give your child both the time and the opportunity to adjust to this quite frightening change in his life.

You can do much to allay your child's fears by familiarizing him with the journey to school, the entrance to the school, his classroom, some of the children who will be in his class, his teacher, where the games are, and what some of the routines are. Most teachers will welcome your taking your child along to the school several times before he starts so that he can feel comfortable in his new surroundings. Make the first visit as casual as possible. Stay for only a few minutes, so that your child doesn't get bored or frightened, and don't make him do anything he doesn't want to.

**Making separation easy**  The first morning at preschool is likely to be difficult for both of you. It may be that you have to stay with your child for the whole morning, but this shouldn't happen more than once. Don't forget that it's a great transition for him to make, so be patient. Many nursery schools will welcome your staying to give your child confidence. Eventually, when your child realizes that you're not going to leave him, he'll be happy to get on with his classroom routines as long as you sit somewhere quiet and discreet.

Maybe during the first morning, but certainly on the second, suggest that you're going out to buy a newspaper, but come back within five minutes, so that your child is reassured. Don't go if your child gets very distressed at the prospect of your leaving. Once he's happy, suggest that you leave again, this time for about half an hour, and come back in exactly the time you said you would. Over the next few days, leave for longer and longer periods according to how your child reacts. Some children adapt quickly to preschool and you won't need to stay after the first few days.

Others may still want you to stay for about half an hour at the end of two weeks. Just fit in with your child. The most important thing is that your child should feel that school is a happy place and that it's not associated with the unhappiness of being separated from you. A good teacher will advise you when she thinks the time is right for you to leave.

▶ **STARTING PRESCHOOL** Once your child is engrossed in some activity she may hardly even notice when you leave.

# Family conflicts

**Your child will become very distressed indeed if he thinks that the people dearest in the world to him, his mother and father, no longer love each other, and that there's a danger that they may separate or leave him.**

Children are extremely sensitive to atmospheres within the home so if you and your partner are going through a bad time, behave caringly and affectionately in front of your child and show that you have concern for each other. Witnessing a row is one of the most harmful experiences you can inflict on your child, so that thought should act as a deterrent.

On the other hand, I don't believe in a united front between parents on every question. Your child should understand that it's all right for mum and dad to have different opinions, as long as they are expressed without acrimony.

Children have to get used to conflict because they're going to meet it very quickly when they leave home. The best place for them to become familiar with it is in the security of their own home.

Most children will blame themselves for any conflict between their parents and will go to great lengths to make you friends again. Reassure your child that he isn't to blame for any anger that you feel towards your partner, and that you love him regardless.

# Physical development

Young children are often said to be "into everything". And so they should be. Their bodies need almost constant activity in order to develop normally. Woe betide the toddler or preschooler who isn't encouraged to run around, or, worse, is left parked with a snack in front of the television.

## Body milestones

When your child first starts to toddle, he has very little control over his movements. But from about 18 months onward, your child will quickly progress in getting around. He'll be very active on his feet, perfecting his walking and balancing skills, and you can encourage this development by involving him in your daily activities. He'll begin to enjoy ball games, playing with toys on wheels, and games that involve hopping, jumping, or climbing. Spend time with your child, encouraging him in his new skills and helping to build up his confidence: it will be vital in his continuing physical development.

**18 months to two years** Your child will be able to go up and down stairs alone, but he'll put two feet on each step before moving on to the next. He'll kick a ball successfully without falling over. Dance with him – it will give him practice in making a wide range of movements.

**Two-and-a-half years** He'll be able to walk on tiptoe, jump in the air, and on and off objects. However, he won't be able to stand on one foot yet. Provide him with a moving toy with wheels that he can sit on and use his feet to propel. He's probably too young for a tricycle, but there are many simpler moving toys you can get that are suitable.

**Three years** By this time your child has become much more nimble, walking up stairs with confidence. Your child can jump off the bottom step and stand on one foot for a second. He can swing his arms when he walks and ride a tricycle. He'll probably enjoy playing jumping games, such as hopscotch, which are also a good way of working off excess energy.

**Four years** Now he is very active and well coordinated. He can even carry a drink without spilling it. He races about, hopping, jumping, and climbing, and can walk down stairs rapidly, with one foot per step. Show him how to use a skipping rope. All his muscles are working together now and play such as this gives him a workout for a wide range of movements.

**Five years** By this age your child's coordination is finely developed. He can walk in a straight line, go down stairs on alternating feet, skip a rope with alternating feet, climb confidently, and enjoy fast-moving toys and games. Take him to playgrounds with a wide range of equipment and, if you have a garden, think about installing a climbing frame on the grass which provides lots of scope for muscular activities.

**Setbacks** If your child has a setback in the development of physical skills, don't worry. He's learning so much at the moment that it's quite understandable that he may slow down in one aspect of his development to concentrate on another; he may also suffer lapses after an illness. Just relax and let your child develop at his own pace, while still providing all the help and encouragement you can.

## Out and about

Your toddler or preschooler will want, quite naturally, to race about as much as possible, but out of doors you'll have to be careful. He'll have no traffic sense as yet, so you'll either have to hold his hand or use reins. I believe that reins are the most satisfactory solution for both of you: they hurt neither your arm nor your child's and they give him far greater freedom than he would have holding your hand. If you're in a hurry, or can't bear the idea of having to make constant stops and starts to look at things, take a pushchair of some sort and use that when you need to.

# Development in boys

The pace of development is affected by many things and gender is one of them; boys and girls develop according to different "timetables". In general, boys:

■ begin to talk at a later stage than girls and are more prone to language disorders

■ tend to be less sociable than girls and more interested in objects than in people

■ usually walk later than girls

■ are more likely than girls to grow in sudden spurts

■ refine jumping, running, and throwing after the preschool years

■ are more aggressive, competitive, and rebellious than girls

■ are more vulnerable to stress than girls and are more likely to have behavioural problems.

◄ **HOPPING AND JUMPING (FAR LEFT)** Contrary to most people's expectations, young girls are better than boys at hopping and jumping games.

◄ **ACTIVE PLAY (LEFT)** Encourage your child to enjoy active play, which helps develop potential. But make sure he understands safety rules, such as wearing a helmet when on a bike.

## Encouraging girls

It's just as important to encourage girls as well as boys to be curious and active, and to let off steam with physical activity.

■ Don't be over-concerned about your little girl hurting herself or getting her clothes dirty; this attitude can inhibit your child from discovering her physical potential.

■ Girls are more naturally sociable, so encourage them to play team or cooperative games such as hopscotch or skipping.

■ Play games with your child that include energetic movements, such as "Simon says".

■ Girls tend to be more gifted at imaginative role-play games, so encourage your little girl to include more physical creativity, with constructional and spatial skills, in her fantasy games.

■ Never hamper your daughter's adventurousness and curiosity; encourage her to climb and swing as you would a son.

# Physical play

If your child is encouraged to be physically active and adventurous, he'll be willing to push himself to the limit and develop his full potential. If you are overprotective and don't allow your child to test his abilities, master a new skill, and move on, you will hold him back and he'll lack coordination and confidence as a result. It's important to separate his fears from yours; his fears will make him circumspect and sensible, while your fears will cripple both his curiosity and spirit. He needs to discover for himself the limits of what is safe and feasible.

## Scope for activity

Through the toddler and preschool years your child has boundless energy, and is ready to tackle more demanding activities, so give him plenty of scope: running, climbing, and pedalling will improve his skill and help him burn off surplus energy. Depending on your child's skill and confidence, he may be ready to tackle roller skating or riding a bicycle with stabilizing wheels. Introducing your child to sports and other activities now could lay the foundations for a lifetime of enjoyment, so give him the chance to try out a wide variety of different activities, such as swimming, dancing, or football. At the very least, make sure he has somewhere he can run, climb, or kick a ball about.

**Give him guidance** You can always help your child to tackle new and difficult tasks at first, holding his hand and guiding him through them so that you are secure in your own mind that he's competent and therefore safe in whatever he's doing. Extend adventurousness and curiosity in your child across the board, not just in physical development but with toys, music, painting, books, and games. Encourage him to find out as much about the world as he possibly can.

▲ **SQUATTING** At 18 to 20 months your child can bend to pick up objects without toppling over. Show him how to squat – this helps the development of his hip and knee muscles, and he'll find it a useful position when he's playing with toys on the floor. He'll soon become more and more confident with this type of movement.

**▼ RUNNING** By 20 months or so your child will be able to run quite well, but will have difficulty turning corners and may topple over if she stops suddenly. The muscles that control running are still not quite strong enough.

**▼ CLIMBING STAIRS** At two years old your child will be able to go up and down the stairs by himself without holding on. But he'll still need to put both feet on each step before moving on to the next one.

# Encouraging boys

Boys are assumed and encouraged to be adventurous in their play, but it is a mistake to assume that all boys are outgoing and active. Some boys have an obvious preference for boisterous games while others prefer quiet contemplative activities.

■ Games on large soft cushions and foam-filled furniture are excellent fun and good for promoting balance and coordination.

■ Boys are usually considered to be better at "spatial relationships".

■ Provide plenty of opportunities for your little boy to be creative. Give him saved-up household items such as toilet roll tubes, egg boxes, and yogurt cartons to play with; these items can be turned into almost anything his imagination can conjure up.

**▲ OUTDOOR PLAY** Tricycles and other wheeled toys are lots of fun for preschoolers and help improve their muscle strength. Pedalling also helps your child to develop his coordination skills. If you have a garden, perhaps you can also set aside a special outdoor activity space for your child, such as a sandpit or climbing frame.

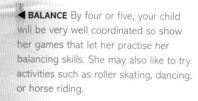

**◀ BALANCE** By four or five, your child will be very well coordinated so show her games that let her practise her balancing skills. She may also like to try activities such as roller skating, dancing, or horse riding.

1

## Encouraging independence

**With so many new skills to learn at this stage, it's important not to expect your child to develop at a rate that is too fast for him.**

All children progress at their own pace, which is decided by the speed that their developing brain and nerves allow. Your child will want to please you, and may try to do things that are more complicated than his development will allow. Failure is demoralizing because he feels he's let you down. A better approach is to give him all the encouragement he needs, showing him how pleased you are with every task he manages, without setting him goals that are beyond his abilities.

# Using hands

From 18 months onwards' you'll notice some dramatic changes, especially in the way your child uses his hands. He'll learn to dress himself and to manage increasingly fine movements. His creative skills improve too, as his building-block houses get more complicated and his drawings more recognizable. Help his development by giving him every chance to do things for himself.

◀ **HAND SKILL MILESTONES** Your child will try an "unscrewing" movement with jar tops and door knobs by the age of two. He'll use crayons more deliberately and may be able to build a tower of four blocks. He may just be able to do up a zip fastener.

▲ **FINE MOVEMENTS** Your child will be able to thread large beads or spools on a string by the time she's about two-and-a-half years old.

◀ **GETTING DRESSED** At two-and-a-half, putting on and taking off clothes will become easier and your child will be increasingly eager to do these things for herself.

## Everyday tasks

As his hand skills improve, all sorts of everyday tasks are now becoming possible for your child to manage by himself, so be patient and give him the opportunity to do things without your help.

**Washing and dressing** By the age of two, your child will be able to cope with a number of dressing skills, though putting on his socks, shoes, and gloves will still be tricky, so let him choose his own clothes and practise getting dressed. Clothes with press studs and fairly large buttons, provided the holes are not too tight, will also encourage him to develop new finger skills. Continue to encourage his dressing ability and he'll soon be able to put on and take off underpants, trousers, and T-shirts.

At three he will probably be able to fasten and unfasten buttons by himself, including the smaller ones, so he'll be able to dress and undress himself completely if he wishes.

A four-year-old will be able to wash his own face and hands so encourage him in this. He'll like to brush his teeth too, but you'll have to go over them again afterwards to make sure they're properly clean.

## Improving dexterity

As soon as your child can turn a door knob with two hands and open a loose-fitting screw-top jar, give him toys that need to be fitted together. More complicated toys, especially construction or craft toys, will help him to practise and develop his skills.

Ensure that your two-year-old has plenty of colourful picture books to hand as he can now turn the pages of a book one at a time by himself. Your child can now build a tower of four blocks and with encouragement he'll make more complicated structures. Building blocks that need pressing and fitting together will help develop the small movements of his hands. Intricate tasks, such as threading large beads or playing with little construction bricks will further boost his manipulation skills. By the time he's three, your child will be able to build a tower nine blocks high and he'll also be starting to use scissors – this is a huge step forward in brain/muscle coordination.

Toddlers and preschoolers are great experimenters, so you can feed your child's curiosity by opening up his world with a variety of other activities.

**Gardening** Give your child a small plot in the garden that's entirely his and show him how to handle tiny seeds and young plants very carefully. Help him plant some quick-growing flowers such as marigolds, or vegetables such as radishes, runner beans, or peas. He'll love to help pick them when they are ready, and may even eat the vegetables!

## Touching himself

Children usually become aware of their bodies, including genital organs, towards the end of the first year but handle them without any obvious pleasure, just curiosity.

By the time your child is a toddler, handling may bring a mildly pleasurable sensation. Later on most children of both sexes fiddle with themselves and it is perfectly normal behaviour.

There is no reason to discourage it or show disapproval. If you do, the child will grow guilty and secretive. If your child masturbates in public, try to distract him rather than scolding or showing disapproval.

1

▲ **CONSTRUCTION TOYS** Building blocks are popular toys for toddlers and preschoolers, and ideal for developing hand movements and dexterity.

# Helping around the home

Your preschooler will enjoy helping around the house, and he'll see this as a form of play because he's keen to copy everything that you do.

■ Show him how to help prepare the vegetables and salad for lunch by snapping the tops of beans and tearing lettuce leaves.

■ He'll love setting the table for meals and getting everything in the right place.

■ Encourage him to keep his own things tidy and put them away at the end of the day.

■ Show him how to sort the clean laundry for you, putting all the socks into pairs.

▲ **LET HIM HELP** Help your child develop his feelings of confidence and independence by encouraging him to do simple tasks, such as preparing a snack, for himself. Show him what to do and leave him to it.

**Taking things apart** Many children of four or five and upwards love taking anything mechanical to pieces, so don't throw away old clocks, cameras, or record players when they break; let your child have fun taking them to pieces.

**Jigsaws** If possible, try to buy puzzles with pieces that are easily identifiable when the puzzle's apart. Your child will find it much easier if he can see that there is an arm, leg, or tree on a piece rather than just a shape. Wooden jigsaws are easier to handle and don't bend like the cardboard variety. If you find your child still has trouble holding the pieces, make it easier for him by gluing on small plastic hooks from a hardware store.

With some jigsaws you may have to show your child exactly how to assemble the pieces. When you do this explain to him why certain pieces go together and interlock: "Look, this bit has two bumps that look like eyebrows and this piece is for the head that always goes on top of the body." Once you've done this and helped your child through it himself a couple of times, he'll happily sit and do it over and over again. If you have a number of puzzles, make them easier to sort by marking the pieces of each one with a different coloured pen.

You can make your own puzzles out of your child's favourite picture by pasting it on to heavy card and covering it with clear contact film. With a craft knife, cut the puzzle into roughly equal-size pieces made up of triangles, diamonds, and squares.

**Drawing and painting** Children from the age of about two enjoy drawing, so give your child plenty of drawing materials, including a range of different crayons, and start him off by showing the effect of all the different colours. He will also enjoy using paints, especially if you allow him to be messy and paint with his hands. You can also help him relate his drawings to the world around him by naming the colours of the crayons and then pointing out the same colours in everyday objects. By two-and-a-half years, his pictures will become more recognizable, and by four to five years, he'll be producing images of people and familiar objects.

**Spatter painting** Your preschooler might enjoy trying out spatter painting. To do this, place leaves, grasses, coins, whatever shape he wants, flat on to a piece of white paper. Then show him how to take a toothbrush, soak it with paint, and gently draw a blunt knife across it so that the paint is spattered randomly across the paper. To make his spatter paintings look even more exciting he can try using several different colours. When the paint is dry, remove the objects.

**▼MAKING THINGS** Your child's ability to use scissors represents a huge step forward in hand skills. Give him simple models to make. Any scissors he uses should be blunt-ended.

**▼HELPING IN THE KITCHEN** Your child will enjoy helping with cooking and preparing meals. She'll like to measure out ingredients, cut out shapes from pastry, and decorate dishes.

# Drawing

Your child's improving manual dexterity is clearly demonstrated by his ability to copy a circle. His skill develops rapidly between the age of two-and-a-half and three-and-a-half years.

**▲TWO-AND-A-HALF YEARS** His earliest attempts at a circle may end up like a spiral.

**▲THREE YEARS** His attempts become more controlled, but the lines may not quite join up or may overshoot.

**▲THREE-AND-A-HALF YEARS** Your child should be able to draw a true circle or an oval shape.

**▲DRAWING PICTURES** Your child will love drawing so give her lots of paper and big fat pencils and crayons to play with. Encourage her by putting some of her pictures up on a big noticeboard for everyone to see.

## Imagination

Most children over the age of 15 months or so begin to develop a vivid imagination, and there are substantial individual differences. In general, the greater the intelligence, the greater the imagination.

Between 15 and 18 months, imagination begins to appear in doll play. At three years your child will have imaginary playmates behind the sofa and he'll tell tall stories and play highly imaginative games with friends. His imagination may lead to the development of fears: of the dark, of noises, or of animals, for example. He may even start to have bad dreams.

▲ FUN IN THE GARDEN Your toddler will love having his own watering can and trowel so he can help in the garden.

# Mental development

Your child is now starting to become an independent person. From now until he starts school, his speech will progress by leaps and bounds. He'll be able to ask for what he wants, and do some of the things you want him to do – if he so chooses. He'll have an insatiable curiosity about his world and everything in it.

**18 months** Your toddler will be able to ask for food, drinks, and toys when he wants them. He probably tells you when he wants to go to the potty, but he can't wait and so has frequent accidents. He'll carry out several simple requests and begin to understand more complex ones, such as "Please get your hairbrush from the bathroom." He may also grab your arm or use other gestures to get your attention. His vocabulary may consist of about 30 words.

**Two years** Your child's vocabulary of names and objects will increase rapidly. He'll describe and identify familiar items. He'll obey complicated orders, and find a toy that he played with before. He'll talk non-stop and ask occasional questions.

Shortly after this, he'll know who he is and be able to say his own name. He'll try to build houses and castles with blocks, and repeat new words when encouraged. He'll begin to pit his will against yours and may become rather negative – saying "no" fairly often and not always fitting in with your wishes. He may know the difference between one and several, but he has little idea of the magnitude of numbers and so anything more than one may be "lots".

**Two-and-a-half to three years** Your child will start to add detail to broad concepts, as in "A horse has a long tail", and be able to draw horizontal and vertical lines. He'll be able to say one or two nursery rhymes and find them in his book, and he'll know some of his colours. He will also begin to ask "why?" and say "won't" and "can't". He may make an attempt at copying a circle that you have drawn for him (see p.189), but probably won't be able to complete it. Your child will now enjoy helping you with household tasks.

He will begin to grasp the concept of numbers and may be able to count to three. A boy will have noticed that his sex organs stick out from his body, in contrast to those of little girls he has seen.

Your child can understand prepositions, such as "in", "on", "under", "behind", and "after". At around three years old, your child will be able to form more complex sentences and his vocabulary may consist of 200–300 words. This, together with his ever-increasing curiosity, will lead him to ask incessant questions. He can distinguish between "now" and "then" and will refer to the past. He knows his own gender. He'll become more sociable and like to play with others.

## Reasoning

As a toddler, your child may have satisfied his curiosity, absorbing a great deal of new information in the process, but rarely related it to anything else in his life. What happens from the third year, however, is that your child starts to think about his experiences and to learn from them. Information is sifted, matched up to other experiences to see if they fit together, or if they differ greatly, and it is then put into similar or different pigeonholes. Your child is learning to reason.

Your child starts to plan ahead, and becomes much more creative and imaginative. Gradually all the information that he has absorbed so far becomes available to apply to a given situation. This new ability to think, imagine, and create changes his perception of the world. Many familiar things in the house or garden no longer contain the same interest. He needs wider horizons; he needs to explore. Your child becomes very interested in how things work and he's greedy for information.

Another huge step is the realization that time is not just in the present: there is today, yesterday, and tomorrow. Planning for the future is a critical aspect of our intellect. It's during his third year that you'll hear him say for the first time, "I'll eat that later" or "We can go tomorrow".

## Forming concepts

This is an important step forward for him. One way in which it will be obvious is when, between the ages of 18 months and two years, he starts sorting objects as a form of play: he might sort his building blocks out from his other toys, for example. You'll notice, too, that he's begun to understand how things are grouped: he knows, for instance, that his ball and an apple are similar in shape and that they roll; that animals that bark and have four legs are dogs.

Some time before his third birthday, your child will begin to give these concepts names – round, dog. He'll use the names in all cases where they are appropriate – whether the dog in question, for instance, is a family pet, a dog he sees on television or in a book, or a toy dog. By the time he is three years old, he'll describe things in a way that shows he also understands their differences: "our dog", "toy dog".

# Colours

To help your child grasp the notion of colour, always mention the colour of something that you're using or wanting.

■ Household items: "I'm looking for the green packet"; "Where's that red tin gone?"

■ Your child's clothes: "That's a pretty pink dress"; "What a nice red jumper".

■ Flowers, animals, and especially birds: "Can you see the robin's red breast?"

■ Show your child how colours are made: "Look, if we mix a little bit of red with this white we will get pink; yellow mixed with blue will make green"

■ Teach your child the colours of the rainbow and get him to pick them out if you see a real rainbow.

# Giftedness

It is tempting to think your child is gifted if he's further ahead than others in one or two areas.

Truly gifted children, however, are advanced in most aspects of achievement and in the acquisition of skills. They will enjoy all kinds of brain exercises and may even find some of them very easy. A gifted child invariably learns quickly and is able to use that learning in a broad and flexible way. If this applies to your child, it will be important to provide him with plenty of stimulation, new games, new ideas for play, and plenty of creative opportunities. Otherwise he is liable to become bored and frustrated if he's not being stretched by his play (see p.251).

## Preschool years

The development of your child as an independent and reasoning individual blossoms during the preschool years. He'll speak much more fluently and he'll start to relate speech to the written word. He'll also be much more imaginative in his play so that he'll keep himself amused for longer periods and rely less on your involvement.

One of the best ways of helping your child is to listen to what he's saying. His world is expanding at a colossal rate; it's important to try to understand his thinking and answer questions in ways he can relate to.

**Three years**  He will want to help with simple household tasks, such as sweeping up or laying the table. His steadily improving grasp of shapes and understanding of sequences will mean he can solve more complex puzzles, such as rearranging pictures into the correct order, or copying a design. His make-believe play will be more vivid as he invents people and objects and puts them into more complex situations, which is why girls enjoy playhouses and boys make camps. And he's beginning to understand that some enjoyable things must be put off to the future, such as a visit to a favourite relative, or being able to buy an ice cream.

**Four years**  He is more independent and more self-centred at the age of four. He may be cheeky, and more argumentative about getting his own way. He will have mastered the concepts of past, present, and future, although he may not understand how near or far off his birthday is.

**Five years**  He'll be more sensible and controlled, and will be able to play games that have more complicated rules. He'll be able to appreciate clock time and it will help him relate to a

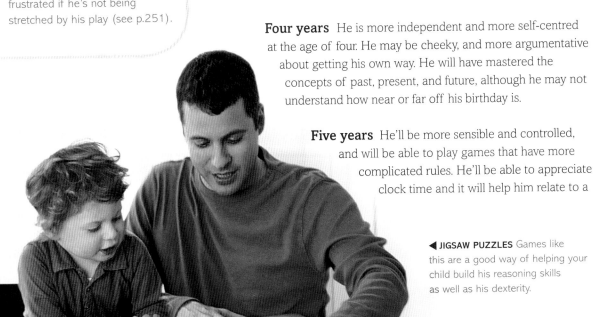

◀ JIGSAW PUZZLES Games like this are a good way of helping your child build his reasoning skills as well as his dexterity.

▶ **MAKE-BELIEVE PLAY** Your child will love creating a world of his own. Put up a play tent in the garden, so he can make a "camp", or make one indoors by draping a sheet over two chairs.

daily routine. His sense of humour will be more developed now and he'll be able to tell simple jokes and act out comical situations.

# Perception

Perceptual style – the way in which a child takes in a situation – depends on whether he is able to shut out the background or takes a lot of notice of it. The former is called field independence and the latter, field dependence.

Measurements of field independence or dependence show a strong difference between girls and boys. Boys are usually more field independent, and are therefore able to pick out a shape from a complicated background more easily than girls. This could be because boys are generally far better at spatial visualization at a much earlier age than girls are.

It can be quite helpful to know if your child is field independent in his interests and personality. If he is, he'll generally be able to focus on objects or tasks, while field-dependent children tend to focus more on people. This may account for the fact that baby girls, being more field dependent, are much more sociable from the outset than boys.

# Testing perception

You can assess your child's field dependence or independence by seeing whether or not he is able to pick out a geometric shape from a complicated drawing. Show your child a shape, such as a circle, square, or triangle, and then ask him to find a figure exactly like that in a more complex drawing.

In order to find the figure, your child has to ignore the background detail (the field) and pay attention only to shapes. Generally speaking, children become increasingly field independent as they get older. After a while you will be able to introduce more complicated shapes – such as a hidden animal – in more and more complex backgrounds.

If your child is more field dependent, he'll need more outside clues, and so will rely on your prompting and your encouragement. In contrast, however, your field-independent child, because of his greater ability to extract parts from wholes, will tend to be better at some cognitive tasks, particularly those that require good spatial sense He may be good at playing games such as chess, for example.

# Learning difficulties

**Children learn at different rates so apparent problems, such as a delay in learning to read, may simply be a normal variation in timing, rather than a sign of any disability. But there may be other signs that might indicate a learning difficulty of which you should be aware.**

■ Learning difficulties rarely occur alone. They are usually part of a broader picture including perhaps poor coordination, poor memory, and the inability to draw and to fit differently shaped blocks into matching holes in a board.

■ Common features that accompany learning difficulties include a short attention span, aimless over-activity, poor concentration, impulsiveness, aggressiveness, and clumsiness. Eyesight and hearing should be tested in a child like this in order to pick up any possible weaknesses.

■ Dyslexia is a learning difficulty that should be spotted early on. Commonly called word-blindness, this condition is part of a wider spectrum of learning problems including difficulty in spelling and writing. Early signs include delayed language development, apparent hearing problems, and clumsiness, but a proper diagnosis can only be made by a professional child psychologist (see p.253).

## A stimulating environment

One of the ways you can really encourage a child's development is to foster creative play with an inviting environment.

Simply the way you display your child's toys can, to a large extent, determine whether they'll be played with or not. When toys are piled higgledy-piggledy in a toy box, they're not inviting to a child. Well-displayed, orderly toys arranged into little scenes stimulate him to play and to make other creative arrangements. It also helps to have particular play areas, like a sand tray, a painting table, and somewhere your child can splash about with water.

# Learning through play

Play encourages learning in many ways. It improves manual dexterity – building a tower of blocks or doing a jigsaw puzzle teaches a child how to make his hands work for him as tools. Playing with other children teaches him it's important to get on with others; he'll discover friendship and learn to be kind to other people.

Social play helps to make a child's language more sophisticated because the more imaginative the play, the more complex the ideas that have to be put into words. Play aids physical development; the freedom to swing, climb, skip, run, and jump helps to perfect muscular coordination and physical skills. Play also improves hearing and vision considerably.

## Play for a toddler

Up to two years of age, your child will spend longer on toys that he can use independently, particularly those that imitate the adult world. Dolls, toy houses, and cars, for example, enable him to act out the scenes he sees in real life. As he gets older, he'll acquire new skills and enjoy anything that tests them – building and knocking down, or constructing and taking apart. Household items, such as plastic containers and cardboard tubes, will stimulate his imagination.

**Dolls** Girls and boys love dolls; dolls are children's pretend families, helping them to create a make-believe world into which they can

◀ **LEARNING TO CLASSIFY** Farmyard animal toys help your child learn how to put things in groups and distinguish whether things are the same or different.

escape. While playing with dolls, your child is understanding human emotions, re-enacting the things that happen to him, such as getting dressed, having a bath, being tucked in to bed and kissed goodnight, and learning to relate them to other people. Even action dolls for boys can bring out protective feelings. A child can also use dolls to get rid of aggressive instincts that might otherwise be directed against others.

**Water play** Children love playing with water, especially in the bath. Give your child empty plastic bottles and containers so that he can create a variety of water effects. Small, blow-up paddling pools are ideal in the summer. Another summer game is to lay a tarpaulin on the ground and spray water over it; your child will enjoy sliding around on the slippery surface. Children love blowing bubbles: put some washing-up liquid in a beaker and shape a pipe-cleaner with a circle at one end.

**Creative activities** Drawing, painting, making shapes with modelling clay, and fitting together puzzles all encourage creativity. Long before he can write or draw formally, your child will love scribbling and using colours, so give him crayons and lots of paper. A box of coloured chalks and a blackboard and easel, set up at his height, will be useful because he'll be able to draw, then rub out his work and start all over again.

Your child will love using paints. Plastic egg boxes make excellent paint palettes. He'll enjoy finger painting and can create interesting prints and patterns with combs, pegs, sponges, cotton reels, or cardboard tubes. Try cutting shapes out of pieces of potato so that he can print his own patterns. Give your child thick brushes or provide pastry brushes, cotton wool balls, corks, straws, and pipe-cleaners for variety.

### Helping around the home

Children love being part of the domestic routine. A young child can be given a little bowl with some flour to mix each time you bake; or give him his own small dustpan and brush so that he can help you with the cleaning.

▲**MIRRORING THEIR WORLD** Children love to play with toys that allow them to copy and re-enact scenes from the world they see around them.

# Outdoor safety

Once your child is old enough to have large toys to play with outside, you'll need to bear new safety precautions in mind. If you take safety precautions the risk of serious accidents can be greatly reduced.

■ Young children should always be properly supervised, and never left alone to play outdoors, especially in paddling pools.

■ Outdoor play equipment, such as slides and swings, should be checked regularly for strength, stability, and signs of corrosion. It should be installed on a soft, flat surface, such as grass or sand – never on concrete.

■ Check all of your outdoor play equipment to ensure that there is no risk of scissoring, shearing, or pinching injuries and that surfaces are free from snags and splinters.

■ Instruct your children carefully on safety and what they can and can't do on play equipment.

■ Ensure that tents, playhouses, and tunnels are made of flame-retardant material.

■ Make sure that sandpits are covered when not in use to stop animals fouling them.

■ Fence off ponds and pools, and if there's a gate keep it locked.

■ Always empty a paddling pool after use.

## Outings

Your child's insatiable curiosity needs more stimulation than your home can offer, so go to the local park regularly and plan outings to a wildlife park or to the beach or countryside.

■ Let your child know in advance what to expect, say by reading a book with him, so he'll get the most out of the experience.

■ Talk about items of interest, take crayons and paper, or a colouring book, and encourage him to draw what he sees.

■ The seaside is full of new sights, sounds, and smells. Don't forget a bucket and spade; sand castles are a perennial favourite.

■ Provide a cheap camera to make a record of the trip and put his photos in an album.

## Play and development – the preschool child

Play will continue to make a positive contribution to your preschool child's development. Once he has practised his creative interests at play, he can apply them to the real world. Sometimes your child will be completely absorbed in a make-believe world of his own and won't need your involvement: at other times you can add to his enjoyment by suggesting new games, or new ways to play with his toys.

**Make-believe play**  Your child will create a little world of his own as part of his imitation of adults. An instant tent or playhouse can be made from a couple of chairs or a small table draped with a blanket. Children love playing with cardboard boxes, as long as they are big enough to climb into. Small ones become boats and cars; piles of them turn into castles and houses. Boxes laid on their sides are tunnels, and laid end to end become trains.

Dressing up is a favourite game at this age: a few simple props can transform your child into a doctor or firefighter and, in his fantasy world, he is the adult, and a teddy bear or doll serves as the child. It often surprised me who my sons thought were family.

**Messy play**  Any play involving water, sand, mud, or dough will stretch your child's intellect. Your child may build a wall in the sandpit, which then becomes a castle, or he may simply enjoy playing with a bucket full of water and floating objects that keep popping up to the surface no matter how often he pushes them down. To make your supervision easier, set aside a time when messy play is allowed and a place where the mess can be contained, and encourage your child to look forward to it.

▶ **MAKE BELIEVE** Playing with puppets and putting on puppet shows allow your child to discover the exciting worlds that she can create using her developing imagination and verbal skills.

▲ **DOMESTIC HELP** Your child will love it when you ask him to help you with domestic tasks and will respond enthusiastically to being involved in the household in this way.

## Simple games

Your child at four or five is old enough to understand simple board games. He'll enjoy uncomplicated games involving a spinning wheel, dice, or moving pieces, as well as card games that rely on pictures, such as "Old Maid" and "Snap".

■ Many games will help him improve his counting skills and also his developing ability to concentrate. Games with rules that have to be followed carefully can serve as an introduction to the concept that the real world is full of accepted standards.

■ He'll have to learn to take his turn and to wait patiently while others take theirs. This will help him to realize that other people have rights and needs that sometimes take priority over his.

■ The winning and losing element of games will teach him to understand and cope with disappointment and to try harder next time, as well as enjoy the success of winning. Don't concentrate too much on winning; it could make him unduly aggressive and competitive in later life.

**Domestic play** By now your child has mastered the coordination needed to help around the house. For him it's play rather than work because he's so keen to copy you. He helps in the kitchen by tearing salad leaves or arranging bread on a plate, and will enjoy laying the table, so improving his manipulative and counting skills as well as his independence and sense of self-worth.

**Musical play** Any child with normal hearing can hear and enjoy musical sounds. He probably won't be able to play melodies, but he may be able to hum them and will enjoy banging out a rhythm. Rattles, wooden clappers, trumpets, and drums are all very good for this purpose, as are old pans, pan lids, or baking tins and wooden spoons. A xylophone will enable him to identify musical sounds and experiment with high and low notes and even play his own tunes. It's best not to buy a xylophone or other musical instrument until he's shown interest over the long term and then it's worth investing in a good-quality one from a music shop, which will be better for your child's developing ear.

## Sharing toys

Your child wants to be sociable so he has to learn the difficult skill of sharing with other people. It's easiest if he learns to share with you first, so set him a good example: "Here's some of Mummy's ice cream for you to share"; "You can have half of my apple". Then introduce the concept of "One for you, one for me". Only then say "May I have your pencil?"; "May I play with your dolly?", and introduce the idea gradually.

## Language in girls

Right from the moment of birth, girls are more responsive to the human voice than boys are, and they have better verbal skills throughout childhood.

Girls talk sooner than boys, and begin to string words into sentences earlier. They have better articulation, pronunciation, and grammar, and are better at verbal reasoning. They also learn to read earlier than boys.

The structure of the female brain is believed to be the reason for girls' superior verbal skills (see p.98): the speech centres are more tightly organized in the female brain than in the male brain, and have more and better connections with other functions of the brain.

# Speech and language

Your toddler is learning new words all the time now and he's also starting to put them together. His pronunciation will sometimes be indistinct, but this is no cause for worry; if he's using words with meaning and putting them together, then his language is developing.

Mild speech defects, such as lisping, are very common in children, and usually disappear without any treatment. There is great variation in the speed at which children acquire speech, so don't compare your child with others, and don't worry if his development doesn't match the timetable outlined below: I give these dates merely as average guidelines.

**18 months to two years**  Your toddler will probably have a vocabulary of about 30 words, including possessives ("mine") and negatives ("won't"), instead of simply "no". He's starting to combine words to make simple statements, such as "ball gone", or questions: "Where Daddy?" He understands that conversation is a two-way thing and will wait his turn to speak, and he uses language to give information, to ask for things, to tell you how he feels, or to relate to other people. Remember that he understands more words than he can use, so you can continue to help him by teaching him new words. Use adjectives whenever you can, and combine them with nouns: "good boy", "hot water", "big dog". Introduce adverbs too: "Run quickly", "Pat the dog gently". When you use prepositions – "on", "under", "behind" – always show him what you mean.

**Two to three years**  He'll probably have a vocabulary of 200–300 words by now, and he can talk at some length. He's interested in learning new words. His attention span is longer, and he'll listen to you when you explain things or give reasons. He'll still mispronounce words, and may lisp, but his fluency and confidence are improving all the time. He can connect two ideas in a single sentence, "I get teddy and play in garden", and can use pronouns such as "I", "me", and "you" correctly. You can help your child to increase his vocabulary by using unfamiliar words in your speech in such a way that he can guess at their meaning. Read to him often, and explain new words as they arise. He'll like to hear the same stories read over and over, and will be able to understand increasingly complicated narratives. Your child's use of language is becoming more social now, and he'll talk more to other children than to adults, so contact with children is the best way to help him to develop his abilities.

## Talking to your child

It's important that you continue to talk to your toddler, and go on introducing new words and making your meaning clear with gestures and facial expression. It's just as important, however, that you allow him to respond so that he learns that conversation works two ways. If he initiates a conversation by showing you something or asking you a question, always give him your attention. If you're impatient, or just respond with "That's nice" without even looking at him, he'll become discouraged. Talk about everything you're doing in detail. When you're dressing him, give a running commentary: "Now we'll do up your buttons … one, two, three." Describe objects you are using: "Let's put the apples in the glass bowl"; "Would you like a yellow sweet or a red sweet?"

While you shouldn't correct your child when he makes mistakes, there's no reason why you should talk to him in his own baby language. If he makes a mistake in grammar or pronunciation – "Granny goed" – just repeat his words giving the correct form: "Yes, Granny went home".

## Language and understanding

You'll be able to observe the way your toddler gradually gains concepts in his use of language. He'll often use the same word to describe similar things, so that apples, oranges, and peaches are all "apple", because they are all round and fruit; and horses, cows, and sheep are all "horse" because they are all large animals with four legs. This is because he doesn't have words to describe all of them, so he uses the nearest one. The questions your child asks you may be simple because he can't express what it is he really wants to know. When he says "What's that?", he may be asking "What is it? What is it called? What does it do? How does it work?" all at once. Give him as much information as you think he can understand: "This is called washing powder. It's like soap. I put it in the washing machine to make our clothes nice and clean." Always try to answer the question he is really asking.

▶ **SOCIAL SKILLS** During the third year a child's verbal skills will be improved by interacting with other children.

**Boys are usually slower than girls at developing language skills, and this discrepancy lasts right through childhood.**

Boys are usually later in talking than girls, are slower to put words together in sentences, and take longer to learn to read. Speech disorders, such as stuttering, are far more common in boys than in girls, and boys outnumber girls in school remedial reading classes by four to one.

Although this difference in linguistic ability levels evens out somewhat during the teenage years, you can help your son's language skills in the preschool years by reading stories, poetry, and rhymes aloud to him and playing lots of word games.

Studies of the way children use language show marked differences in the way girls and boys speak to each other, which can be seen even in the preschool years.

The reason for these differences has to do with the way the sexes behave in groups. Girls want to be part of the group, so their talk is aimed at promoting unity and reaching compromises. Girls:

■ use language as a way of forming close, intimate friendships

■ make suggestions when playing in groups – "Let's play house"

■ give reasons for their suggestions: "Let's play in the garden because there's more room".

▲ **GIRLS AT PLAY** Close friendships form the basis of a girl's social world, and this will be reflected in her choice of language.

# Language skills

As your child's world becomes wider, his language will have to keep pace with new experiences and ideas. His perception of the world is becoming more complex, and so is his vocabulary; for example, he'll start to realize that mauve is different from purple, and look for the words to express this subtle difference. While he is learning more and more words, it's still important not to overtly correct his mistakes. If he hesitates over a word, supply it instantly to maintain his momentum and interest.

**Three years**  Your child will enjoy learning new words, so he listens to adult conversations carefully, and his attention span is increasing. He can understand words that describe how he feels, such as "cold", "tired", and "hungry". He's also beginning to understand words such as "on", "under", and "behind", although this will take longer. He'll probably be able to give his first and last name when asked and it's good to practise this with him. Because his mind is racing ahead of his ability to form words at this stage, he may start to stutter, but this is likely to be temporary and he'll soon gain his fluency again. If he hasn't overcome his stutter by about four-and-a-half, or earlier if it's severe, it might be worth consulting a speech therapist for specialist advice.

**Four years**  Children of this age talk a great deal: they boast, exaggerate, tell tall tales, and even have conversations with imaginary friends. Your child will ask lots of questions, as much out of a desire to keep you talking, as out of any real curiosity, because he loves conversation. He'll enjoy inventing silly words, and may even indulge in mildly obscene verbal play, especially to do with the lavatory and the potty. He'll probably start to use slang, and he may call you names and threaten you. Try not to over-react to this, as the attention you pay him will in fact encourage him to repeat the behaviour.

**Five years**  Your five-year-old will ask innumerable questions, and now he really is seeking new information. He loves to be read to (and this will last for years to come). He's aware that there's a "right" way to say things and will often ask you what it is. He can understand opposites, and it's very easy to make a game out of this, where you give a word such as "soft", "up", "cold", and he has to give the opposite. He'll also be able to define words if you ask him, and this is a very good way of getting him to use his skills of classification as well as develop his verbal skills. In fact all word games are excellent mental exercise, because clear speech goes hand in hand with clear thinking.

## Books and reading

Encouraging an interest in books is probably the best single thing you can do for your child, so read to him often; his attention span is increasing now and he'll be able to listen to stories with sustained interest. Words are crucial to the way our brains work; they're our main means of communicating, and they form the basis for everything your child will learn in school. Books will provide your child with new words and new ideas, and will explain to him how the world works.

Let your child know that you regard reading as a pleasure. Have plenty of books in the house and make it clear to your child that they're all available for him to look at. Store his own books on low shelves where he can easily browse through them.

Choose books for your child that are visually appealing; first reading books should be short, with only a few pages, and should have large illustrations, large print, and a simple vocabulary. Be willing to read your child's favourite books over and over again; eventually he'll memorize the words, and when he's ready to start reading himself, the familiar words will be easier to recognize.

## Learning letters and numbers

Take every opportunity to help your child become familiar with letters and numbers. Show him how his own name is spelled, and let him try to copy it. As you read to him, pick out a simple word like "cat" and point it out every time it recurs. Then show him again what the word looks like, and ask him if he can find it on a certain page. When you're doing routine tasks, such as doing up the buttons on your child's cardigan or laying the table, count out loud. When you're out shopping, you could ask your child to fetch things for you: three packets of soup or two oranges.

◀ AIDS TO LEARNING Give your child numbers and letters to play with. Magnetic ones can be attached to the fridge door for the whole family to enjoy.

## Identifying with others

By the time your child reaches the age of three he'll begin the process of identification, both with himself and with other people around him.

You'll start to see evidence of his self-awareness as he takes steps to command and control himself, showing that he can put himself in the position of others. You may overhear your child scolding himself when he thinks he has done something that you would disapprove of. He will begin to act out the part of the adults known to him, particularly you, often adopting words and phrases that you use regularly.

This will all become part of the process of him exploring and getting to know the way the world works and his own part in it. Now is the time to introduce him to the idea of a wider circle of people, teaching him to respect and be polite to them. Introduce him to visitors to the house – delivery people, postman, and window cleaner – as well as your own friends, and make meeting people part of his daily routine.

# Social behaviour

From his first moments your child looked to you as the centre of his world. As he gets older and his self-awareness develops, he'll begin to see you as a separate person and will extend his interest to other people. Although you can't make friends for him, you can introduce him to a few first companions. He'll soon learn to adapt and develop the social habits of older children.

**18 months to two years**  At this age you can encourage your child to interact with other children. Invite children to the house and give him games and play material to facilitate socializing. Be patient; although his initial reaction may be self-centred, he will modify selfish behaviour if it's played down. Avoid rivalry by praising your child's achievements – this will give him a good sense of self-worth. Praise all sharing.

**Two to two-and-a-half years**  As he's learning to share, encourage games that involve giving to others and respecting their wishes. He may demonstrate feelings of rivalry as a consequence and try to force his will on others. You'll need to use discipline fairly while still encouraging and supporting all his efforts and achievements, since approval is more important at this stage. Start teaching your child manners and respect for other people's property. Be consistent about unbreakable rules like those concerning safety.

**Two-and-a-half to three years**  As your child continues to socialize, he'll become more independent from you and more outgoing towards other children. He will start to be more generous and unselfish in play with others, and form stronger friendships with adults and children, showing signs of sympathy when others are in distress. It's never too early to introduce the need for truth and honesty. Always reward it even if it involves a confession to a misdemeanour. Reward the truth and deal with the misdemeanour next time. NEVER punish truth.

## Right and wrong

Your child will only learn the differences between right and wrong if these are clearly pointed out. You can act out why hot or sharp things are dangerous using sounds and actions. If your child understands why you want him to do something, he is much more likely to do it willingly, so try

**▲ TOYS FOR SHARING** Help your child learn to cooperate with others by encouraging him to share his toys, such as modelling dough and cutters, with a companion.

to explain and then ask his opinion. There are situations that are non-negotiable: where your child's safety is threatened, when the thoughts and feelings of others should be considered, and where your child is tempted to tamper with the truth. Be very firm on these points; he'll gradually learn a sense of responsibility for disciplining himself as he grows up. Cheekiness can often be mistaken for impertinence, but unless your child is imposing on the feelings of others, he may be displaying nothing more than a healthy resistance to authority.

A spoilt or over-indulged child will behave in a self-centred way and this may be the result of the over-protectiveness, favouritism, or high expectations of his parents. The best cure is to let him go to preschool at two-and-a-half to three as a leveller. He'll get used to mixing with other children and start learning how to get on with them.

## Sharing

Young children are naturally selfish and usually begin to think of others only when they're taught to do so. When your child understands that other children feel as he does, he'll be able to grasp the importance of thinking of other people's feelings. Learning to share is very difficult, but with your patience he'll successfully acquire this skill. Help by making sharing a game. Initiate games that involve giving things to others.

Your child's ability to make friends could be slow to develop, so introduce the idea of friendship to him gradually. Invite friends around, one at a time to begin with, to your home, where he's sure of himself. Be near at hand to give help and support should he need it. He'll begin to build up a circle of friends and gain confidence by having his own place within it – an essential way to learn the ground rules for future friendships.

# Tantrums

Toddlers between the ages of two and three often have temper tantrums as a means of giving vent to frustration when they don't get what they want.

This is quite normal because your child won't have sufficient judgement to control his strength of will or the language to express himself clearly, but as his knowledge and experience of the world broadens, the occasions when his will is pitched directly against yours start to become less frequent.

A tantrum may be brought on by such feelings as frustration, anger, jealousy, and dislike. Anger is brought on by not getting his own way; frustration by him not being sufficiently strong or well coordinated to do what he wants. It will usually involve your child throwing himself on the floor, kicking and screaming.

The best thing you can do is to stay calm, since any attention on your part will only prolong the kicking and screaming. If he has a tantrum in public, remove him firmly but gently and without fuss from the spotlight of attention.

At home an effective technique is simply to leave the room. Explain to your child that, while you still love him, you have to leave the room because you're getting angry. Never confine him in another room because this denies him the option of coming back and saying sorry.

## Growing up like mum

By the age of three your little girl is aware of the fact that she's female and that she'll grow up to be a woman.

This makes her very attentive to you – her mother. Her view of gender roles will be influenced by your attitudes. If you:

■ regard yourself as equal to your partner, your daughter will see this as normal

■ treat other women as close friends and confidantes, your daughter will see relationships with adult women in this way

■ see working as integral to family life, your daughter will view a career as compatible with having a family.

▲ A ROLE MODEL When your little girl starts to realize that she will grow up like her mother, she'll take a special interest in your activities.

# A changing identity

Your preschooler faces many changes in how he sees himself as his independence grows and his personality matures. Sudden upheavals can cause your child to have quite violent changes of mood as he tries to relate his changing identity to his family life and the guidelines he has learned for social behaviour, both of which are relatively constant. Be patient and allow your child to mature in his own time. You'll find that any difficult stages are easily outweighed by the thrilling ones, and your child must experience both in order to grow and become a socially adept member of his community.

**Three years** If your child has been brought up to relate to new friends he'll separate from you easily from the age of three-and-a-half onwards, at about the same time as he is learning to play interactive games, such as tag. He is generous and generally sympathetic when someone else is distressed. Unselfishness comes from being a team member so encourage your child to pull his own weight at home. Give appreciation whenever possible if he does something helpful.

**Four years** During the fourth year your child has an expanding sense of self, indicated by bragging, boasting, and out-of-bounds behaviour. He begins to realize that other children are separate entities. Your four-year-old wants to be grown up. He becomes argumentative, and may be selfish, rough, or impatient, especially with younger children or brothers and sisters. He'll express affection at bedtimes but might be jealous of you and your partner together. Four-year-old boys, in particular, often have a silly, boisterous sense of humour.

**Five years** During his fifth year, your child may become rather serious, business-like, and realistic. He gets very excited in anticipation of the future. At this age your little girl is sympathetic, affectionate, and loves to be helpful. She has a strong feeling for the family, and appearance is very important to her. She is not afraid to call people names. For a little boy, his mother is the centre of his universe. He takes others and himself for granted and is interested in immediate experiences.

## Sexuality and gender

**Three years** By the time children are about three years old, they are already interested in their own gender and the differences between girls and boys. For example, at about the age of three-and-a-half a boy will express "I like" and then slightly later "I love" and he will affirm, if questioned, that he is a boy rather than a girl. Children also begin to express interest in physiological differences between the genders and in boys' and girls' postures for urinating.

You child will make no distinctions between gender at play and realizes that people touch out of friendship as well as out of love. He begins to become interested in babies and wants his family to have one. He will ask questions such as "What can the baby do when it comes?", or "Where does it come from?" and most three-year-olds don't understand when they get the answer that the baby grows inside its mother. It's still vital, though, to answer your child's questions as frankly and honestly as possible so that his trust in you is not undermined.

**Four years**  By the age of four, children are extremely conscious of their navel and under social stress they may grasp their genitals and may need to urinate. They may play a game of "show", indulge in verbal play or name-calling, and make jokes about passing urine or stools. They have an interest in other people's bathrooms and may demand privacy for themselves, but be extremely interested in the bathroom activities of others. They may begin to segregate themselves along gender lines. All your answers to your child's questions on sex should stress the aspects of loving, caring, and the responsibilities that an intimate relationship demands. Treat your child's questions seriously and always try to give accurate, truthful answers, but don't feel you always have to tell the whole story. Supply as much information as you feel your child can cope with and understand at the time.

Your child may also question how babies get out of their mothers' tummies and may spontaneously think babies are born through the navel. This is a time when any gender-stereotyped behaviour is learned more from peers than parents.

**Five years**  By now your child will be familiar with, but not especially interested in, physical differences between the genders. He'll be more modest and less self-exposing and will play less in the bathroom than earlier. He'll be aware of sex organs when he sees adults undressed; he'll wonder why, for example, his dad doesn't have breasts.

Most children of five take the opposite sex for granted and there's little distinction between the role of gender in play. There may be frequent boy–girl pairs. Interest in babies continues. Your five-year-old will constantly ask, "Where do babies come from?", and will accept "Mummy's tummy" as an answer, but some fix on the idea that you buy a baby at hospital. He'll make little connection between the size of a pregnant woman and the presence of a baby inside her.

# Growing up like dad

**Your little boy will have realized by the age of three that he will grow up to be a man, and he'll become particularly interested in his father.**

Your little boy will watch your partner and learn from him what it is to be a man. If your partner:

■ treats women, particularly you or his daughters, in a caring and considerate way, your little boy will believe that this is the correct way to treat women

■ sees other men as friends, your son will also find older men approachable

■ enjoys and participates fully in family life, your child will follow this example

■ resolves disputes with rudeness and violence, your son will too.

▲ **A SENSE OF IDENTITY** Your little boy will gain his idea of what it is to grow up as a man by observing his father.

2

## Favouritism

**It is all too easy to favour one child above the other, or at least to treat him in a way that seems like favouritism.**

If a child is born several years after a previous one and is much wanted, for example, he may be treated preferentially. Sometimes it may be that the mother's favourite is the boy, the father's favourite is the girl, and a third-born child is no one's favourite.

Favouritism reveals itself in many different ways, some of them apparently inconsequential, but very important in the mind of a child. A favoured child may be:

- reprimanded less

- allowed to do a greater variety of activities

- given more treats, such as rides on father's back, or sweets

- defended when he gets into trouble for being naughty

- given more time and attention.

Of course, all children have different needs, and it is impossible to treat them absolutely equally all the time, but you should beware of favouring one child, or even appearing to; children are quick to notice such behaviour and a child who feels left out will suffer a blow to his confidence.

# Family relationships

Children who grow up in a stable, secure environment and feel loved by their parents are likely to become well-adjusted adults. Ideally, you and your partner will have equal but complementary roles, and agree on strategy, so that your child can't play one of you off against the other. The way a child interacts with his parents and siblings evolves gradually between the ages of three and five.

## Mother and child

**Three years** At the age of three, children generally have good relationships with their mothers. Quite often the mother is the favourite parent with whom children like to talk about and relive past events. By about three-and-a-half the mother–child relationship can sometimes become more difficult. A child may refuse to eat, dress, or take a nap for his mother, but be quite compliant with someone else.

**Four years** By the age of four, your child will take pride in you, quote things that you say, and boast about you to friends, though at home he'll still resist your authority.

**Five years** The mother–child relationship is generally smoother: your child likes to do things that you request, enjoys playing around you, and needs to be aware of your presence without having your full attention. Children quite often express affection, such as "I like you, Mummy", and, although they accept punishment from you, it may not have a great impact on them. Boys may talk about marrying mummy.

## Father and child

**Three years** At this age the mother tends to be the favourite parent, but the father can take over in many situations. For instance, a child may cling less at bedtime and go to sleep more quickly in the presence of his father. At the age of three-and-a-half, girls may express closeness to their fathers.

**Four years** Children boast about their fathers outside the home, and quote them as an authority. Some children may feel jealous of their father spending a lot of time with their mother and feel they are being deprived of her attention. If this is the case, a child may express dislike for his dad.

**Five years** By five years of age, children are likely to accept fathers taking a caring role if their mother is busy, ill, or away. Relationships with their father are generally smooth, pleasant, and undisturbed at this stage and children often value special outings with their fathers. They usually accept punishment better from mothers than fathers, although fathers can have more authority and so tend to be disobeyed less often.

## Siblings

At the age of four, relationships with siblings can be turbulent. A child is old enough to be a nuisance to older siblings and can be selfish, rough, and impatient with younger siblings. Quarrels and physical fights over toys are common and there will be complaints about fairness. A five-year-old is usually good with younger siblings. Having said this, a five-year-old is still too young to be responsible for younger siblings; and although he may be caring while an adult is present, he may resort to teasing when left alone with a sister or brother.

## The only child

Although there are benefits to being an only child, such as lots of love and attention, there are also disadvantages. The only child can sometimes feel lonely, and reticent about mixing in groups. Encourage him to visit friends and invite them home, and arrange outings with other young children.

There is also the tendency for some parents to be possessive and overprotective with their only child. This can be dangerous for both parent and child. If you don't allow your child a sense of adventure and the freedom to experiment and explore, he may become timid and wary of new people and experiences. An only child needs the same amount of discipline as other children. Try not to be over-indulgent, and make your child realize that he can't always expect to have your undivided attention.

# Rejection

**Although unusual, some parents emotionally reject their children and this can express itself in criticisms and unfavourable comparisons to siblings.**

The consequences can be acute. Signs of profound insecurity in a rejected child include:

■ excessive fear or shyness

■ crying a lot

■ aggressiveness and tantrums

■ jealousy and attention-seeking

■ excessive clinging to mother, thumb-sucking, or masturbation

■ bedwetting or soiling

■ physical tics

■ headbanging

■ bullying, stealing, or lying

■ cruelty to animals.

◀ **SIBLING RELATIONSHIPS** Your child will enjoy the companionship of a sibling to play with, but don't be surprised by quarrels, since these are quite natural.

## Shyness

This is something that affects many children at some stage. Common types of shy behaviour include disliking new experiences, reluctance to join in social gatherings, unwillingness to talk to unknown people, and difficulty in making new friends.

Don't think of shyness as something wrong with your child; many well-adjusted adults are quite shy. The best way of dealing with it is not by criticism or forcing change, but by preparing your child for any situation he's likely to find difficult, perhaps with stories or role-playing. In most cases, time and patience are all that are needed. See opposite for ways to help a shy child at school.

Don't worry if your preschool child is not too popular at this stage. Friendships in this age group are casual and unstable, here today and gone tomorrow, and they are not likely to have important or lasting effects on your child's personality.

# Making friends

By the time your child reaches the age of four, he's likely to be able to play with other children in an interactive, imaginative, and sustained way. Although group play demands some cooperation from children, this is quite superficial, since children can often play with their own ends in mind, and have little concern for the group as a whole.

## Social groups

Although children do not fit into rigid stereotypes, there are some common features in most groups of preschool children. The "star" is the child who's popular with everyone; the "rejectee" tends to be least popular; the "neglectee" doesn't evoke strong feelings in other children and, although he doesn't have any enemies, he probably has no friends; and the "clique" is a small group of children who repeatedly seek out each other's company. The problems experienced by the rejectee are obvious and are usually quickly spotted by nursery staff. Neglectees, however, may suffer from a form of social isolation that is more subtle, but equally, if not more, damaging.

## The loner

Isolation in the early years of childhood can have several long-term negative effects. Studies have shown that children who have problems interacting with their peers not only suffer in the preschool years but have more emotional disturbances in later life than "sociable" children,

and this can incline them to suicide in adolescence and adulthood. The loner is also more likely to play truant and be involved in vandalism and petty crime. For this reason, making efforts to help an unpopular child is always worthwhile. Encouragingly, preschoolers seem better able to develop new social skills than older children or adults.

The first signs that a child is a loner may appear when he starts playgroup or preschool. Whereas other children pair off or form groups, this child remains solitary. When children are asked to find a

▶ PLAYING TOGETHER Although by the age of five, children tend to select a single playmate, they do not necessarily play together, but "in parallel".

partner, the loner will be the last one left without a partner and, when asked to stand in a line, he will find himself at the back.

If you think that your child is being neglected it's important to take steps to help his social development. Fortunately, preschool children can learn new social skills easily if helped by sympathetic staff and you.

# How to help

If your child has poor social skills, there are various ways that you or your child's teacher can help. These include attaching a child to something or someone that raises their standing, or giving a child a responsibility that will boost confidence.

**Opposite pairing**  This involves pairing a neglected or unsociable child with a child who is outgoing and sociable. By being seen as the friend of a popular child, the neglected child will gain a significantly higher level of social acceptance in a short time.

**Younger pairing**  Pairing a child with poor social skills with a younger child can be another way of conferring status. A study showed that when unpopular children between the ages of four and five played with children younger than themselves, their level of popularity increased by at least 50 per cent. Younger playmates offer positive social experiences to neglectees and rejectees, which helps build their self-esteem.

**Clique activities**  Although it might seem bad for children to form small, exclusive groups within a large group, allowing them to mix in their preferred clique motivates them to get on with their peers outside the clique. Clique-based activities give children a sense of security and confidence about all social relationships.

**Small groups**  It's sometimes assumed that an unsociable child will become sociable when surrounded by a big group. In fact, small groupings are better at facilitating friendships because in a large group the unsociable child can remain in the background; in a small group he can't be ignored. A nursery school teacher can help by placing the child in a small group, then gradually extending the size of the group.

**Star responsibility**  Establishing definite roles, such as giving the most popular children responsible tasks to do, appears to have a settling effect on all children of nursery school age. Tasks could include giving out the straws for milk, or organizing tidying up. Unsociable children appear to benefit from this strategy as much as other children.

# Your child's new world

Now that your child is socializing with children of his own age, whether at preschool or at play, he'll have new concerns of which you will become aware.

■ Clothes are one of the first ways of expressing individuality and children may identify themselves with a particular peer group by the clothes they wear. By the time your child reaches preschool age he'll probably want to select his clothes each day. You can encourage his sense of identity and his independence by having a fairly flexible attitude towards his choice of clothes.

■ Toys, sports equipment, any sort of collection, such as a stamp or sticker collection, books, and comics are all powerful indicators of status among children. Even earning money for doing odd jobs is a sign of prowess.

■ Academic or athletic success, or popularity, also confer distinction. Some children also derive status from their parents – a high-profile or professional career, being well travelled, or affluence are all things that carry prestige.

■ If you feel that your child attaches too much value to a particular thing, or values something that is inappropriate, help him to reassess priorities and perhaps reward him for some achievement that you consider worthy.

## Explaining about lying

**If your child makes a habit of exaggerating the truth, it's important that you stress why telling lies is such a bad idea.**

If he is old enough to understand, you could try telling him the story of "The boy who cried wolf!". Afterwards, talk about the story and make sure that he understands that if you can't tell the difference between what is true and what is not true, you might not know when something really important has happened to him.

▼ **TALKING IT THROUGH** If you discover that your child has been lying, explain what she has done wrong patiently but firmly, rather than getting angry.

# Lying

In order for a child to tell a lie he must have reached a stage in his psychological development when he can distinguish fantasy from reality. For example, if a 15-month-old baby is chastised by his mother for daubing poster paint on a wall, and he shakes his head vigorously in denial, he isn't lying – it may be that he has genuinely forgotten the action, wishes that he hadn't done it, or simply cannot recognize the difference between fantasy and reality. Only when a child reaches the age of three or four years will he be capable of lying, and most children will lie if they find a situation sufficiently threatening.

## How serious is lying?

Children lie for many different reasons, and some types of lying are more serious than others. For instance, a make-believe lie is a natural part of a child's fantasy life, whereas a cover-up lie is a conscious attempt to avoid getting into trouble for something he knows is wrong.

**Exploratory lying** This is done simply to see your response. For example, a four-year-old child might tell his mother that he didn't like his dinner even though he ate it all. This is designed to see how you'll react. In most cases, your response to this kind of lying is enough to discourage him from doing it again. Some children, however, recognize that it wins attention and will use this tactic over and over again as they grow up. For this reason it's serious and must be discouraged.

**Bragging** This type of lying usually takes the form of a greatly exaggerated story and is done to boost the child's self-confidence. A five-year-old will state boldly that he's received many expensive birthday presents or that he lives in a huge house in an attempt to impress his friends. Although bragging is generally harmless, it's a good idea to discourage your child from this type of lying by reinforcing his genuine achievements. For a small number of children, bragging can become a permanent habit. Children who brag frequently do so because they desperately want to impress their friends and parents and they want to be loved. The danger is that people will come to view everything your child says with scepticism. Bragging lies can become a child's hallmark and he may lose many friends as a result.

**Make-believe lies** These are lies that mix reality and fantasy, and they serve to add excitement to everyday experiences. For instance, a four-year-old may have a vivid imaginary world consisting of fairies, monsters, and invisible friends, all of which he can describe in colourful detail. These childhood fantasies aren't really lies, and it's best to treat them as a normal phase in your child's development.

**Cover-up lies** Lies that aim to deliberately mislead are the type that parents worry about most. Children tell cover-up lies to avoid getting into trouble, and they learn this tactic at a relatively early age. In one survey mothers were asked to identify the most common reason for their four-year-olds lying to them. Nearly half of them said that it was a lie to escape a reprimand. Cover-up lies become more sophisticated and plausible as a child gets older.

Lies to avoid punishment can put parents in a difficult position. If you punish your child every time he does something wrong, he may learn to lie in response. On the other hand, if you don't reprimand your child then he's likely to carry on behaving in the same way. You need a balance between being too liberal and too punitive. I tried to encourage the truth with my children by saying that a child who told the truth would never be punished. They realized I was aware of the effort taken to be honest and promised not to lie; they rarely did.

# Dealing with lying

A study carried out several years ago investigated the impact of different parental responses on lying. It was found that children whose parents used moral principles to explain to their children why lying is wrong effectively reduced the frequency of lying. A parental response involving punishment increased the frequency of lying.

Children sometimes tell cover-up lies, not to escape punishment, but because they fear that their bad behaviour will stop you from loving them. Therefore any punishment for lying should be accompanied by reassurance. A child needs to be aware that punishment and parental love are not mutually exclusive. There is much research to show that parents who are honest with their children receive honesty in return. Make it easy for your child to confess to his misdeeds by speaking to him calmly rather than getting angry and making accusations. If the punishment for breaking rules is too severe, your child will go to great lengths never to admit he has broken them.

Children often say things that are inaccurate or untrue, and one important reason is that they hear their parents doing it: adults frequently tell "white lies" to avoid hurting other people's feelings unnecessarily. Your child may hear you saying something that contradicts what you normally say. If the reason for such tactful conversation is not explained to him, he can't understand why it is wrong for him to do the same.

# Helping a child who lies

Because children lie for different reasons, every child must be treated individually. There are, however, a number of dos and don'ts that apply to all children.

■ Act calmly – the child may genuinely be confusing reality and fantasy.

■ Try to understand the motive for a lie. Your child might be lying not because he wants to be malicious, but because he's afraid of the punishment he'll receive.

■ Explain to your child why it is wrong to lie. Use examples that he can understand.

■ Make punishments reasonable. If you over-punish your child, he will be more determined to lie in the future.

■ Make your child aware that although you are angry with him, you still love him.

■ Don't ridicule the child who persists with bragging lies. Bragging indicates low self-esteem and you'll need to increase your child's self-confidence with praise and affection.

■ Set a good example. You may tell a fib for a good reason, for example, by saying there are no sweets left when there are some hidden, but your child will have trouble seeing why his lies are wrong and yours aren't.

# When things go wrong

▲ **BEDWETTING** Don't scold your child if she wets the bed. Reassure her and try to understand why it is happening.

There are two broad categories of abnormal social development: habit disorders and behaviour disorders. The chart below sets out some of the most common and lists some of the factors that cause them. These are never sole causes, however, only characteristics of the environment created by parents. Many other factors may be involved. Of course by no means will all children respond to these family traits with any kind of a disorder. The table is suggested only as a guide to help parents.

Habit disorders involve problems with eating, passing stools, sleeping, or speaking, and behaviour disorders involve problems with social conduct, such as stealing. Parents may sometimes feel that their child with a behaviour problem is being manipulative or vindictive, but preschoolers are generally too young to behave in a calculated way.

## Common problems

| FACTOR | HABIT DISORDER | BEHAVIOUR DISORDER | WHAT YOU CAN DO |
|---|---|---|---|
| Overstrictness | Bedwetting | Bullying, smacking other children, biting | Relax over-authoritarian attitudes to toilet training. Don't scold. Give your child dedicated time. Show more affection and praise more. |
| | Faecal soiling (see column, right) | Lying, blaming others, stealing, refusal to share | More relaxed attitude to bowel control. Never "toilet train". |
| | | Destructiveness | Your child needs outlets for aggressive behaviour. Allow boisterous play. |
| Overprotection | Undereating (due to overfeeding) | Antisocial behaviour, refusal to "join in" | Be more flexible and relaxed about food. |
| | Negativism, "cissy" | Becomes a loner | Encourage your child to be independent. Develop his self-respect and sense of self-worth. |
| Lack of affection | Overeating to compensate | Stealing, lying, delinquency | Show your child affection and give praise. |
| Neglect or disorganized home | Pica (see p.214) | Lying, stealing | Give focused attention once a day. |
| | Faecal soiling (see column, opposite) | Destructiveness, bullying | Give more dedicated attention every day. |
| Prudishness, repressiveness about nudity, overstrictness | Possibly obsessive masturbation | Prurient interest in sex, very early sexual intercourse | Be open. Don't discourage questions about the facts of life. If you can, be relaxed about nudity. |

Problems such as bedwetting, faecal soiling, overeating, and faddy eating occur in most normal children and, as long as they only happen occasionally, they shouldn't be seen as disorders. However, when a child repeatedly wets his bed past the age when you would expect him to be dry, or overeats to the extent that he becomes obese, help should be sought. Habit disorders usually result from family factors, emotional trauma or conflict (such as a new baby in the family, a new home, or a change of school), or delayed development. Occasionally, there's a physiological basis for bedwetting and this possibility needs to be eliminated first.

**Stress** Children as well as adults can suffer from stress. Clinginess and habit or behaviour problems can be signs of stress. If your child is showing these symptoms, ask yourself if he's under strain or if you're expecting too much of him.

## Habit disorders

**Enuresis (bedwetting)** This is the most common habit disorder and is never the child's fault. It usually happens at night, and the most common reason is developmental delay. Most children are dry during the day and night by the age of five. Habitual bedwetting in a seven-year-old child could be considered abnormal, but it is probably the result of stress and it will improve when the stress is removed. Occasional bedwetting is common and is often caused by excitement, fear, or illness so don't worry about it.

In some families there's a history of bedwetting; a child should never be blamed for his slowness. Only about one in ten children suffering from enuresis has a physical or emotional disturbance, and these children usually suffer from enuresis during the day as well as the night. Physical causes include physiological or anatomical disturbance of bladder function, urinary infection, nocturnal epilepsy, and congenital abnormalities of the bladder.

Bedwetting is sometimes an emotional response to excessive parental pressure to be clean and dry. Insufficient or inconsistent encouragement or unrealistically high expectations before the child is developmentally ready are common reasons. Bedwetting is made worse by parental disapproval and teasing by siblings. Never scold or ridicule bedwetting, and always praise success.

Measures such as restricting fluid before bedtime, and waking and lifting during the night are occasionally helpful. The pad and buzzer method of treating enuresis, in which a buzzer sounds when the bedclothes become wet, is successful in some cases, but it shouldn't be used on children under seven. The best approach to bedwetting is to treat it as lateness rather than illness and not to draw attention to it.

# Faecal soiling

Unlike bedwetting, faecal soiling is unusual in toilet-trained children and almost always indicates stress or emotional disturbance.

Nevertheless, a physical cause should be ruled out. There are three types of faecal soiling: soiling that has been present from babyhood; regressive soiling, in which a toilet-trained child reverts to an earlier stage of development; and aggressive soiling, which is an emotional response to overstrict parenting, or over-severe or out-of-date toilet training (see pp.170–72).

Aggressive soiling usually occurs in children who have been "toilet-trained" too early in life, because the parents place exaggerated emphasis on being clean. If a child feels stifled and isn't allowed to play and get dirty, he may express his frustration through soiling.

The most effective way to deal with soiling is to reduce a child's anxiety. Overstrict parents need to become more relaxed, and stressful or traumatic events need to be dealt with sympathetically.

# Depression

Children become depressed when they face stress they can't cope with, such as moving house, separation from parents, divorce, or being the subject of abuse.

It is now believed that any evaluation of learning difficulties in a child should include routine checking for depression, since the two often go hand in hand.

A depressed child may cry more than normal, lack interest in games and friends, and be irritable when you try to rouse him from his apathy. Depression rarely occurs on its own in children; it's usually combined with compulsive behaviour. Sleep disturbance, anorexia, lack of concentration, which in turn causes difficulties at school, and tense, restless behaviour are common features. Chronic depression affects the development of a child's personality – he may become antisocial as he grows up.

There are many ways to help a depressed child. If his environment is insecure, a period as a day-patient or in-patient in a children's unit may be useful, provided it's combined with help from the whole family. Psychotherapy can help to relieve unconscious conflicts in the child, whether they are about growing up or over-dependence on parents. Parents, too, may need help and therapy. Every effort should be made to identify the stress on the child and then reduce it.

**Eating disorders**  Refusing to eat, overeating, being excessively fussy or faddy, and pica (eating things not usually considered edible) may all be classified as eating disorders if they happen often. Faddy or fussy eating is common in otherwise healthy children and many children go through phases of faddiness that pass. Faddy eating, unless excessive, is not really a problem. It is often a child's natural way of selecting a balanced diet.

Persistent refusal to eat or picking at food is common in preschool children. Poor appetite may be caused by anxiety or it may indicate a problem between parent and child. Parents may be overanxious, with exaggerated ideas about nutritional needs, or food may be used as a symbol of affection. Overfeeding results in undereating. Fortunately, food refusal in young children rarely leads to undernourishment – the best treatment is to be flexible about meals and offer a wide range of food.

Overeating is a more serious problem than food refusal or faddiness in that it can lead to obesity. Obesity is bad for a child's health, and means that he may be teased by his peers and suffer from low self-esteem. Children overeat for many different reasons; sometimes a child uses food to compensate for the fact that he feels unloved and insecure; sometimes a parent who feels inadequate will overfeed a child to make up for not giving him enough love. To prevent overeating, it is essential to identify the underlying reason, whether it is insecurity on the part of the child, or conscious or unconscious overfeeding on the part of the parent.

Pica is the consumption of substances without any nutritional value, such as soil, gravel, chalk, paint, clothing, or even faeces. It occurs most frequently among children from neglected, poor, or disorganized homes. Children with pica may show other signs of disturbed behaviour.

## Behaviour disorders

Antisocial behaviour usually stems from a problem within the family or in the family's inability to adjust to society at large. An affected child may fail to identify himself as part of a family and to accept parental attitudes and standards of behaviour. This is most likely to happen in disorganized or disordered homes, where there are no consistent adult role models, or where a child is constantly being moved around, scolded, punished, or being mentally, physically, or socially abused. Common symptoms of behaviour disorders are bad language, temper tantrums, disobedience, aggression, stealing, and lying.

Psychologists, child psychiatrists, and social workers can provide a diagnosis of a behaviour disorder, and in some cases psychotherapy may be recommended. Since the problem often indicates an underlying problem in the family, the whole family rather than just the individual child may receive counselling, and be assigned a social worker.

**Negativism** Stubbornness, selfishness, and disobedience are all characteristics of negativism. To some extent, all preschoolers are negativistic. They may seem to delight in doing the opposite of what they are asked: when you want your child to go out, he'll decide to stay in, or when you want him to eat his food, he'll refuse it.

There are many reasons for resisting parental authority and parents can misinterpret them. A child may be negativistic, not because he wants to revolt against authority, but because he wants to continue what he's doing. He has no conception of time, and sees no reason why he should stop playing an enjoyable game. Reasons such as a meal time or going to bed are irrelevant if he isn't hungry or tired.

Another explanation for negativism is that a young child can't distinguish between two opposites. He's inexperienced, his life is charged with alternatives, and often he finds it impossible to differentiate between yes and no, give and take, or push and pull. His interest in these double alternatives is so evenly balanced that he goes from one extreme to the other. Flagrant negativism may be the result of insufficient parental encouragement. Even if your child is slow to perform a task or makes a mess, it's important that you encourage learning early on.

**Stealing** Between the ages of two and five or six, a child may be so attracted to an object – a toy, coins left on a table, or a sweet – that he takes it when he hopes no one is looking. Sometimes he'll do it in such a way that his theft will be discovered. Neither is a sign of a deep-rooted problem. Rather, it's the normal result of overwhelming desire unchecked by social inhibitions. Don't punish the act, but don't ignore it. Tell your child clearly and calmly that this is unacceptable and insist that the object be returned. In all likelihood, one or a few such interchanges are all that's required to end the behaviour.

**Resistance to school** A child who says he doesn't want to go to school or, more commonly, who complains of a stomachache or headache on school mornings: he may be coming down with a mild illness; he may be unhappy about something in school; or he may not wish to leave you because of shyness or something he is worried about at home. It's best not to force your child to go to school at first, unless this is a recognized and often-repeated pattern. If an illness doesn't reveal itself in a day or two, or if your child perks up once the threat of school is removed, you should talk to his teacher to help uncover any problems. If all is well at school and reluctance to leave home is the possible cause, try a loving but firm goodbye and a warm but restrained welcome home. If the behaviour persists, speak to your doctor.

# Sexual misbehaviour

**Adults tend to classify some aspects of normal development (such as games of "show") as prurient. They are quite normal stages of development, and it is only adult interference that leads to exaggerations of sexual play.**

True sexual misbehaviour may occur in isolation or together with other forms of antisocial behaviour, such as truancy. Sexual curiosity and masturbation are common and normal features of childhood, and become abnormal only because of their frequency or the circumstances in which they occur. Unless you consider a child's sexual behaviour completely unacceptable, it is important to retain a sensible attitude to this feature of childhood. Even if you do consider behaviour questionable, speak to your doctor before labelling your child's behaviour abnormal.

2

## Choosing a preschool

**When he's three or four years old your child will be able to go to preschool, if you choose.**

Before making a decision, visit several preschools in your area. Prepare a list of important points to check. For example, are the teachers relaxed or formal? Is it a happy environment? What is the standard of facilities? How many children are there, and are they well supervised? What are the children taught? Does the school feel safe? Are the children happy?

Sit in on a few classes and speak to parents whose children already attend. You'll then have the information you need to decide which school is right for your child.

▼ **PART OF A GROUP** Going to preschool helps to widen a child's horizons. He'll have a chance to try new activities and interact with children his own age.

# Early education

The choice as to whether or not you decide to send your child to preschool, or nursery school, will depend largely upon the options available and whether or not they suit his needs. Find out what there is in your area and try to visit the preschools. Talk to the teachers and other parents so as to get a good idea of what's provided.

## Choosing preschool education

There is no single kind of preschool that is best for every child. Each child should be in a school that fits his particular needs. All evaluations of preschool education show mixed results. One long-term assessment showed that boys in Montessori programmes sustained gains in reading and maths throughout their school careers. Other research shows that intellectual gains are found in all but the poorest of programmes. But it's difficult to know how long these benefits last. Evaluations of Head Start, an American-based preschool organization, for example, show that apparent IQ differences between children in Head Start and those who don't attend preschool diminish over time. Whatever the benefits of preschool education, there's no substitute for a loving home environment.

## What preschool can do for your child

Preschool has some benefits other than just education. Your child can develop a greater sense of confidence and therefore more self-control, as well as learning to share, to be concerned for the needs of others, and to take turns. Your child's skill in planning ahead and cooperating with others will improve through fantasy and group play. The opportunities for play in preschool will enhance the various ways that your child thinks – that is, imaginatively, speculatively, and inventively. These are characteristics that are often found in intellectual and creative children.

Some preschools are also designed to help disadvantaged children by building up their confidence. Children who attend such schools turn out to be less likely to repeat a year in primary school than their peers who did not attend preschool. They are also less in need of special education, and less likely to show delinquent behaviour when they reach adolescence.

Playgroups often take children from as early as two-and-a-half years old. They provide the opportunity for interaction with other children of the same age and help develop early social skills, but in a less formal atmosphere than preschool.

## Settling in to preschool

You can help your child adjust to preschool by taking him along for one or two visits well in advance of his start date. Encourage him to play with the other children, or with some of the equipment. But try not to push him to socialize with other children if he doesn't seem keen at first. Some children are naturally more gregarious than others and he'll adjust in his own good time. The aim is to make his visits as enjoyable as possible. If you stress all the fun things he will do, his eager anticipation for school will be stronger than his worry about leaving you. If he's having trouble adjusting, most preschools will let you stay with him on the first day, and for steadily decreasing periods of time on the following days. Make sure you collect him yourself for the first week when he's most insecure. Once he is confident that he's not being abandoned, you'll be free to make other arrangements for collection.

Your child's personality, maturity, place in the family, and willingness to leave home will all influence the way he settles at preschool. In general, boys are more likely than girls of the same age to cry when their mothers first leave them and they tend to cry when frustrated or angry with a teacher or helper.

Although your child is now going to preschool, this doesn't mean that your part in his education is finished. Ask him what he's done at school and who he played with. By getting him to talk about his school experiences, you'll be consolidating the new words and skills he is learning. You can help him to improve his use of language by repeating what he says in the correct form, although not by directly correcting him. Your child will be constantly seeking new information and you should always try to answer his questions truthfully. If you don't know the answer, suggest you both look it up in a book rather than just try to fob him off.

## How children behave at preschool

As a rule boys are more task-oriented in preschool play and little girls talk more about being friends, recognizing similarities in each other, admiring one another's clothes, discussing who's friends with whom, and so on. Dominant and aggressive behaviour in little boys is very much in evidence in a preschool setting. Intelligence and ability to get along with others are as important to popularity in preschool as a boy's size or physical prowess. Popularity fluctuates from day to day.

Hitting is a common form of aggressiveness. A few girls strike out at other girls, but their hitting is usually not effective. Boys take longer to learn not to hit others and make unprovoked, if mild, attacks on girls. They will, for example, push little girls or gesture menacingly at them.

## Approaches to preschool

No single method of preschool has proved to be significantly better for every child. Many parents send their children to preschool to give them an opportunity to play and be sociable; other parents send them simply because it allows their children physical outlets away from home, avoiding their making a mess at home.

Structured classes are better suited to the needs of most small children. A chaotic environment may cause some boys to react in a way that some teachers describe as hyperactive. Structures vary within different preschools. Some follow a timetable for certain activities each day along the lines advocated by Dr Montessori, and organize the school around an orderly child-sized environment with specific behavioural guidelines, such as putting things away when they are finished with.

A child who finds tasks easy and has lots of local friends may be suited to a structured traditional school. However, a child who has few local playmates and wants to socialize may enjoy a less structured preschool.

## Girls at school

In general, girls have a greater aptitude for subjects involving language skills, such as reading. They're also more likely to prefer games that involve social interaction with other girls.

This innate tendency may be reinforced by parents and teachers who steer them towards certain activities that involve "playing quietly" and away from others more associated with boys. Whatever the reasons, girls at school generally follow certain patterns of behaviour.

■ Girls prefer to play with other girls in games involving a strong element of cooperation. They will often shy away from boys, especially those engaged in boisterous or aggressive play.

■ Girls tend to choose activities involving books (with words or pictures). On the other hand, they may be more anxious than boys about maths and other number-based activities.

■ Girls are generally well motivated and more willing to conform. However, this may mean that teachers assume they are coping well with lessons and so they may receive less attention than boys.

# Going to school

Starting school will be a great milestone for your child, and for you. You'll both have to make adjustments: your child will discover a new, exciting world, and you'll have to adjust to his growing independence.

## Is your child ready?

There's a legal maximum age by which your child must have begun school – in the UK, five years – but many parents are keen to send their children earlier if places are available, to give them a "head start". It's biology and not the calendar that determines your child's readiness for school. Certain physical skills are therefore usually taken as signs that he's reached the level of mental development necessary for school success. These include being able to catch a large ball, hop on one foot, and run and stop on a signal. Your child must be capable of taking care of his bodily needs, such as going to the toilet independently, doing up his shoes, and dressing himself. He should also know his full name and be able to ask clear and concise questions. Many five-year-olds are proud of learning numbers and their ability to count. They also demonstrate their maturity by making strong efforts to keep themselves under control. You can begin to introduce these things to your child before he starts school.

If you are unsure whether your child is ready, ask a preschool teacher. A teacher with ten years' experience has probably taught around five hundred children and so should be very accurate at predicting whether your child will do well at school.

## School readiness checklist

Your child needn't have mastered every skill on the list. Use it as a guide, and talk to a teacher at the school. A child's ready when he:

■ joins in the shared activities of a group
■ listens to a story and re-tells events in sequence
■ joins in and readily follows instructions for games or new activities
■ expresses ideas and needs clearly to others
■ hops, skips, and jumps
■ helps about the house doing simple tasks
■ recognizes basic colours and shapes
■ recognizes similarities and differences in sound
■ joins in songs and knows some simple ones by heart
■ copes with buttons, shoelaces, and zip fasteners, and can cut with scissors
■ can copy simple figures, including a circle, square, and triangle
■ is able to attend to personal toiletry needs.

# Helping your child to like school

Your child is more likely to succeed at school if he has the right frame of mind to begin with. You can help with this by preparing your child before he starts so that he is physically and mentally ready for the demands that school will make on him. Encourage him to carry out simple tasks so that he understands the concept of responsibility. Make sure his play involves imagination and creativity, as well as opportunities for learning and developing his memory. It's important, too, that the school provides the right environment for your child's education, with motivated teachers who have a good relationship with their pupils.

Your child will undoubtedly benefit if you take an interest in what he's doing at school and you can help him at home. However, there's a real danger that you can do more harm than good if your methods are very different from those being taught at school. Talk to your child's teacher about the school's particular approach and find out at first hand about what is being taught. Some schools actively encourage parents to sit in on lessons as observers, or you may even be able to help out. But don't overdo the schoolwork. Home should also be a place of comfort and refuge, so you will need to strike a balance between helping your child progress with his education and overloading him with work.

# Your changing relationship

Your child's first days at school mark a change in his relationship with you. Up to now he has been dependent on you for everything, but now he'll have to begin to learn to become independent and responsible for all his own decisions and actions. This change doesn't happen overnight, but it is important to begin the process by encouraging your child to take on more and more responsibility. By now he should already wash and dress himself and he might be expected to lay out his school things for the next day.

He'll feel very grown-up, and won't want to be fussed over, but you should always be ready to give a cuddle whenever he shows he needs one. It is hard for your child to accept that he isn't fully grown-up, and the emotional drain of daily social interaction may occasionally be too much for him. As with most things, a cuddle from you is the best remedy and will set him up for the next day.

You may find that your child won't want such public displays of affection as he used to have, particularly not in front of his new friends. Don't feel snubbed. He is simply asserting himself as independent – grown-up enough not to need a kiss from mum. More than anything else, it's important not to push too hard, even in asking what happened during his day. Clever prompting will be all you need to hear about his time at school, but prying will only make him secretive.

# Boys at school

**Generally, boys have a greater aptitude for activities involving spatial skills, such as building games. They're more likely to prefer games that involve competition and physical activity.**

As with girls, this innate tendency may be strengthened by adults. Boys may be encouraged to take up "boyish" activities that allow them to "let off steam" or involve construction, and unconsciously discouraged from contemplative pursuits, such as reading. As a result they too tend to behave in certain ways at school.

■ Boys prefer playing with other boys, especially in energetic games that involve physical activity, such as climbing or mock fighting.

■ Boys concentrate on toys that aid mathematical and spatial skills. They will also persevere with a difficult maths question until they solve it.

■ Boys become more disruptive if they do not get attention or are having difficulty with a subject. This may mean that the teacher will spend a disproportionate amount of time with the boys compared with girls.

# Family life

A new baby is a 24-hour-a-day commitment and you'll find that your lifestyle will change enormously. This will be all the more true if you have twins or even triplets.

Your relationship with your partner will also be different. There'll be less time for intimacy and companionship and you may find you need to stop and take stock of your joint responsibilities. Men can look after children just as well as women and shared parenting will reap benefits for you and your partner, as well as your child.

You may want to involve other members of your family in helping to bring up your baby, especially if you're a single parent, or if you and your partner both go out to work. Or you may decide to employ a nanny or childminder, or send your child to a day nursery or crèche. Whichever choice you make, it's vital to plan ahead and organize your time.

## Mum knows best?

**The argument that women are better equipped for parenthood than men is no longer valid.**

At one time it was not uncommon for a woman to have ten children or more, and young girls were more likely to be involved in looking after them. Nowadays most mothers have never seen, let alone held, a newborn until they give birth.

If a woman does have more experience of looking after a baby than her partner, it's important that she doesn't mock his efforts, since he may respond by withdrawing his help altogether. When this happens, the role of each parent becomes polarized, increasing pressure on the mother and isolating the father from the family unit.

▲SHARED PARENTING Spend time with your partner getting to know your child and learning to be parents together.

# Becoming a family

No matter how many baby books you read, and no matter how well prepared you are, you can still be knocked sideways by the impact of a newborn baby on your life. As well as the physical requirements of looking after a baby, your normal domestic chores, such as washing, will at least quadruple.

After the first few weeks, when relatives and neighbours stop dropping around to offer congratulations, the novelty of being home alone with a new baby can wear off rapidly. You may miss social interaction with friends and colleagues. In particular, you may miss the difference between work and home. With a young baby you don't have the luxury of leaving your work behind.

Many people also find that making the transition from being a couple to being a family can prove more traumatic than they imagine. The dynamics in a relationship need to adapt to a new addition. Problems can arise when a couple find it difficult to fit another person into the complex equation of human emotions that makes up a relationship.

## New responsibilities

The arrival of a child means that choices become stark: beforehand, for instance, if neither partner wanted to clean the bathroom floor, it could be left until later. But a baby can never be left until later. Her needs take priority and somebody has to take immediate responsibility for meeting them. Time that was previously spent on other things must now be given to the baby. Ideally these lifestyle changes are shared equally within a partnership, but in practice women very often end up taking on the main burden. Depending on individual expectations, this can lead to deep resentment within a relationship, causing a couple to move apart after the birth of their baby.

Research in the US has shown that one in every two marriages goes into decline after the birth of the first child. All of the couples in the study, no matter how well adjusted, experienced on average a 20 per cent increase in conflict within their marriage during the first year of parenthood. Although conflict can sometimes be healthy, it is often not what new parents expect.

To reduce the stress placed on a partnership, it is vital that each partner has at least some idea of what to expect and is able to compromise. Having a baby means rearranging your life.

▲ **A LOVIING FAMILY** Your child can't have too much love and attention, so both of you should give her as much as you possibly can.

# Dads – your new role

The way to conquer your new role is to take it on fully. There's nothing more unsatisfactory than having imagined yourself a headliner and being reduced to a walk-on part.

If you grasp fatherhood with both hands by sharing the care of your child with your partner, you'll establish yourself as pivotal in your family and the rewards for you will be in the depth of the relationship with your child and in the strengthening of your relationship with your partner.

If you feel your life has been turned upside down by the arrival of your baby, you're one of the only two people who can put it right. Life won't ever be the same again, but that will only be a cause for regret if you stand on the sidelines of family life instead of embracing it.

## Equal parenting

Although the role of men in parenting has changed, some people still take the attitude that childcare is primarily a woman's responsibility. Ideally, discuss your respective roles with your partner before your baby is born. Help your partner understand that being a good father doesn't just mean helping: it means fathering the child as well.

It's important for you and your partner to share the childcare as far as possible. If a father isn't involved in caring for his child, it can be limiting in two ways. First, his relationship with his partner may suffer if she feels resentment at a lack of help and support. Second, if a father doesn't play an active role in the early months and years of his baby's life, he may lose the chance to form a close bond with his son or daughter. A detached father will have a negative effect on his child. Girls may have trouble interacting with men, and boys will be deprived of a male role model.

## Fathering

There's no reason why a child can't enjoy an equally close relationship with both parents. A baby's relationships don't operate on an either/or basis, and you should never worry that if a baby spends an equal amount of time with her father, she might love her mother less. All young children need as much love as they can get, and both parents should do their utmost to provide it.

Today it may be economic factors that determine who's left holding the baby. If a woman earns more than her partner, or if he is unemployed, many couples can't afford to let misplaced male pride reduce their weekly income. While the rise of the house-husband has undoubtedly benefited lots of families, it is important to bear in mind that the man left at home needs just as much support as a woman does.

# A father's story

Anna and Henry Richards experienced a bad few months after their son Alex was born. Anna was exhausted, depressed, and overwhelmed, and Henry didn't feel very paternal.

Henry puts this down to the fact that he measured fatherhood in terms of doing things, and that Anna quickly took all responsibility for the baby.

Henry's frustration made Anna's difficulties worse. For the first three months she had periods of postnatal depression. Their sex life deteriorated and Henry started to feel rejected by Anna, physically and emotionally.

"Then we found out Anna was pregnant with Leora only ten months after the birth of Alex. I realized then that I had to give Anna enormous credit for being able to cope with it all. I half expected her to cave in, but instead she became stronger, perhaps because of having to cope with Alex."

During the third month of Anna's pregnancy she had a threatened miscarriage. She was advised to stay in bed, and Henry decided to take unpaid leave from work so that he could look after her.

"At last I felt I was the linchpin of our family unit. Despite the emotional strain, I'm glad we went through it. It has made me an equal parent with Anna, whereas before I felt like an observer."

## Grandparents

With the arrival of a first child, grandparents can be supportive, or they can be the source of increased tension, especially if family relations are already strained. You will probably find that you see more of your in-laws once your baby is born, and hopefully this will contribute to a happier family life.

Sometimes, however, the intimacy and interdependency of family relations means there is a thin line between helpfulness and interference. Ideally, you and your partner will have discussed the role you want grandparents to play. Once you've decided how much help you do or don't want, you'll find it easier to establish your authority by setting out the rules in advance.

Many grandparents, particularly grandmothers, want to show you how they coped with a crying baby or a disobedient toddler. This advice is usually well-meant and may be welcome. If it isn't, say so. Point out that she's your baby and caring for her is your responsibility. If you occasionally make mistakes they will be your own. It's certainly worth persevering to overcome problems so that your child can benefit from a secure and loving relationship with her grandparents.

## A special relationship

A good relationship between a grandparent and grandchild is rewarding for the whole family. Grandparents can offer a more relaxed perspective toward your children. Parents can rest, secure in the knowledge that when a child is with her grandparents she'll be well looked after, and she can learn to form an important emotional bond beyond her mother and father.

Grandparents can form special relationships with their grandchildren for several reasons. First, they see them less frequently than their parents, which alleviates the strain of day-to-day care. Second, ultimate responsibility for a child rests with her parents. This frees grandparents to enjoy the thrill and pleasure of parenthood without the accompanying worries and stresses. Third, a grandparent has already brought up at least one child, and problems are always easier to cope with the second time around. Grandparents are also likely to have more quality time to spend with their grandchildren.

▲ **SECOND TIME AROUND** Your parents and your partner's parents are likely to have a relaxed attitude towards childcare.

As children become young adults with problems of their own, grandparents can offer a broader perspective on the difficulties facing them. A grandparent is likely to be the oldest person that your child will ever know as a friend, and he or she can give your child an insight into how things were in the past.

Not all families, however, can enjoy the benefits of an extended family. This is particularly true today, as financial pressures force couples to move to where they can find work. Divorce can also limit grandparents' access to their grandchildren. This can be terribly upsetting for both grandparents and grandchildren alike, and it helps if a child continues to see her grandparents regularly.

## Love and security

The most basic needs of any young child are physical care and emotional love and security. If a child feels well cared for, she'll grow into a more outgoing and relaxed person. A child who's given lots of love and security at an early age is likely to become less demanding as she grows older. Conversely, a child who's emotionally neglected may grow up insecure, clingy, and fearful. It's important that parents don't shy away from giving their child adequate love and security for fear of "spoiling" her. Although it's true that a child shouldn't get into the habit of thinking she can have anything she wants, it's even more important that she doesn't get into the habit of thinking she isn't loved.

Remember, your child's way of seeing things is very different from yours. Small and apparently trivial displays of affection (a hug, a pat, a kiss) will do much more to shape the personality of your young child than anything else. It's no good loving your child and trying not to show it, in the mistaken assumption that this will make her a "stronger" person. In fact the opposite is true.

Affection produces emotional and physical results. For instance, when young babies are held in their mother's arms they breathe more slowly, have steadier respiration, cry less, and sleep more. This isn't so surprising, as cuddling takes a child back to the comforting sensation of the uterus when she was warm and secure. Hugging is also the best way of communicating to a young child that you love and care for her. If your child sees you and your partner hugging each other she'll know that, in spite of any arguments you might have, you still love each other.

Even if your child can feel that you love her through your physical affection, it's also important that she hears it. Toddlers especially need to be told that you love them. They've reached the stage when they can tell you that they love you, and they need to hear this from you. Never be shy of showing your love – it's the most important thing you'll ever share.

# Showing love

**Loving touch is crucial to our wellbeing and, in the case of babies, has even been shown to promote physical development.**

If you're not sure how to increase the amount of physical affection you show your child, have a look at some of these suggestions. These combine physical attention with love and companionship – exactly what every child needs.

■ Try carrying a young baby in a sling; almost all newborn babies love the sensation of being strapped close to you.

■ Every so often give your baby a soothing rub with baby lotion or a massage (see pp.58–9).

■ Share a bath together, or take your baby swimming at the local pool. Hold her tightly in the water so that she feels warm and secure.

■ As she gets older, do some exercise together – this doesn't have to be anything more complicated than putting music on and dancing around the room.

■ Have a few rough-and-tumble games; many mothers leave this to the father or to other children, and particularly neglect to play boisterous games with girls.

■ Curl up in bed with your child, and every now and then have a lie-in, so that your child starts the day knowing she is well loved.

# Miriam's casebook

# Single parent

When Nicole, a manager in a fashion store, became pregnant with Matthew three years ago, she found herself in an unexpected situation. At the time she was having a non-committal affair with a work colleague. "I found myself in a quandary because throughout my whole life I never once envisaged myself as a single mother. I had grown up thinking a child should be the product of a loving relationship. But I knew that this wasn't a relationship I wanted to remain permanent."

## First reactions to pregnancy

"Whether it was circumstance or coincidence I don't know, but when I found out I was pregnant with Matthew, it seemed as though I was being given a chance to actively take control of my life, instead of waiting for someone else – who might never arrive – to do it for me.

The thought of becoming an unmarried single mother took a lot of getting used to. Initially, my own mother, who is quite conservative, reacted very badly, which made things even harder. She's come round to the idea, but that's because Matthew is a lovable toddler whom she adores madly."

## Making choices

In the end, Nicole took six months' maternity leave after Matthew was born. The first three months went smoothly as Matthew was quite a placid baby. By the eighth week, he usually slept five hours each night. "In fact, although I was exhausted, Matthew gave me so much joy that I took an unexpected delight in having him all to myself." After three months' maternity leave, Nicole was torn between staying at home and going back to work, but in the end, despite financial pressures, she decided to stay at home. "I felt Matthew was just too young to leave with an unknown childminder. It was only towards the end of the fifth month that I started to experience problems."

## Coping with illness

"The worst bit was never having anyone to moan to at the end of the day. You can't moan to a six-month-old. Little problems and nagging worries soon developed into overblown crises that kept me awake for hours at night. The week before my six-month maternity leave was up, Matthew got a mild chest infection. Although it wasn't serious, I became so worried that I developed severe insomnia and was prescribed tranquillizers."

Matthew's chest infection lasted for three weeks and the doctor then diagnosed asthma. Nicole was immediately convinced that Matthew was an "ill" baby who would be sick for the rest of his life. "If there had been someone else to share the worry with, I'm sure I wouldn't have reacted so badly," she recalls. "I felt I had to put off returning to work for another month. Then when the day finally arrived I was surprised by my own anxiety – not so much because I had to leave Matthew (I left him asleep with my mother) but because half way to work I started to wonder if I could still do my job. The job I have is quite high-pressured — part of my salary is based on commission – and things have to be up and running from 9am to 6.30pm without a break. I worked four days a week, and it wasn't easy worrying all day at work, and then worrying all night at home."

## Finding the best childcare

At this point Nicole's mother moved in with her so that she could have some time to adjust to being a single working mother. Having her there made Nicole realize that, although she couldn't really afford it, she had to consider full-time help at least until the end of Matthew's first year. She contacted a local parents' group, who sent her advice on hiring a nanny or an au pair.

## Employing a nanny

When Matthew was eight months old, Nicole hired her first full-time live-in nanny. The cost, for someone on her salary, was prohibitive. She also realized that, although she got a bit more sleep, most of the time she found it impossible to stay in bed and leave it to the nanny when she heard Matthew crying. "It may have been that his asthma made me over-protective, or it may simply have been that I didn't like sharing my home with a relative stranger – whatever the reason, after two months I asked the nanny to leave and decided I'd muddle through, continuing to work part-time and asking friends and family to look after Matthew while I was at work."

This helped ease the financial situation, which by that point had become quite critical. It was still hard for Nicole to go out, because she couldn't afford to spend money on a babysitter and an evening's entertainment. She realized, nearly a year after the birth, that she hadn't been out socially.

## Rebuilding a social life

"That was when I had the idea of having my first post-Matthew dinner party. About eight friends came around, each with a homemade dish, and we had a fabulous evening without waking Matthew once. Having the dinner party made an enormous difference to me. It was the first time I felt as though I was a social being again, rather than just a single working mother with no social life outside work and home. About a week later I managed to come off the tranquillizers permanently."

Two months after Matthew's first birthday, Nicole arranged regular day care with a nanny who looked after him three days a week, and he continued to stay with his grandmother one day a week.

"This was the first time that things seemed to calm down enough for me to enjoy being a parent. I got used to the asthma attacks, and no longer panicked unduly. My job was more under control and I even began to nurture an irregular social life. I no longer feel any guilt about having Matthew on my own, because I know he is always well looked after and that he receives a huge amount of love."

## Be nice to yourself

Learning to look after your new baby in the first weeks can be overwhelming, so look after yourself, too.

■ If you and your partner share the care of your baby you can both have time to yourselves.

■ Don't expect to be a perfect mother straight away. You have a lot to learn, and your baby is learning too.

■ Let the housework go. Do only the essential tasks, and get someone else to do them for you if you can.

■ Low potassium levels can contribute to a feeling of exhaustion. Eat plenty of potassium-rich foods, such as bananas, tomatoes, dried apricots, and plain yogurt.

■ Don't be surprised if you get the "baby blues" – up to 80 per cent of mothers do, and they will pass after about ten days. Seek help quickly if your feelings of depression continue.

# Organizing your life

As any mother knows, the physical, emotional, and social demands on your life seem to multiply unendingly with the arrival of a new baby. Interrupted nights and hectic days, coupled with the psychological pressure of taking responsibility for a new person, combine to heap unexpected stresses onto a new mother.

Organization can be the key to survival. Pregnancy is the ideal time to sit down and take stock of the situation before you are swept away by the joys and traumas of parenthood. But no matter what stage you are at, it's never too late to organize your time so that you get more out of it.

When you are planning your post-baby life, try dividing up things you have to think about into different areas: baby-related, work-related, home-related, partner-related, and you. This last category is usually under-valued, but happens to be one of the most important. If you aren't happy, your baby won't be happy. There are certain things that you'll find helpful to think about in advance. For instance, if you're going back to work, have you spoken to your manager about when you're returning? Have you considered doing fewer hours? Is it possible for you to do a job-share?

If you're going to be working part-time, will any of your working rights be affected? They shouldn't be, but you should check now rather than later. You don't want to discover that you might be facing a wage cut when you've already committed yourself to expensive childcare.

**Establishing a routine** A lot of the work you do in caring for your baby involves repetitive tasks, and these will be much easier to manage if you can work out some sort of timetable. Your routine should follow your baby's needs, not vice versa, so you won't be able to establish it straight away; it will take your baby three to six weeks or longer to settle into a pattern of feeding and sleeping.

Be careful not to confuse organization with regimentation. You don't want your life to be inflexible, as the needs of a young child can change hourly. What is important is that the routine you create for yourself doesn't either bore you or ignore you.

## Time for yourself

You are your child's universe, so it's best for her if you're not irritable, grumpy, and jaded. While you must make every effort to meet your baby's needs, you must also look after your own needs.

Plan at least half an hour each day to devote entirely to yourself – you may want to have a bath, read a book, watch television, phone a friend, meditate, exercise, or just relax. Before the baby arrives, finding half an hour for yourself seems simple, but once she's born it can seem like an impossible task. If you are to make some space for yourself, the first thing to do is learn to accept offers of help graciously. Too many mothers feel they are failures if they don't personally attend to their child's every need. This can be a dangerous route to go down. It's based on unrealistic expectations and eventually leads to exhaustion or even breakdown.

## Getting away

If you and your partner have already discussed how you are going to share the new workload (see Equal parenting, p.223), the next stage is discussing how you can make some time for each other once your baby has arrived. Try to arrange for a babysitter to come at least once a month, or better still once a week, so that parenting doesn't take over every single waking second of your lives. Look into the possibilities of nanny sharing (see p.241) or, if you're not working full-time, see if you can arrange a "baby-swap" with another mother. Find out about courses or activities that offer a crèche. This is an ideal way to meet friends, take up an interest, or increase your qualifications while your child is cared for and socializes with other children of her own age.

Spending time apart from your child doesn't necessarily make you a worse parent – in fact, in most cases it makes you a better one. If you spend all your time with your child she'll develop unrealistic expectations of relationships in general, and is likely to become overly demanding of friends and teachers alike.

It's also important to realize that although your child needs a close and loving relationship with you, it's a mistake to think that she must have your company every second of the day. She'll gain confidence and valuable social skills by learning to interact with adults and other children.

▶ **HANDING OVER** Your baby doesn't need you every minute of the day, so let someone else take care of her now and then while you go out.

# Time as a couple

As well as making time for yourself, it's important to have some time as a couple, without your baby. It's hard to be spontaneous now, so planning to spend time together becomes very important.

It may seem odd to make a formal appointment to spend time with your partner, but it really can help you keep up a healthy relationship once your baby's been born. You needn't make an elaborate arrangement – it could be something as simple as always having a cup of tea and chat at the end of the day or planning to go swimming together every Sunday while a friend or relative looks after your baby. Don't feel guilty – keeping your relationship strong is as important for your baby's happiness as it is for you.

# You and your partner

When your baby arrives your relationship with your partner changes immediately. All the common interests and experiences that previously held you together (your social life, your sex life, hobbies, holidays, and so on) suddenly go out of the window overnight. You're likely to be so exhausted that your partner's needs are the last thing on your mind.

The discipline that a new baby imposes on your life makes keeping excitement and sparkle in a relationship a great effort. That's why many couples feel it's just never the same – and they're right. Sometimes it's better than it ever was before, but problems arise when one partner, inevitably the father, feels excluded.

## Your partner's feelings

Although it's widely acknowledged that a mother undergoes huge upheavals during and after pregnancy, there's less appreciation of the effects that a new baby has on a father. Most fathers who support their partners through labour are in some state of shock after the birth. They're often traumatized by seeing their partners in considerable pain and distress. In fact, research has shown that nearly one in ten fathers suffers serious postnatal depression. One of the reasons suggested is that parental roles have changed so much, making it more difficult than ever for fathers to adjust to parenthood.

Unless you make an effort with your partner, he may start to feel that "three's a crowd" and that he's being pushed out. It's unwise to let this type of situation develop, not only because you need your partner's help, but because he needs to spend as much time as possible with your baby at an early age so he can build a loving relationship with her.

## The "rejected" father

Be aware that barriers between you and your partner are likely to spring from the fact that, as one psychologist put it, "although men and women become parents at the same time, they don't become parents in the same way". There

◄ **SHARING FEELINGS** Always make time to talk to your partner so you can avoid misunderstandings.

are many sociological, financial, and environmental reasons for this, but the result is often straightforward resentment or jealousy.

A man can quickly feel isolated within the family unit. He suddenly finds his partner's time monopolized by the new addition, and he may no longer be sure where he fits in. It's quite common to find a father becoming jealous of his own child. This situation may be exacerbated if there were differences of opinion about having the child in the first place.

Your partner may find these feelings particularly difficult to deal with if he also feels rejected on a sexual level. Often men take a new mother's diminished sex drive as a personal rebuff. If possible, discuss the effects this may have on your relationship before the baby arrives.

## Making love again

If you haven't lost your desire for sex, that's wonderful and you should make the most of it. There's no reason to wait for your first six-week checkup to have sex if you feel fit enough. For some women, however, especially those who have had episiotomies, sex isn't on the agenda. After the baby arrives, your partner may share your lack of interest in sex, but if he doesn't, one sure way to make him understand is to let him feel your episiotomy scar – most men will be very sympathetic.

A reduced sex drive is natural in that nature is doing her best to furnish you with the most reliable contraceptive of all – abstinence. After all, the last thing any new mother wants is to find that she's pregnant again so soon after her first baby. Try to impress upon your partner, however, that there may be emotional as well as physiological reasons for your not wishing to have sex, and he needs to respect these equally.

## Keep talking to each other

During the initial months of parenthood, both of you should make real efforts to keep the lines of communication open between you. No matter how exhausted or disorientated you may be, keep talking.

Having a child changes things forever. If you are the one to spend most time with your new baby, you'll be distracted from the fact that you have temporarily lost your lover. The same can't necessarily be said for your partner – if he isn't so involved in the day-to-day care of your baby, it's only natural that he feels the change in your relationship more keenly. Share the care as much as possible. Too often, women involve their partners by giving them tasks that are only indirectly linked to the baby. When a mother says, "I'll get Samantha ready while you run the bath", she is sharing some of the work, but not the child. Try reversing some of these options so that your partner spends sufficient time with the baby, and make sure that both consider each other's needs.

# Tips for new dads

Once your baby is born, it's important to be sensitive to your partner's needs and prepared for the physical and emotional difficulties that she may experience after the birth.

■ Don't leave the entire care of your child to your partner, even if she doesn't seem to mind. There'll be hidden resentment, and you'll lose the chance to be a real father.

■ Spend some time alone with your baby to increase your confidence and give your partner a break.

■ If you are working, talk to your employers about the new addition to your family. Take paternity leave when your baby's born, and see if you can change some of your working hours afterwards.

2

▲ **AN ACTIVE FATHER** A father who helps care for his child will feel needed by both his partner and the baby.

## What to take: young baby

When you go out with your young baby you'll need to take some essentials such changing and feeding equipment with you. Here are some suggestions:

■ changing bag or mat, change of clothes, fabric or disposable nappies, baby wipes, nappy cream, and container for dirty nappies

■ change of breast pads if you're breastfeeding, or flask of hot water, bottle, and feed if you're bottlefeeding

■ sunhat or woollen hat

■ cardigan.

▲ BABY SLING A sling can be the easiest way of taking a young baby out and about and she'll enjoy the close contact.

# Travel and outings

Time spent in planning your outing or travel schedule with your baby is never wasted. The younger your baby, the more you'll have to plan. In the first few months, your baby's feeding schedule may not be very predictable, so you'll need at least one spare bottle if you're not breastfeeding and, of course, whatever changing equipment you normally use.

When you go out, plan your route so that you know where you can stop, where you can change your baby, and where you can feed her without embarrassment or inconvenience. If you're planning to shop, it's worth checking with stores to find out if they have a mother-and-baby changing room, and avoiding those that don't. Lightweight baby-changing bags containing a portable changing mat are a great help.

With a very young baby it's simply not worth undertaking a very busy outing during which you may have to walk a great deal, carry heavy loads, or make lots of changes of transport. Be easy on yourself. Try to take a friend or your partner with you if you can, so there's always an extra pair of hands and someone to help you should you have problems. Your baby can go with you anywhere as long as you're well enough prepared and have something in which to carry her – a sling, pram, or car seat.

## Using a pushchair

If you don't want to carry your baby in a sling, a pushchair is ideal for a small baby, who will fit comfortably and snugly into its shape. Babies are interested in their surroundings from an early age, so as soon as your baby can sit up, angle the pushchair so that she can see what is going on around her when you're out and about.

You'll need to be adept at collapsing and opening the pushchair within a few seconds without any problems, so practise it at home before your first outing. If you can't fold up the pushchair efficiently, you will find people jostling to get in front of you when you are in a queue, which will only add to your frustration. And don't forget you'll have to do all this while holding your baby. Here are a few safety tips:

■ When you open your pushchair, always make sure that it's in the fully extended position with the brakes fully locked.
■ Always make sure your baby's safety harness is fastened.

- Never, ever, leave your baby in a pushchair unattended.
- Should your baby fall asleep in the pushchair, adjust it to the lie-back position so that she can sleep comfortably.
- Don't put shopping on the handles of the pushchair; it can unbalance the pushchair and your baby may be injured.
- When you stop, always put the brakes on because you could inadvertently take your hands off the pushchair and it could run away.
- Check your pushchair regularly to make sure the brakes and catches work well and that the wheels are solid.

## Public transport

Using public transport can really be a trial, as neither buses nor trains are equipped or serviced for mothers and young children. Picture yourself with a pushchair, a heavy and wriggling baby, the baby bag, your handbag, a coat, and possibly a toddler in tow, and public transport is the last thing you want to face.

Of course, you can make things easier by never travelling in the rush hour or, with a young baby, carrying her around in a sling. For an older baby, a backpack makes you much more independent, and you can manage everything more easily with your hands free. Always prepare yourself well ahead of time. I simply would not leave home with my children without some distracting toys and favourite books and snacks. Gather everything together in good time so that you can check them over to make sure that you haven't forgotten anything. The same goes for when you are getting off a bus or train; be ready to get off in plenty of time for your stop. Always ask for help from fellow passengers.

## Special outings

Your baby is never too young for an outing; indeed, with a young baby you can go just about anywhere and, provided she can look about her, she will enjoy the change of scene even if she doesn't understand much of what's going on. When planning an outing for an older child, always try to consider what your child's personality can cope with best. If you have a quiet child who has a long concentration span, you can take her to a flower show or an antique market, and point out the things around her. If, on the other hand, she is very active, she will need more space to run around in, so a trip to the zoo, a playground, or a fair is more appropriate. Wherever you go, be ready to make endless stops to look at anything that catches your child's attention. Always take enough drinks and snacks to keep your child happy for the full duration of the trip. Don't take on a trip of any kind if you or your child are feeling out of sorts; the day is bound to be a disaster, so don't feel guilty about cancelling the outing altogether.

2

## What to take: older baby

You'll need to take food or snacks, and feeding and changing equipment. Here are some ideas:

- changing mat, fabric or disposable nappies, baby wipes and nappy cream
- sealable container for nappies
- baby food, dish, spoon, and bib
- snack, such as fruit
- water or diluted fruit juice
- sunhat or woollen hat
- cardigan or sweater
- comforter and favourite book and/or toy.

▲ **HANDLING A PUSHCHAIR** Make sure that you can kick it shut, open it up one-handed, and operate the brakes.

When going out with your baby, always plan all your movements and stops in detail, so that you can use your time efficiently.

■ Try to fit in a shopping trip between feeds or, if you think that it is going to be a longer trip than the usual interval between meals, take a snack with you.

■ Always bring basic changing equipment in case your child needs a clean nappy. Many stores these days have special dedicated areas for mothers and babies.

■ If you are travelling by car, adjust your baby's seat to a reclining position so that she can sleep.

▲ HARNESS AND REINS Keep your older baby safe on busy streets with a harness and reins. These harnesses can also be used in a highchair with anchor straps.

# Shopping trips

Taking a baby shopping brings its own problems. Your baby can easily become bored, hungry, fretful, and difficult to manage, so it's worth planning ahead quite carefully to minimize stress. Going by car will make a world of difference: you can feed and change your baby in privacy in the car, you can stack your shopping in the boot, and you don't have to worry about catching buses and trains. If you don't own a car, it might be worth asking a friend who does to join your shopping expedition, or ask a relative if you can borrow his or her car occasionally.

Try to shop fairly early in the day, because the streets and shops are less busy, and there are fewer distractions for your baby or child. Always try to give a baby a good meal before you leave; that way you may have two or three hours to complete your purchases without her getting hungry. Try to undertake a shopping trip with your partner, so that one of you is free to make the purchases.

Bring whatever equipment you would bring on any other trip. Toys may seem something of a burden, but they will more than pay their way. You can attach them to a backpack, pushchair, or supermarket trolley for your child to play with without her being able to throw them on to the floor. Bring some kind of small snack, too, because shopping seems to make children either hungry or fretful, and a snack will deal with both.

## Shopping with your baby

You need to have your hands free for shopping, and so how you carry your baby is worth some thought and attention. Most of the time you can use a pushchair, make sure she is strapped in. Once your baby is able to sit up with good head and back control, you can put her into your shopping trolley in a supermarket. Many supermarkets now have trolleys with integral baby seats and harnesses, but with the older, tip-up seats you need to strap your baby in with a harness. Because babies are always grasping and reaching for interesting objects, try to walk down the centre of the aisle so that your baby isn't tempted to dislodge tins and packets. A backpack is ideal for carrying your baby on shopping trips; her interest will always be engaged, she'll feel very secure with such close physical contact, and she should be well behaved and cry very little. Best of all, your hands will be left free.

## Occupying a toddler or older child

Once your child is a little older, make shopping trips more fun by talking about everything you do and see. Keep up a running commentary, with observations or questions that engage your child. Your young child will love being involved in shopping decisions, and she'll feel very important and needed if you act on her preferences. With items where brand is not important to you ask your child to point to the one she'd like you to buy.

As my children got older and could toddle around the shopping aisles, I used to ask them to put all their choices into the trolley themselves, so that they were constantly engaged looking for their favourite things. They felt a great sense of pride in finally finding what they wanted, and a sense of achievement in filling up the trolley.

One of the ways I used to distract and entertain my children on a shopping trip was to ask them if they were thirsty or hungry immediately on entering the supermarket, and buy them a drink or a healthy snack. That way they could munch or sip their way around the supermarket and feel quite happy and occupied the whole time.

**Keeping your child with you** Reins are a very good idea for an older child because she will feel a sense of freedom and independence, but she'll never be able to get very far away from you; a wrist link that's securely attached to her reins will prevent you becoming separated from her. If you have a child who keeps on getting into mischief, this may be the only way to prevent her from wandering off and getting lost.

## Learning

You can use your shopping trips as opportunities to teach your child all sorts of things – about colours, for example: "This tin is red; that packet is blue; that jar has a yellow wrapper." Your child will recognize the cornflake packet that she sees at breakfast every morning and will soon understand what the words mean, so that from quite an early age, say, 18 months, you can say to her, "Can you see the cornflakes? Now I wonder where the jam is?"

Early reading can be encouraged by teaching your child to associate the contents of a packet or tin with things that she actually eats at home. For example, if she drinks cocoa regularly, you only have to take the tin of the brand she sees every day from the shelf and ask "What does this word say?" for her to respond with "cocoa", because she has learned from experience that cocoa is what comes out of that tin. All my children began to read food packets before they read anything else.

Trips to the supermarket will also teach your child about the act of shopping itself, and the choosing and decision-making that is involved. You can introduce her to the value of money, and to a certain degree you can teach her about manners and sociability, because she will very quickly learn the justice of allowing other people to get to the shelves when she has a great interest in doing so herself.

# Shopping with your toddler

Once your child can walk, losing her in a crowd can be a worry, so take precautions against this.

■ Use reins or a wrist strap in busy places so that she can't wander.

■ Dress your toddler in something brightly coloured so that you can spot her from a distance.

■ Have some sort of family code for your children to come back to you. I used to carry a small whistle around my neck.

■ All shopping trips can be lessons even if you only teach your child about healthy eating (for example that fresh vegetables are better than tinned).

■ From as early an age as possible make your child learn her name, address, and telephone number, so she can repeat it if she gets lost.

■ Teach her never to walk off with any stranger.

■ Make sure your child recognizes her surroundings when she's near to home by pointing out landmarks on every journey: "There's the pillar box on the corner, and there's the blue gate, and our house is the next one along."

## Baby on board

Plan and prepare for your journey well in advance. These tips will all help to make things go more smoothly for you.

■ By law, you must have a car seat for each child under the age of 12, correctly fitted and with safety harness (see p.312).

■ Never put a child seat on the front seat of a car with an airbag.

■ Fit a blind over the passenger windows to block out bright sun.

■ Keep a bag in the car with basic changing and feeding equipment; restock it often.

■ Always have a box of tissues and some baby wipes in the car.

■ Take a few toys, a rug, and some CDs out with you – stories are always popular.

■ Carry a bag of spare clothes for each child in the car. Don't worry about accidents, just change your child quickly into dry clothes.

■ For safety, tape cutlery to the inside of food containers.

■ Always take some soft clothing like an anorak or sweater that your child can use as a pillow.

■ Always have a supply of bags for rubbish or wet clothes.

■ Try to start travelling early in the morning, or at night when the roads are empty.

# Car journeys

Children can be very active on car journeys. They're learning and taking great pride in newly acquired physical skills, like jumping, skipping, hopping, climbing, and running, and it's difficult for them to be confined in a small space. All this is intensified in hot weather because your child will become tired, touchy, and tearful more easily than usual. Never leave a child alone in a car in hot weather, because the temperature inside the car can rise much higher than the temperature outside, causing her to become quickly overheated and even dehydrated. Always screen your child from bright sunlight by putting a purpose-made blind over the window through which the sun is shining. You might also think about attaching a canopy to your baby's seat, which serves the same purpose.

A long car journey is hard for everyone, so make sure that your child is cool, fed, given enough to drink, has plenty to occupy her, and is taken to the lavatory without a fuss; accept accidents philosophically.

## Safety

Whatever else, your baby must be transported safely in a car. A young baby should sit in a rear-facing car seat. This can be in the front or rear of the car but is safer in the rear. Do not use a baby seat in the front of the car if there is a passenger airbag. An older baby or toddler should sit in a front-facing car seat in the rear of the car. Children over four can use a booster seat and seat belt.

After any accident, you should replace your seat belts, your child's car seat, and the anchorage kit, as they will have been badly strained and may be damaged. For the same reason, you should never buy secondhand car seats, harnesses, or anchorage kits.

Misbehaviour like shouting or kicking should not be tolerated; it is extremely distracting for you while you are driving and could even be dangerous. If your child does behave badly, pull straight over to the side of the road, stop the car, and sort out the difficulty. Tell your child that you are going no further until she starts to behave herself properly.

## Longer journeys

Most children will become restless if they have to travel for longer than an hour and a half. Your child has no idea of time, so she'll be constantly asking you when you are going to arrive, or whether you are nearly there. Restlessness can be alleviated by stopping the car every hour for about five minutes and allowing your child to run around, explore, and generally get rid of excess energy. Warn her in advance about the stops so that she can get herself ready by putting on a coat and hat if it's cold outside.

**Feeding a baby**  A car journey – especially a long one – is when breastfeeding comes into its own, because you have no preparations to make. Never feed when the car is in motion, because your baby would be very unsafe. If you're bottlefeeding, use disposable bottles and feeds, or mix the formula in a sterilized bottle when you need it, using some boiled water from a thermos flask. Never try to keep made-up feeds warm because you are only letting germs multiply.

Once your baby is weaned, you'll need to take food, a feeding dish, a plastic spoon, a bib, a cup with a spout, a supply of drinks, and something your baby can nibble on, such as pieces of dry toast or rusks. You can feed your baby directly from the jar, but remember to throw away anything she doesn't finish afterwards, because the food will be contaminated with saliva, and germs will grow in it very quickly.

**Changing a baby**  Even if you normally use fabric nappies, forget the expense and take disposables with you on a journey: they're just so convenient, quick, and easy for both you and your baby. You can always change your baby on the back seat of the car or in the boot if she lies on a rug or a towel. There is no need to do any more than top and tail your baby while travelling, but be meticulous about cleaning the nappy area. Wipes are an essential, as is a sealable container for dirty nappies.

**The older child**  Your child will get bored and hungry, so always have some healthy snacks like raisins, sugarless cornflakes, or pieces of cheese in plastic bags, and take more drinks than you ever think you'll need – your child often wants to drink more when she's travelling. Seedless grapes are good snacks, as they quench your child's thirst and satisfy her hunger.

Take some toys to distract your child while travelling (books may be a bad idea, though, if she suffers from motion sickness), and these can be arranged in different ways for safety and convenience. Buy or make a special cover for the front headrest of your car with pockets in the back which can carry drinks, snacks, and toys, or tie toys to coat-hooks or handles so that they don't get lost under seats. Magnetized games are particularly useful in cars because the bits cannot get lost, and you can stick Velcro on certain toys so that they will adhere to the car seat and stay in one place while your child is playing with them.

CDs of music or children's stories may give you at least half an hour of peace, so always have one at the ready. Word games are fun too. "I spy" is always a favourite, particularly if you join in, and will keep your children occupied for quite a long time if you make the object interesting. Keep a special treat tucked away in the glove compartment with which to relieve tension or tears.

# Motion sickness

If you have suffered from motion sickness, or there's any history of migraines, eczema, or allergies in the family, then your child is quite likely to suffer from motion sickness too. There are some things that you can do to help minimize motion sickness.

■ Don't give your child a rich or greasy meal before a journey, or too many snacks on the journey.

■ You can give your child a motion-sickness drug, available from doctors; always give it at least half an hour before you leave.

■ Stay calm. If you're anxious your children will become anxious too. Motion sickness is brought on by anxiety and excitement, and is much more likely to happen on the outward journey, so be patient when you leave home.

■ Snacks that can be sucked are a good idea, because they don't create a mess, so take along a supply of glucose sweets.

■ Keeping your child occupied or distracted will help prevent motion sickness, but don't let her read, as this may bring it on.

■ If you notice your child becoming pale or quiet, ask her if she wants to stop. Be very sympathetic if she actually is sick and give her time to recover before you continue with your journey.

■ Give your child a drink after she's been sick to get rid of the taste of vomit from her mouth.

## What to pack

Use the following checklist to make sure you've got everything you need for your child.

- Passport and immunization documents.
- Your changing bag.
- Travel cot.
- Pushchair or sling.
- Car seat if necessary.
- Changing equipment or potty.
- Feeding equipment.
- A vacuum flask for cool drinks.
- Toys and games.
- Her favorite comforters.
- Sunhat and sunscreen.
- Cotton, drip-dry clothes.
- Plenty of clothes to protect your child from sunburn or heatstroke.

# Planning a holiday

Never think your baby is too young to travel. Children nearly always surprise us, and rise to the occasion in ways we never think possible. I'm told that when I was only six weeks old, my mother and father took me camping, living under canvas for two weeks by the sea! When my third son was only ten weeks old we took him to Italy, and while we were finding our lost luggage in Rome, he was by far the best behaved of us all.

## Before you go

A golden rule if you are going abroad on holiday is to make sure that your hotel has facilities for children, and really likes children. Things to look for in a hotel include such child facilities as a crèche, a place where you can take your child for early supper, a children's menu, highchairs and cots, a playroom, and an outdoor play area with trained attendants. It's worth going to some trouble to ensure these things are available because if your children are not happy, you will not enjoy the holiday yourself. If you are going to the seaside, make sure that the beaches are safe.

**Vaccinations** Well ahead of time – six months at least – you must take advice on what vaccinations or immunizations are needed, because regulations are constantly changing all over the world. The reason for starting early is that some vaccinations need quite a long lead time, and for others, as with hepatitis, you may have to wait four to six weeks between injections, or you may not be able to follow one vaccination immediately with another. You can get information from your doctor or practice nurse or from major outlets of your travel agent. Check for any other items you might need, such as water sterilizing tablets.

## Air travel

Most airlines make special facilities available to children as long as they're given warning. If you have a baby, ask for bulk-head seats, which have special folding tables for a Moses basket or cradle. If these are not available, ask for any seat that might have more leg room. Travel cots may be available in-flight. Families with young children are usually allowed to board first, or you can arrange for priority boarding. Most travel agents will make all these enquiries on your behalf. Here are some things to think about before you travel:

- Aim to reach the airport early enough to avoid long check-in queues, and give yourself plenty of time to get there. You may be able to check in on the Internet, so ask your airline.

- Put all travel documents in a special bag, inside a loose, lightweight shoulder bag. If you can, fit in your baby bag too, with spare nappies, spare clothing, and anything else your baby needs. Be sure to check the airline's latest regulations on hand baggage, though.
- Make sure that everything you take on board has an indestructible label, including your baby bag.
- Take a few of your baby's favourite toys with you or see whether any of the games suggested for use in the car (see pp.236–37) would work on a plane to entertain your child.
- Carry your baby in a sling so that your hands are free.
- Change your baby's nappy just before getting on the plane.
- Take a folded pushchair on the plane with you; the crew will take it from you as you enter, and return it to you as you leave.
- Babies and children feel some pain during takeoff and landing, so keep aside a little treat or your baby's comforter so she can suck on it to equalize the pressure in her ears.

## Sun safety

Children can get heatstroke (see p.338) in a surprisingly short time and this is a dangerous condition. Most often it occurs when the nape of the neck is exposed to hot sun, which interferes with the temperature-regulating centre in the brain. Children sweat a lot more than adults do in a hot climate, so always have water with you and give your child as much water to drink as she wants.

If your baby is under six months, never expose her skin to direct, strong sunlight. Keep her as cool as possible, with light, cotton clothing that covers almost all of her body. When she's in her pushchair or pram, shield her with a sunshade.

Make sure older children wear loose cotton clothing and sunhats when they're out in hot sun; good-quality sunglasses are also helpful. There are now special T-shirts and sun suits that filter UVA and UVB rays for additional protection. Sunhats should have a wide brim, so that they shield the back of the neck as well as the face – the wider the brim, the more protection the hat will provide. Children need to wear a high-factor sunscreen (see column, right) on any exposed skin all the time that they are outdoors – even if they are swimming or if the weather is cloudy, as they could still burn. Try to make sure children spend time in the shade between about 11am and 3pm when the sun's rays are at their strongest.

Damage from the sun is accumulative so that cancers that develop in the elderly are the result of their lifetime exposure to the sun. It's wrong, therefore, to let children think there's no need to worry about sunburn at their age. Instead, teach them to enjoy the sun safely from the start.

# Sunscreens

**There are many sunscreens available and most protect against both UVA and UVB rays. Choose one with a sun protection factor (SPF) of at least 30.**

Apply the sunscreen 30 minutes before going out in the sun and then every two hours, or after swimming. Many sunscreens say that they are waterproof, but if your child is running in and out of the sea or swimming pool, it's safest to re-apply often.

Experts now believe that although sunscreens allow longer in the sun without burning, the carcinogenic effects of sun exposure are still occurring. This falsely perceived "safe" exposure is leading to the rapidly rising incidence of skin cancer throughout the world. For this reason, it's vital to make sure you protect your child in the sun.

▲ **SUN PROTECTION** Dress your child in a sunhat and T-shirt and apply sunscreen regularly when she's outside playing in the sun.

## Feeding

**You'll need to decide how you want your baby to be fed while you're out at work.**

If you begin working before she's six months old – that is, before any mixed feeding – you'll need to plan. Introduce a routine so that feeding times are predictable and constant. If you feed your baby at breakfast and around 6pm, the person who looks after her during the day need give only the expressed milk or milk formula for the other two daytime feeds.

If you don't want your baby to take any milk substitutes, freeze expressed breastmilk (see p.44). It should take around two weeks to get into this routine. You will need to run down your daytime milk production before returning to work or you will be most uncomfortable during the day.

# Returning to work

When it's time for you to return to work, you may realize that you haven't given yourself enough time to readjust after pregnancy. It's always a good idea to check with your doctor, as there are health factors to consider about which she can advise you. Some mothers find that they can't bring themselves to leave their baby, while others – even though they adore the baby – are climbing the walls and have to "escape".

If you've decided to return to work, be assured that as long as you arrange good childcare (see column, opposite), you won't be neglecting your child. There's no danger of your young baby forgetting who you are, or transferring her affection to her daytime carer. The really important thing is that when you get home you spend quality time with your child.

I know from my own experience as a working mother that guilt pangs are inevitable. I felt certain, however, that my baby would instinctively know I was her mother. I was reassured when I later came across research showing that very young babies are quite able to single out their parents (whether biological or adoptive) due to the loving, interested attention that only parents can give. Similarly, it has been shown that premature babies

► **CHILDMINDERS** You will be able to tell from your child's reactions whether she feels loved and secure with the childminder you have chosen.

can distinguish between the touch of their parents' hands through an incubator and the more matter-of-fact handling of nursing staff.

The important point is that it is the quality of the time you spend with her that counts more than the quantity. Love isn't measured in time: love is what you put into time, no matter how short.

## Combining two roles

The job you face at home is twice as demanding as the one you face at work, and your terms of employment are worse. Your efforts will go largely unnoticed by society and, of course, you won't get paid a penny. In fact, you will have to pay for the privilege of being a parent – but as most parents will tell you, it's a privilege worth paying for!

Your child's first step, first smile, and first word are all priceless personal achievements. Helping to mould a tiny baby into a thoughtful, well-adjusted individual is a task requiring sacrifice, responsibility, and, above all, love. It also yields huge emotional dividends. To my mind this makes parenting one of the most important and rewarding jobs in the world. Given this, it is disturbing to see the low status attached to parenting, particularly for women, who shoulder much of the burden. Being a good parent involves helping your child's personality to develop in a positive sense, and being a good role model. If you want your children to grow up and work hard, then the fact that you work hard at your own job sets them an excellent example.

Having to combine the role of principal parent with full-time career is not easy, but women are doing it with imagination and sheer hard work. The rise of the mythical "super-mum" has meant that we are often expected to do it all without any help. There are a lot of "super-mums" around: they are the ones who manage everything day after day, at home and in the office, without failing to give love and energy to their children.

**Finding help** If you want to use a day nursery, you'll probably have to register while you are pregnant. If you want home-based care, start looking for reliable childcare at least six weeks before you plan to return to work. Getting help from a relative can be the perfect solution for many mothers, but think carefully. You can start to feel uncomfortably indebted, or conversely, they can feel taken for granted. Because you don't have a "professional" relationship, it may be difficult to stipulate rules and guidelines, particularly if your views on child-rearing diverge.

However, if these problems are dealt with early on, you can benefit immeasurably from the security, flexibility, and low cost of this type of arrangement. If you ask a friend, not a relative, to help on a regular basis and you pay her, she must by law be registered as a childminder.

# Choosing childcare

Your baby doesn't only need to be changed and fed: she needs the kind of loving attention that you would give her yourself if she is to learn to interact and become a sociable child.

**Childminders** These are usually mothers themselves, and must be registered with the local social services department. Your local council will provide a list, but you should arrange payment and hours with the childminder.

**Day nurseries** Run privately, these often have long waiting lists and usually only a small number of places for babies. Put your name down as soon as you know you are pregnant if you want your child to go to a particular nursery.

**Nanny or mother's help** This kind of help can be expensive, but you might consider sharing a nanny with another family. You can find one through agencies, or by advertising locally, or in a newspaper or magazine. Parents' groups may be able to put you in contact with other mothers interested in sharing a nanny.

**Crèche** Perhaps you are very lucky and have enlightened employers who make it possible to take your baby to work with you. This means you can continue breastfeeding and have your baby close by all day. If there's a crèche at your workplace, ensure you arrange a place well before your baby is born.

## Effects on your children

**Research suggests that children can be better off with two unhappy parents than with divorced parents.**

However, the research gives no indication of the different divorce situations, which are critical in determining the effect on the child.

An amicable divorce may be barely damaging and its effect entirely different from that of a bitter, acrimonious divorce. The main reason for this is that in an acrimonious situation, each parent usually does his or her best to turn the children against the other parent. This has a very negative and damaging effect on children, and should be avoided at all costs.

# Separation and divorce

At some stage in every relationship, problems arise. Some couples live happily ever after, but many don't. This doesn't necessarily reflect a lowering of moral values; it is more an indication of the complexities and pressures of modern life. Support systems are weaker and expectations higher.

## Periods of change

The problem for nearly all couples is that in the long term people change. Although this can be difficult, it can also be invigorating and constructive. If you learn to develop together, you will prevent boredom and stagnation building up in your relationship.

At the end of periods of change, which are often fraught with emotional insecurity, you'll either grow together or grow apart. Whatever happens, it's vital that your children feel secure at all times. For young children, change within the family (or fear of change) is very damaging. Children don't have the defence mechanisms to protect themselves from the severe emotional insecurity that a breakup can cause.

## Explaining to your children

A young child is like a sponge that soaks up emotional signals, whether or not they're directed at her. If you are happy, the chances are your child will be happy; if you are sad, she'll be sad. Although it's worth making an effort "for the sake of the children", don't fall into the trap of thinking they won't know what's going on. They usually sense when something is wrong, whether or not you have a smile on your face.

Because of this, it's always best to explain, at least partially, what is going on. If you don't, children will invent their own explanations, mistakenly blaming themselves for problems in the family. This is because children under five conceive the world only in relation to themselves. If you don't give a plausible explanation of why you and your partner are arguing or splitting up, they may come up with explanations that are inconceivable to an adult, but make perfect sense to a child, such as: "Daddy has left because I don't tidy my room properly", or "Mummy is upset because I wet the bed/I'm clumsy/I lost my pocket money". Feelings of guilt are very damaging, especially for a child already

▲**LOVE AND REASSURANCE** Your child will need extra love and reassurance if you and your partner have relationship problems. He needs to know you both care for him, no matter what happens.

struggling to come to terms with the emotional turmoil and insecurity that marital breakups can trigger. Doubt is one of the worst fears in a child's mind, so never leave your child in any doubt that you love her.

## Divorce

If you reach the point where the only option left is divorce or separation, don't assume automatically that your children will be devastated. Some will be, but the effect on your child will depend greatly on age, personality, the circumstances of the divorce, and the prevailing social attitudes.

I know of one primary school class in London, for instance, where out of 35 children, only five had parents who were still together. They were regularly teased by the others from "broken homes" who saw these five children as materially disadvantaged: the children whose parents were still together got only one set of presents on their birthday or at Christmas and they had only one house. Although having divorced parents is nothing to boast about, many of these children did. This may be deeply shocking to a lot of people, but it is just one more indication of the changing times.

## Moving out

If the time comes when one of you has to move out, it's vital your child knows that both parents still love her in the same way and that both will continue to be active parents. Your child should know exactly when she will see the parent who has moved out and, no matter how difficult it is, every effort should be made not to break these arrangements.

If you are the parent left with full-time responsibility for your child when your partner has moved out, try not to be upset if she misses her father or mother. Don't try to make her forget that the other parent exists, and don't speak abusively about the other parent, as this will only confuse your child further. Even if your child appears to be unaffected by a marital split, keep a close eye on her and ask her teachers if they notice any difference in her at school. Some children have fewer questions than others and keep their feelings of insecurity to themselves, but they may still need extra attention and love. Increased bedwetting, thumb-sucking, and "clinginess" are all signs that your child needs extra reassurance.

Grandparents can be a great boon at the time of the divorce. If possible, do encourage your child to see both sets. Don't let bad feeling act as a cut-off. Think of your child first – she needs continuity, security, and reassurance, and grandparents are second to none at providing these, as long as they don't bad-mouth either parent.

Ask your children about their worries and anxieties and give them space to voice them. Listen and take them seriously. Act upon them. They'll almost certainly be things you haven't thought of.

## Access

**Whatever your feelings are about your partner, it's best for your child if you're easy-going and generous about access.**

Don't be stingy and don't be confrontational – it causes your child such anguish. Try to meet somewhere civilized like one of your homes, not in a park or shopping mall, or your child will feel like a commodity.

Plan well ahead, don't break promises at the last minute, and if your partner is late be breezy about it, otherwise your child will worry about both of you. Don't make it an opportunity to denigrate her father or mother; be offhand, and keep your child calm: "Oh, I expect the traffic's bad" or "Shall we have a game of snap till Daddy gets here?"

If your partner is consistently late or unreasonable, arrange a separate meeting to discuss this, out of earshot of your child. The only time to consider preventing your ex-partner having any access to your child is if you think she's at risk of being kidnapped or otherwise harmed. In such cases, it is best to seek professional advice, either through counselling services or a lawyer.

## Getting help

New parents are often surprised at the amount of work involved in caring for a newborn, and this is even more true for mothers who have multiple births.

■ Many mothers of twins don't realize how much help they will need, although mothers who have already had one baby tend to be more realistic about this. Don't underestimate the task of caring for twins, and don't for one minute imagine that asking for help reflects badly on your adequacy as a parent.

■ Helpers can create extra work. This is particularly true of a friend or relative who moves in to "help" you and then expects you to cook for her every evening, so consider this carefully before accepting long-term help.

■ You may find that everyone wants to help with the babies and no one wants to do the housework. Don't be afraid to be firm about what kinds of help you most need.

# Multiple births

Twins are by far the most common multiple births. Identical twins are formed by the splitting of a single fertilized egg: the two babies develop from one egg and one sperm, and share a placenta. Non-identical, or fraternal, twins develop from the fertilization of two eggs by two sperm and have a placenta each. Multiples can occur in any combination of identical and fraternal.

## Pregnancy and birth

Early rapid weight gain is a common sign of twin pregnancy. The minor complaints of pregnancy can become more uncomfortable and there are a few clinical conditions that are relatively more common in multiple pregnancies, such as anaemia or fluid retention. Make sure you eat well and get plenty of rest.

For a mother carrying two babies, pregnancy is naturally more tiring than for a mother carrying only one. But it's usually shorter – 37 weeks rather than 40 weeks. Delivery is reassuringly straightforward and, while it's been known for the birth of the second baby to be delayed by days, this is rare and the gap between babies is usually less than half an hour. Twins are more likely to be premature.

## Breast or bottle?

| BREASTFEEDING | BOTTLEFEEDING |
|---|---|
| Breastfeeding is slightly more difficult to establish than the bottle and it's not easy when you're on an outing. | An advantage is the freedom for your twins to be fed by their father (or anyone else) if you're tired, and in public. |
| There are all the usual advantages of breastfeeding, especially protection against infection – very important to twins because prematurity is more common than with single babies. | Neither you nor your babies will find your return to work such a difficult transition to make, as bottlefeeding is already established. |
| You can hold both your babies and feed them at the same time, giving them equal attention and nourishment. | It's virtually impossible to bottlefeed your two babies at the same time, at least not holding them close to you in the crook of your arm, while making eye contact. |

## Feeding your twins

There are some special considerations if you are trying to feed twin babies and, while I would always advocate breastfeeding, you may want to consider the pros and cons set out in the chart opposite. Many mothers of twins settle for a combination of breastfeeding and bottlefeeding. When you come to establishing daily routines, there are several ways in which you can try to get your twins to feed and sleep at similar times, although initially one may wake early and want feeding and the other may simply sleep on. You could feed the baby who wakes first while waiting for the second to wake, then reverse them; or feed both at once and spend time talking or playing with them afterwards.

## Should twins sleep together?

Almost serendipitously it was found that premature twins, if placed in the same incubator, were happier, more contented, and gained more weight than when they were nursed separately. A moment's reflection is enough to understand why this must be so. After all, twins share a very confined space for nine months and solitude will be quite difficult to bear.

Once at home you can extend this theory into the nursery by placing both your babies in the same crib. This will suit tranquil sleepers, but restless babies may well disturb each other. The next step might be to try adjacent cots. Another equally good approach is to treat twins simply as siblings, and have them sleep in the same room, but not in particularly close proximity. The crying of one twin doesn't usually seem to bother the other unduly.

## Nappy changing

Try to share the nappy changing between you, otherwise life becomes one long nappy change for one of you. Most parents of twins opt for disposable nappies, and there's a special small size for preterm babies. You'll probably find that it will be several weeks before your twins are big enough for the next size of disposable nappies. Unless two of you are working together, it's best to change your twins one at a time.

## Importance of play

Because of the demands they make on your time, twins are likely to receive less adult stimulation through play and physical contact than single babies, but they get far more peer stimulation and company. Loving interaction with you is essential to their physical, mental, and social development. Set aside time for play every day, or arrange the babies' sleeping times so that they are awake in the evening when both parents can play with them.

## The father's role

Most fathers want to be closely concerned with the care of their babies and so will enjoy looking after either or both of them to give you a break.

A father fulfils a pivotal role in a family with twin babies and a couple should discuss in some detail the sort of activities he'll be helping with or have sole responsibility for when the babies come home. Some are obvious, like going to the supermarket, doing household chores, cooking, and laundry. Night duty is particularly important to give respite to a mother who is overtaxed during the day and exhausted at night.

▲ **ATTENTION FROM YOU** Twins enjoy being together, but they also need lots of individual love and attention from both of their parents.

## Dressing twins

**Many parents wish to dress twins alike, especially if they are identical, and this can look very appealing.**

However, from the outset it's only fair to twins to think of them and treat them as individuals. It's difficult enough for a single child to achieve a sense of self and self-worth without having to battle with a doppelgänger who looks alike and is dressed identically. Not only that, twins find they have to distinguish between themselves to friends, relatives, and strangers; dressing them individually goes a long way to avoiding such embarrassment.

As your twins get older, I think it's much better to let them decide for themselves what they wear, and if you've always dressed them differently they'll probably continue to do so themselves.

# Being a twin

Twins have a close and intuitive understanding of each other and enjoy the companionship of a child of the same age. Having the support and approval of another person can be very reassuring as they grow.

## Physical development

Don't make the mistake of expecting your twins to do too much too soon and don't compare them to other babies of the same age, or each other. Like any other babies born preterm, if your babies were premature, their progress will be slower than that of babies who went the full 40 weeks.

The development of a preterm baby can be slow and erratic, and for some every day can be an uphill struggle. It's very encouraging to know, however, that twins born after 32 weeks will develop quite normally, although they may achieve their milestones somewhat later than full-term babies. So for each milestone add on their period of prematurity to the dates given for full-term babies. If progress seems slow, be consoled by the knowledge that, in an American study, twins were shown to have caught up in height by the age of four and weight by eight. Don't make the mistake of expecting your twins to develop identically even though they look alike. Non-identical twins rarely do, and of course a boy and a girl develop in different ways at different rates anyway. In boys and girls growth spurts and skill acquisitions don't happen at the same ages.

## Twins as individuals

Much of family life militates against twins being treated as individuals. It's just easier and simpler for them to be placed alongside each other in their highchairs and fed from the same dish, even with the same spoon! When young they may have played together with the same toys at the same time. It's irresistible for parents, family, and friends to treat twins as a single identity, where individuality is submerged. But there are some safeguards that can be put in place. You can

**◄ ENCOURAGING INDIVIDUALITY**
Encourage each twin's sense of identity and individuality by dressing them in different clothes or colours.

choose names that don't sound similar, and dress them in different clothes. Different coloured bed linen and towels help too. Also, try to be on the alert for individual personality traits and help them to flower.

## The special bond

The extra strong bond that exists between twins is legendary. Even after separation, twins can seem to be governed by a unifying force, marrying on the same day, buying the same sort of house, even choosing identical cars. Very often each relates to the other more intimately than with any other person, including parents and, later on, even partners. It's as though there are unspoken ties that defy explanation and love that outweighs all others. And, of course, twins do understand each other in a way no one else can because they spend so much time together, attending to one another, covering each other's weaknesses, and fortifying their strengths. Also, they often face up to situations together, which makes them feel strong and confident as a team, but also gives each one a unique insight as to how the other ticks.

## Talking to twins

You may find that your twins are slow to talk and there may be several reasons for this. An Australian study suggests that twins generally have more difficulties to deal with from the outset and so milestones can be late, not just with speech, but with handling skills too. But it must be remembered that twins share the parental attention that a single child would enjoy undiluted and so there are fewer opportunities to learn and, in particular, busy or tired parents feel less like talking to their babies.

## Becoming sociable

Make sure your twins feel at home with any social group, be it family or friends, or toddlers, from a very early age. There's a danger of twins not mixing with other children because they have each other for company. Indeed, they may seem rather bossy and self-centred to other children. However, because of their self-sufficiency, you may find that your twins are quite happy to be left with strangers from an early age as long as the other twin is present.

Twins may opt to play exclusively with each other as a twosome and will have to be persuaded to join in with other children. Gradual separation can often work if activities are split between parents and friends. Dad might get one twin to help in the garden, while Mum takes the other shopping. Invite a friend of each twin to play on different days. Later on, encourage teachers to place your twins in separate activity groups, or even classes, to give them a chance to make their own friends.

## Siblings

The arrival of twins can put everyone under strain, not least other brothers and sisters. The "dethronement" that follows the arrival of a new baby is a double whammy when twins arrive.

It's very difficult to give older children the attention they're used to (and deserve) when twins absorb all your time and energy. But for their sake plans should be laid and a real attempt made to soften the blow, otherwise children are in danger of feeling neglected, unloved, and insecure.

Twins should be heralded throughout the household with charts, pictures, and story books so that siblings can grow accustomed to the idea and role-play with dolls. Involvement with equipping the nursery helps make the absent babies seem real, and their return from the hospital can seem acceptable if mum's arms are free to gather up the children waiting excitedly for the new arrivals, while someone else carries the twins. Each child should receive a small gift from each twin (named) and it helps to set aside the first half-hour for playing with them before seeing to the twins.

Ensure that an older child has half an hour a day of your undivided attention, so that he feels valued. And perhaps you and your partner can take older children out on their own so that they have you to themselves, and feel secure in your love despite the new arrivals.

# Special needs

There are many reasons why a child may need more care and attention than his peers. Your child may have a chronic condition, such as asthma; a learning disorder, such as dyslexia; a developmental disorder, such as autism; or he may simply be very advanced for his years. Whatever the case, he'll need extra support and consideration in order to maximize his potential. This may take the form of special medical treatment, home care, or special education. This care is as important for a very bright child who might outstrip older siblings, and even parents, as it is for the child with learning difficulties.

Early identification of special needs is very important. A severe condition such as cerebral palsy will be apparent soon after birth, but others, such as dyslexia, can go unnoticed for years. Never be afraid to act on your suspicions; seek professional advice if you're at all worried and make sure you seek out specialist help. The better informed you are, the more you can do to help and support your child.

# The special child

Although all children develop at different rates and the range of what doctors and psychologists consider "normal" is wide, a small number fall at either end of the developmental spectrum. At one end are children who are unusually advanced for their age in both motor and intellectual skills; at the other end are children who haven't acquired basic skills such as language, and children who learn very slowly. In between are children with developmental or learning disorders such as autism and dyslexia.

Perhaps surprisingly, very advanced children have similar needs to children who have a learning disorder – lots of stimulation, attention, and love. You might say that all children need these things – and you'd be right – but without them, children with special needs will suffer more. If such children don't receive the correct stimulation, they may not turn out to be "just average"; they could develop serious behavioural problems.

The monitoring of a child's growth, development, and behaviour may involve a number of people, including your doctor and health visitor as well as a paediatrician and school nurse.

## Recognizing the signs

If your child does have special needs, an early diagnosis is very important so that he can have the right help. Some learning disorders are difficult to spot, especially if they are characterized by behaviour that may be considered positive, such as quietness, little crying, or excessive sleeping.

Autistic children, for example, are often described by their parents as well behaved before other signs of their illness emerge. A gifted child, on the other hand, may be very disruptive and not do well at school, making it hard for parents and teachers to recognize his potential.

The following are some signs that might indicate that your child has special needs. However, bear in mind that children vary enormously so what you regard as delayed speech in your child, for example, could be just a normal variation in development. If you're worried, check with your doctor.

## Developmentally delayed child

■ Not speaking by the age of two-and-a-half years.
■ Failure to interact with other people – to join in appropriately in conversation, for instance.
■ Repetitive routines or habits beyond the normal age, such as asking the same question over and over.
■ Problems reading and writing, inability to tell left from right, and poor coordination.
■ Overactivity and very short concentration span.

## Gifted child

■ Very early and fluent language skills.
■ Very independent behaviour, or a preference for the company of adults.
■ A tendency to become bored by repetitive tasks.
■ Precocious development accompanied by bad behaviour such as temper tantrums.
■ Unusually long concentration span.

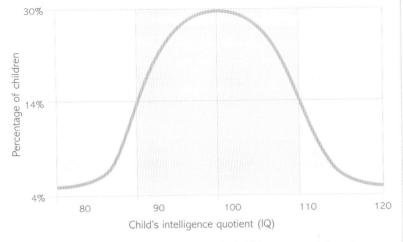

▲ **INTELLIGENCE QUOTIENT (IQ)** The few very gifted children appear at the extreme right of the curve. At the left is the small group of children who have impaired mental abilities. Most children fall between these extremes.

# Giftedness

A gifted child is one who has advanced cognitive (understanding) skills for his age. He will be a high achiever in most areas, and he may have an IQ over 150. Having a gifted child is rare. Although many children may be advanced for their age in a particular skill at a particular time, only about two per cent of the population are truly gifted. If your child is gifted, however, it is likely that you as a parent will be the first to notice.

## Recognizing the signs

Identifying a gifted child becomes easier as the child gets older, but one of the first signs is early language acquisition, particularly speaking fluently before the age of two. Early reading may be another sign of giftedness: many able children learn to read at the age of three or four. Other possible qualities of gifted children are as follows:

■ Good powers of reasoning.
■ A good memory for places and names.
■ A strong creative and imaginative drive.
■ Sharp powers of observation.
■ Being curious and always asking questions.
■ More at home with adults than with children.
■ An ability to grasp abstract ideas.
■ Independence.
■ Ability to solve problems or puzzles.
■ Having an extensive vocabulary.
■ Assimilating facts very quickly.
■ Long concentration span.
■ Ability to describe events, people, and situations accurately and vividly.
■ Eagerness to spend time studying or learning.
■ A specific talent, such as artistic ability.
■ A high IQ.

## Special needs

Although you may perceive giftedness as an asset rather than a problem, your gifted child may not always be provided for adequately at school and he'll have specific emotional needs that are different from those of the average child.

The gifted child may find it hard to relate to his peers. He may be impatient with other children for being slow and this may make him unpopular with his peer group. Although your child may be condescending towards other children, he will probably still want to be part of their group and this may lead to frustration and isolation.

Alternatively, your child may try to conceal his talents in order not to seem different, so that he will be accepted by other children.

Interacting with adults can also be a problem for some gifted children. Teachers may treat gifted children as arrogant, precocious, or cheeky. Gifted children are likely always to know the answers to questions and to be able to point out inconsistencies; they often question the reasons for doing something. The gifted child does not mean to be attention-seeking or trouble-making, and the negative response he gets from adults can make him withdrawn and antisocial.

A gifted child who is denied the chance to exploit his potential may show a confusing mixture of intellectual prowess and immaturity. He may sulk and have temper tantrums; he may be bored by basic school subjects; and, if he's restless and inattentive, his teachers, far from recognizing his talents, may believe that he is of low ability.

If your child is having problems at school, you may have to intervene. Talk to his teacher about the kind of specialized learning your child requires and make sure that he gets it.

## Can giftedness be cultivated?

Intelligence is wholly innate and overrides all cultures and backgrounds; cleverness is partly innate and partly environmental. Evidence suggests that some gifted children come from relatively affluent homes with educated parents who spend time stimulating and encouraging their children; the extra boost can turn a very bright child into a gifted one. On the other hand, there is very little evidence to show that the parents of gifted children are "pushy" and force their children to study against their will. Being overly pushy as a parent will not help to cultivate giftedness in a child. While you can help a child fulfil his potential, you can't change that potential.

# Helping a gifted child

It's important to know that your child is gifted since it may help to explain a lot of his behaviour, especially behaviour that's construed as deviant: social withdrawal, aggressiveness, and so on. It's also important in that it means you can start to cater for your child's specific needs. Gifted children need lots of intellectual stimulation, and they will be deprived if they don't get it.

If your child's of school age, enlist the help of his teacher. If a teacher doesn't understand that your child is gifted, then he or she may perceive him as a threat or a problem. A sensitive teacher will help your child to integrate with others and will prevent him becoming isolated. Some schools have provisions for gifted children and there are enrichment programmes that will supplement your child's learning. Contact the National Association For Gifted Children (see Useful addresses, p.344).

As a parent, it's important that you treat your child sympathetically. He may be very advanced in some ways, but he'll still be emotionally immature, so avoid treating him as a "little adult". There are many ways to provide stimulation for your child.
■ Provide him with toys that promote interactive learning. Limit television, as it is a passive way of learning.
■ Give your child freedom to play and try not to intervene too much, unless he asks for your help.
■ Encourage any specific talents such as painting.
■ If you have a particular talent of your own, share it with your child and try to communicate your enthusiasm to him.
■ Send your child to summer schools and introduce him to other gifted children.
■ Encourage him to ask questions and, if you don't know the answer to a question, help him to look up the information in a book.
■ Read him stories that will enrich his imagination.
■ Involve him in everyday tasks around the home.

# Underachievers

Whereas gifted children acquire skills very early, underachievers or developmentally delayed children acquire skills at an unusually slow rate. Some of the first indications that your baby is "behind" are docility, quietness, and sleeping for very long periods.

Your baby won't make much noise and won't interact with his environment in the same way as the average child. He'll be late in smiling, responding to sounds, and learning to chew. When you try to engage your child in activities, he'll have a short attention span, and he'll spend brief periods doing lots of different things rather than devoting all his energy to one task or game. As he grows older, he may demonstrate a tendency to be overactive and he may have a lower than average IQ.

## Diagnosis

A developmentally delayed child will be later than usual in achieving some developmental milestones (see right). It's important, however, to eliminate the possibility that your child has a physiological problem, such as partial deafness or blindness, a severe developmental disorder, such as autism (see p.258), or whether he's simply developing at a rate that is below average. Ask your doctor to refer your child to a psychologist for assessment. Your child may need remedial help.

## Behavioural milestones

There are clues or signs that your baby or child is developmentally delayed or underachieving. Although children vary in the speed at which they develop, if your child has not reached the following stages then it's possible that he may have a developmental disorder.

**Hand regard** A baby becomes aware of his hands at the age of six to eight weeks, then he begins to play with his feet. Between the ages of 12 and 16 weeks he will stare at his hands and waggle his fingers. Hand regard may go on for as long as 20 weeks, however, in developmentally delayed children.

**Grasp reflex** If you put your finger into a baby's palm he'll close his fingers around it in a tight grip. This reflex usually lasts about six weeks after birth, but persists longer in developmentally delayed children.

**Mouthing** At about four months your baby will put everything that he can into his mouth. This lasts until around a year in a normal child and longer in a developmentally delayed child.

**Casting** From the age of nine months children will throw objects out of the pram – a behaviour called casting. Developmentally delayed children may continue to do this for much longer.

**Dribbling** Slobbering and dribbling should stop at around one year. But developmentally delayed children may still be dribbling at 18 months.

## Helping an underachiever

Intellectual development is determined by both nature (inherited qualities) and nurture (things such as physical and social environment, and diet). Your child's IQ is decided before birth, but it can flower through the stimuli that your child is exposed to after birth. If your child is not encouraged to interact with other people from an early age, and he's not encouraged to engage his senses in the world around him, the chances are that your child will not reach his full potential, even if that potential is limited.

If you suspect that your child is lagging behind, spend lots of time reading aloud and talking to him, playing with him, taking him out, showing him new things and new people, and encouraging him to play imaginative games with his toys. Give him toys that are educational and plenty of colourful books and pictures to look at.

Behaviour modification techniques may be helpful. Put simply, this means rewarding your child's responses with praise and affection and being patient with his efforts, however slow they are. If you punish him for slowness, he may become discouraged and lose his incentive to learn.

2

# Dyslexia

This is a learning difficulty that affects reading, spelling, and written language. Although dyslexia particularly affects a child's mastery of written symbols – letters, numbers, and musical notation – he may have difficulties with spoken language too. Dyslexia is a specific neurological disorder and is not the result of poor hearing or vision, or low intelligence. One in 20 children is dyslexic.

## Diagnosis

Many bright children are dyslexic, and the condition is often diagnosed earlier in these children since parents become aware of the gap between their child's obvious intelligence and his level of achievement in specific areas. The main symptom of dyslexia is difficulty in reading and writing. Your child may have problems perceiving letters in the correct order, or he may confuse similarly shaped letters such as b and d, and p and q. Labelling a child dyslexic if he is not is just as harmful

as failing to recognize it if he is. A correct diagnosis can only be made by an expert. The following may help you to spot dyslexia in your child.

■ Poor spelling and poor coordination.
■ Difficulty in remembering lists of words, numbers, or letters.
■ Difficulty in remembering the order of things, such as days of the week.
■ Problems telling left from right.
■ Jumbled phrases, such as "tebby dare" instead of "teddy bear" and difficulty learning nursery rhymes.

## Dyscalculia and dyspraxia

Dyscalculia and dyspraxia are related conditions. Dyscalculia is rarer than dyslexia, but shares many of the same features. The child's core problem is in handling numbers and mathematical concepts. Common signs of dyspraxia are clumsiness, poor posture, awkward gait, and confusion about which hand to use to perform a task. The child may also have difficulty catching a ball, poor body awareness, and find it difficult to hop, skip, or ride a bike. Both conditions are treated in the same way as dyslexia.

Dyspraxia is also treated with occupational therapy and physiotherapy, and the benefits of treatment will have a knock-on effect on problems with specific learning difficulties.

## Effects of dyslexia

The problems noted on page 253 may occur in children who don't have dyslexia. The difference is that dyslexic children suffer more severe symptoms and they won't grow out of them.

Recent research suggests that, as well as having problems with literacy, dyslexic children also have problems with distinguishing different sounds, and with memory. If there is associated dyspraxia (see p.253) they will have balance problems too. Such children, for example, will find it much more difficult to balance on one leg than non-dyslexic children. A dyslexic child's strengths are likely to be sensitivity, intuition, and impulsiveness. Skills associated with the left side of the brain, such as dealing with symbols, responding to instructions, and putting things in order, are weak in the dyslexic child. Some dyslexic children are very creative and have an aptitude for drawing and painting.

## Special needs

One of the main problems that dyslexic children face is incorrect diagnosis. It is common for children to attempt to learn to read and write, fail to do so, and then be labelled "slow" or even disabled. This is very demoralizing for the child and is bound to affect his school performance overall. Parents and teachers often confuse dyslexia with a low IQ, but in fact most dyslexic children have an average or above-average IQ.

If dyslexia is recognized early, remedial education is very effective. If a child is diagnosed as dyslexic at the age of four or five, when he goes to school, he'll probably only need about half-an-hour's extra tuition a day for a period of six months to bring his reading and writing up to normal standards. If dyslexia is not diagnosed until a child's seven or eight, he'll have a lot of catching up to do.

# Helping a child with dyslexia

You can do three things to help your dyslexic child at home. First, and this is sometimes overlooked, acknowledge that your child actually has a problem. If you're told that your child will catch up or will learn to read eventually, don't listen – dyslexia is a specific learning disorder that only responds to the appropriate remedial treatment. Second, be supportive and positive, especially if your child is having problems at school. Third, play lots of learning games with your child.

**Emotional support**  If your child is at school and is lagging behind other children, his self-confidence may be low, and it's very important that you make him feel successful at home. Don't show any impatience. Encourage him to do the things that he is good at and help him do things for himself.

Give him self-help aids, such as left and right stickers on his tricycle, and, if he finds a particular task difficult tell him to take it slowly. The British Dyslexia Association (see Useful addresses, p.342) gives advice on coping strategies and remedial education for children with dyslexia. They can also provide you with helpful leaflets and books.

**Home learning games**  Playing games with letters, words, and sounds can be very useful. The following tips are all ways in which you can have fun and enhance your child's learning.
■ Say nursery rhymes out loud together or try making up your own rhyming poems or limericks. This will familiarize your child with the concept of rhyming words.
■ Teach your child rhymes or songs that involve sequences of things such as days of the week.

■ Play "Simon Says". This will help your child to follow instructions.
■ Play "Hunt the Thimble". This will encourage your child to ask questions involving relationships such as under, on, and inside.
■ Introduce your child to the concept of left and right.
■ Ask your child to lay the table at meal times.
■ Play clapping games. Give one clap for each syllable of a word and get your child to repeat it. Clap a rhythm to his name.
■ Give your child groups of words and ask him to pick the odd word.
■ Get your child to think of as many words beginning with a particular letter as he can.
■ Play "I Spy". If your child has difficulty with letter names, make the sound of the letter instead.
■ Encourage your child to trace words and letters, or to make letters out of plasticine.

# ADHD

This stands for Attention Deficit Hyperactivity Disorder and is one of the most common childhood disorders seen by psychologists. Children with ADHD are impulsive, inattentive, and easily distracted. Although they are not noted to be "overactive" from birth as such, they are likely to have been colicky, demanding babies.

## What causes ADHD?

The current theory about ADHD is that it is a disorder of perception and understanding. Four times as many boys as girls have ADHD, and it is caused by both genetic and environmental factors. In the past, problems such as ADHD and hyperactivity were thought to have a dietary origin. Diets high in chemical additives and lacking in essential vitamins and minerals were thought to cause aberrant behaviour in some children, though this has proven not to be the case.

## Effects of ADHD

A child with ADHD may be unpredictable and disruptive. Even before he goes to school he may have problematic relationships with adults and have acquired a reputation for rebelliousness. This has a negative effect on his self-esteem, so that when he does go to school he starts off on an unequal basis with other children. His performance may be variable: one day he might be quite compliant; the next he won't be able to sit still for more than a few minutes and will fidget incessantly. He may become a low achiever at school, with a reputation for poor concentration, and he may be thought to have a low IQ, though he may not. Certain early physical symptoms are associated with ADHD. In babies these include colic and difficulty feeding either by breast or bottle. In children they include poor appetite and sleeping problems. Boys with ADHD seem to suffer more than girls, in that girls are likely to be more achievement-orientated and better adjusted socially. Boys in particular may be criticized for overactivity and this can make things worse.

## Diagnosis

If your child is having problems at school – if he is irresponsible, impulsive, careless, disorganized, and suffers from poor concentration and motivation – you need to eliminate the possible causes. Consider the possibility that he is dyslexic (see p.253) or gifted (see p.251). If his behaviour has started recently, has he experienced a traumatic event? Does he have any other behavioural problems such as lying (see p.218) or is he resistant to school (see p.219)?

Your child may need to be referred to an educational psychologist who will be able to diagnose ADHD and decide on appropriate action that meets your child's individual needs. Discuss his problems with his teacher too.

## Helping a child with ADHD

It's important for a child with ADHD to have an orderly home life and a structured routine. If your child knows that he has to do certain things at set times of the day, he's less likely to be unruly. Remember, too, that if your child has problems with self-control, he probably has low self-esteem because he meets with adult disapproval all the time. Always praise and reward good behaviour and he'll learn that certain types of behaviour win your approval, while others don't. When you want your child to do something, make requests clear and simple and give them one at a time. Praise effort as well as achievement.

Drug treatment is reserved for severe ADHD in children over the age of six and the main drug used is methylphenidate hydrochloride (Ritalin). It has significant side effects, so use is closely monitored.

Parenting a child with ADHD can be very demoralizing, since your child may have a reputation for being a troublemaker. Many parents feel isolated because their child is rejected by preschools, and even banned from friends' homes. Don't blame yourself for your child's behaviour and take time away from your child if you can when it all gets too much. Organizations such as the Hyperactive Children's Support Group (see Useful addresses, p.342) can offer help and advice.

# Stammering

When your child is learning to talk it's normal for him to stumble over words, repeat words, and hesitate. It's only when hesitations dominate your child's speech and cause him considerable distress that he's said to have a stammer. Whereas normal hesitation is the relaxed repetition of a word at the beginning or the end of a phrase, a child with a stammer will get stuck on a word, and repeat one of its syllables over and over again.

## Is it serious?

When children are learning language they are not always able to convey their thoughts in words as quickly as they would like to. Your child lives very much in the present and he will want to convey the intensity of his feelings immediately. When his vocabulary isn't wide enough or his language skills aren't advanced enough, he may stammer in his rush to get the words out.

Most children stammer at some stage. Your child may stammer on some days and not others; he may stammer when he's tired, excited, or in a particular situation or environment. It doesn't matter, though, unless he stammers in a lot of situations and gets upset because of it. Never make a fuss about occasional stammering or you child will become anxious.

## What causes stammering?

If your child is to become a fluent speaker, then he needs to have plenty of support and encouragement to boost his confidence. A combination of the following three conditions can cause a child to develop a stammer:

■ Parental demands that overestimate the child's ability, such as asking lots of questions; insisting on clear speech; and expecting fast replies and grown-up behaviour.
■ Your child wanting to perform well to impress people before his vocabulary is large enough.
■ Stressful situations in which your child is tired, anxious, or frightened, or where people are talking very fast, or there are lots of interruptions.

A stammering child believes that speaking hesitantly is in some way wrong or bad. He becomes acutely self-conscious and focuses on the way he speaks, which leads to worse stammering. He may avoid situations that involve speaking, especially to new people, and if your child is of school age he may pretend that he doesn't know answers to questions to avoid having to speak in front of the class.

## Special needs

If your child has a severe stutter he may need the help of a speech or language therapist. A therapist may visit your child at school or liaise with parents and teachers. The British Stammering Association (see Useful addresses, p.342) provides contacts, advice, and a helpline.

◀ **IMPROVING FLUENCY** Singing, or any kind of rhythmic speech, can reduce stammering. Tapping out a rhythm to rhymes and songs can help your child feel more confident.

## Delayed speech

At the age of about 12–15 months your baby will probably be able to say simple words, such as "mama", "dada", "dog", and "cat", and by two years he'll probably be able to form simple sentences, such as "daddy in garden". Speech will become progressively more sophisticated during his third and fourth year. As with all aspects of development, the age at which milestones are achieved varies widely, but if your child is very far behind other children of the same age, then there may be something wrong.

There are many causes of delayed speech, the most important being deafness – have your child's hearing tested at once if you suspect he may be deaf (see p.96). Deafness can lead to late development of speech, which is why routine hearing tests are so important. A baby will not learn to speak if he is severely deaf. Chronic glue ear (see p.285) can also result in hearing problems.

Your child may also be late in speaking because he hasn't received the correct stimulation, which can happen to children who have been institutionalized or those whose parents simply don't talk to them enough. Boys are generally more prone to delayed speech than girls, and twins may also speak later than average (see p.247).

Very occasionally, delayed speech is due to a physiological defect or a disease of the speech muscles, larynx, or mouth. There are also disorders that affect the part of the brain that controls speech.

Children vary in the age at which they begin to speak, but if your child is not talking at all by the age of two-and-a-half, you should seek advice from your doctor.

If your child is deaf, he may need to have a hearing aid; and if he has a severe speech defect, he may need some help from a speech therapist.

## Helping a child with a stammer

You can influence your child's speech by the way you talk to him. If you speak very quickly and you appear distracted, your child may feel that he has to keep up and that you are not interested in what he has to say.

Always try to speak slowly and appear attentive and interested. Look at your child and, if possible, talk to him on the same physical level. Use language that is simple and talk about very immediate things that can be seen. Avoid asking too many questions – instead describe your own feelings or experiences; this will encourage your child to contribute. Above all, never react negatively to your child's stammer or he will become more self-conscious and the stammer will get worse. When your child is struggling with a sentence try not to complete it for him or supply a word.

If your child is very anxious about stammering talk to him about it. If he knows that you understand, this will lessen his sense of suffering alone. If you don't talk about his stammering, your child may feel that it is something to be ashamed of. If your child is very young and is having problems with speech, return to games and activities that involve looking or listening rather than speaking. If your child is at school, talk to his teacher. Some of the following strategies can help.

■ Your child may need extra help with reading. If he is worried about particular words this can cause him to stammer. Reading aloud in unison with another child may reduce stammering.

■ Children tend to be more fluent when they are talking about something personal or a subject that they know a lot about. This should be encouraged whenever possible.

■ If a teacher is observant about what encourages fluency or what increases stammering he can prevent your child feeling embarrassed. When he needs information from your child, it may help if he asks questions that require a "yes" or a "no" answer, particularly if your child is getting distressed about it.

■ Some methods of speaking to your child promote fluency and should be encouraged. These include saying words that have a rhyme or a rhythm, saying words that have actions to go with them, reciting lists, or counting, acting, or singing.

■ It may be a good idea for your child's teacher to broach the subject of stammering with him in a matter-of-fact way, since your child will then feel that it has been noticed by a sympathetic adult and that he doesn't have to hide it.

# Autistic spectrum disorder

Also known as autism, this is a condition in which a child has problems relating to people and situations and may show an obsessive resistance to any change in routine. Autism varies from mild to severe and typically appears within the first three years of life. It's four times more common in boys than in girls. It used to be thought that autism was caused by emotional deprivation or some negative aspect of the child's background or upbringing. We now know that it has a physiological origin and results from an abnormality in the brain. There may be a genetic basis.

## Diagnosis

Because autism is a developmental disorder it may take a while for you to realize that your child is different from others. You may notice that your baby is uncommunicative in the first year of his life, but you may not attach any significance to this until later, when other signs become apparent. Most parents know that their child is autistic or that "something's wrong" by the time he's about three.

## Effects of autism

Children with autism vary considerably in their abilities, but there are three main traits that all autistic children share: problems with social interaction, communication problems, and impaired imagination. Many also display repetitive behaviour, and some have very sophisticated memories.

**Social interaction** If autism is severe, your child will be indifferent to other people. In babies this manifests itself as crying that can't be appeased by holding and cuddling, quietness, poor eye contact, and failing to return or respond to gestures such as smiling.

In other autistic children it manifests as a lack of interest in interacting with other people, particularly children.

They don't make friends and, when they do approach people socially, they may behave inappropriately: they may repeat snatches of conversation that have just been spoken, they may be aggressive, or they may use confusing language. In less severe forms of autism, your child may accept social contact, but will not be very responsive or respond in a stilted, repetitive way.

**Communication** From an early age most children show a desire to communicate with other people. Even before they can form words they will communicate non-verbally using facial expressions and body language. Autistic children seem to lack this desire. Even if your child does speak he will tend to speak at people, rather than with them, or his speech may be restricted to conveying his immediate needs. Your child may exhibit echolalia (repetition of words that he has just heard), and he may use specific words or phrases in a repetitive or inappropriate way. It is common for autistic children to be confused about when to use "I", "you", or "he".

**Imagination** An autistic child doesn't use his imagination when he's playing with toys and, rather than perceiving

things in their entirety, he may become overly interested in a small detail of a toy, person, or object. When playing with a toy train, for example, he might concentrate on one small part, such as a wheel or the buffer, rather than using it as a make-believe train. Some autistic children do pursue activities that engage the imagination, such as reading, but these tend to be repetitive and stereotyped. For instance, your child may read a book again and again.

**Repetitive behaviour** Repeated tapping, rocking, head-banging, teeth grinding, grunting, screaming, finger flicking, spinning objects, and standing up and jumping from the back foot to the front foot, are some of the behaviours that can occur in autism. The type of repetitive activity that your child indulges in is dependent on his level of ability. More sophisticated types of behaviour include arranging objects in complex, repeating patterns, and collecting large numbers of a particular object. Your child may be interested in a particular topic and will ask the same questions about it and demand the same answers over and over again. You may also notice that your child likes repetitive routines, even inappropriate ones, to be observed without fail. For example, he may want exactly the same sequence of activities carried out at bedtime each night.

**Memory** Some autistic children are able to store a memory and retrieve it exactly as it was first perceived, and the results can be very impressive. An autistic child may, for example, draw perfectly from memory a building he has seen or repeat whole conversations or lists of information.

## Special needs

The severity of your child's condition depends on several factors: whether he has any other learning disorders (such as dyslexia, see p.253); the type of education he has access to; and his personality or disposition, which will affect how he reacts to his disabilities. It is important to diagnose autism and associated disorders as early as possible so your child's needs are met.

The National Autistic Society (see Useful addresses, p.342) helps parents with autistic children. They have various publications on care and education, and also organize conferences and workshops.

Depending on the severity of your child's autism, he may be able to go to an ordinary school where he may receive extra help, or he will need to go to a specialist school for children with learning or developmental disorders.

▲ HELP AND SUPPORT If your child is having difficulty with speech, you can use sign language to help him. It should complement speech, though, and not replace it.

# Helping a child with autistic spectrum disorder

You will probably find that your child's behaviour is most problematic between the ages of two and five, and there may be an improvement between the ages of six and 12. As he grows up, your child will probably become more responsive and sociable. Although no cure exists for autism, there are many different therapies designed to improve the behaviour and adjustment of your child.

**Behaviour modification** This therapy concentrates on replacing dysfunctional behaviour (tantrums, head-banging, aggressiveness, and so on) with desirable behaviour, using a system of rewards.

**Relaxation and massage** The child is taught how to relax using massage, music, touching, and verbal cues. Later, the verbal cues can be used on their own when the child shows signs of tension; because he associates them with feeling relaxed, they should dissipate the tension. Massage helps autistic children bond to people through touch.

**Holding therapy** This involves giving the autistic child plenty of hugs and cuddles, regardless of his indifference. The theory is that if you insist on holding your child, he'll be comforted and reassured without the problem of having to initiate the interaction in the first place.

**Speech therapy** Some cases of autism are diagnosed by speech therapists, because poor language development is often the first sign. Speech therapy can also improve your child's communication skills. If your child doesn't speak or his speech is very limited, it may help to teach him a sign language such as Makaton, which complements rather than replaces speech.

**Psychotherapy** This involves working with all the family so that parents understand the behaviour of the autistic child and its consequences. In some cases, the child himself might receive individual psychotherapy.

# Living with chronic conditions

The word "chronic" is used to describe an illness, such as cerebral palsy or asthma, that is long-lasting, in which the symptoms are present on a daily basis, or they flare up occasionally. In contrast, an acute illness, such as tonsillitis, comes on suddenly, and the duration of symptoms is quite short. Chronic conditions may be lifelong and you, your family, and your child, will need to make some changes in your lifestyle in order to cope with the condition on a day-to-day basis.

## Dealing with illness

The most common emotional reaction to the news that your child has a chronic condition is anxiety, combined with fear, bitterness, and possibly guilt that you yourself have done something to cause the condition. After the initial shock, many parents become very involved in learning about their child's condition and how to manage it. The first thing you need to know is what the treatment programme entails – this may be daily injections, occasional blood transfusions, or just making sure that your child always carries an inhaler. You'll also need to familiarize yourself with the symptoms of an attack or the possible dangers to your child, and learn what to do and how to help your child in an emergency.

When your child first shows signs of a chronic condition, apart from the physical unpleasantness of being ill, he will most likely find the experience of visiting doctors and hospitals quite stressful. Stay calm in front of your child and don't fuss and panic. He'll see your anxiety and interpret it in his own way and become more anxious himself; he may even become terrified that he's going to die. Talk to your child rationally about his condition and explain what is happening to him. If he doesn't understand what's wrong with him this can be more frightening than the illness itself.

Because you are worried about your child's health, it is quite natural for you to pay special attention to him. You'll need to be careful, however, that you don't exclude other members of your family, especially if you have other children.

Research is being conducted into chronic conditions and management programmes are becoming progressively more advanced – many children with these illnesses can live a near-normal life. (For self-help groups on the conditions described here, see Useful addresses, p.342.)

# Asthma

This condition affects one in ten children at some time in childhood. The symptoms – cough, wheezing, and shortness of breath – are caused by narrowing of the airways and episodes are brought on by various triggers. A child with asthma may have other allergic conditions, such as eczema and hay fever, and there may be a family history of such conditions. Asthma may improve as a child gets older.

**Risk factors** The reasons for the increase in rates of asthma are not entirely known, although pollution, viruses, low birthweight, and bottlefeeding instead of breastfeeding are possible factors. Smoking is a proven, and very important factor, particularly if you smoke during pregnancy, and you or your partner smokes during your child's early years. There's good research to suggest that children who are not exposed to a wide variety of viruses and bacteria in early childhood and who therefore fail to have their immune system challenged are more vulnerable to developing asthma. Children who are raised on farms are less likely to have asthma than city dwellers. Boys are twice as likely as girls to have asthma. Breastfeeding may help improve a child's resistance.

## Diagnosis

As many as one in three young children have wheezing episodes during winter with a cold, cough, rapid breathing, and difficulty feeding, but this doesn't make them asthmatic. It's the pattern of symptoms that develops over time that shows whether a child has asthma or not.

It can be quite difficult to spot asthma in very young children for three reasons. First, a third of all children have at least one attack of wheezing during their first five years and most of them will never have breathing problems again, even though wheezing may be severe enough to warrant hospital admission. Second, doctors may not link individual episodes, so may describe flare-ups as wheezing, wheezy bronchitis, chesty coughs, or colds. Third, a "peak-flow meter", the device normally used to measure how well the lungs work, can only be used with children over five.

Before reaching a diagnosis, your doctor should wait and see how the pattern of symptoms develops. It's this pattern, not individual symptoms, that confirms the diagnosis. Typical symptom patterns for asthma are:

■ Repeated attacks of wheezing and coughing, usually with colds.
■ A persistent dry irritating cough.
■ Many restless nights caused by attacks of wheezing or coughing.
■ Wheezing or coughing between colds, especially after exercise or excitement, or when exposed to cigarette smoke and allergens such as pollen or house-dust-mite droppings.

Many people believe that wheezing is the only symptom of asthma, but for young children a persistent dry and irritating cough may be the only symptom. Healthy children don't cough persistently. Children under the age of one year are most likely to

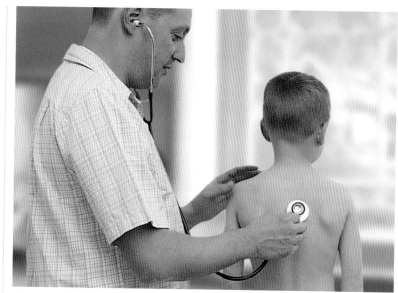

▲ DIAGNOSING ASTHMA A doctor will need to monitor the pattern of your child's symptoms over time before he can diagnose asthma.

suffer from wheezing set off by virus infections such as a cold. In fact viruses are an almost universal trigger for children. However, if the wheezing is only ever brought on by viruses the child may not have true asthma.

## Triggers

You'll find that certain substances or activities can trigger an attack. Once you've identified triggers, help your child to avoid them!

**Smoking** Help your child avoid cigarette smoke because it's especially harmful to growing lungs, and can trigger asthma attacks. Never smoke around children and don't allow visitors to your home to smoke.

**Cold air** Your child may cough or wheeze initially on going out of doors. Keeping your child indoors, however, is not the answer. A dose of reliever medicine (see p.262) just before going out may be all that's needed.

**Activity** If laughter, excitement, or exercise trigger asthma in your child, it may be a sign that the asthma is not properly controlled. Consult your doctor, since it is very important for children to enjoy themselves. The symptoms of activity-induced asthma may be prevented if your child takes a dose of reliever medicine beforehand. Your child should warm up before playing games – several 30-second sprints over five to ten minutes will allow him to exercise for up to an hour or so. Swimming provides an excellent form of exercise and it seldom provokes an attack unless the water is very cold or heavily chlorinated.

**Allergies** Minimize your child's exposure to potential allergens, such as mites, pollen, and fur. Complete avoidance of house dust is impossible, but avoid feather pillows, duvets, and fitted carpets; cover a child's mattress with a plastic sheet; clean and vacuum your child's room when he's not there.

# Treatment

Your doctor can prescribe medicine that will control your child's symptoms, although they won't cure asthma. Most medications come in the form of an inhaler ("puffer"). There are two types: preventers and relievers. Young children should use their inhalers with a device called a spacer, which delivers the drug directly to the airways.

**Relievers** When an asthma attack occurs, a reliever, or bronchodilator, (generally blue) makes breathing easier by relaxing the tiny muscles in the narrowed airways and allowing them to open up. They may also be taken several times a day to stop symptoms developing. A child who suffers occasional asthma attacks must have a reliever medicine to hand at all times.

**Preventers** Your child will probably have to take a preventer (generally white or brown) if he usually needs to use a reliever more than once a day. These stop asthma from starting by reducing inflammation in the airways and making them less sensitive to irritants. Preventers must be taken regularly, even if your child is well. They take about 7–14 days to become effective from the time they are first taken. Once the symptoms are under control your doctor may reduce the treatment. If a child uses a preventer and a reliever, label the puffers clearly.

**Treatment devices** The drugs can be given in different ways, depending on the age of the child and his ability to coordinate his breathing with the use of the inhaler. The following is a general guide:

| | |
|---|---|
| **up to 2** | Nebulizer or spacer with face mask |
| **2–4** | Aerosol puffer with spacer |
| **5–8** | Powder inhaler |
| **8 up** | Powder inhaler or aerosol puffer |

With an aerosol puffer a metered dose of medication is inhaled directly into the lungs. Without a spacer this requires very good coordination by the child. A dry-powder inhaler is good for giving preventer medicines, but they can't be inhaled very well when the child is wheezing or is tight chested because a good breath is needed to trigger the device. An aerosol may still be needed for relieving these symptoms.

Some very young children need a nebulizer, a machine with a mask attached that produces a very fine mist of medicine. For most children, however, spacers with face masks are the best solution. A measured dose of the drug is delivered into the spacer and the child then places the mask on his face and inhales it over several breaths. You can turn the spacer into a toy by putting stickers on it, or play games in which you count out loud as your child takes five breaths from the spacer. Nebulizers or steroid tablets may be needed for severe attacks.

Studies such as Gaining Optimal Asthma Control have shown that it's possible to control asthma by using a combination of drugs treatments. These medicines are a combination of an inhaled cortico steroid to reduce inflammation and a long-acting bronchodilator to help airways stay open for a long time. They help treat the underlying cause of asthma – inflammation – and are taken on a daily basis to help prevent asthma symptoms and attacks. There are also non-steroid oral treatments available.

◀ **SPACER** Plastic spacer devices make inhalers easier for young children to use and allow more effective dose control.

# Helping a child with asthma

Although there's no known cure for asthma, modern asthma management can effectively reduce a child's symptoms and allow him to lead a full and active life. Regular contact with your doctor and close monitoring of your child are important. Many GP surgeries now run specialized asthma clinics with highly trained practice nurses.

Your doctor will develop an asthma management plan with you, and explain when to use the preventer and reliever, and what to do if your child's symptoms get worse. This should be written down for you to keep. A vital part of any plan is a review meeting with a doctor or nurse every few months. Monitor your child's symptoms closely and speak to your doctor if you notice any of the following:

■ Wheezing and coughing in the early morning.
■ Increased symptoms after exercise or exertion.
■ Waking at night with a cough or a wheeze.
■ Increased use of reliever therapy.

**An emergency plan** Any asthma attack can be life-threatening, so have an emergency plan of action agreed with your doctor for very severe attacks. If your child has a history of brittle asthma with the sudden onset of severe breathing difficulties, call an ambulance after ten minutes.

■ At the start of the attack give your child his usual reliever. Wait about ten minutes and if there is no improvement, call an ambulance.
■ Repeat the treatment every five minutes until the breathing improves or help arrives.
■ Give your child corticosteroid tablets if they've been prescribed.
■ Keep your child upright.
■ You should call your doctor or an ambulance or take your child to the nearest hospital if he needs to use his reliever inhaler more often than every four hours.

# Cystic fibrosis

An inherited condition that affects mainly the lungs and the pancreas, cystic fibrosis (CF) is also known as mucoviscidosis because it produces thick and sticky mucus in the lungs and the pancreas. CF is the most common inherited disease in the UK. It affects about one in every 2,500 children, in differing degrees. The genes responsible for CF have been discovered and there's now a chance that there'll be a cure by the time your child is grown up.

## What causes CF?
The disease occurs when both parents carry the gene for the disorder. One person in every 25 is a carrier of CF, but a CF gene is masked by a normal gene from the other parent, and even when two carriers of CF have a baby, there is only a one-in-four chance that the baby will have CF. These chances apply anew for each pregnancy. They don't change the more pregnancies you have. CF affects both girls and boys in equal numbers. Parents with an affected child who are planning a further pregancy will be offered genetic counselling.

## Diagnosis
Most babies born in the UK have a sample of blood taken when they are one or two weeks old, usually from a prick in the heel. These spots of blood are tested for the signs of several diseases, one of which may be CF.

Another test measures the amount of salt in the sweat; children with CF have more salt in their sweat than normal children. (Some parents say that their child tastes salty when they kiss him or her, even though children with CF don't sweat more than other children.) This sweat test is carried out on any baby who has recurrent bouts of pneumonia or fails to thrive, and on the siblings of a CF child.

**Your feelings** Once the diagnosis is made, you may have trouble accepting it, especially if your child seems well. You may feel angry, or guilty, but very soon you will realize that no one is to blame. Recriminations are not only pointless, they'll do great harm to relationships within the family and to your CF child.

You may seek a second opinion or even consider alternative therapies. You should discuss this with your doctor. Write down the questions you want to ask as you think of them, in case you forget later. Doctors will be happy to provide a second opinion, particularly if you have not yet had the chance to visit a special clinic for CF. All children with CF should be treated in specialist clinics.

Some people find complementary therapies helpful, but they must be taken in addition to conventional therapy and should be discussed with the child's doctor. It is essential for the future health of your child that conventional medicines are given in the prescribed way.

It's important to try not to overprotect your child. Remember he is a normal child who happens to have CF. He will be naughty and have all the same emotions as other children, and there's no reason to treat him differently in relation to discipline, education, or physical activities. If you do, you will not only be doing him a disservice, but will also be creating problems for yourselves in the long run. If you're the parent of a newly diagnosed child, you may find it helpful to talk to other parents with CF children. Support groups can put you in touch.

**Learning about CF**  Much of the treatment for CF is carried out at home, and to be as effective as possible, you should try to understand as much as you can about the disorder. CF is a very complicated condition, however, and each child will be differently affected, so other people's experiences may differ from yours.

Bear in mind, though, that you can't expect to know everything immediately and no one will expect you to. Moreover, you will be given a huge amount of information and advice from many different sources.

## Digestive problems

The pancreas is a gland in the abdomen. It produces insulin, which passes directly into the blood, and digestive juices containing enzymes, which pass into the intestines where they help with the digestion of food. In CF, the small channels down which these juices flow to reach the intestine become blocked with sticky mucus, and the enzymes can't reach the intestines to digest food. CF children often have large appetites, but fail to thrive and pass large, pale, greasy stools because their food can't be absorbed properly.

**Treatment**  Most of the missing digestive enzymes can be replaced with pancreatin, which is given in a powder or capsule form. For a young baby the powder can be mixed with a little cooled boiled water or milk, and given before each feed from a spoon or feeding bottle. It should not be mixed with a whole bottle of milk, because it will curdle the milk. Once your baby is on solids, he should eat whatever the rest of your family is having. Vitamins are not well absorbed in CF, so your child will need vitamin drops each day.

## Respiratory problems

Inside the lungs there are lots of tiny tubes, the bronchioles, down which air passes to reach special air sacs, the alveoli; here, oxygen enters the bloodstream and carbon dioxide leaves the blood to be breathed out. CF children have normal lungs at birth, but the mucus produced in them is abnormally thick, so it blocks some of the smaller airways and leads to infection, and later to lung damage.

# Helping a child with cystic fibrosis

Even with pancreatic supplements, a child with CF may not absorb all the nourishment he needs in order to grow normally. Your child will therefore need more calories, so high-energy snacks between meals, such as milkshakes, are helpful. It's important to be sure that your child is growing well as this shows he's absorbing nutrients; you can plot his measurements on the growth charts on pp.318–23.

You can only learn how to clear the thick mucus from your child's chest from a physiotherapist and with lots of practice, so don't be afraid to ask for help. You should start the physiotherapy from the time of the diagnosis, and it's important to get into a routine early on. You will need to do it twice a day when your child is well, and more often when he has a chest infection.

You should liaise very closely with your doctor about the prevention and treatment of chest infections. Should an infection occur, your child will need extra physiotherapy and prompt treatment with antibiotics.

**Treatment** The aim of treatment is to keep the lungs as normal as possible by:

■ Clearing the sticky mucus with physiotherapy, breathing exercises, and physical exercise.
■ Prevention and prompt treatment of chest infections, usually with antibiotics.

## When to see the doctor

Your CF child is vulnerable to chest infections, so it's important to seek medical help promptly if necessary. The following symptoms may indicate that a doctor's visit is needed:

■ Decreased or poor appetite
■ Weight loss
■ Tummy aches
■ Frequent or loose stools
■ Increased or frequent cough
■ Vomiting
■ Increased sputum
■ Change in the colour of sputum
■ Breathlessness
■ Unwillingness to exercise
■ Fever
■ Cold symptoms

# Immunizations and CF

Babies with CF are particularly at risk from the common childhood infectious diseases, especially those that may affect the lungs.

**Immunization schedule** A child with CF must stick rigidly to the normal schedule (see p.283), and injections should only be postponed in very exceptional circumstances and always after consultation with your doctor. Having a cold or a cough is not sufficient reason to delay immunization. CF children should also be immunized against flu every winter.

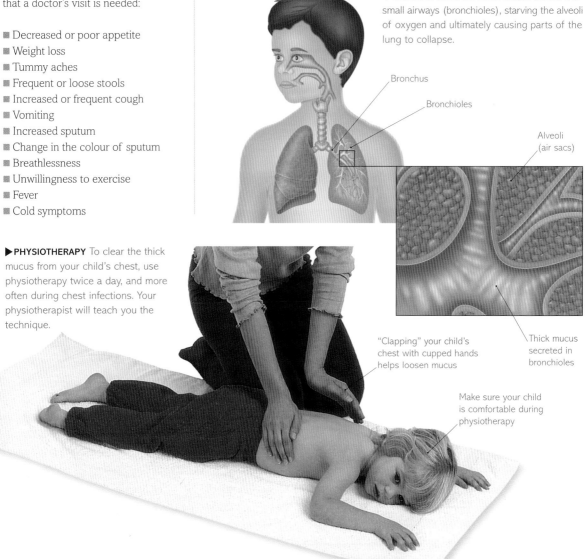

▼**BLOCKED AIRWAYS** Thick mucus blocks the small airways (bronchioles), starving the alveoli of oxygen and ultimately causing parts of the lung to collapse.

Bronchus

Bronchioles

Alveoli (air sacs)

▶**PHYSIOTHERAPY** To clear the thick mucus from your child's chest, use physiotherapy twice a day, and more often during chest infections. Your physiotherapist will teach you the technique.

"Clapping" your child's chest with cupped hands helps loosen mucus

Thick mucus secreted in bronchioles

Make sure your child is comfortable during physiotherapy

# Diabetes mellitus

In children diabetes mellitus is due to a lack of insulin from the pancreas. This results in an increase in blood glucose (sugar) concentration (hyperglycaemia), causing excessive urination and constant thirst and fatigue. An accumulation in the body of chemicals called ketones occurs when there is a severe lack of insulin. A high sugar level is not in itself dangerous, but high ketone levels are. Most diabetic children need insulin injections and a strictly controlled diet.

## Is there a cure?

Diabetes occurs because cells of the immune system attack the insulin-producing islet tissue in your child's pancreas. Any cure must therefore replace the damaged tissue in some way. For this reason, transplantation offers the only viable therapeutic approach, but rejection of the transplanted tissue does pose a serious problem.

There is promising research going on that suggests we might be able to graft tissue into the body that will not be recognized as foreign. Already this approach has worked experimentally and has been used to reverse diabetes in a number of animal models, without the need for anti-rejection therapy. It

is quite possible that diabetes will be cured with transplants in your child's lifetime. Progress has also been made with genetic research, and the recent discovery of two new genes has opened up the possibility that the condition could be prevented.

## Adjusting to diabetes

It can be frightening when you're told that your child has insulin-dependent diabetes (type I diabetes), but the disease will not prevent your child from leading a full and active life.

How you and the family handle your child's diabetes helps to determine the way in which your child accepts or denies the disease and becomes a

balanced, mature person. As parents you'll need to exercise skill to help your child accept his condition with the minimum of fuss. You'll soon know a lot about diabetes itself, the need for insulin, and the technique for injection, as well as about the importance of proper food intake and exercise. You will also need to know how to recognize the signs of a low/high blood sugar level.

## Controlling diabetes

The aim of diabetes treatment is to keep your child's blood sugar levels as near to normal as possible. Too high a level (hyperglycaemia) can lead to fatigue, excessive urination, constant thirst, weight loss, and an increased level of ketones in the body. Too little blood sugar (hypoglycaemia) can lead to weakness, dizziness, confusion, and even seizures. Proper levels are achieved by a combination of dietary control and regular meals, with particular attention paid to the intake of sugar and carbohydrates, insulin injections, and regular exercise.

After a diagnosis is made treatment is started by the hospital consultant paediatrician who specializes in diabetes, usually supported by specialist diabetic nurses and dieticians. There are many different insulin preparations available, but essentially they are of two types – short-acting and longer-acting. Short-acting insulins are used before the

▲ INSULIN INJECTION Pinch the skin gently and insert the needle at 90°. A needle will deliver the insulin to the layer of fat just below the skin.

◄ INJECTION SITES To avoid scarring, vary the injection sites. Suitable sites include the upper arms, thighs, buttocks, and stomach.

main meals of the day whereas longer-acting preparations are used twice a day. It is likely that your child will need to use a combination of the two. These are now available in cartridge form and they can be given conveniently via a cartridge pen. The hospital team will also talk to you about the value of blood glucose self-monitoring, which both you and your child can do at home to help control the diabetes. A system is available that enables you to measure your child's blood sugar accurately at any time. Precise monitoring and testing of blood sugar may reduce and even reverse some of the complications of diabetes.

The hospital diabetic team will want to see your child regularly. In particular they will be aiming to keep blood glucose under control and will monitor his growth and development. This is likely to involve regular blood tests.

Perfect control is too much to hope for. Even if your child is completely trustworthy about insulin and food, he'll still occasionally have a raised blood sugar. If your child eats sweets occasionally, this act of breaking the rules isn't life-threatening, so don't make too much fuss. One bit of chocolate will not make any child unwell, not even a child with diabetes. Even if your child has followed your advice, you'll have to accept that blood sugars can sometimes be a little high or a little low. Be realistic.

## Immunizations and diabetes

Diabetic children are more vulnerable to infection so annual flu jabs are recommended. Your child must also have the usual childhood vaccinations (see p.283), including pneumococcus, which is now part of the immunization programme for all children.

# Blood glucose self-monitoring

You begin the blood glucose testing by obtaining a drop of blood from a tiny finger-prick. In one method the blood is dropped onto a chemically sensitive strip. The strip is inserted into a machine that measures the blood glucose and the result shows up on a digital display. Another method relies on comparing the strip visually with a colour-coded chart. Each method gives accurate results.

Blood glucose self-monitoring allows you to measure your child's blood sugar levels frequently and accurately without visiting the doctor and waiting for lab results; with it you can respond promptly to a low blood sugar count by giving your child high-carbohydrate foods, or to a high blood sugar count by giving an insulin injection. Your doctor will recommend the proper insulin dosages or other medications according to your child's blood glucose levels.

While it involves a small element of pain, blood testing is more accurate than urine tests, since there is a delay between the rise of blood sugar and the time it shows up in the urine. Another problem is that urine tests only show high glucose readings when the levels are well above acceptable limits.

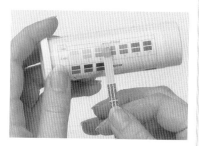

▶ **TESTING STRIPS** The strip will change colour to indicate your child's glucose level. Read the blood glucose level by comparing the strip with the colour chart on the side of the strip container.

# Helping a child with diabetes

You'll need to supervise discreetly while giving your child some responsibility so that he learns self-care and control.

Children with diabetes tend to worry more than children without the disease, and this is only to be expected; they have to assume important responsibilities and they know, or will come to know, that diabetes can do some very unpleasant things. Diabetes makes children feel tired and confused, and can make them lose consciousness. A child who is diabetic has to plan ahead when leaving home, and remember always to take along some sweets or sugar and insulin and syringes. Your child is threatened both physically and psychologically by diabetes, so you need to be sympathetic without becoming over-protective. As your child grows older, he'll be better able to understand what has to be done.

# Cerebral palsy

In the UK each year roughly one in 500 babies is born with or develops cerebral palsy. It is a disorder that affects both boys and girls from all races and social backgrounds.

## What causes cerebral palsy?

Children with cerebral palsy suffer from abnormalities of movement. In most cases the condition is caused by an injury to the brain, usually before, around, or soon after the time of birth. The injury may occur during a difficult or premature birth. It may occur because the baby fails to breathe properly, or because of cerebral bleeding, or bleeding into brain cavities (intraventricular haemorrhage). Injury can also be due to an infection in the mother in early pregnancy – rubella (German measles), for example. Rarely, the brain forms abnormally for no obvious reason, or the disorder is inherited even if the parents are healthy.

The treatment consists of trying to develop the child's physical, mental, and social capabilities to the full. It is important that the child is fully assessed by a specialist and a physiotherapist so that he can be given treatment from an early age.

## Types of cerebral palsy

If a child has cerebral palsy, part of his brain does not function normally. The affected area is usually one of the parts of the brain that controls certain muscles and body movements; the disease interferes with the messages that normally pass from the brain to the body. In some children cerebral palsy is hardly noticeable at all; others are more severely affected. No two children will be affected in quite the same way. There are three main types of cerebral palsy:

**Spastic cerebral palsy** Here, the cortex, the outer layer of the brain, which controls thought, movement,

# Helping a child with cerebral palsy

It's difficult to predict the effects of cerebral palsy, particularly on a young child. It doesn't become more severe as your child gets older, though some difficulties may become more noticeable, and your priorities will change: when your baby is young, for example, you might concentrate on helping him to sit up, but later you will be more concerned with communication skills and talking.

There is no cure for cerebral palsy, but if children are lifted, held, and positioned well from an early age, and encouraged to play in a way that helps them to improve their posture and muscle control, they can learn a lot and lead fulfilling lives.

There's no question that you're going to have to work very hard with your child and there will be difficult moments when you feel that it's all too much. These feelings are natural, and most parents feel that they gradually get less severe. Indeed, many parents say they find bringing up a child with cerebral palsy a challenging and fulfilling task.

Children with cerebral palsy often tend to lie or sit in certain ways, because their muscles are sometimes in spasm, and they can have problems with their joints. Having physiotherapy treatment as soon as cerebral palsy is suspected can help reduce the risks of these complications developing. You can help your child in several ways.

■ Your child may get stiffer and have more muscle spasm when he's lying on his back, so lie him on his side or tummy instead, supporting him with a cushion if necessary. It's also a good idea to change his position every 20 minutes or so.

■ Help your child to learn to use his hands right from the start by letting him feel things with different textures, and encouraging him to hold toys and other objects. Toys securely strung over his chair can be useful.

■ Enable your child to learn about shapes by showing him different simply shaped objects, and encouraging him to handle them and play with them.

■ A child of three or four years with cerebral palsy may want to help with everyday tasks around the house like any child his age. Explain to your child what you're doing, let him watch you, and if possible let him join in.

and sensation, is affected. Tight and sometimes jerky muscle movements result from this.

**Athetoid cerebral palsy** This type involves the basal ganglia, which are groups of cells that lie deep within the brain. The basal ganglia promote organized, graceful, and economical movement, so an abnormality can cause movements that are bending and wave-like.

**Ataxic cerebral palsy** This indicates that the cerebellum, which is located at the base of the brain, is affected. Because the cerebellum is responsible for coordinating fine movement, posture, and balance, an abnormality can result in an uneven gait and difficulty in walking.

## Effects of cerebral palsy

Some children with cerebral palsy will have difficulty talking, walking, or using their hands, and most will need help with everyday tasks or appliances to improve mobility. Very often, a child's other abilities – such as vision or hearing – may be affected.

The child with cerebral palsy may suffer slightly or severely from slow, awkward, or jerky movements, stiffness, weakness, floppiness, or muscle spasms. Some children are prone to involuntary movements.

There are also a number of other disorders associated with cerebral palsy that are due either to poor muscle control or to other abnormalities in the brain.

**Eyesight** The most common eye problem is a squint, which may need correction with glasses or, in severe cases, an operation.

**Hearing** Children with cerebral palsy are more likely than other children to have severe hearing difficulties. It is important that hearing difficulties be diagnosed early (see p.96). If a child is affected, he may be able to wear a hearing aid.

**Speech** The ability to control the tiny muscles in the mouth, tongue, palate, and voice box is necessary for speech. Difficulty in speaking and problems with chewing and swallowing often occur together in children with cerebral palsy. Speech therapists can help with both sorts of difficulty and ease communication problems.

**Spatial perception** Some children with cerebral palsy can't perceive space and relate it to their own bodies; for instance, they're not able to judge distances or think in three dimensions. This is due to an abnormality in a part of the brain that is not related to intelligence.

**Epilepsy** About one-third of children with cerebral palsy are also affected by epilepsy (see p.270), but it's impossible to predict whether, or when, your child may develop epileptic seizures. In some children these start in infancy; in others, not until adulthood. If your child does develop epilepsy, it can be controlled with medication.

**Learning difficulties** People who are unable to control their movements very well, or to talk, are often assumed to have a mental disability. While some people with cerebral palsy do have learning difficulties, but this is by no means always the case. Many people with cerebral palsy have average, or higher than average, intelligence.

◀ HELP FOR YOUR CHILD It's important to help children with cerebral palsy to lead as normal a life as possible. This little girl is having fun with a toy while sitting in a special physiotherapy seat and table designed to support her and correct her postural problems.

## Choosing and using toys

Despite their difficulties with movement, children with cerebral palsy need stimulating play just as much as any child, but choosing toys can be problematic. Most toy companies make goods suitable for children with cerebral palsy. If you are planning to buy an expensive toy, ask your physiotherapist or occupational therapist for advice, or join a toy library and experiment to find out which toys your child will find most rewarding. Wedges, for support, and standing frames can help children with cerebral palsy to enjoy their toys. Once again, your occupational therapist can help.

■ Help him to use his imagination by telling him stories about his cuddly toys while you play with him, for example, or encourage him to have a tea party with them.

■ Always show your child how a new toy works, not once but many times.
■ If your child doesn't seem to want to play, start showing him how much fun it is by starting to play with his toys yourself, and ask him to join in.

■ When your child is playing let him choose from two or three different toys, then put away the ones he doesn't want to play with now. If he's surrounded by too many toys, he'll be easily distracted.

## Conductive education

This is a learning system designed to help adults and children with certain kinds of motor disabilities, including children with cerebral palsy, to become much more independent. It was developed at the Pëto Institute in Hungary and has helped some children to gain skills that their parents never believed possible. The aim is to help people to function as normally as possible – physically, intellectually, and socially. It is based around a consideration of the child as a whole person, intensive group work with parents and children, and the encouragement of every small movement towards gaining independence.

In the UK, Scope (see Useful addresses, p.342) is establishing a network of schools where parents and their preschool children can learn the basics of conductive education together.

# Epilepsy

The most common disease of the brain in the UK, epliepsy affects five in 1,000 school-age children. It occurs when the normal electrical impulses in the brain are disturbed, which causes periodic seizures. There are different forms, including "grand mal" and "petit mal".

## Epileptic seizures

Tonic-clonic, or "grand mal", seizures start with difficulty breathing and loss of consciousness. This is followed by stiffening of the body, lasting a minute or less, and then a series of rhythmic jerks of the limbs, clenching of the teeth (when your child might bite his tongue), and frothing at the mouth.

In absence, or "petit mal", seizures, there are no abnormal movements, only a second or two of unconsciousness, very much like daydreaming. Your child's eyes will glaze over and he'll appear not to see or hear anything. This is not easily recognized, and may even go undiagnosed. Although not as dramatic as tonic-clonic, absence seizures can interfere with a child's life, particularly with paying attention and performance at school, and with some physical activities when loss of control could pose a danger.

## How serious is it?

Epilepsy is by no means life-threatening. Most children grow out of the absence form by late adolescence; those who suffer from the tonic-clonic form can also improve with age and may grow out of it. Some children with tonic-clonic epilepsy need attention all their lives, even though the condition can usually be controlled by drugs.

It can take time to establish the level of medication required, and a child may go through times when the epilepsy is not absolutely controlled by drugs. If this happens, consult your doctor, who can adjust the dose.

Dosage of the anti-epileptic treatment will need to be increased as your child grows and puts on weight as treatment is based on weight. If your child has a seizure of any kind, check with your doctor immediately.

Epilepsy is not to be confused with febrile seizures (see p.281), which are

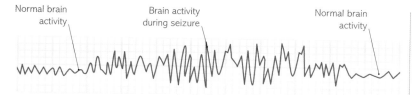

Normal brain activity

Brain activity during seizure

Normal brain activity

▲ **EEG TRACE** An electro-encephalogram, or EEG, can detect levels of electrical activity in the brain. During a seizure brain activity becomes unregulated and chaotic, as shown on this trace.

caused by a high fever preceding or during an infectious illness.

## What to do during a seizure

■ Loosen the clothing around your child's neck or chest, and clear a space around him.
■ As soon as your child stops moving violently, put him in the recovery position (see p.329).
■ Make a note of what happens during your child's seizure, as well as how long it lasts so you can tell your doctor.
■ Don't try to restrain the limbs.
■ Don't try to hold your child's teeth apart if they are clenched, or put anything into his mouth.

## Treatment

If your child has a seizure, your doctor will ask you about it and examine him to decide what form of seizure he's had. If the doctor suspects the seizure may be the onset of epilepsy, the child will be referred to hospital for an examination that may include an electro-encephalogram (EEG), blood tests, and a brain scan.

Anti-convulsive drugs taken on a daily basis will reduce the frequency of tonic-clonic seizures and eradicate them in most children. Selective drugs are now available that can target a precise area of the brain and don't cause the side effects associated with older drugs.

Your child's condition will be reviewed periodically by your doctor, and if there are no seizures for a year or two, he may try phasing out the drugs. Surgery may be used if drugs are not effective and if damage to a single area of the brain is thought to be the cause. Your doctor will advise you as to whether this might be appropriate.

## The outlook for your child

The aim of caring for a child with epilepsy is to control the seizures with a minimum of side effects and enhance his quality of life as he grows up. Seizure control should never be established at the cost of drug side effects, as they may result in cramping of important brain functions that allow your child to develop normally.

Monitoring your child's condition is very important. Don't rely on your doctor to do this; establish a plan of action that involves regular visits and if your child has more than one or two seizures, visit the doctor immediately for reassessment; the medication may need to be adjusted.

# Helping a child with epilepsy

It can be a shock to realize that your child has epilepsy, but you must try to remain calm. You and your child will both need to get your confidence back. You can do this with the help of your doctor, who can advise you on how to cope with the seizures and prescribe medication.

It is important to observe your child's condition so that you can report back to your doctor. Make a note of the frequency of your child's seizures. If he's on

medication, watch him carefully and report any mental or personality differences that may be caused by the drugs. You should never stop your child's medication without seeking medical advice first. To do so could result in a severe, prolonged seizure after a few days.

Treat your child as normally as possible all the time. Tell his friends and teachers about the condition so that they're not frightened and shocked if your child has a seizure when they're there. Your child should

always wear a bracelet or medallion engraved with information about his epilepsy.

When your child is old enough, teach him how to recognize the signs of an oncoming attack. Many people with epilepsy experience sensations such as an unpleasant smell, distorted vision, or an odd feeling in the stomach just before a seizure starts. If your child can identify these sensations as warning signs he may be able to avoid having an accident.

# Sickle-cell disease

This inherited disease is most common in people of African or West Indian descent, but may also occur in people from the Indian subcontinent, the Middle East, and the eastern Mediterranean. A sufferer will have bouts of pain and may be at risk from other disorders, but will be quite well most of the time.

## Types of sickle-cell disease

Sickle-cell disease (SCD), is caused by an abnormality of haemoglobin, the oxygen-carrying substance in red blood cells. The three main types are: sickle-cell anaemia, the most common and severe form, haemoglobin SC disease, and sickle beta-thalassaemia.

**Sickle-cell anaemia** When oxygen levels are low, the abnormal haemoglobin (known as type S) becomes crystallized, making some red cells fragile and rigid. These sickle cells – so called because of their characteristic sickle, or crescent, shape – can then become trapped in the blood vessels, causing a blockage that prevents blood flow. This accounts for the excruciating pain that is characteristic of an SCD attack.

Sickle cells survive only about 20 days in the body, as opposed to the usual 120 days for normal red cells, and the early death of red cells leads to anaemia. Sometimes aplastic crises occur, in which the blood-forming activity in the bone marrow is reduced temporarily. When this happens, the number of red blood cells becomes dangerously low. This condition can be life-threatening.

**Haemoglobin SCD** In this form of SCD there are two abnormal haemoglobins, type S (the abnormal type in sickle-cell anaemia) and type C.

The disease appears later, and in a milder form, than sickle-cell anaemia.

**Sickle beta-thalassaemia** This is similar to sickle-cell anaemia in that there is an abnormality in the haemoglobin that results in abnormally shaped cells. Sufferers inherit a sickle-cell gene from one parent and a beta-thalassaemia gene from the other.

## Sickle-cell trait

The sickle-cell trait is found in areas where malaria was or is endemic, and offers some protection against it. It's not surprising, therefore, that around ten per cent of Afro-Caribbeans, 25 per cent of Nigerians, and a smaller but significant number of Middle Eastern and Mediterranean people have the trait.

A child can only develop SCD if both parents pass on the abnormal trait, and even then the chances are only one in four. If only one parent passes on the trait, then the sickle-cell gene will be masked by a healthy gene from the other parent. A carrier is unaffected, but the trait shows up in blood tests.

## Effects of SCD

Apart from causing anaemia and acute attacks of pain known as "crises", SCD can cause other problems including infections and jaundice. In addition, there's a small risk of a stroke occurring during a crisis.

**Infections** Children with SCD are particularly vulnerable to infections – for example in the lungs or bones. An overwhelming infection can cause a dramatic loss of blood cells in the spleen or liver, resulting in a massive drop in haemoglobin levels, which is potentially fatal if treatment is not given immediately.

**Pain crises** When sickle cells block a blood vessel, there may be oxygen starvation of tissue supplied by that blood vessel; this can occur nearly anywhere in the body, although the feet and hands are particularly vulnerable.

These crises are one of the most distressing aspects of SCD. The pain is violent and unpredictable, and as a parent it is very difficult to watch your child in pain and be unable to help him. The crisis can be treated with painkilling drugs, however. Sometimes pain crises are brought on by infections, strenuous exercise, low temperatures, or dehydration caused by vomiting or diarrhoea.

**Jaundice** The rapid breakdown of red cells can result in increased levels of a pigment called bilirubin (see Jaundice, p.25). This causes a yellowish appearance in the whites of the eyes, which often increases with the severity of the crises. Skin may also have a yellowish tinge.

**Development** Children with SCD may experience slowing down of their growth (both height and weight) and the onset of puberty may also be later than usual. They may exist in a permanent state of chronic anaemia leading to a rapid decline in their condition when ill.

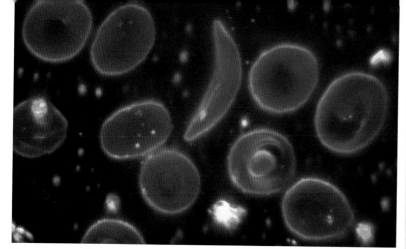

**▲ SICKLE CELLS** Haemoglobin is the protein contained in red cells in the blood. Abnormal haemoglobin leads to the production of red blood cells that are fragile, short-lived, and sickle-shaped, hence the name of the disease.

## SCD screening

Genetic and supportive counselling are essential for couples at risk or who have SCD in their families. In some areas, all babies are screened for haemoglobin abnormalities regardless of their ethnic origin. Early detection means the condition can be managed properly right from the start, and in particular that long-term treatment with penicillin can begin promptly. This minimizes the risk of lung infections and sickle-cell crises.

Antenatal screening is available to find out if a baby's haemoglobin is normal and can be carried out at the time of amniocentesis. Screening is advisable for pregnant women who are aware that they have the sickle-cell trait. Couples at risk will be also offered counselling to clarify the risks of having children with SCD.

## Treatment

If your child has SCD, he'll need frequent doses of penicillin to nip bacterial infections in the bud. This should be given from the time of diagnosis throughout life.

All affected children need folic acid supplements. A child with SCD should drink plenty of fluids to prevent dehydration and should always keep warm, to encourage normal circulation. Although over-exertion can cause problems, your child should exercise regularly and find his own energy tolerance level – exercise will improve the health of his heart and his circulation. Pain and any symptoms of infection should always be treated promptly.

Where millions of red blood cells have been destroyed, exchange transfusion in hospital may be necessary. Sometimes many exchange transfusions will have to be given. Although this is a lengthy procedure, it will allow your child a near normal life. Painkillers, fluids, and possibly inhaled oxygen and antibiotics may be given too. With experience, parents can learn to manage mild SCD crises at home.

# Helping a child with sickle-cell disease

Although knowledge about the disease is incomplete, it is important that you are as well informed as possible, so that you can help your child avoid pain crises. Counselling will give you a safe, confidential way of exploring your feelings, and provide a source of encouragement and support (see Useful addresses, p.342).

When your child starts school, you should inform his head teacher as well as his class teachers of his condition, making them aware of the problems it can impose on education. Your child may miss out on classes, for example, because of hospital admissions or a crisis. Reassure your child and encourage him to express his anxieties.

Your child's feelings must be given great consideration. Many children with SCD experience difficulties with their classmates at preschool and school. Ask your child's teachers if they can educate the other children in the class about the condition so that your child does not suffer from feelings of alienation or isolation – as he might if, for example, the children in his class thought they could catch the disease from him.

Many SCD children express a fear of dying or being deformed. Others feel different and alienated, thinking they're the only ones who are suffering from this condition and that nobody understands them. Yet others are afraid of expressing when they are in pain in case nobody believes them. You can help enormously by making sure that your child knows he has your sympathy, understanding, and care whenever he needs it.

# Medicine and healthcare

Most childhood illnesses are minor and others
are easily preventable; immunizations are
effective against most infectious diseases. In
a baby, however, seemingly minor illnesses can
cause complications: a cold that develops into
a throat infection, for instance, may cause
breathing difficulties.

Sometimes it's hard to know whether to seek
medical help. You should never worry that you
are being too cautious – if you find yourself
wondering whether it's worth consulting a
doctor, then you probably should.

The main cause of death in young children is
accidents. Reduce the likelihood of accidents by
making your home safe and taking precautions
when your child is away from home. Learn
first aid. Don't just read this book; attend an
approved first aid training course (see p.325)
and learn the emergency procedures on
pp.324–29 by heart.

# Dealing with illness

It's fairly easy to recognize when your child is ill: she'll be pale, listless, and off her food. You can treat her at home for most things, but if you're ever worried or in two minds, call your doctor. Other sources of help are NHS Direct, NHS walk-in centres, and a hospital accident and emergency department. Some symptoms require immediate medical attention (see opposite). Even when you're sure your child is ill, you might not know what's wrong. To help your doctor, observe all you can about your child's symptoms; the more information he has, the better the chance of an accurate diagnosis.

## Warning symptoms

There are a number of symptoms that indicate that your child may be unwell, and possibly needs to see a doctor.

**Raised temperature** The normal body temperature for a child is 37°C (98.6°F). If a baby has a raised temperature seek medical advice.

For an older child with a raised temperature, always consider her overall condition to decide how unwell she is. Take into account how alert and communicative she is, whether she's eating and drinking, and any other symptoms she might have such as earache. Also bear in mind that your child's temperature does vary according to how active she has been and the time of day. Her temperature is lower in the morning than during the day, and higher in the evening. It will also be higher if she's been running around a lot.

**Diarrhoea** Loose, watery bowel movements mean the intestines are inflamed and irritable, and there's not enough time for water to be reabsorbed from the stool. Gastroenteritis is the most common cause, but diarrhoea can also be caused by an infection elsewhere in the body. Diarrhoea is always serious in babies and young children because it can lead to dehydration. If your baby is under one year old and she has had

## Taking your child's pulse

The pulse is the wave of pressure caused by a heartbeat. It can be felt where arteries are close to the skin. A rapid pulse may indicate that your child is unwell.

**Pulse rate** This varies according to health, age, and physical exertion. The average pulse rate for a baby is 100–160 beats per minute; this slows to 100–120 for a one-year-old, and 80–90 by about seven. When taking your child's pulse, use your first two fingers – not your thumb as it has a pulse. Count the number of beats in 15 seconds and multiply this figure by four.

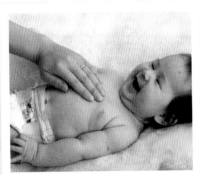

▲ **CHECKING HEARTBEAT IN BABY** For a child under a year, the best way to take a pulse is to put your fingers on her chest at the level of the nipple and count the number of heartbeats (you'll also find a pulse on the inner side of the arm above the elbow).

▲ **RADIAL PULSE** If your child is over one year, it should be relatively easy to find the pulse on her wrist. Hold her hand, and place the middle and index fingers of your other hand on the spot on her wrist immediately below her thumb. Count the beats.

diarrhoea for three hours, you should consult your doctor immediately.

**Vomiting** Check with your doctor if your child has been vomiting during a six-hour period or more, especially if she has diarrhoea or fever. Vomiting is usually caused by gastroenteritis or food that doesn't suit, but there may be a more serious cause.

**Pain** You should check with your doctor if your child complains of headaches, particularly after she's bumped her head or if the headache comes on a few hours after a head injury, or if there is blurred vision, nausea, or dizziness. Stomach pain, particularly on the lower right side of her abdomen, should be checked too.

**Breathing difficulty** This is a medical emergency and requires immediate help. Breathing may be laboured and you may notice that your child's ribs are drawn in sharply each time she takes a breath. If your child's lips go blue, you should treat this as an emergency and call an ambulance.

**Change in appetite** Sudden changes in appetite may indicate underlying illness, especially if your child has a fever, even a mild one. Call your doctor if your child refuses food for a day and seems lethargic, or, if she's under six months old, has a poor appetite, and doesn't seem to be thriving.

## Calling the doctor
It is only natural for a new parent to be anxious, and you may worry because you are not sure whether your baby is genuinely poorly. Along with many doctors, I quickly learned that the one person whose opinion can't be dismissed is the mother's. So your

guideline should be, whenever in doubt, call a doctor. Don't feel shy about asking your doctor questions if something is worrying you, however trivial it may seem.

**What to tell your doctor** In order to make a diagnosis a doctor will need the following information: a description of your child's symptoms; when they started; in what order they occurred; how severe they are; and whether anything precipitated them (eating something poisonous, for instance). In addition to this, your doctor will need to know your child's age and medical history.

Be prepared to give details of any injury or accident. Did your child lose consciousness? Has she had anything to eat or drink (in case she needs an anaesthetic)? Was she bitten by an insect or animal? What was it and what were her symptoms? If she has swallowed a toxic substance or plant, keep it to show to the doctor.

The specific questions your doctor may ask about an illness are: has your child vomited or had diarrhoea? Does she have any pain? Where is it? How long has it lasted? Have you given her anything for it? Is her temperature raised? How quickly did the fever come on and what was her highest temperature? Has she lost consciousness at any time? Have you noticed swollen glands or a rash? Has she had any dizziness or blurred vision? The doctor will also ask general questions about your child's appetite and sleeping patterns.

**What to ask your doctor** If your child is prescribed drugs, make sure that you know when the drugs should be taken (some need to be taken on a full stomach), how long they should

be taken for, and whether there are any side effects. Find out how your child should be nursed and how soon her symptoms can be expected to go away. Ask your doctor about preventive measures for a child who has a recurring condition like cold sores.

With an infectious disease, you'll need to know whether it's safe to have visitors, how long your child will have to be off school, and whether the illness has any long-term effects.

## Emergencies
Some situations demand immediate medical attention. Call an ambulance right away or take your child to the nearest hospital accident and emergency by car should any of the following serious situations happen.

■ A bone fracture or suspected fracture (see p.337).
■ A severe reaction to a sting or bite from an insect or animal (see p.339), or after eating nuts.
■ Head injury (see p.335).
■ Symptoms of meningitis (see p.304).
■ Pale blue or grey colouration around the lips.
■ A burn or scald (see p.334) larger than the palm of your child's hand.
■ Poisoning or suspected poisoning (see p.332).
■ Unconsciousness (see pp.326–28).
■ Severe bleeding from a wound (see p.333).
■ Contact with a corrosive chemical, especially involving the eyes (see pp.332 and 336).
■ Difficulty breathing or choking (see p.331).
■ Any injuries to the ears or eyes (see pp.284, 287, and 336).
■ An electric shock (see p.332).
■ Inhalation of toxic fumes such as smoke or gas.

# Temperature

Take your child's temperature whenever you suspect she's ill. Normal body temperature for a child is between 36°C (96.8°F) and 37°C (98.6°F). Anything over 38°C (100.4°F) is classed as a fever. Never take your child's temperature immediately after she's been running about or when she's just eaten something hot or cold.

## Taking a temperature

A hot forehead may be the first sign of a fever, but to be sure, take your child's temperature with a thermometer. Take it again after 20 minutes. A digital thermometer is the most accurate. Ear thermometers are also very accurate and give a reading in seconds. Strip

▲ **DIGITAL THERMOMETER** Window shows the temperature reading.

▲ **EAR THERMOMETER** Window shows the temperature reading.

▲ **STRIP THERMOMETER** A glowing panel indicates your child's temperature.

thermometers are less accurate than others, but simple and safe to use.

## Using a digital thermometer

A digital thermometer can be used in the mouth or under the arm. To take the mouth temperature, place the thermometer gently under your child's tongue. Ask her to place the tip of her tongue firmly behind her lower front teeth – this will hold the thermometer in place. Then ask her to close her lips – but not her teeth – over it. When the thermometer beeps, remove it and read the number in the window. With a young child you may find it easier to take her temperature under her arm. Put the thermometer into her armpit, hold her arm down until you hear the thermometer bleep, then remove it and read the number in the window. Wash a thermometer in soap and cold water after use and store in its case.

## Take care

Don't use a mercury thermometer in your child's mouth; she may bite it and swallow mercury, which is a poison. Digital thermometers are harder to break and are safe and easy to use with children of all ages. They are battery-operated, so be sure to have some spare batteries available.

## Using an ear thermometer

Digital ear thermometers are a quick, safe method of taking a child's temperature. Gently insert the thermometer tip into your child's ear and read the temperature from the display. The ear thermometer has a hygienic disposable tip.

## Using a strip thermometer

The strip thermometer is easy to use. Carefully position the heat-sensitive side on your child's forehead and hold it there for a minute or so, keeping your fingers clear of the panels. The temperature should light up on the outside of the strip.

▲**DIGITAL THERMOMETER** Taking your child's temperature by placing the thermometer in her armpit is probably the easiest method with a young baby.

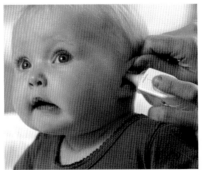

▲**EAR THERMOMETER** Digital ear thermometers work quickly and produce a reading on an LCD to within 0.1°C degree accuracy, but can be expensive.

▲**STRIP THERMOMETER** Unbreakable, accurate, and simple to use, strip thermometers are easily stored at home or carried with you when travelling.

# Medicines

Most medicines for children come in syrup form. Using droppers or letting your baby suck the medicine from your finger are the best ways to give medicine if your child can't swallow from a spoon. If your baby refuses medicine, ask your partner to help you, or wrap her up in a blanket so you can hold her steady. With older children, promise a favourite food to take the medicine's taste away.

## Giving medicine

Whether you are using a syringe or a plastic measuring spoon to administer medicine to your child, you'll need to hold her securely. It's best to hold her hands gently out of the way, to prevent her knocking the medicine out of your hand. If you're using a syringe that's too big to fit into the neck of the medicine bottle, you'll need to decant some medicine into a universal adapter (see picture, right) first, and from that fill the syringe to the required dose.

**▶ LOADING A SYRINGE** Put the adapter into a medicine bottle and fit the syringe tip into it. Press the plunger down into the empty syringe, tip the medicine bottle up, then draw medicine into the syringe.

Syringe

Universal adapter

Medicine bottle

**▲ USING A SYRINGE** Introduce the syringe tip into your baby's mouth and then under her tongue. Gently press the plunger down to release the medicine in a controlled flow so that your baby can take small swallows and doesn't gulp or choke.

# Applying drops

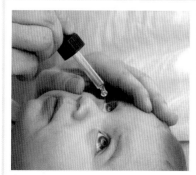

**▲ EYE DROPS** Lay your baby on her back and tilt her head in the direction of the affected eye. Draw the right amount of liquid up into the dropper. Gently pull her lower eyelid down with your finger and raise her upper lid. Let the drops fall into the corner of her eye. Get someone to help if necessary.

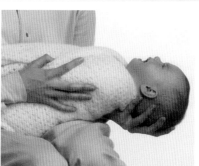

**▲ NOSE DROPS** Lay your baby on her back with her head tilted backwards, supported by your hand. Draw the right amount of medicine into the dropper. Then hold the dropper just above your baby's nostrils and let the required number of drops fall into each nostril. Hold her still for a minute or two.

**▲ EAR DROPS** Lay your baby on her side. Draw the right amount of medicine into the dropper. Hold the dropper over your baby's ear opening and let the required number of eardrops fall into the centre of her ear. Keep her still for a few moments while the drops spread into the ear canal.

# Nursing your child

You don't need special skills or medical knowledge to look after your sick child. Relax the rules and try to hide your anxiety. Don't insist that she eats while she's ill, but do encourage her to drink lots – electrolyte rehydration solution will help.

## General nursing

As well as whatever treatment the doctor recommends, the following routines will help your child to feel more comfortable while she is ill:

■ Air your child's room and bed at least once a day.
■ Leave a bowl by your child's bed if she's vomiting or has whooping cough.
■ Leave a box of tissues by your child's bed.
■ Give small meals frequently; your child may find larger portions of food off-putting.
■ Dress her in a vest and pants if she has a fever, so she doesn't get too hot
■ Give paracetamol elixir or ibuprofen for pain relief or if she has a fever.

## Should your child be in bed?

At the beginning of an illness when your child is feeling quite poorly she will probably want to stay in bed and she may sleep a lot. As she starts to feel better she will still need bed rest, but she'll want to be around you and may want to play. The best way to accommodate this is to make up a bed on the sofa in a room near where you are so that she can lie down when she wants to. Don't insist that your child goes to bed just because she's ill – children with a fever, for instance, don't recover faster if they stay in bed. When your child is tired, however, it's time for bed. But don't just leave her alone. Make sure that you visit her regularly

(every half an hour), and stay to play a game, read a book, or do a puzzle. When she's on the road to recovery make sure that enough happens in her day to make the distinction between night and day.

## Giving drinks

It's essential that your child drinks a lot when she's ill – when she has a fever, diarrhoea, or is vomiting – because she will need to replace lost fluids to avoid becoming dehydrated. The recommended fluid intake for a child with a fever is 100–150ml per kg (1½–2½ floz per lb) of body weight per day, which is the equivalent of 1 litre (2pt) per day for a child who weighs 9kg (20lb).

Encourage your child to drink by leaving a drink bedside her (preferably water or fruit juice). Try putting drinks in cups that are especially appealing, or that she normally can't have, and by give her bendy straws to drink with.

## Occupying your child

Illness is an occasion when you can completely indulge your child. When she's not resting, spend time playing games and talking to her. Relax all the rules and let her play whatever games she wants to, even if you've previously disallowed them in bed. If your child wants to do something messy like painting, just spread an old sheet or a sheet of polythene over the bed. If you can, move a television into her room temporarily – this will keep her entertained and make her feel special as well. Or let her sleep on the sofa.

Let her do some painting; read aloud to her; get out some of her old toys and play with them together; buy her small presents and let her unwrap them; sing songs or make up a story together; ask her to draw a picture of what she is going to do when she feels better; and, unless she has an infectious illness, let some friends visit her for a brief period during the day. As your child gets better, let her play outside for a while, but if she has a fever discourage her from running around too much.

Position of fontanelle

▶ **DEHYDRATION** If your baby is under 18 months and has vomiting or diarrhoea she may be dehydrated. If she has sunken fontanelles, dry mouth and tongue, sunken eyes, and fewer wet nappies, she needs immediate medical attention.

## Vomiting

Your child will probably find vomiting a distressing experience so try to make her as comfortable as possible. Get her to sit up in bed and make sure there's a bowl or a bucket within easy reach, so that she doesn't have to run to the toilet. Hold back long hair, and when she's being sick hold her head and comfort her. Afterwards help your child to clean her teeth, or give her a mint to suck to take the taste away.

When your child hasn't vomited for a few hours and she's feeling hungry, offer her bland foods, such as pasta or mashed potato, but don't try to make her eat if she doesn't want to. More important than eating is having plenty of fluids. Avoid milk and give her water, diluted juice, or rehydration solution.

## Treating high temperature

The first sign of a raised temperature is often a hot forehead, but to check that your child is feverish take her temperature (see p.278). Call your doctor if the fever lasts more than 24 hours or if there are any accompanying symptoms.

Temperatures over 38°C (100.4°F) should be taken very seriously in children under six months, but doctors

▲ **TRUST YOUR INSTINCTS** If you suspect that your child isn't well, don't hesitate to get medical advice. You know your child and you're the best judge of her health.

do believe a high temperature is a protective mechanism for killing off viruses and bacteria. To reduce fever, lower the temperature in your child's room and give iced drinks. It's important for her to drink lots of fluid as she'll be perspiring a lot.

Try to cool your child down by undressing her down to the minimum clothing and bedclothes if her temperature is over 40°C (104°F) – there's a risk of you child suffereing from febrile seizures if the temperature is too high. Never sponge your child

with cold water as this will cause her blood vessels to constrict, preventing heat loss and increasing temperature.

Paracetamol can be given to babies and children over three months old and is available in liquid form. Children of one year and over can be given ibuprofen (also available as liquid), but avoid ibuprofen if your child has asthma as it can bring on an attack. Children under 16 shouldn't have aspirin. Follow dosage directions carefully and check with your doctor if you are unsure what to give a child.

## Febrile seizures

The most common cause of seizures in babies and children between 12 months and four years is a raised temperature that accompanies an infection. It's known as a febrile seizure.

**What happens** During a seizure the muscles of the body twitch involuntarily due to a temporary abnormality in brain function. The child loses consciousness. Other symptoms include stiffening of the body, rhythmic jerking of limbs, and clenching of teeth. Afterwards she may be sleepy and confused. The child may also be incontinent.

**What you can do** Undress her down to her vest and pants to reduce her temperature. Clear a space around her so that she can't damage herself. Wait until her body has stopped jerking and then place her in the recovery position (see p.327). Don't leave her alone, and don't try to restrain her or put anything in her mouth. Call your doctor. If the seizure last more than 15 minutes, call an ambulance.

# Hospital

At some point in your child's life she may have to go into hospital. This could be because she has had an accident, she needs an operation, or she has a chronic condition, such as sickle-cell disease (see p.272), which requires regular blood transfusions.

## Preparing your child

Given a little forethought on your part, a stay in hospital does not have to be upsetting or frightening for your child. If you don't like hospitals and you convey this attitude to your child you may inadvertently make her stay in hospital more difficult than it has to be. Try to teach her that a hospital is a friendly place where people go to get better. Whenever the chance arises – if you have a friend or a relative in hospital, for instance – take your child along when you go to visit and be matter-of-fact, not gloomy, about their illness. If your child's first experience of a hospital is when she becomes sick, it will seem more alien than it would otherwise.

If you know that your child is going to hospital, read her a story about a child who goes into hospital, and role play doctors and nurses with toy stethoscopes. Be as honest as you can about why she's going to hospital, and emphasize that it's to make her better. Reassure her that you will be with her as much as you can, and if she is old enough to understand, tell her when she'll be well enough to come home.

If your child needs to have an operation she'll probably be curious about what's going to happen to her. Answer her questions as honestly as you can – if she asks you whether the operation will hurt, don't pretend that it won't, but tell her that doctors have medicines that will make the pain go away quickly.

## What to take

You can help your child prepare for a stay in hospital by packing a bag with her. One of the most unsettling things for her will be the unfamiliar surroundings and the change of routine, so let her have some of her own things with her: a personal stereo and CDs or a radio, travel games, cuddly toys, and a photograph for her bedside. On a practical level, for a short stay pack the following items:

- A toilet bag containing a hair brush, comb, soap, flannel, toothbrush, and toothpaste.
- Three pairs of pyjamas or three nightdresses.
- A dressing gown and a pair of slippers.
- Three pairs of socks.
- Three pairs of pants.

## In hospital

Most hospitals expect parents to stay in with their children 24 hours a day. Whether yours does or not, try to spend as much time as possible with your child, especially at first, when her surroundings are unfamiliar. Let her know when you are going to come,

▶ **HOME COMFORTS** Give your child lots of reassurance if she has to go into hospital and let her take some home comforts, such as favourite toys.

and always keep your promises about visiting. Ask the nurses on the ward whether you can bathe, change, and feed your child. If she's well enough read to her and play games. If you can't stay at the hospital all the time, encourage your friends and relatives to visit at different times so that your child has someone she knows well with her most of the time.

## Coming home

Depending on how long your child has been in hospital, you may notice some changes in her habits. She probably woke up and went to sleep much earlier in hospital than she does at home, and these patterns may carry on for a while. She may have been indulged a little, and she may be reluctant to go back to school. Your best approach is to be tolerant, as your child will soon adapt to life at home.

# Immunization

The incidence of potentially fatal childhood diseases such as diphtheria has declined dramatically since the introduction of vaccination programmes, which provide immunity. Some vaccines are long-lasting (rubella), others need to be "boosted" at regular intervals (tetanus).

There are two types of immunization: passive and active. The former works by introducing already-formed antibodies into the body. The latter involves injecting a weakened form of the disease-causing organism, which encourages the immune system to produce its own antibodies – this is why immunization can sometimes produce mild symptoms of the disease it is intended to protect against.

In the first five years of your child's life, she will need immunizations for polio, meningitis C, and pneumococcal infection as well as measles, mumps and rubella (German measles), and *Haemophilus influenzae* type b (Hib), diphtheria, tetanus, and whooping cough. Vaccines don't provide instant protection; in some cases they take up to four weeks to be effective. Give paracetamol to ease any discomfort.

## Importance of immunization

Because immunization programmes have been so successful, it is easy to forget how prevalent diseases like whooping cough or polio once were. Many first-time mothers nowadays have never seen a child in leg-braces – a common sight in their grandparents' day when the possibility of paralysis or even death from polio was very real.

Immunization protects both individuals and whole communities from infectious diseases. Every child should therefore be properly immunized. Some mothers are alarmed by stories about the side effects of vaccinations, but these are actually quite rare.

Your child shouldn't be vaccinated, however, if she has an acute illness with a fever, or if she's had a severe reaction to a previous dose of vaccine. Your doctor or health visitor will advise you on what best to do.

## Childhood immunization programme

| WHEN | WHAT GIVEN FOR | HOW IT IS GIVEN |
|---|---|---|
| Two months | ▪ Diphtheria, tetanus, pertussis, (whooping cough), polio, and Hib | ▪ One injection |
| | ▪ Pneumococcal infection | ▪ One injection |
| Three months | ▪ Diphtheria, tetanus, pertussis, (whooping cough), polio, and Hib | ▪ One injection |
| | ▪ Meningitis C | ▪ One injection |
| Four months | ▪ Diphtheria, tetanus, pertussis, (whooping cough), polio, and Hib | ▪ One injection |
| | ▪ Meningitis C | ▪ One injection |
| | ▪ Pnemococcal infection | ▪ One injection |
| Around 12 months | ▪ Hib and meningitis C | ▪ One injection |
| Around 13 months | ▪ Measles, mumps, rubella (MMR) | ▪ One injection |
| | ▪ Pneumococcal infection | ▪ One injection |
| Three years and four months or soon after | ▪ Diphtheria, tetanus, pertussis, (whooping cough), and polio | ▪ One injection |
| | ▪ Measles, mumps, rubella (MMR) | ▪ One injection |

# Common complaints

Any illness in a child is different from, and more serious than, the same illness in an adult because a child's immune system is not fully developed and complications can occur. A throat infection in a child, for example, can easily spread to the chest because the airways are so short. In this section I've described the most common childhood complaints, and given advice on when you need a doctor, and what you can do at home. Try to become familiar with the material in these pages; it'll help you to take prompt and appropriate action whenever your child complains of feeling ill.

# Ears

Ear infections are common in children because the tubes between the middle ear and the throat (Eustachian tubes) are narrow, short, and horizontal, so drainage is poor and they are easily blocked, leading to middle ear infections.

## Waxy ear

Ear wax is produced by glands in the outer ear canal and protects the ear from dust, foreign objects, and infection. Children tend to produce more ear wax when they have a cold or sore throat, and if this dries and hardens, it can result in hearing loss. Although it's not usually serious, you should consult your doctor.

**Symptoms**  Ear wax can become hard and compacted and cause impaired hearing, a ringing sound in the head, or a sensation of fullness in the outer ear. It may be possible to see the wax buildup.

**Treatment**  Ear drops may be effective. Drops are more likely to be used if the wax has formed a hard plug, as they will soften it, allowing it to come out. You should never try to insert anything into your child's ear to try to clear wax, not even a fingernail

or cotton bud. It will only push the wax further into the canal or even damage the lining of the ear.

## Outer-ear infection

The passage leading to the eardrum from the ear flap can sometimes become infected as a result of swimming, excessive cleaning or scratching, or the presence of a foreign object in the ear. This can be painful, but is not usually serious.

**Symptoms**  Your child will complain of earache and her ear flap and outer ear passage may be red and tender. You may notice a pus-like discharge from the ear, and a dry scaly look. If your child is in great pain, she may have a boil in the ear canal.

**Treatment**  Home treatment includes keeping the ear flap clean, and giving paracetamol elixir to relieve pain and keep the temperature down. Your

doctor may prescribe antibiotics or ear drops. Any foreign object or boil in the ear must be dealt with in hospital.

## Middle-ear infection

Otitis media, or infection of the middle ear, is quite common in children. It is caused by bacteria entering the middle ear from the nose and the throat via the Eustachian tube. If left untreated, middle-ear infections can result in permanent hearing loss.

**Symptoms**  Severe earache and loss of appetite are the most prominent symptoms. Your child may also have a fever or a discharge from the ear, and there may be some hearing loss. A baby with a middle-ear infection may be distressed and pull and rub her ear, which will be very red. She may also have general symptoms such as loss of appetite, vomiting, and diarrhoea.

**Treatment**  The usual treatment is pain-relieving medication. At home you should keep your child comfortable and cool and give lots of drinks as well as her medicines. Your child should avoid getting water in her ear until the infection has cleared up.

Antibiotics may be prescribed in severe cases, especially if the child is feverish and vomiting.

## Glue ear

If your child has repeated infections of the middle ear it can gradually fill with jelly-like fluid. As the fluid can't drain away through the eustachian tube it becomes glue-like and impairs hearing because the sounds are not being transmitted across the middle ear to the inner ear, where they are actually heard. Most cases clear up without any treatment, but if the condition persists your child may need treatment to prevent hearing loss leading to poor learning and speech development.

**Symptoms** Glue ear generally causes no pain, but partial hearing loss and a feeling of fullness deep in the ear may occur. A child with chronic glue ear may sleep with her mouth open, snore, and speak with a nasal twang. If chronic glue ear is not treated it can cause prolonged deafness.

**Treatment** The fluid may drain away if left for a few weeks. Your doctor may prescribe decongestants to help drainage. If the fluid doesn't clear, surgery may be recommended. A tiny hole is made in the eardrum and the fluid is sucked out. Then a grommet may be inserted – this is a tiny plastic tube that allows air to circulate in the middle ear. Any fluid that forms can drain away through the grommet or down the Eustachian tube.

The grommet usually falls out after a few months and the eardrum heals.

Children can go swimming while the grommet is in, but shouldn't dive. When washing hair, use ear plugs to stop water getting into your child's ears. Occasionally, the operation has to be repeated if the fluid reaccumulates.

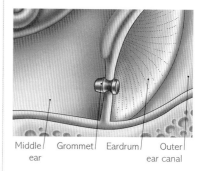

Middle ear | Grommet | Eardrum | Outer ear canal

▲ **EAR GROMMET** This is a tiny plastic tube that's fitted to allow air to circulate in the middle ear. Any fluid that forms can drain away through the grommet.

# Nose

A blocked nose, due to a cold, flu, or more rarely an allergy, is quite common in childhood and not usually serious. There's no need to call a doctor unless your child is unwell. Minor nosebleeds are also quite common, and again are not generally serious.

## Blocked or runny nose

Excess mucus in the nose, which results in sniffing or a runny nose, is usually caused by a cold virus (see p.294). The mucous membranes lining the nasal passages become inflamed and congested and hence block the nose. Other causes include allergic rhinitis (see p.293) or a foreign object, like a bead, in the nose (see p.341).

**Symptoms** The secretions produced by a cold virus usually start off being clear and runny, but may become thick and yellow by the time the body's defences attack the infection.

**Treatment** Encourage your child to blow her nose often. Demonstrate how to clear one nostril first, and then the other. Inhaled menthol in the form of a chest rub or drops on your child's pillow or clothes may help.

Call your doctor if a runny nose lasts more than three days and your child is unwell.

## Nosebleed

Most nosebleeds can be stopped quite easily. If a nosebleed is severe, lasts more than 20 minutes, or follows a blow to the head, take your child to the doctor. Nosebleeds in children are often caused by nosepicking. A foreign object in the nose may also result in a nosebleed. The bleeding usually comes from tiny blood vessels just inside the nostril. A clot may form in the nose as the bleeding stops; it shouldn't be removed.

**Treatment** Sit your child down with her head forward over a bowl or a sink while you gently squeeze the soft part of her nose. Keep applying pressure for about ten minutes, after which the bleeding should have stopped; if it hasn't, repeat for another ten minutes.

Don't let your child blow her nose for at least three hours afterwards. Never put your child's head back, as she may swallow blood and be sick. If a nosebleed is severe and doesn't stop after squeezing the nose for 20 minutes, take your child to hospital.

# Throat

Throat infections such as tonsillitis are rare in babies under one year. They are more common in children who have just started school and are being exposed to a new range of bacteria. As resistance to infections increases, attacks should become less frequent.

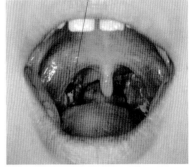

▲ **TONSILLITIS** Swollen, infected tonsils cause a sore throat and difficulty in swallowing. Yellow or white spots may also appear on the tonsils.

## Sore throat

This is usually due to infection by a bacterium such as streptococcus, or a virus such as a cold or flu virus.

**Symptoms** Your child may tell you that she has a sore throat, or you may notice that she finds it hard to swallow. Depress her tongue with a spoon handle and tell her to say "aaahhh" so you can look down her throat for inflammation or enlarged red tonsils.

**Treatment** Give lots of drinks, and liquidize your child's food if she finds it difficult to swallow. Your doctor may prescribe an antibiotic if there is a bacterial infection or tonsillitis. Use paracetamol to ease pain and fever.

## Tonsillitis and adenoids

The tonsils, situated on both sides of the back of the throat, prevent bacteria that invade the throat from entering the body by trapping and killing them. This can result in the tonsils becoming swollen and infected. The adenoids, which are at the back of the nose, are usually affected too.

**Symptoms** Your child will have a very sore throat and may find swallowing difficult. The tonsils will be red and enlarged, possibly with whitish spots. She may have a raised temperature, swollen glands in her neck, and her breath may smell. If the adenoids are swollen, her speech may sound nasal.

**Treatment** Consult your doctor, who may take a throat swab and examine your child's ears and glands. As for a sore throat, give lots of drinks and liquidize your child's foods. Use paracetamol to ease discomfort and fever. Antibiotics may be prescribed for bacterial tonsillitis. Removal of the tonsils (and sometimes the adenoids) is considered after many severe recurrent attacks or if the ears are badly affected too.

## Laryngitis

An infection of the larynx, or voice box, may accompany any cold or sore throat. As long as it doesn't develop into croup (see p.296), laryngitis is rarely a serious condition.

**Symptoms** The most common symptoms are hoarseness or loss of voice. Your child may find it uncomfortable or painful to swallow, and may have a dry cough and a mild fever. Sometimes laryngitis develops into croup (see p.296).

**Treatment** Most cases of laryngitis are short-lived. Your child should rest, preferably in a humid environment in which the air can circulate. Give her lots of fluids and encourage her to rest her voice. If her temperature remains high, she may need antibiotics. Make sure she doesn't overheat (see p.281) and should croup develop (see p.296), seek medical help as soon as possible.

## Lymph nodes

With a local infection, extra white blood cells are produced at the lymph nodes nearest the site of the infection, to mop up and kill the bacteria nearby.

**Feeling lymph nodes** The production of white cells causes lymph glands to become inflamed and sore because they are filtering bacteria or viruses from the blood. To feel them, run your finger down your child's neck from a point just below his ears; they feel like a string of beads.

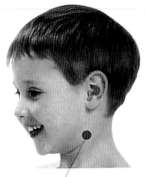
Lymph nodes

# Eyes

The most common childhood eye problems are infections or inflammations that can be cured with good hygiene, and sometimes antibiotic eye drops. It's common for babies to squint until they are six to eight months old, but if a squint gets worse, see your doctor.

## Blepharitis

This is inflammation of the eyelid margins, found in conjunction with eczema and cradle cap, and is usually recurring. It is not serious and can usually be alleviated with simple self-help measures. Check with your doctor if your child's eyes become sticky or if the condition does not clear up within a week.

**Symptoms** The eyelid margins appear red, scaly, and inflamed and you may notice tiny crusts of dried pus on your child's eyelashes.

**Treatment** Tell your child to close her eyes and, using cotton wool dipped in a solution of warm boiled water and half a teaspoon of salt, wipe each eye from the nose outwards. Use a fresh piece of cotton wool for each wipe. Do this every morning and night until the skin has healed. Your doctor may prescribe eye drops or ointment if there is an infection.

## Conjunctivitis

In this common eye complaint the membrane covering the eyeball and lining the eyelids (the conjunctiva) becomes inflamed and red. There are three main causes of conjunctivitis: infection by a virus or bacteria, damage due to the presence of a foreign body, and an allergic reaction. Infective conjunctivitis is very contagious and if one eye is infected, the other one is likely to become

infected too if you don't take precautions. Make sure your child doesn't touch her eye and doesn't share towels and flannels.

**Symptoms** Inflammation causes pain on blinking and your child may find it uncomfortable to look at bright lights – a symptom called photophobia. When conjunctivitis is caused by an infection, the eye will be sticky and there may be a collection of pus in the lower eyelid. Allergic conjunctivitis produces clear, watery tears and swollen eyelids.

**Treatment** Always seek medical advice for a child who has a "red eye". If there's an infection your doctor will prescribe antibiotic ointment or eye drops – even if the infection is only in one eye, both eyes will need to be treated as it can easily transfer from one eye to the other. Anti-inflammatory eye drops and antihistamines may be used to treat allergic conjunctivitis. You can help relieve discomfort by gently wiping the eye with a saline solution or cooled, boiled water to remove the discharge. For foreign object in the eye, see p.336.

## Stye

When the follicle of an eyelash is infected, a stye, or small abscess, develops on the margin of the eyelid. Rubbing the eyes may encourage them. A stye usually comes to a head within four or five days, then clears up. It may need treatment if it's very sore.

**Symptoms** At first the eyelid appears red and a bit swollen, then the swelling fills with pus and the stye may protrude noticeably from the eyelid.

**Treatment** If the eye is very sore, warm compresses may help. Styes are not as contagious as other eye infections, but you should still keep your child's flannel and towel separate. For recurrent infections your doctor may prescribe antibiotic ointment.

## Squint

Your baby's eyes may appear to be pointing in different directions, sometimes convergent (towards each other) and sometimes divergent (away from each other). Until the age of about eight weeks, this is perfectly normal, but if your baby's eyes have not aligned by six to eight months, or if they get worse, seek advice.

The usual causes of a squint are an imbalance in the muscles of the eyes, or one eye being long-sighted and the other being short-sighted.

**Symptoms** If you suspect that your baby has a squint, confirm by observing how light is reflected in her eyes. It should be reflected from exactly the same place in each eye; if not, then she almost certainly has a squint. Consult your doctor.

**Treatment** The usual treatment is to cover the strong eye with a patch, since this forces the muscles in the weak eye to become stronger. The eyes should become aligned within about five months, though it can take longer. If your child's squint is related to long- or short-sightedness, she should be prescribed glasses.

# Mouth

Childhood mouth problems are generally minor; thrush is the only condition that needs immediate medical attention, since it does not respond to the usual self-help measures. Your child may refuse food when her mouth is sore. Give her liquidized bland foods that she can suck through a straw.

## Teething pain

A child's teeth usually begin to come through at about six months and are complete by her third birthday (see p.145). When the teeth are erupting, the gums are red and swollen.

**Symptoms** If you touch the swollen, red gums you may feel a hard lump beneath. Your baby will salivate and dribble more than usual and will chew objects. She may have trouble sleeping and be more irritable and clingy than usual. Eating may be painful. Other symptoms, such as loss of appetite or vomiting, are not caused by teething.

**Treatment** Paracetamol may be used for pain relief, but medical treatment is not usually necessary.

▲ **PAIN RELIEF** Chewing on a cool teething ring — never frozen — or firm-textured foods such as carrot fingers or pieces of apple can ease the pain.

## Mouth ulcers

Open sores (ulcers) in the mouth can occur inside the lower lip, on the tongue or gums, and inside the cheeks. Aphthous ulcers are the most common and appear as round or oval yellow spots with an inflamed outline. They should go away by themselves in ten to 14 days, but if they're recurrent, or prevent eating, seek medical help. Ulcers may be the result of minor injury and can also be caused by infections such as herpes simplex.

**Symptoms** All mouth ulcers are painful. Your child may have difficulty eating, especially food that is acidic or salty, and may refuse food.

**Treatment** If your child has an aphthous ulcer, try applying an antiseptic jelly (ask for something in orobase, a base that doesn't dissolve in saliva) to the affected area and giving your child paracetamol. Your doctor may prescribe an anti-inflammatory cream if the ulcer is severe. Avoid anything containing a local anaesthetic as allergies may occur. Try to eliminate the underlying cause: if rough teeth are rubbing, ask your dentist to file them down; discourage your child from biting her cheeks; or, if you are bottlefeeding, try using a softer teat.

Whatever the type of ulcer, you should liquidize your child's foods, give her a straw to drink through, and avoid giving her salty or acidic foods.

## Thrush

The mucous membranes can sometimes become infected by the fungus *Candida albicans* – a condition known as thrush The growth of candida is usually kept in check by the presence of other bacteria, but when these bacteria are eradicated by taking antibiotics candida begins to multiply unrestrictedly. Alternatively, thrush can be passed on from a mother at the time of birth when the baby passes through the vagina.

In children, thrush may only be obvious in the mouth, but it can infect the whole gastro-intestinal tract and the anal area, where it is sometimes confused with nappy rash (see p.77).

**Symptoms** Thrush produces white, curd-like patches on the gums, cheeks, tongue, and roof of the mouth. If you attempt to wipe them off they become raw and may bleed. Around the anus thrush appears as red spots or a rash. If your child has nappy rash as well, there may be white flaky patches.

**Treatment** Thrush can be treated quickly and simply with anti-fungal medications, in liquid form or gel for oral thrush, and cream form for anal thrush. These are available from a pharmacist. It's important to treat anal or nappy area thrush both orally and topically or it usually recurs.

Liquidized, bland, cold, or lukewarm foods are best if your child has oral thrush. Natural yogurt is particularly good (but not for very young babies).

Fungi flourish in warm, moist conditions, so if your baby has anal thrush keep her as dry as possible. Be meticulous about hygiene, and always keep your child's hands clean.

# Skin

Childhood skin complaints may be caused by an infection or an allergy, or it may be a response to very high or low temperatures. Most of them are minor and can easily be treated. Rashes occur with a variety of complaints, some of which are serious; if you are at all worried about a rash, consult your doctor.

## Chapped skin

Chaps are little cracks in the skin, sometimes raw and deep. Exposure to the cold makes skin dry and prone to chapping. This particularly affects the extremities, where circulation is poor – the hands, fingers, and ears. Damp skin around the lips chaps too. Failing to dry properly after washing, and washing so frequently that the skin's natural oils are removed, can both contribute to chapping.

**Symptoms** Chapped skin has a dry, cracked appearance. If the cracks are deep there may be some bleeding and severe pain, and if they become infected you may notice some pus and inflammation.

**Treatment** Unless chapped skin becomes infected or is very slow to heal, you can probably solve the problem with self-help measures. Apply rich emollient creams to your child's skin, use lip salve on her lips, avoid using soap (use baby lotion instead), and dress her warmly in cold weather. Avoid icy winds and sudden changes in temperature. Infected chapped skin should be treated by your doctor.

## Chilblains

Children who are sensitive to cold may get chilblains. Constriction of blood vessels in the skin is a normal reaction to cold, but in a cold-sensitive child the fine network of blood vessels beneath the skin may overconstrict, and then overdilate when your child returns to a warm environment. Where over-dilation occurs, a bump, or chilblain, will form in the skin.

**Symptoms** A chilblain is a red or purple lump of any size. The main symptom is intense itchiness when the body starts to warm up after exposure to cold. Chilblains usually occur on the feet, the backs of the lower legs, the hands, the tip of the nose, and the edges of the ears.

**Treatment** Chilblains, although irritating, are not serious and usually heal themselves if kept warm. A simple application of talcum powder or calamine lotion can often alleviate itchiness and discourage your child from scratching.

If your child is susceptible to chilblains make sure that she's dressed warmly when she goes out in cold weather, paying particular attention to vulnerable areas of the body. As damp conditions increase the likelihood of getting chilblains, make sure that she has waterproof clothing to wear in wet weather.

## Cold sores

The virus responsible for cold sores is called herpes simplex and is a relative of the virus that causes chickenpox and shingles. All sufferers from cold sores carry the virus in their skin, where it lies dormant in the nerve endings. The virus is transmitted from parent to child during kissing. A rise in skin temperature due to intense sunlight, flu, a cold, stress, or over-exertion can reactivate the virus and result in a cold sore.

Cold sores are not usually harmful except near the eye where, rarely, they can cause ulceration of the conjunctiva (the covering of the white of the eye).

**Symptoms** There is usually warning of an attack in the form of a hot, itchy, tingling sensation for 24 hours before the cold sore appears. The skin becomes red and then tiny blisters appear, usually around the lips or the nostrils. The blisters enlarge, join up, and then burst, revealing the classic cold sore. Fluid from the blisters then forms a crust, which gradually shrinks and falls off as the skin underneath heals. This takes ten to 14 days.

While a cold sore is at the blister and weeping stage it will be very painful and your child may complain of pain over the whole side of the face, earache, and pain when she chews because the facial nerves are inflamed by the virus.

Cold sores are very contagious, and your child can spread them to other parts of her face by touching them with her fingers.

**Treatment** Your pharmacist can recommend, or your doctor will prescribe, an anti-viral cream to be applied every two or three hours as soon as the skin begins to tingle. This will prevent future cold sores from developing into their full-blown form. An antibiotic cream may be prescribed if the cold sore becomes infected.

Discourage your child from touching her face, from kissing other children, and from sharing her flannel and towel for the duration of an attack. Applying petroleum jelly may stop a cold sore from cracking; surgical spirit may help to dry the sore out, but it stings and I don't approve of its use on children.

It's helpful to identify the triggers that bring on your child's cold-sore attacks. For instance, if it is strong sunlight, your child should wear a high-protection sunblock around her lips in summer.

## Boils

When a hair follicle becomes infected a red pus-filled swelling can result. Boils are rarely serious if they are treated appropriately, but they can cause pain, particularly if they are in an uncomfortable place such as the armpit or buttock. Boils rarely heal by themselves, and left untreated can form a carbuncle (a cluster of several boils).

**Symptoms** Initially the skin will be red and swollen. As the yellow pus collects beneath the skin the swelling increases. Boils usually appear singly, but, because hair follicles are so close together, it's possible for the infection to spread easily and for a crop of boils to appear.

**Treatment** Seek medical help if your child has several boils, if there are signs that the infection is spreading, if the boil is causing severe pain, or if it has not burst after a couple of days. Your doctor may decide to lance the boil to drain the pus away, which provides immediate pain relief. Crops of boils require antibiotics and investigation of the cause. Don't try to burst or squeeze a boil at home;

this will be excruciatingly painful and will spread infection. Instead, dab the affected area with antiseptic cream and cover it with a gauze dressing to protect it.

## Impetigo

The bacterium staphylococcus, which is present in the nose and on the skin, can sometimes cause a skin infection around the nose, mouth, and ears and elsewhere. Impetigo is characterized by a bright yellow, crusted rash or small pus-filled blisters; it is highly contagious and so it's important to keep your child away from school until it has cleared up.

**Symptoms** The first sign of impetigo is reddened skin. This is followed by the appearance of blisters full of pus, which burst leaving patches of oozing skin. The fluid dries into a yellow crust. Impetigo spreads rapidly if left untreated.

**Treatment** Take your child to your doctor, who will prescribe an antibiotic cream and dressings to keep the skin covered, and possibly oral antibiotics. Be meticulous about hygiene – wash away crusted areas with warm water and pat dry with a paper towel. Use disposable flannels and towels for your child to protect the rest of the family from infection.

## Infantile eczema

This inflammatory skin condition takes two forms in children: atopic eczema and seborrhoeic eczema. Atopic is the most common and it's caused by an inherited tendency, plus a trigger factor such as an allergy or an infection, or occasionally, stress. Seborrhoeic eczema has no known cause and may simply be a response to stress. The

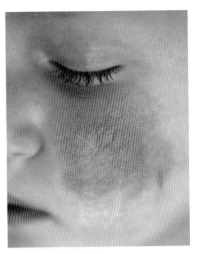

▲ **ECZEMA RASH** Baby eczema is very common and develops at a few months old. The affected skin is red and sore. Itchiness is the most irritating symptom.

reason for including this here is that it appears in the first weeks or months of life and is a worry for parents, who are at a loss as to how to manage it.

**Symptoms** Skin affected by atopic eczema is raw, dry, scaly, red, and itchy, and there may be small white blisters, like grains of rice, that burst and weep if scratched. Common sites are the face, hands, neck, ankles, and the knee and elbow creases. Seborrhoeic eczema looks similar, but is less itchy and affects the face, scalp, neck, armpits, and nappy area.

**Treatment** If you suspect your child has eczema see your doctor, who may prescribe an anti-inflammatory cream and antihistamines to curb itching and combat any allergy. If the skin is infected antibiotics may be necessary. Your doctor will also try to identify the cause: a pet, washing powder, or food, for example. Don't, however, try to eliminate any foods from your child's diet without your doctor's supervision. Keep contact with water to a minimum, and if you have to bathe your child, put unguent emulsificants or unscented bath oil in the bath. Stop using soap, and make sure that clothes and anything else that's in contact with her skin, even bedding, are rinsed and contain no trace of washing powder or fabric conditioner.

Minimize her contact with potential allergens, apply emollient cream to her skin, and keep her fingernails short so that she can't scratch. Dress your child with cotton next to her skin at all times. At each nappy change use lashings of aqueous cream – and I mean lashings – to keep the skin moisturized.

Underplay the condition in front of your child. Your anxiety can make the condition worse.

## Dermatitis

This is an inflammation of the skin that occurs in response to stress, to an allergy such as nickel sensitivity (contact dermatitis), or occasionally to light (photodermatitis). Seborrhoeic eczema (see opposite) is in fact a type of dermatitis.

**Symptoms** Dermatitis, no matter what type, is a red, itchy, and scaly rash, sometimes with blisters. With contact dermatitis the rash usually appears where the skin has been in contact with the allergen. Photodermatitis appears as clusters of spots or blisters on skin that's been exposed to the sun.

**Treatment** If dermatitis is very severe your doctor may prescribe a weak corticosteroid cream. Make sure that your child keeps the affected areas clean, doesn't scratch them, and doesn't expose them to defatting agents such as soaps and detergent.

## Heat rash

A hot, poorly ventilated environment in which the skin can't cool encourages heat rash; the body responds by sweating excessively and the sweat glands become enlarged and red. Heat rash is quite common in babies as their sweat glands are not working properly yet.

**Symptoms** A faint red rash appears on the parts of the body that get hot easily and where sweat glands are most numerous. Typical areas include the neck, the face, and skin folds such as the groin, elbows, armpits, and behind the knees.

**Treatment** Don't overdress or swaddle your baby. Bathe her in tepid water and pat her dry, leaving her skin slightly damp. Make sure the temperature of her room is not too high and keep air circulating by opening a window slightly.

If your child's rash has not cleared up after 12 hours, consult your doctor in order to exclude other possible causes of the rash.

## Sunburn

Spending too much time in the sun or being exposed to sunlight that is too intense can cause sunburn. Babies under 12 months should not be exposed to the sun at all.

All children should wear a high-factor sunscreen (at least factor 30), which should be applied 30 minutes before going out in the sun and reapplied every two hours or after swimming. Chldren should also wear a sunhat and T-shirt. If your child is fair-skinned or unused to being in the sun, be especially cautious about letting her play outdoors. Children should be well protected from very hot sun, especially if abroad (see p.238). Sunburn can be painful and, in extreme heat, may be associated with heatstroke (see p.338).

In the long term, however, sunburn can lead to skin cancer, particularly in fair-skinned people. We now know that sun damage is accumulative, so that cancers that develop in later years are the result of lifetime exposure to the sun. It's wrong to let children think that they don't need to worry about sun damage when they are young.

# Rashes

Infectious diseases like chickenpox, German measles, or measles, as well as allergies and blood disorders, may all cause rashes.

A rash may be discrete or blotchy, flat or bumpy, it may disappear on pressure or not, and it may contain blisters. If your child has a rash, check to see if she has a fever (this may indicate an infectious disease), and consider whether she has been exposed to any potential allergens (see p.292).

**Serious rashes** A rash that doesn't disappear on pressure, called a purpura rash, is nearly always an indication of something serious and can result from a fault in the blood-clotting mechanism or from bacterial toxins, as in meningitis.

You can spot a purpura rash by pressing a drinking glass to your child's skin to see if the rash remains visible through it. If you see the rash, check with your doctor immediately.

**Symptoms** The affected skin will be hot, inflamed, red, and tender. Sometimes the skin looks "bubbly" and blistered. After a few days the dead skin flakes and peels, at which point your child may complain of itchiness.

If sunburn is severe, particularly on the back of the neck, look out for symptoms of heatstroke: fever, vomiting, and dizziness (see also p.338). If they are present, seek medical help immediately.

**Treatment** Immediate relief from sunburn can come from applying calamine lotion and cold sheets or towels to the affected areas. Paracetamol may also be helpful to keep your child's temperature normal. Treat sunburned skin very gently; let your child go without clothes indoors, and cover the skin with loose-fitting clothes and bare skin with total sunblock if she's going outdoors. A hat should cover the nape of the neck. Your doctor may prescribe an anti-inflammatory cream for sunburn.

## Warts and verrucae

Caused by a virus, warts may occur singly or in great numbers. Most disappear without treatment after two years. There are more than 30 different types of wart virus. Children usually get common warts on the hands or areas subject to injury, such as the knees, and verrucae, which are warts on the soles of the feet. Although contagious, they are not at all serious.

**Symptoms** Common warts, such as those found on the hands, appear as firm, flesh-coloured or brown growths. They are composed of dead skin cells. Although they may look unsightly, they warts should not be painful unless cracked and bleeding. Verrucae are flat warts on the sole of the foot. Unlike other warts, they may be very painful because they are pressed into the sole of the foot.

**Treatment** Unless warts are painful, unsightly, or at risk of being passed on to other children, don't worry since they may disappear spontaneously. If you do decide to treat a wart at home, there are several products available in pharmacies. Never use them on the face or the genitals, as they can scar delicate skin. If you consult your doctor, she will discuss treatment options with you and may refer your child to a wart clinic to have the warts or verrucae removed. If you suspect that your child has genital warts see your doctor straight away. Verrucae should always be covered to prevent them from being passed on.

# Allergies

An allergy is an abnormal response of the immune system to a specific chemical or substance. The most common form of allergy is hay fever, which is an allergy to pollen, but children may be allergic to a range of things, from foods and plants to light and drugs.

## Urticaria (hives)

This is an allergic skin rash that takes the form of itchy, raised red blotches with white centres. It's most commonly caused by a reaction to a particular food, drug, or plant (nettles for example), to light, or to an insect bite. Histamine (a chemical found in cells throughout the body) is released in response to contact with an allergen and it causes fluid to leak into the skin from the blood vessels, leading to the typical weal. Newborns sometimes have an urticaria rash (see p.14).

**Symptoms** The skin is extremely itchy and there are raised white lumps (weals) surrounded by a flare of inflammation. The weals are small and circular or large irregular patches. The rash usually appears on the limbs and the trunk, although it can appear anywhere on the body. Urticaria lasts for a few minutes, disappears, and then reappears at a different site. It can be accompanied by facial swelling (angioedema), for which you should consult your doctor without delay. Swelling of the mouth, tongue, and

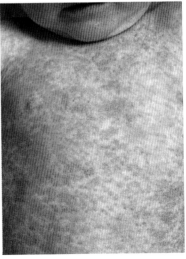

▲**URTICARIA RASH** Raised white lumps form, surrounded by inflammation. Sometimes these join together, forming large patches on the surface of the skin.

throat, can cause difficulties with breathing (anaphylaxis). This should always be treated as an emergency.

**Treatment** Apply calamine lotion to your child's skin or give her a coolish bath. Your doctor may prescribe antihistamine syrup. If your child has had a previous severe allergic reaction, your doctor may advise you to carry a preloaded syringe of epinephrine (adrenaline). You may want to consult an allergist to help identify the allergen.

# Hay fever (acute allergic rhinitis)

When the mucous membranes lining the nose and throat are exposed to an allergen (usually pollen) they become inflamed and the child suffers from the symptoms of allergic rhinitis (see below). The condition usually occurs in the spring and summer months when the pollen count is high. Hay fever is relatively unusual under the age of five. It tends to run in families, and it may disappear spontaneously.

**Symptoms** Hay fever symptoms include sneezing, a runny nose, and red, itchy, watery eyes. Hay fever is distinguishable from a common cold in that it is seasonal and there is no fever.

**Treatment** While it's impossible to prevent your child being exposed to pollen, you can note the pollen count each day and discourage her from playing outside if it is high. Antihistamines often help relieve symptoms. Your doctor may also arrange for skin tests to identify the particular pollen causing your child's symptoms and may prescribe a course of desensitizing injections. Eye drops and corticosteroid nasal sprays are additional treatments.

# Chronic allergic rhinitis

Chronic or perennial allergic rhinitis is just like hay fever, but happens all year round. It starts in the same way as hay fever (see left), but the culprit is usually house dust mites. Other causes are feathers and cat and dog fur.

.

**Symptoms** The symptoms of chronic or perennial allergic rhinitis are the same as those of hay fever – runny nose, watering of the eyes, and itchy nose and eyes. Diagnosis is confirmed by skin tests.

**Treatment** The most effective treatment is avoidance of the allergen or allergens. You may have to get rid of a favourite pet, change bedding, and/or vacuum clean frequently.

Antihistamines and other drugs help prevent symptoms occurring. Intranasal corticosteroids, given in small, safe doses, often bring rapid relief.

# Photosensitivity

This condition is an allergy to light, or rather to certain wavelengths of light. A very rare form is inherited, but more commonly it is caused by swallowing a photosensitizing substance or applying it to the skin. Examples of such substances are some drugs, dyes, chemicals, and plants.

**Symptoms** Photosensitivity usually shows as an urticaria rash, easily distinguishable because the skin that's covered by clothes is not affected and there's a clear line demarcating the skin that has been exposed to light.

**Treatment** The photosensitizer and/or sunlight should be avoided until the rash clears up. A susceptible child should always cover up well outdoors and wear total sunblock.

# Flea bites

Children quite often get one flea bite, develop an allergy to it, and then come out in a crop of spots. These spots are often mistaken for more bites, but it is in fact an allergic urticaria rash. The rash will be very itchy, but it will subside in ten to 14 days.

**Treatment** The family cat or dog will have to be sprayed for fleas. You will also have to spray any carpets or soft furnishings that may harbour flea eggs. Your doctor may prescribe an antihistamine medicine to contain the itching and scratching.

# Drugs

The most common drug allergy is to penicillin and its derivatives. Once diagnosed, your child should wear a bracelet or medallion stating she is allergic to it so that she won't be given it again. It should also be noted on her records at your doctor's surgery.

Any drug at any time, however, can cause an allergy, particularly if there's a family history of allergies, eczema, and asthma. The worst form of drug allergy is anaphylaxis, in which blood pressure drops and the tongue and throat may swell up; it needs emergency treatment.

**Symptoms** Urticaria rash appears up to ten days after exposure to the drug, possibly with swelling of the face and tongue. Problems with breathing, vomiting, and diarrhoea need urgent medical attention.

**Treatment** For mild allergies antihistamines are usually sufficient. An immediate injection of epinephrine (adrenaline) is needed for anaphylaxis. Once a drug is identified as an allergen it must be avoided for life.

# Colds and influenza

Infections with cold or flu viruses are common in childhood because children haven't yet developed immunity to specific viruses. There are roughly 200 cold viruses, which all produce similar symptoms – your child will never get the same cold twice.

## Common cold

Colds are not serious unless your baby is very young, or a complication such as bronchitis (see opposite) sets in. Colds are more frequent when your child starts nursery, because she's suddenly exposed to lots of new viruses. Babies are less likely to catch colds because of the antibodies they receive from their mothers, especially if they are being breastfed.

**Symptoms** Most cold viruses start with "catarrhal" symptoms (blocked or runny nose, cough, sore throat), fever, and listlessness. The nasal discharge is first clear and then thicker and yellow as the body's defences take over. The rise in temperature can cause cold sores (see p.289), hence their name. If you child complains of other symptoms such as sore throat or earache, check with your doctor as she may treatment.

▲ **CLEARING SINUSES** Dissolve menthol crystals in water and get your child to inhale the vapours. Cover his head with a towel to keep the vapours in.

**Treatment** Only symptoms can be treated, not the virus itself; there's no cure for the common cold. If a secondary infection such as sinusitis or bronchitis supervenes, then your doctor will prescribe antibiotics; otherwise, home remedies suffice. Give our child plenty of fluids, encourage her to blow her nose frequently, showing her how to clear one nostril at a time, and apply petroleum jelly to her nostrils and top lip if they become sore or chapped.

When congestion is severe, make sure that your child sleeps with her head propped up with pillows, and try applying a menthol rub to her chest. In a young baby a cold can prevent breathing during feeding. Your doctor will prescribe nose drops if a blocked nose interferes with your child's sleeping or feeding.

## Sinusitis

The sinuses are cavities in the bones around the nose and cheeks and above the eyes, and are lined with mucous membranes. Mucus usually drains from them into the nose. Sinusitis occurs when drainage is impaired, usually with a cold or flu or if an infection spreads to the sinuses from the throat.

**Symptoms** Nasal secretions are clear and runny at first with a cold. A change to a thick, yellow discharge is normal, but if it is persistent, sinusitis has probably developed. Other symptoms include a feeling of fullness and discomfort around the top of the nose, headache, diminished sense of smell, blocked nose, and sometimes fever.

**Treatment** At home, keep the atmosphere humid, prepare menthol inhalations for your child, and give her paracetamol syrup if she complains of pain in her face and forehead. Decongestants may also help. If symptoms get worse or don't improve after three days, seek medical advice.

## Influenza

This is a viral infection similar to the common cold, but it produces more severe symptoms. Influenza, or flu, can be very debilitating, and is potentially serious because it can weaken the body and make the ears, sinuses, and chest vulnerable to secondary infections by bacteria.

**Symptoms** Flu symptoms resemble cold symptoms, but in addition your child will also have quite a high temperature, a headache, and backache, and she may complain of feeling hot or cold and shivery. She will be lethargic and weak, and may feel nauseous.

**Treatment** The only remedies available for flu are symptomatic ones. Let your child rest in a warm, ventilated room, and give her paracetamol elixir and plenty of fluids. Take your child's temperature regularly – if it fails to come down, or other symptoms develop such as a persistent nasal discharge, earache, or a chesty cough, seek medical advice. Paracetamol or ibuprofen syrup reduces the temperature and eases aches and pains.

# Chest infections

In very young children the air passages, sinuses, ear, nose, and throat are really all one system because the tubes are so short. A chest infection can therefore develop from an infection elsewhere in the upper respiratory tract. Chest infections are always serious. The airways may become so narrow that breathing is impaired, and pneumonia may develop. If your child's breathing is ever laboured you should always seek medical help immediately.

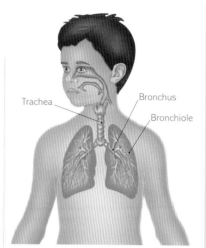

Trachea     Bronchus

Bronchiole

▲ **RESPIRATION** Air flows from the trachea through the bronchi to the bronchioles. Finally oxygen enters the blood via tiny air sacs called alveoli.

## Coughs

The cough is a reflex action that clears the throat of any irritant such as mucus, food, dust, or smoke. A cough may be due to the irritation of a cold, sore throat, tonsillitis, a chest infection, or asthma. The cause should be treated, not just the cough alone, which is merely a symptom of an underlying condition.

**Symptoms** There are two types of cough: a productive cough, in which phlegm is produced, and a non-productive cough, in which there is no phlegm. The first has a "wet" sound, while the second is dry and hacking. Both will prevent sleep. In a small baby mucus running down the back of the throat can cause vomiting. A cough may also be a nervous symptom. If a cough is hacking or croaking your child may have croup (see p.296). Violent coughing can cause vomiting.

**Treatment** If you suspect that your child has croup (see p.296) or asthma (see p.260), you should seek medical help straight away. An underlying acute infection such as tonsillitis (see p.286) should be treated separately. As long as they don't stop your child from sleeping or eating, most other coughs can be treated at home. Discourage your child from running around, as breathlessness may bring on a coughing fit, and get her to lie on her stomach or side at night; this prevents mucus running down the throat. Give your child plenty of warm drinks and if she is coughing up lots of phlegm use an expectorant elixir, and lay her over your lap and pat her on the back. Only give cough suppressants for a dry cough, never for a productive one.

## Bronchitis and bronchiolitis

The larger airways in the lungs are called the bronchi and the smaller are called the bronchioles. Bronchitis or bronchiolitis occurs when a viral infection causes the linings of these airways to swell and mucus to build up. Bronchiolitis tends to be more serious because it can cause severe breathing difficulties. Bronchiolitis is most common in babies and very young children. Bronchitis is not usually serious in children over a year old.

**Symptoms** The symptoms of bronchiolitis are a cough and breathlessness, which may lead to difficulty in feeding. Your child may have a raised temperature and may wheeze. She may be pale and appear quite ill. There may be indrawing of the chest (in the struggle to get air into the lungs) and the lips and tongue may appear blue. If this happens you need urgent help so call an ambulance.

The symptoms of bronchitis are a dry cough that develops into a cough producing green or yellow phlegm, raised temperature, and possibly the loss of appetite. If your child swallows the phlegm she may vomit it up. If your child becomes more unwell, possibly with difficulty breathing, this may indicate severe infection or even pneumonia.

**Treatment** You should consult your doctor if you suspect that your child has a lung infection. She will prescribe antibiotics as necessary. Laboured breathing and a grey or blue complexion should always be treated in hospital, where your child will be put in an oxygen tent to help her breathe.

Keep your child warm and rested, give plenty of fluids, and encourage her to cough up the phlegm. If she has a fever of more than 40°C (104°F), sponge her down with tepid water (see p.281) and give her paracetamol to keep her temperature down. Don't give your child a cough suppressant as it is important to bring up the phlegm.

## Pneumonia

This is a severe and serious inflammation of the lungs, caused by a virus or bacterium. Your child will be ill for two reasons: first because of the bacterial or viral toxins, and second because the affected lung is out of action. The initial cause of pneumonia is often a cold or flu. Conditions like asthma, cystic fibrosis, whooping cough, and measles increase the risk of pneumonia. Pneumonia is always serious and small children are often treated in hospital if they're in need of oxygen therapy.

**Symptoms** Pneumonia usually starts with a fever and cough and your child may be breathless. She may look pale and unwell and seem lethargic. Her breathing may be shallow. and more rapid than usual.

**Treatment** Laboured breathing is always a reason for you to seek medical advice urgently. You should consult your doctor straight away if you suspect your child has pneumonia. Your doctor will prescribe antibiotics and may decide that immediate hospitalization is necessary.

## Croup

When a small child's air passages become inflamed and congested as a result of an infection, breathing can become difficult and croup can result. The croup sound is due to air being drawn in through a swollen and narrowed larynx, usually as a result of a viral infection. Croup usually occurs in children between the ages of one and four years. It can come on suddenly: your apparently well child will wake in the night with croup.

**Symptoms** The main symptom is a barking cough, accompanied by hoarseness and noisy breathing. Lack of oxygen may result in pale skin, anxiety, and sweating. In severe cases your child may be fighting for breath and her face may turn grey or blue. Attacks occur at night and are often short-lived.

**Treatment** Stay calm. If your child is upset her breathing will become even more laboured. Make sure the air around your child is damp – get her to lean out of a window, take her to the bathroom and run the hot taps, or use a humidifier.

If your child's face turns blue, you must get medical help immediately. Croup may need hospital treatment or treatment with an oral corticosteroid. Even if croup is mild tell your doctor..

# Parasites

Parasites are very contagious, so if your child has lice or worms the whole family should be treated. Always inform your child's nursery, playgroup, or school of the infestation. Infestations can be uncomfortable, but they're not serious and can be eradicated.

## Lice

Head lice are common in children of school age. The louse is a small insect that lives on blood from the scalp, lays eggs, and cements them to the base of the hairs; the eggs, called nits, become visible as the hair grows. Contrary to the belief that lice are a sign of lack of cleanliness, head lice prefer to live on clean hair.

**Symptoms** Your child will complain of an itchy scalp, which is worse in hot weather. You may see white eggs firmly attached to the hair near the scalp.

**Treatment** Tell your child's school that she has nits. To treat, wash the hair and then saturate it with conditioner while damp. Comb the hair thoroughly for 30 minutes with a nit comb, wiping the comb clean after each stroke. The eggs can be difficult to dislodge and you may need to slide each one off the hair individually. Rinse the hair as usual. Repeat this treatment every two or three days until the hair is clear of nits – this will take at least two weeks. Alternatively, wash your child's hair in insecticidal shampoo. All the family should be treated.

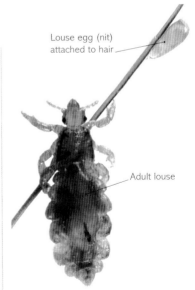

Louse egg (nit) attached to hair

Adult louse

▲ **LOUSE AND NIT** The adult louse lays its eggs (nits) at the root of the hair. The eggs become firmly attached and hatch after about two weeks unless they are removed by combing or the hair is treated with insecticidal shampoo.

## Scabies

This is an infestation by a microscopic mite that burrows into the skin and lays eggs. Although it is not serious, it can be very itchy, especially at night, and it's highly contagious. A child can get scabies by physical contact with someone suffering from scabies or from infested bedding.

**Symptoms**  The backs of the hands, finger clefts, feet, ankles, and toes are affected by an intensely itchy rash. Burrows are usually visible as grey, scaly trails across the skin with a black pin-head spot (the mite) at the end.

**Treatment**  Your doctor will probably prescribe a lotion to treat scabies. This should stay on for 24 hours and the treatment should be repeated after a day. The whole family will need to be treated.

Try to stop your child scratching affected areas. This may hinder the doctor's diagnosis and cause sores to form that could become infected.

Mites can live independently of human skin for up to six days, so you should wash all your clothes and bed linen to prevent re-infection.

## Threadworm

Threadworms are extremely common in children, but are not serious and are easily eradicated. Eggs and larvae enter the child's mouth, and as they mature, the females move down the intestine and lay eggs around the anus. This causes itchiness and a child can easily pick up the eggs on her fingers and transfer them to her mouth, thus the cycle of infestation begins again.

**Symptoms**  The most distressing symptom of threadworms is the intense itchiness around the anal area,

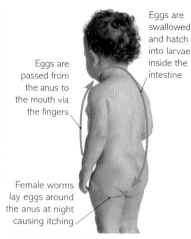

Eggs are passed from the anus to the mouth via the fingers

Eggs are swallowed and hatch into larvae inside the intestine

Female worms lay eggs around the anus at night causing itching

▲ **CYCLE OF INFESTATION**
Threadworms enter the body through the mouth and lay eggs around the anus. A child can become re-infested by scratching the anus, then transferring the eggs to her mouth.

which feels worse at night when your child is hot and can prevent her from sleeping. There may also be tiny white worms present in the stools.

**Treatment**  If you notice worms in your child's stools or find she's suffering from anal itchiness and is scratching her bottom, especially at night, tell your doctor, who will prescribe a medication for the whole family. Pay special attention to hygiene:

encourage hand-washing often and always after she uses the lavatory. Keep your child's fingernails short, and get her to wear pants in bed to discourage scratching.

## Roundworm

This type of worm is very rare in the West and is usually only brought in by people living in tropical climates, especially in areas where hygiene is poor. The parasite is a cylindrical worm approximately 15–40cm (6–16in) long that enters the body in egg form via contaminated food. Once in the body, the eggs hatch and the worms mature and lay new eggs, which may be passed in the stools.

**Symptoms**  Roundworms inhabit the intestine and produce few or no symptoms. Sometimes the worms may be visible in your child's stools. Your child will appear undernourished and she will fail to thrive.

**Treatment**  Roundworm is treated with tablets that kill the worm. Laxatives may also be given so that the worms pass quickly and easily in the stools. Scrupulous hygiene is absolutely essential if treatment is to be successful.

## After travelling abroad

**Amoebic dysentry** If you have recently been in the tropics and your child is suffering from persistent diarrhoea, she may have contracted amoebic dysentery.

This is caused by an amoeba – a tiny single-celled organism that lives in the large intestine – that is only picked up in tropical countries. It

causes serious illness with fever, diarrhoea, and stomach pain. If you suspect amoebic dysentery, take your child and a sample of her stools to the doctor as soon as possible. She will need drugs to get rid of the parasite as well as rehydration therapy if diarrhoea has been severe.

# Stomach and abdomen

Babies are affected by few of the conditions that cause abdominal pain in adults, like gallstones and peptic ulcers. But several causes of abdominal pain in infants and children are potentially very serious so call your doctor immediately if a child with abdominal pain is distressed or if the pain is accompanied by a temperature, diarrhoea, or vomiting. Any tension in the house, between parents or siblings, or at school, can cause a child to feel nauseous, vomit, and suffer from abdominal pain. When all other causes have been eliminated consider stress as a cause of pain. Ask your doctor for advice.

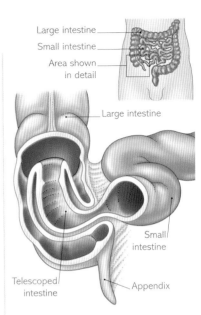

Large intestine

Small intestine

Area shown in detail

Large intestine

Small intestine

Telescoped intestine

Appendix

▲ **FOLDED INTESTINE** In intussuception a section of the small intestine telescopes in on itself, like a finger in a glove being turned inside out. Intussuception is a rare and very serious condition.

## Colic

This type of crying usually occurs in the first four months of life, then disappears spontaneously without treatment. It's thought to be due to spasm of the intestines, though there is no proof of this and the cause remains unknown. The condition is harmless, though distressing for parents.

**Symptoms** Your baby, who is otherwise well, will have bouts of crying when she screams and draws her legs up towards her abdomen.

**Treatment** No drugs are needed. Your baby may be soothed by any rhythmic activity, such as rocking, swaying, being taken in the car for a ride, or being laid on her tummy on your lap while you pat her back. Often, nothing will calm a colicky baby, but try to remain calm yourself. Since colic often occurs at the same time each day, typically in the evening, you should try to plan your day accordingly so as to reduce the stress on you.

## Gastroenteritis

Inflammation of the stomach and intestine causes diarrhoea and vomiting; pain is a lesser symptom. In the UK, 90 per cent of cases of gastroenteritis are viral and contracted from other people, not from contaminated food. There are also various non-infectious forms of gastroenteritis caused by food intolerance, spicy foods, and antibiotics. The complaint is extremely common and fairly mild. It rarely lasts for longer than three days and the child tends to recover without any specific treatment other than replacement of fluid and minerals. A young baby can't tolerate dehydration, and if she vomits or has diarrhoea for more than three hours contact your doctor.

**Symptoms** The first symptom is going off feeds, followed by vomiting and possibly diarrhoea. Your baby may become dehydrated, in which case the fontanelles of her skull will be sunken (see p.280) and her mouth dry.

**Treatment** Mild cases can be treated at home by your doctor, but if vomiting or diarrhoea continues, your baby must be treated in hospital, where she will be given fluids intravenously.

## Intussusception

In this rare and unexplained condition of babies, the intestine telescopes in on itself, forming a tube within a tube, usually causing a blockage of the intestine, which is very serious. It's most common at the junction of the small and large intestines.

**Symptoms** Your baby may scream intermittently and draw up her legs. There may be vomiting and diarrhoea and she may pass blood and mucus. Her abdomen may be swollen and she may become dehydrated. The condition may be complicated by a ruptured bowel and peritonitis (inflammation of the lining of the abdomen) if left untreated.

**Treatment** Passing air into the bowel can cause the intussusception to unfold. If it doesn't, then in practically all cases surgery is successful. In severe cases a segment of bowel may have to be cut out.

## Appendicitis

Inflammation of the appendix, a small, finger-like sac that branches off the first part of the large intestine, is a common cause of abdominal pain. The cause is not known, but it may be obstruction by a small piece of faeces or very occasionally by threadworms. The appendix becomes inflamed, swollen, and infected.

Appendicitis is not a serious condition if it is diagnosed early enough. If the symptoms are mistaken for something else such as constipation, and there is any delay in treatment, the appendix can burst, resulting in an abscess in the abdominal lining or even peritonitis (widespread inflammation of the abdominal lining).

**Symptoms** The first symptom of appendicitis is pain around the navel which, after a few hours, shifts to the right lower side of the abdomen where it becomes intense. Your child may also have a slight temperature and refuse food. The tongue may become coated and there may be vomiting, diarrhoea, or constipation.

**Treatment** Consult your doctor immediately as your child's appendix must be removed before it ruptures. If the appendix has ruptured, resulting in an abscess, this must be drained, and the appendix removed after treatment with large doses of antibiotics. Peritonitis also requires antibiotics and removal of the appendix.

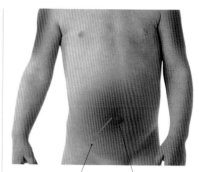

Sharper pain in lower right side

Initial pain around navel

▲ **SITE OF PAIN** The first symptom of appendicitis is a slight ache in the navel area. This develops into a sharper, more localized pain, which is usually most intense in the lower right-hand side of the abdomen.

# Abdominal pain

| TYPE OF PAIN | OTHER SYMPTOMS | CAUSE |
|---|---|---|
| Sudden pain causing your baby to scream and draw her legs up | Common in babies under four months | Colic (see opposite) |
| Crippling abdominal pain that causes your baby to scream | Blood and mucus in the stools and vomiting | Intussusception (see opposite) |
| General mild abdominal pain | Vomiting and diarrhoea | Gastroenteritis (see opposite) |
| Severe pain near the navel that moves towards the lower right of the abdomen | Slight temperature, refusal of food, coated tongue, vomiting | Appendicitis (see above) |
| Generalized tummy ache | Anxiety, clinginess, tearfulness, aggression, and nausea | Stress (see introduction opposite) |
| Sudden crippling pain in the lower abdomen | Swelling and pain in the scrotum. | Torsion of the testis (see p.301) |
| Generalized tummy ache | Sore throat, nasal congestion, and slight fever | Throat infection (see p.286), common cold (see p.294), or middle ear infection (see p.284) |
| Dull abdominal ache spreading round into the back or down into the groin | Pain on urinating, bedwetting when previously dry, and rarely blood in the urine | Urinary tract infection (see p.300) |

# Urogenital complaints

Symptoms such as painful urination or blood in the urine may result from an infection of the bladder, a kidney disorder, or rarely an injury. Correct diagnosis is important in all such complaints so they don't become chronic. One of the most common genital emergencies is torsion of the testis (see opposite).

## Urinary tract infection

The urinary tract consists of the kidneys, where urine is produced from water and waste products; the ureters, which carry urine from the kidneys to the bladder; the bladder, which stores urine; and the urethra, which carries it away from the bladder. The female urethra is much shorter than the male one, so bacteria entering the female urethra have a much shorter distance to travel to the bladder, increasing the likelihood of infection.

The most common cause of urinary tract infection is poor hygiene. The most common type is cystitis (inflammation of the bladder lining), which mainly affects girls. Kidney infection can be caused by a congenital defect that results in a backflow of urine into the kidneys. Kidney infection can also be the result of a bladder infection that spreads upward towards the kidneys.

**Symptoms** Urgent, frequent urination is the most prominent symptom of a urinary tract infection. Your child may complain of a burning or stinging sensation at the beginning and end of urine flow. This is due to the bladder muscle contracting down on the inflamed lining. Your child may also pass urine involuntarily, and start to wet the bed again at night. Pain in the lower abdomen and back is common. Severe back pain, fever and chills, refusal to eat, and headache mean your child has a kidney infection and she will be very ill in this situation. Blood in the urine indicates a severe infection or kidney damage.

**Treatment** All urinary tract infections require medical treatment. Your doctor will take a sample of urine to confirm the presence of a bacterial infection and prescribe the most suitable antibiotic to treat it.

All children who have a urinary tract infection are referred to a paediatrician for assessment. The paediatrician will look for anatomical abnormality and check there is no kidney damage. Give your child plenty of fluids to keep the bladder flushed out, and encourage her to urinate as often as possible. Paracetamol elixir and a wrapped hot-water bottle on the lower abdomen can help to relieve pain.

Show your daughter how to wipe herself from front to back after she has passed a stool. If you have a bidet, encourage her to use it every time she passes a motion. For the duration of an attack washing should be very gentle, as the urethra is sensitive.

## Balanitis

This is an inflammation of the foreskin and head of the penis, usually as a result of bacterial infection. The foreskin is nearly always tight. Products such as washing powder can also cause balanitis.

**Symptoms** The glans (tip of the penis) and foreskin are red, swollen, and tender to the touch and you may notice pus coming from inside the opening. Your child won't let you retract his foreskin and he will have pain on passing urine.

**Treatment** Medical treatment is always necessary to prevent your son developing a stricture of the foreskin, which will make it too tight to retract

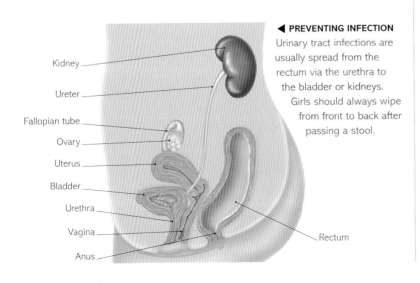

Kidney

Ureter

Fallopian tube

Ovary

Uterus

Bladder

Urethra

Vagina

Anus

Rectum

◀ **PREVENTING INFECTION**
Urinary tract infections are usually spread from the rectum via the urethra to the bladder or kidneys. Girls should always wipe from front to back after passing a stool.

and require circumcision. Your doctor will give you an antibiotic cream to apply to the affected area and suggest the following measures: change your son's nappies frequently; keep his penis clean; apply antiseptic cream to any soreness and a barrier cream to the entire genital area. You should also always make sure your child's clothes are thoroughly rinsed to remove any traces of detergent.

## Undescended testes

Before a baby boy is born, his testes develop inside his abdomen, and descend into the scrotum (the pouch below the penis) shortly before birth. Occasionally, one of the testes fails to descend. The testes need to hang outside the body, where the temperature is lower, for efficient sperm production to take place; a testis at body temperature can't produce sperm. Even if only one testis is undescended, treatment is carried out to achieve the best possible fertility later in life, because there is an increased risk of malignancy in an undescended testis, and for cosmetic purposes. Retractile testes withdraw into the

abdomen in response to cold or touch. This is normal in young children, and can persist into adulthood. It doesn't affect fertility.

**Symptoms** One or both testes are absent from the scrotum. This condition is otherwise symptomless and will not cause your child any discomfort at all.

**Treatment** Often the testes descend by themselves during the first year of life. If they don't, corrective surgery may be carried out when your son is older, usually between the ages of one and two years.

## Torsion of the testis

If one of the testes becomes twisted on its stalk the blood supply will be interrupted and it will become swollen and very painful. If the condition is left untreated, the testis will be irreversibly damaged, so you should seek medical treatment straight away.

**Symptoms** The first symptom is severe pain in the groin area. Later the testis becomes swollen and tender.

Your son could feel sick and may vomit. The scrotum will turn red and purple, and then blue.

**Treatment** The testis must be surgically untwisted as soon as possible in order to restore blood flow. Occasionally, the testis will untwist spontaneously, but you mustn't wait for this to happen.

## Blood in the urine

The medical name for blood in the urine is haematuria. It may be only a streak or sufficient to colour the urine deep red. The cause may be in any part of the urinary tract from the kidneys to the urethra. Cystitis (inflammation of the bladder) and urethritis (inflammation of the urethra) are two common causes. Nephritis (inflammation of the kidneys) is less common but more serious.

If you notice blood in your child's urine you should seek medical advice immediately. Although infections such as cystitis are not serious, they cause great discomfort and it's important to stop bacteria spreading from the bladder up to the kidneys.

**Symptoms** Slight bleeding may be invisible, and found only when urine is examined under a microscope, or when a special diagnostic dipstick is put into the urine. The symptoms of a urinary tract infection (see opposite) may be present.

**Treatment** Since blood in the urine is only a symptom of an underlying disorder, your doctor will do tests to determine the cause and treat it. The urine must be cultured to find an infection and your child may have an ultrasound scan of the urinary tract to check for anatomical abnormalities.

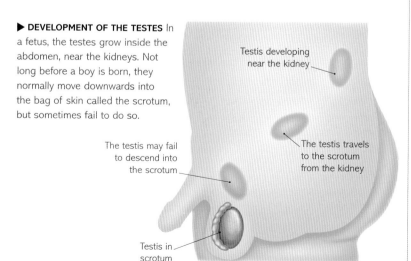

▶ **DEVELOPMENT OF THE TESTES** In a fetus, the testes grow inside the abdomen, near the kidneys. Not long before a boy is born, they normally move downwards into the bag of skin called the scrotum, but sometimes fail to do so.

The testis may fail to descend into the scrotum

Testis developing near the kidney

The testis travels to the scrotum from the kidney

Testis in scrotum

# Infectious diseases

An infectious disease is one that's caused by a micro-organism – that is, a bacterium or a virus. The infection is most commonly spread via the air or by direct contact, though it may also be spread via food, water, or insects, particularly in poor conditions.

In countries where standards of sanitation are high, appropriate drugs are readily available, and health and nutrition are generally good, infectious diseases pose far less of a threat than they once did. In addition, many serious infectious diseases have been virtually eliminated in developed countries by immunization (see p.283). The characteristics of many childhood infectious diseases are similar: a rash on the body, a fever, general malaise, and cold symptoms. If you notice a rash and your child's temperature is raised, consult your doctor. It's an emergency if you notice a rash that does not go away when pressed with a glass (see p.304).

The dangers with most illnesses are that your child may become dehydrated from vomiting and/or diarrhoea or refusing food and drink, have difficulty breathing due to constricted airways, or suffer from febrile seizures (see p.281). Some diseases can lead to complications if left untreated.

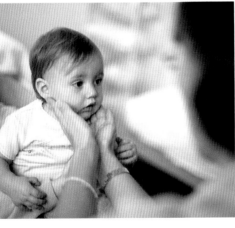

◀ **MUMPS** The salivary glands will swell up, changing the shape of your child's face; the swelling may appear on either or both sides of the face, just below the ears or the chin.

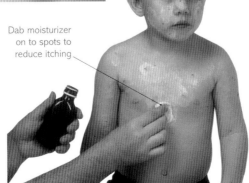

Dab moisturizer on to spots to reduce itching

▶ **APPLYING LOTION** The rash that accompanies chickenpox is very itchy. Rub moisturizer such as Oilatum Plus in to soothe the itch; the spots may leave scars if they are scratched vigorously.

## Disease

**Chickenpox** A common and usually mild viral disease.

**Incubation** 10 to 21 days

**Rubella (German measles)** A viral infection, which is usually mild in children.

**Incubation** 14 to 21 days

**Mumps** A viral illness, which is seldom serious in children.

**Incubation** 14 to 21 days

**Measles** A highly infectious and potentially serious viral illness.

**Incubation** 8 to 14 days

**Whooping cough** A bacterial infection that causes inflammation of the airways.

| Possible symptoms | Treatment | Complications |
| --- | --- | --- |
| Red, itchy spots that become fluid-filled blisters and then scabs. Headache and slight fever. | Acyclovir may be prescribed in the early stages for severe cases in very young children. Apply moisturizer with antiseptic to the rash. Your doctor may prescribe paracetamol and antihistamine. Never give aspirin to a child under 16. | In rare cases, chickenpox leads to encephalitis (inflammation of the brain). Reye's syndrome, a serious illness with symptoms of vomiting and lethargy can develop if aspirin is given to a child under 16. There's also a risk of eczema herpeticum if the blisters become infected with the cold sore virus. |
| Small red spots, first on the face and then all over the body, slight fever, and enlarged lymph nodes at the back of the neck and behind the ears. | There is no specific medical treatment. You can give your child paracetamol elixir if she has a fever and you should try to keep her in isolation. | The biggest risk is to pregnant women who are not immunized and come into contact with a child with German measles, since it causes birth defects. There's a slight risk of encephalitis. |
| Tender, swollen glands below the ears and beneath the chin. Fever, headache, and difficulty chewing and swallowing. An affected child may complain of earache. A less common symptom is painful testes in boys – very rare before puberty. | There is no specific medical treatment. You should keep your child away from school, give her paracetamol elixir and plenty of fluids, and liquidize her food. | Occasionally, meningitis, encephalitis, and pancreatitis. Occasionally, one of the testes is affected, and decreases in size. If both testes are affected, this may result in infertility, but this occurs very rarely. |
| Brownish-red spots appear behind the ears and spread to the rest of the body. White spots in the mouth (Koplik spots) before the rash are a diagnostic sign. The child is feverish, has a runny nose, cough, and headache. May have sore eyes and find it hard to tolerate bright lights. | Keep your child in bed for the duration of the fever and keep her off school for seven days after the appearance of the rash. Give her paracetamol elixir and plenty of fluids. Your doctor may prescribe eye drops for sore eyes and antibiotics for secondary infections. | Ear and chest infections that require treatment with antibiotics may occur. There is also a slight risk of pneumonia, encephalitis, and seizures. |
| A severe paroxysmal cough with a distinctive "whoop" sound as the child tries to breathe, common cold symptoms (see p.294), and vomiting. Coughing may stop your child from sleeping. | Your doctor may prescribe antibiotics, which reduce infectivity but don't cure. In severe cases, your child may need to go to hospital for oxygen therapy and treatment for dehydration. Don't let her exert herself, and keep her away from cigarette smoke. | Sometimes a severe attack of whooping cough can damage the lungs and make your child prone to chest infections. Small babies are most at risk. They may stop breathing for short periods and are also at risk from seizures, pneumonia, brain damage – and very rarely, death. |

# Meningitis

Putting myself in the position of the parent of a child, I'd want to know how to be alert to the possibility of meningitis. The warning signs are:

- vomiting and a high-pitched cry
- headache and sensitivity to bright lights
- stiff neck – your child won't like pulling her head forward when lying on her back
- loss of contact and responsiveness to her surroundings
- a rash that doesn't disappear when you press a glass on it.

If you spot any of these signs, call your doctor immediately.

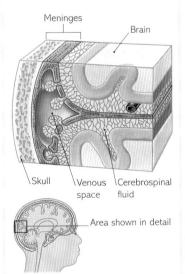

Meninges | Brain
Skull | Venous space | Cerebrospinal fluid
Area shown in detail

▲ **MENINGITIS** Three layers of protective membranes, known as the meninges, cover the brain and spinal cord. Inflammation of the meninges is called meningitis.

# Disease

**Hepatitis** Inflammation of the liver caused by a viral infection. There are many viral causes but infection with the hepatitis A virus is the most common in children.

**Meningitis** Inflammation of the membranes that cover the brain and spinal cord. There are many viral and bacterial causes of meningitis. Immunization (see p.283) protects against meningococcal group C meningitis, pneumoccocal meningitis, and meningitis due to *Haemophilus influenzae B* (Hib).

**Scarlet fever** A bacterial infection that causes tonsillitis accompanied by a rash. It is not very common, and rarely serious.

**Roseola** A viral infection whose symptoms resemble those of scarlet fever.

**Diphtheria** A serious and highly contagious bacterial infection. It is now very rare because of widespread immunization.

**Tuberculosis** A highly infectious bacterial infection that can affect the lungs, bones, kidneys, or meninges.

# Possible symptoms

Extreme fatigue, loss of appetite, nausea, and jaundice. In some cases, your child may pass dark brown urine and pale stools.

Fever, stiff neck, lethargy, headache, drowsiness, and intolerance of bright light; there may also be a purple-red rash (purpura, see Rashes, p.291) covering most of the body. Children may also become unresponsive. In babies under 18 months old, one noticeable symptom is that the fontanelles will bulge slightly.

Fever, enlarged tonsils, and a sore throat. A rash of small spots that starts on the chest then spreads across the body, but doesn't affect the area around the mouth, and a furry tongue with red spots.

A high fever for about three days. Red or pink spots on the trunk, limbs, and neck appear as the fever wanes. The rash fades after about 48 hours.

The tonsils are enlarged and may be covered by a grey membrane. Your child may have a mild fever, a cough, and a sore throat. Breathing difficulties may develop.

Persistent coughing (possibly with blood and pus in the sputum if the lungs are affected), chest pain, shortness of breath, fever (especially at night), poor appetite, weight loss, and tiredness.

# Treatment

Your child should be isolated and rest in bed for at least two weeks. Be meticulous about hygiene – hepatitis is highly contagious – and give her plenty of fluids. If she won't eat, add a spoonful of glucose to her drinks.

Intravenous antibiotics are used to treat bacterial meningitis, and painkilling drugs relieve the symptoms of viral meningitis. If a purple rash develops on the skin that doesn't disappear under pressure, your child should be taken straight to hospital.

Your doctor may prescribe antibiotics. Home treatment includes giving your child plenty of fluids and liquidizing food to make it easier to eat. Give paracetamol elixir to lower temperature.

If your child's temperature is above 40°C (104°F), cool her and give her paracetamol elixir (see p.281). Keep her rested.

Diphtheria is very serious because of the possibility of breathing difficulties and your child should be hospitalized immediately. She will be given strong antibiotics and she may need a tracheotomy to help her to breathe – that is, a small tube will be inserted into the windpipe to bypass the blockage in the throat.

Tuberculosis is a serious disease if left untreated. The disease can usually be treated at home. Your doctor will prescribe antibiotics.

# Complications

Some children suffer from post-hepatitis symptoms for up to six months. These may include moodiness and lethargy.

Viral meningitis is not usually serious and clears up within a week. Bacterial meningitis is potentially fatal because of the risk of septicaemia, and so should always be treated as a medical emergency. It can also affect vision and hearing and can cause hydrocephalus (see p.29).

If your child is sensitive to the streptococcus bacterium it may cause complications, including nephritis (inflammation of the kidneys) and rheumatic fever (inflammation of the joints and heart). These are rare.

If your child's temperature is very high, she may have febrile seizures (see p.281).

Without treatment, diphtheria can cause other serious and potentially fatal complications. Bacteria can release a toxin that damages the heart and nervous system. This can cause heart failure and paralyse the muscles needed for breathing.

Possible complications of tuberculosis of the lungs include pleural effusion (collection of fluid between the lung and chest wall) and collapse of areas of lung tissue (air between the lung and chest wall).

# Safety

Every year a large number of children are admitted to hospital because they have fallen from windows, burned themselves on cookers or been scalded by hot drinks, choked on small objects, or swallowed household chemicals. In fact, poisoning and accidents are the commonest causes of death in previously healthy children under one year old. By taking simple precautions, you can minimize the potential risks in your home. It is all too easy to underestimate the dangers your child faces as she explores her environment.

## Falls

The causes of accidents from falling vary according to the age of the child. Babies under the age of one are most likely to fall from a pram or a pushchair, or from a raised surface, such as a table top, whereas children aged between one and four are more likely to tumble down stairs, fall out of windows, or topple off play equipment.

You can minimize the risk of your child's falling by careful supervision – make sure you never leave your baby unattended on a raised surface – and by making a few changes in your home, such as installing window locks and safety gates on the stairs. Check that the railings on balconies and banisters are no more than 6cm (2½in) apart or your child may fall through or get his head stuck between the rails.

If you don't have a harness for your baby's highchair, pram, or pushchair, you'd be wise to purchase one. The built-in harness that is supplied may not always be adequate. Full harnesses are available from department stores and baby shops – look for one that is easy to fasten and adjust. It's important to make sure you buy one and use it.

## Windows and doors

The types of accidents associated with windows and doors include falling out of an open window, being cut by broken glass, and getting limbs and fingers trapped in closing doors. Various door slam protectors are available, which prevent fingers being trapped in closing doors.

The glass that is usually used for doors and windows is particularly dangerous as it breaks into long, sharp shards. Safety glass, on the other hand, is less likely to break and when it does break it doesn't form sharp pieces. There are two types: laminated glass, which stays in one piece when it is broken, and toughened glass shatters into small rounded pieces. A cheaper option is to use safety film, but this can only be used on unpatterned glass that is completely flat, and, once applied, can't be removed.

Never place furniture under windows – children will not be able to resist climbing up on it, creating a greater risk of a fall. To prevent your child falling out of a window you can install window locks that only allow the window to open by a maximum of 10cm (4in).

Bear in mind, though, that windows can be an essential escape route if there should be a fire in your home, so work out how you would escape from the window in an emergency. Consider taping the key to part of the window frame that's out of reach of young children but there if you need it.

## Fire safety

House fires can be fatal if you or your child inhales smoke and toxic fumes. Fortunately, there are lots of ways in which you can minimize the likelihood of a fire and lessen any damage.

- Don't smoke indoors.
- Don't leave pans containing hot fat unattended.
- Keep flammable liquids locked away.
- Use fireguards on open or gas fires.
- Store matches well out of your child's reach.
- Buy flame-resistant furniture.
- Make sure your child's clothing is flame-resistant – check the manufacturer's label for details.
- Fit a fire extinguisher in your kitchen and replace it every year.
- Keep a dry powder extinguisher and a fire blanket in the kitchen.
- Fit smoke alarms, and check them regularly to make sure that the batteries are working.
- Fit a carbon monoxide detector – available from DIY hardware stores.
- Smother a chip pan fire with a fire blanket, damp cloth, or pan lid.
- If you light candles in your home, keep them well out of the reach of children and pets. Never leave a lit candle unattended.
- Make sure everyone in your home knows what do if there's a fire.

## Burns and scalds

Scalds occur when a child is exposed to hot liquids – they usually affect the face, neck, chest, and arms. As a child gets older and her hand–eye coordination improves she'll be able to pull saucepans, mugs, and kettles containing hot liquids off work surfaces. Another cause of scalding is putting a baby in water that is too hot, or leaving her unsupervised in a bathroom where there is a bath or sink full of hot water. A child can be scalded by less water, at a lower temperature, than an adult.

A good way to avoid scalds is to turn your hot water thermostat down to 54°C (129°F). At this temperature scalding will only start to occur after 30 seconds of exposure. When running a bath for your child, put the cold water in first and then add the hot water afterwards. Never leave a young child unsupervised in the bathroom.

In the kitchen you can prevent your child pulling things off work surfaces by making sure that there are no trailing flexes. Try to buy coiled flexes for your kettle and iron or shorten the existing flex and use hooks to prevent trailing flexes. After you've finished with a mug, kettle, or pan full of hot fluid, empty it immediately. Fit a guard to your cooker, and, when cooking on the hob, use the back rings in preference to the front ones and always keep saucepan handles turned in.

## Electrical safety

Regulations covering domestic electricity supplies and electrical fittings are frequently updated. To be sure that your wiring complies with current regulations and is safe, ask a Part P registered electrician to conduct a periodic inspection at your home. Fit dummy plugs over any unused socket covers and secure any trailing flexes.

## Poisonous substances

Children aged between one and three years are most prone to accidental poisoning because they learn how to climb and open cupboards. Before the age of 18 months children can't tell by taste whether something is likely to be bad for them. Common household poisons include bleach, paraffin, disinfectants, detergents, medications such as antidepressants and tranquillizers, and painkillers such as aspirin (only suitable for children over 16 years of age) and paracetamol. Fortunately, only one in 500 incidents of accidental poisoning has very serious consequences, but it's important to take measures to lessen the risk as poisoning is one of the commonest causes of death in healthy children over the age of one.

Poisoning is largely preventable with a little thought and forward planning. Keep all drugs and household chemicals out of reach of your child, preferably in a locked cupboard or medicine cabinet. When using them, watch your child the whole time – this is when most accidents happen. Both prescribed and proprietary drugs are best kept in bottles with child-resistant lids – avoid taking medicines out of their original containers – and always dispose of any out-of-date or unused drugs safely.

Store household chemicals, such as bleach and all domestic cleaning creams and fluids, in an inaccessible place or a locked cupboard, and never put chemicals into bottles that are familiar or attractive to children, such as lemonade or fruit juice bottles. Keep pet food bowls away from children, as they can harbour bacteria, and don't keep toxic plants or flowers, such as daffodils and irises, in the house.

## Safety equipment

| | |
|---|---|
| Smoke alarms | Your home should be protected with smoke alarms on each level. These alarms are inexpensive and easy to fit. They must be attached to the ceiling, not a wall, to be totally effective. |
| Fire extinguisher and blanket | The kitchen is the most likely place for a fire to start, so you should keep firefighting equipment there. Extinguishers need to be checked regularly for pressure, and may need to be replaced annually. |
| Safety locks | Make sure that windows remain firmly closed, or can be opened only a little way, especially on upper storeys. |
| Stair gates | These can be installed at the top or bottom of the stairs. The bars need to be vertical, not horizontal, so that your child can't climb on them, and the gate should be fitted with a childproof lock. |

# Safety at home

There are some general rules that apply to all rooms of the house. These include avoiding having trailing flexes, loose carpets, rugs, and flammable items of furniture, and choosing furniture that is child-friendly – for example, avoid tables with sharp corners. Keep all electric plug sockets covered, and have windows fitted with window locks. Teach your child from an early age that hot things such as fires and ovens are dangerous and that she should never go near them, but maintain safety precautions until your child is at least three years old.

When your child visits other people's homes, scan the room for potential dangers. If you are in a house where there are no children, carry out a quick check for breakable items, heavy ornaments that can be pulled off surfaces, open, low-level windows, and sharp objects.

## Kitchen

■ Fit a cooker guard and always point saucepan handles towards the back of the cooker, out of reach of little hands.

■ Install a fire extinguisher at an easily accessed point in the kitchen and make sure you replace it annually.

■ Fit a smoke detector on the kitchen ceiling and check its batteries regularly.

■ Keep matches and cigarette lighters out of your child's reach.

■ Set the hot water thermostat to a maximum of 54°C (129°F) – at this temperature it will take half a minute for serious scalding to occur. Check that the thermostat is working properly.

■ Keep plastic bags out of reach.

■ Store sharp knives and cutlery in a drawer with a child lock fitted.

■ Place sharp utensils and cutlery point down in the dishwasher cutlery tray in case your child falls onto it.

■ Fit drawers and cupboards with child-resistant locks to safeguard both the contents and your child.

■ Don't use tablecloths. Your toddler can pull them and everything on the table on to her head.

■ Don't leave hot pans or mugs containing hot drinks around.

■ If you spill fat or liquid on the floor, mop it up straight away.

■ Always keep harmful cleaning products in a secure place.

■ Keep hot items, such as trays that have just come out of the oven, away from the edge of counters so that children are not able to reach them.

■ Turn your washing machine, tumble dryer, and dishwasher off at the mains when not in use.

■ If you are not using the iron, put both the iron and the ironing board away. Never leave your child unattended if the iron is on.

■ Keep bowls of pet food out of reach to avoid bacterial infection.

■ Keep wastebins in a cupboard with a child-resistant lock.

■ Never leave your child unattended while she is eating – she could choke.

■ Stay in the kitchen while cooking. If you must leave the kitchen briefly, turn off appliances.

▶ **STAIR GATES** Make sure that your stair gates have vertical bars that are no more than 6cm (2½in) apart and fit them with childproof locks.

## Hall and stairs

■ Install a safety gate at the bottom of the stairs; gates at the top can be a trip hazard.

■ Make sure halls and stairways are well lit.

■ Don't leave clothes or objects lying on the stairs that you or your child could trip over.

■ The stairway should be protected on both sides by walls or banisters.

■ The gaps between the banisters should not be more than 6cm (2½in) wide so your child can't get her head, arm, or a leg caught in them.

■ Stair carpets should fit the stairs exactly so that your child can't trip on any badly fitting edges.

■ Replace any loose or frayed carpet on the stairs without delay.

■ Make sure that it's impossible for your child to get out of the front door.

## Bathroom

■ Store all medicines, both prescribed and over the counter, in a locked cabinet or on a high shelf and dispose of any unused or old medicines safely.
■ Keep disinfectants, cleaning fluids, and bleach locked away in their original containers, with child-resistant tops, and make sure they are always out of your child's reach while you are using them.
■ Never leave a child alone with a filled bath or sink.
■ When preparing your child's bath always add hot water to cold, never the other way round.
■ Use non-slip mats in the bath.
■ Keep the lavatory lid closed.
■ Fix heated towel rails out of your child's reach.
■ Make sure that your child stands still or sits on your knee when brushing her teeth – running around with a toothbrush in her mouth is dangerous.

## Bedroom

■ Cot toys should not have strings that are longer than 30cm (12in).
■ Never leave your baby with the cot side down.
■ Never leave your baby alone on the changing table, even for a second.
■ Install window locks to prevent windows opening more than 10cm (4in).
■ Avoid lights with trailing flexes.
■ Cot bars should not be too widely spaced (6cm or 2½in apart is the maximum safe space between bars), as your child could get part of her body stuck between them.
■ Don't use a pillow in your baby's cot until she's one year old.
■ Choose furniture with rounded, padded (if possible) corners.
■ Don't leave gas or electric fires on when your child is on her own.

▲ **ELECTRICAL SAFETY** Plug socket covers fitted over any unused sockets in your home prevent your child sticking her fingers or small objects into the holes.

## Living room

■ Patio doors must be fitted with laminated glass or toughened glass.
■ Use a floor-standing or wall-mounted fireguard in front of the fire, but always make sure that it's securely fitted to the wall. Don't put cups, mugs, or ashtrays on the fireguard.
■ Use socket covers to stop your child poking objects into plug sockets. Neutral coloured covers are best so they don't attract your child's attention.
■ Avoid trailing flexes from lights, TV, stereo, and DVD equipment.
■ Don't have poisonous houseplants such as irises and daffodils.
■ Don't leave alcohol, cigarettes, matches, or lighters lying around.
■ Keep fragile, breakable items well out of your child's reach.
■ Don't place hot or heavy objects on low tables.
■ All bookcases and shelving should be securely fixed to the wall.
■ Avoid furniture with sharp corners.

## Play areas

■ Keep older children's toys separate from your younger child's toys. Toys with small parts, modelling kits, and chemistry sets can also be dangerous to babies and toddlers.
■ Store toys safely in a box and don't leave them lying around on the floor where you might trip over them or stand on them.
■ Check the manufacturer's details to make sure that your child's furniture and toys use non-toxic paints.
■ Check your child's toys regularly and throw away any broken or damaged toys, which could injure your child.
■ A playpen is a good way of keeping a young child out of potential danger. Make sure that it is at least 60cm (2ft) deep so that your child can't climb out.
■ Store toys and games within your child's reach so he doesn't have to stretch or climb to get them.
■ Make sure children wear safety helmets when on bikes.

# Safety at play

The most common accidents that result from playing are cuts and bruises from falling over or off toys, or injuries from swallowing part of a toy or inserting it into a nostril. Sometimes an accident occurs because a child is not properly supervised, or because a toy is broken, of a poor standard, or simply too sophisticated for the child. Construction kits, toy cars and trains, and rocking and wheeled toys cause the most injuries. Even soft toys can choke or suffocate a child.

## Toy safety checklist

■ Check packaging and labels to ensure the toy is appropriate to your child's age. In general, toys with small components are not suitable for children under the age of 36 months.
■ Check the manufacturer's warning labels for information about flammability or for any harmful or toxic ingredients.
■ Don't stick pictures on the inside of your baby's cot as she may peel them off and put them in her mouth.
■ Cot toys should not be hung on strings of more than 30cm (12in) long or your child could get tangled up.

■ If your baby can stand up in her cot, remove toys from the side, as she can use them as a stepping stone to climb up and over the bars of her cot.
■ For a child under three, avoid toys with small detachable components, as these can be swallowed easily by very young children.
■ If you have children of different ages, store each child's toys separately.
■ Show your child how to use a toy.
■ One- and two-year-olds can easily fall off rocking toys, and trundle trucks, so keep an eye on your child at all times, especially if she is playing on hard ground.

■ Regularly check the batteries in battery-operated toys. Replace them if there's leakage.
■ Make sure toys have no sharp or abrasive edges.
■ Throw away broken toys or toys with sharp edges rather than giving them to charity or to a jumble sale.
■ Store toys safely away in a box with a lid that doesn't slam shut.
■ If a toy comes wrapped in a plastic bag, unwrap it for your child, and dispose of the plastic bag.

## Outdoor safety

Your child will enjoy playing out of doors – she will be able to run around freely, get dirty, and explore a different

▼ **TOYS** It's tempting to buy toys on impulse, but check for potential hazards first and always make sure the toy is appropriate to your child's age.

Edges should be curved or flexible, not sharp or rigid

Eyes should be firmly attached

Ears should be firmly stitched on

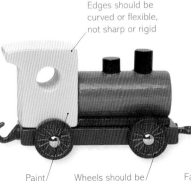

Paint should be non-toxic

Wheels should be non-detachable

Fabric should be flame-resistant

Check for splits or tears; loose stuffing might be eaten or inhaled

## Choke hazards

**Once your baby acquires the pincer grasp, she is able to pick up small objects that she might put in her mouth and swallow.**

A choke hazard tester checks if an object is small enough to lodge in a child's windpipe. If the object slips into the tester, you will know if it's potentially dangerous for your child.

environment. The main danger associated with playing outside is that she may run out of the garden or playground and into the road. Drowning is also possible if there is water or a pool in the garden. You can prevent this by making sure that your child always plays in an enclosed environment and that garden gates are locked with child-resistant locks. Drain or fence ponds, and empty paddling pools after use. The other main dangers include ingesting poisonous plants, animal faeces, or chemicals that are used in gardening.

## Garden safety checklist

■ Make sure that any poisonous plants (see right) are removed, and pull up all types of fungi as soon as they appear.
■ Store all garden tools and chemicals, such as weedkiller or fertilizers, in a locked garden shed.
■ Make sure that garden chairs are

always put up properly – injuries can be caused by unstable deck chairs and loungers.
■ Check the safety of play equipment regularly and watch for wear and tear.
■ Put climbing toys on grass, not on paved areas.
■ Make sure that your child can't run out of the garden into the road – fit child-resistant locks.
■ If you have a pond or a swimming pool and your child is under the age of two you should drain it, cover it, or fence it off.
■ Fix broken glass in greenhouses straight away.
■ Don't use power saws or mow the lawn if your child is running around. Always put power tools away after use.
■ Cover sandpits when not in use to prevent fouling by animals.
■ Don't allow animals to defecate in the garden.
■ Cover up drains and water butts.

## Poisonous plants

Although eating garden plants is rarely fatal it can cause unpleasant symptoms, ranging from irritation of the skin, mouth, throat, and stomach, to serious digestive upset, nausea and vomiting. Tell your child never to eat any plants or berries from the garden and remove any trees, plants, and shrubs that you know are poisonous.

Treat unknown plants with respect and teach your child to do the same. Daffodils, narcissi, hyacinths, irises, buttercups, snowdrops, sweetpeas, and privet cause irritation of the gastro-intestinal tract, and rhubarb, many fungi, tomato leaves, yew, willow, laurel, rhododendron, mistletoe, jasmine, nightshade, and lily of the valley cause general poisoning. Laburnum and oleander leaves and branches are also dangerous and can cause fatal poisoning, as can wisteria seeds and seed pods.

# Playground safety

**Young children need challenging equipment to test their skills and use up energy, but make sure they're safe and supervised at all times.**

■ The play area should be surrounded by a fence so animals can't get in
■ Young children should sit in box swings, not on open swings designed for older children
■ Swings should be enclosed by a fence
■ Climbing equipment is safest if it is situated on grass or sand so the softer surface helps break a child's fall, should she tumble off
■ Do not let your child put her feet under a roundabout or jump off a roundabout when it's moving
■ Slides constructed on an earth mound will break a fall
■ The surface of a slide should have no joins in it
■ Equipment at ground level, like tubes and tyres, is safest for toddlers.

▲ **SAND SAFETY** Sand pits should be shallow so a child can't get buried. Cover with a waterproof sheet when not in use.

# Car and road safety

The most basic car safety rule is to make sure that your child is always strapped in. Rear-facing seats are best for infants and can be used in the front or back of the car. Never buy secondhand car seats in case they're damaged. Fit child locks on the rear doors of your car, and don't let your child lean out of the window, or stick her hands and arms out. Be aware that a child can get her fingers stuck in car doors or windows as they are being closed. Explain to your child that it's safest to get out of the car on the pavement side. Don't take your eyes off the road to turn and talk to your child when you're driving; if she needs your attention, pull over and stop the car in a safe place.

## Baby car seats

The safest way for your baby to travel by car is in a rear-facing baby seat buckled into a seat belt. This means that in a crash any impact is against the baby's back, and not the delicate pelvic organs. An adult seat belt alone is not sufficient for a child under the age of 12 because her pelvic bones are not strong enough to protect the pelvic organs from the pressure of the belt in the event of a crash. Rear-facing baby

▲ **BABY SAFETY** The best car seats for babies from birth to nine months are rear-facing, in the back seat of the car.

seats also provide better protection for your baby's head. There are two types for babies: from birth up to 9 months (10kg/22lb) and up to 15 months (13kg/29lb). They can be used in the front or back seats of cars, although they're safer in the back and must never be used in the front of a car if airbags are fitted (see below). Some models will convert to a forward-facing child seat for when the child is older.

It's not safe for your baby to travel in a carry cot in the back seat, even if it's secured with a seat belt. Never travel with a baby on your lap or inside your own seat belt either; she could be thrown out of the car, or crushed by your weight in a crash.

## Take care

It is illegal to use a baby seat in the front of a car that has a safety airbag fitted on the passenger side, unless the airbag can be switched off. In the event of a crash, the airbag would inflate with such force that the impact could seriously injure the baby's head.

## Child seats

By the age of one year, or when your baby has reached the recommended maximum weight for her rear-facing seat, she'll need a forward-facing seat fitted into the car. These seats are suitable for children up to the age of four to six years (about 18kg/40lb). Some are fixed in place with a four-point anchorage kit, although these are not practical for all types of car. Other types are secured with the adult seat belt, and some have an integral harness that fits over a child's shoulders, across her hips, and between her legs. Many new cars are now fitted with special ISO-fix seat fittings, which makes it easier to install a seat. Make sure you fit your child seat according to the manufacturer's instructions, since a badly fitted seat won't offer any protection in a crash.

When your child has grown out of a car seat (either because she's exceeded the weight limit, or the top of her head is higher than the top of the seat), she must use a booster seat with an adult seat belt. A booster seat raises her so that the adult seat belt does does not cut across her neck and makes sure that the lap strap lies across her hips. In the UK, a booster seat must be used with an adult seat belt until a child is 12 years old or over 1.35m (5ft 3in). The car must have a three-point seat belt as a lap strap on its own is not enough to support a child.

## Road safety

Road accidents are usually more serious and require longer hospitalization than any other childhood accidents, so this is an area where safety is of paramount importance. The responsibility for your child's safety when out in traffic lies with you, of course, not just when she's in her pram but when she reaches school age. Children don't develop the ability to judge the speed of traffic until they are about ten or 11 years old and they are not good pedestrians until the age of 12. You can, however, instil the basics of road safety from an early age, by teaching her yourself and, more importantly, by setting her a good example when you're out and about together.

## Teaching your child

The first thing that your child must learn is that roads are dangerous places. It doesn't matter what the circumstances are – whether she has lost her ball or pet, or wants to greet someone – she must never run out into a road. Unless your road has no traffic don't let your child play on the pavement – encourage her to play in parks, playgrounds, or in the back garden instead, and make sure that these areas are secured with a fence or a locked gate. Tell your child that she must never play on a pedal bike or scooter near the road, that she shouldn't stand in between parked cars, and that if she loses a ball in the road, she should ask an adult to retrieve it.

## Setting an example

The best way to teach your child road safety is to show her how you should behave as a pedestrian. Most of us develop bad habits as adults, such as weaving through traffic, or crossing a road without allowing ourselves sufficient time, possibly even talking on a mobile phone. When you're with your child you should practise the Green Cross Code, even if it takes you longer to reach your destination. This way your child will learn by example

– and children do copy what they see. When you cross the road with your child, hold her hand and explain what you are doing and why. Go to the kerb and tell your child that it is the safety line that must not be crossed without an adult. Look left and right and wait for a clear break in the traffic before you cross over. If you are pushing a buggy, keep it on the pavement until you are ready to cross. Demonstrate to your child how to press the buttons at pelican crossings, and how to wait for the traffic to stop before you cross a zebra crossing. Never run across the road in front of traffic when you are with your child.

Your child's awareness of road safety is in part determined by the area she grows up in. A child who grows up in the country and only has to cross quiet country lanes may need extra supervision when she goes to a town or city because she hasn't made a strong association between roads, traffic, and danger. If this is the case with your child, you can still teach her about road safety when you're driving in the car. When you stop at a pedestrian crossing, point out what they're for and how pedestrians use them to cross the road safely. Where

there are no pedestrian crossings, show your child sensible places to cross, such as straight stretches of road, and point out the dangers of crossing at places such as sharp bends or between parked cars, where you can't see traffic coming. Point out pedestrians who are crossing well or badly, and explain why.

## Environment

Make a careful assessment of the traffic and road conditions on your street. Although traffic speed is an important factor, recent research has shown that main roads pose six times as great a risk to pedestrians as residential or local roads. If you live on or near a main road you should never allow your child to go out of the house on her own – make sure your front door is properly secured so that she can't open it.

If you live in a residential area you could ask your local council to install speed ramps, to impose extra speed restrictions, or to narrow the road at specific points. Try getting together with other parents in your area and discuss a campaign for safe neighbourhood play. Your local authority can play an important role in helping you achieve this.

## The Green Cross Code

This simple road safety routine is really intended for children of eight years and upwards, but you should start to teach it as soon as your child is old enough to follow your example.

**Teaching the Code** Repeat these four simple steps to your child every time you cross the road.

■ Find a safe place to cross the road, such as a zebra crossing or pelican crossing.
■ Stop, look in both directions, and listen for traffic.
■ If there is any traffic, let it pass.
■ Look in both directions, and when the road is clear, walk across. Keep looking and listening as you cross the road.

# Personal records

Your baby's milestones seem unforgettable, but as time passes your memory may become hazy, not just for small details, but about crucial dates such as immunizations.

## Birth record: first baby

Name ...............................................................................
Date and time ...............................................................
Place ...............................................................................
Estimated date of delivery.........................................
Length .............................................................................
Weight .............................................................................
Blood group ...................................................................
Duration of labour .......................................................
Type of delivery .............................................................
Midwife/consultant ......................................................
People present ...............................................................

## Development record: first baby

First smile ...............................          Stands ...................................
Achieves head control .........          Bowel control .......................
First tooth ..............................          Bladder control ...................
Sits unsupported ..................          Walks .....................................
Starts solids .........................          Makes simple statements ......
Feeds self .............................          Dresses self .........................
Responds to own name ........          Obeys simple requests ........
Uses mature "pincer" grip .....          Climbs stairs unsupported ......
Learns to "ungrasp".................          Runs .......................................
First word .............................          Jumps .....................................
Understands "No"...................          Counts to ten .......................
Crawls ...................................          Draws a circle .......................
Fully weaned ........................          Starts preschool ...................
Jargons ..................................          Starts school .........................

These pages will help you keep track of these important events. The medical records on pp.316–17 are particularly important. Use them to refresh your memory each time you take your child to the doctor; they may remind you of some forgotten detail that seems relevant. Make a note of your own medical history, too, and that of your partner; these can often provide important clues to your child's state of health.

## Birth record: second baby

Name ..................................................................
Date and time ......................................................
Place ..................................................................
Estimated date of delivery ....................................
Length ................................................................
Weight ................................................................
Blood group ........................................................
Duration of labour ..............................................
Type of delivery ..................................................
Midwife/consultant ............................................
People present ....................................................

## Development record: second baby

First smile ...............................
Achieves head control ..............
First tooth ...............................
Sits unsupported ......................
Starts solids ............................
Feeds self ................................
Responds to own name ............
Uses mature "pincer" grip ........
Learns to "ungrasp" .................
First word ...............................
Understands "No" .....................
Crawls .....................................
Fully weaned ...........................
Jargons ....................................

Stands .....................................
Bowel control ..........................
Bladder control ........................
Walks ......................................
Makes simple statements .........
Dresses self .............................
Obeys simple requests .............
Climbs stairs unsupported ........
Runs ........................................
Jumps ......................................
Counts to ten ..........................
Draws a circle ..........................
Starts preschool .......................
Starts school ...........................

## Notes

# Mother's medical history

### Illness

_____

_____

_____

_____

_____

_____

_____

### Allergies

_____

_____

_____

_____

_____

_____

_____

### Chronic conditions

_____

_____

_____

_____

_____

_____

_____

# Medical records: first baby

| Illness | Date | Comments |
|---------|------|----------|
|         |      |          |
|         |      |          |

| Injuries | Date | Comments |
|----------|------|----------|
|          |      |          |
|          |      |          |

| Allergies | Date | Comments |
|-----------|------|----------|
|           |      |          |
|           |      |          |

# Immunizations: first baby

| TYPE | DATE | REACTION |
|------|------|----------|
| **Diphtheria, tetanus, pertussis (whooping cough), and polio with Hib** <br> One injection at two months <br> One injection at three months <br> One injection at four months <br> One DTP and polio booster <br> (without Hib) at three years <br> and four months | | |
| **Pneumococcal infection** <br> One injection at two months <br> One injection at four months <br> One injection at 13 months | | |
| **Haemophilus influenzae b (Hib)** <br> One injection at 12 months | | |
| **Measles, mumps, and rubella (MMR)** <br> One injection at around 13 months <br> One booster between three <br> and five years | | |
| **Meningitis C** <br> One injection at three months <br> One injection at four months <br> One injection at 12 months | | |

# Medical records: second baby

| Illness | Date | Comments |
|---------|------|----------|
|         |      |          |
|         |      |          |
|         |      |          |

| Injuries | Date | Comments |
|----------|------|----------|
|          |      |          |
|          |      |          |

| Allergies | Date | Comments |
|-----------|------|----------|
|           |      |          |
|           |      |          |

# Immunizations: second baby

| TYPE | DATE | REACTION |
|------|------|----------|
| **Diphtheria, tetanus, pertussis (whooping cough), and polio with Hib** <br> One injection at two months <br> One injection at three months <br> One injection at four months <br> One DTP and polio booster (without Hib) at three years and four months | | |
| **Pneumococcal infection** <br> One injection at two months <br> One injection at four months <br> One injection at 13 months | | |
| **Haemophilus influenzae b (Hib)** <br> One injection at 12 months | | |
| **Measles, mumps, and rubella (MMR)** <br> One injection at around 13 months <br> One booster between three and five years | | |
| **Meningitis C** <br> One injection at three months <br> One injection at four months <br> One injection at 12 months | | |

# Father's medical history

**Illness**

**Allergies**

**Chronic conditions**

# Growth measurements

The most important criteria in assessing your baby's progress are happiness and general well-being. If she's happy and healthy, you don't need to worry about measuring her at home; your health visitor or local baby clinic will it for you.

You may find it interesting to plot your baby's increasing height and weight on the following charts.

The range of "normal" heights or weights at a given age is very wide. A newborn boy may weigh anything from 2.5 to 4.5kg (5½ to 10lb) without giving cause for concern; a five-year-old boy from 13.5 to 26.5kg (30 to 58lb).

Each chart shows the range of heights or weights into which the vast majority of children will fall. The black line in the middle of each coloured band represents the 50th centile; that is, 50 per cent of children will fall below the line, and 50 per cent above it. The outer lines represent extremes beyond which very few children (fewer than 0.5 per cent) will fall. If your child does fall outside these lines, you should consult your doctor or health visitor.

A child's measurements, plotted regularly, should form a line roughly parallel to the central centile line (see right). If her growth pattern veers from the line, check with your health visitor, baby clinic, or doctor. It's important though not to compare your child to others of her age.

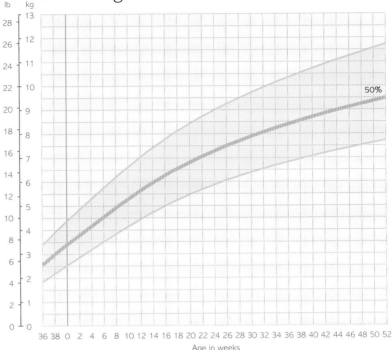

## Girls' weight 0–12 months

## Girls' weight breastfed 0–12 months

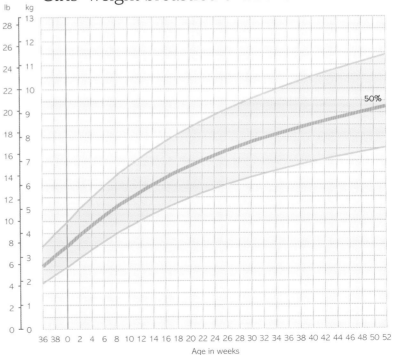

## Boys' weight 0–12 months

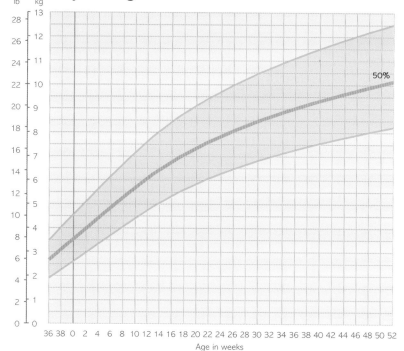

lb | kg

28 | 13
26 | 12
24 | 11
22 | 10
20 | 9
18 | 8
16 | 7
14 | 6
12 | 5
10 | 4
8 | 3
6 |
4 | 2
2 | 1
0 | 0

50%

36 38 0 2 4 6 8 10 12 14 16 18 20 22 24 26 28 30 32 34 36 38 40 42 44 46 48 50 52

Age in weeks

## Boys' weight breastfed 0–12 months

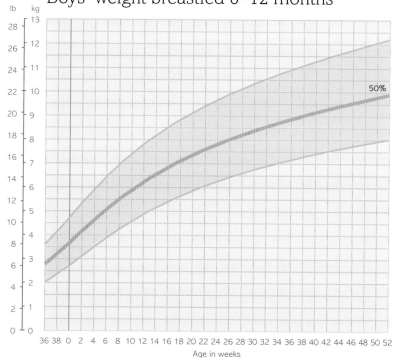

lb | kg

28 | 13
26 | 12
24 | 11
22 | 10
20 | 9
18 | 8
16 | 7
14 | 6
12 | 5
10 | 4
8 | 3
6 |
4 | 2
2 | 1
0 | 0

50%

36 38 0 2 4 6 8 10 12 14 16 18 20 22 24 26 28 30 32 34 36 38 40 42 44 46 48 50 52

Age in weeks

# Using the charts

I believe that no baby needs weighing and measuring if she's thriving, but we've included charts for parents who are keen to follow their child's progress.

■ You'll probably need to ask your midwife or doctor for your baby's weight, length, and head circumference at birth.

■ Fill in the charts using the measurements taken by your doctor or health visitor, or from readings done at the baby clinic.

■ For a preterm baby, you'll have to adjust her age at least until she's a year old. If, for example, your baby was born at 36 weeks, start recording her measurements at the appropriate point to the left of zero on the chart, and subtract four weeks from her age each time you fill in the chart.

■ To measure your child's height, once she's three or four get her to stand against a wall with her feet together and her heels and shoulder blades touching the wall. Make sure she holds her head up straight by gently tilting her chin upwards. If you like, measure her again at six-monthly intervals so she can see how she's growing.

■ To enter your child's measurements on the chart, find her age along the bottom axis and draw a straight line up from it. Now find her weight or height along the vertical axis, and draw a line across. Mark a solid dot where the two lines meet.

# Notes

## Girls' length 0–12 months

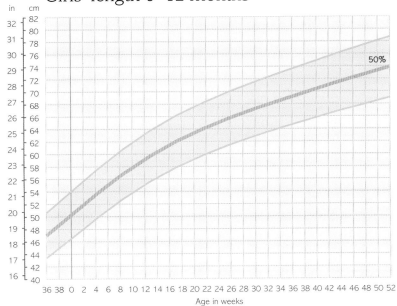

## Girls' head circumference 0–12 months

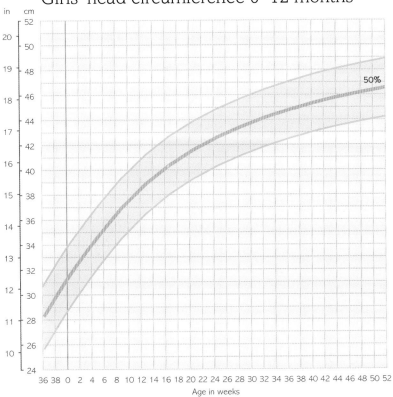

## Boys' length 0–12 months

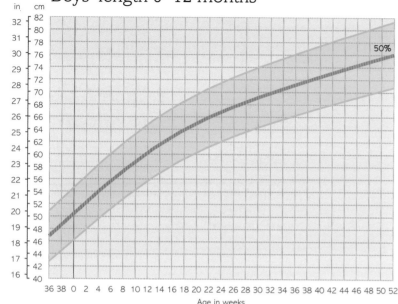

50%

Age in weeks

## Boys' head circumference 0–12 months

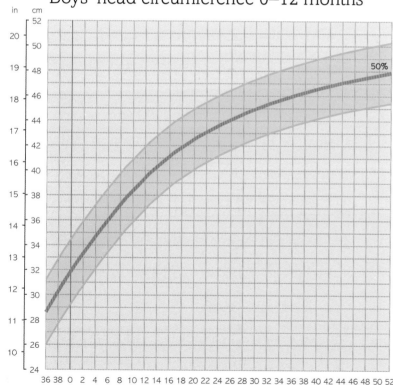

50%

Age in weeks

# Notes

## Girls' weight 1–5 years

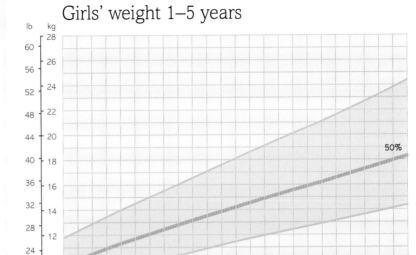

## Girls' height 1–5 years

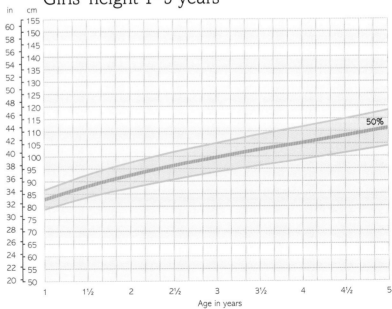

## Boy's weight 1–5 years

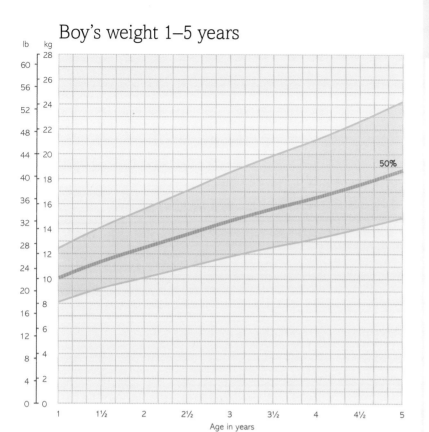

50%

Age in years

## Boys' height 1–5 years

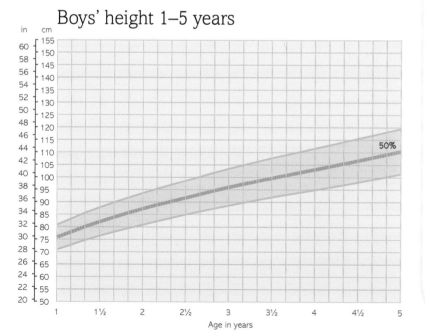

50%

Age in years

# Notes

# First aid

You will inevitably have to cope with minor accidents and cuts and bruises as your child grows up, but you should also be equipped to cope with major emergencies if necessary. All parents should know the basic first aid techniques to deal with accidents quickly, effectively, and calmly. To give first aid effectively you need to understand and practise the techniques detailed on the following pages, and you should keep a first aid kit accessible in an emergency, but keep it out of your child's reach.

## Emergency first aid

An accident that results in the loss of much blood or other body fluids may precipitate shock (see p.332), which is always serious. Other first aid emergencies include choking (see p.333), a very severe respiratory tract infection that blocks the child's airways, drowning, and unconsciousness. Prompt action on your part in an emergency can be lifesaving.

## Priorities

When a child has an accident you must get your priorities right. Ask another adult to summon help while you go through the list of questions given here. Detailed instructions for the procedures are shown on pp.326–31.

If there isn't anyone to help you, work through the list of questions and, if it's necessary, give rescue breaths and chest compressions (CPR) for one full minute, before you call for emergency help.

**Is there any danger?** Make the area safe. Don't put yourself at risk, so don't approach your child if doing so puts you in danger. If it's safe, it's better to remove the danger from your child.

**Is she conscious?** Keep calling her name clearly and loudly. Tap her foot

## Home first aid kit

Keep these items in a clearly marked box with an airtight lid. Make sure you know how to use each one properly. You may also like to keep some infant paracetamol elixir and ibuprofen for treating pain or fever in young children. It is a good idea to keep another first aid kit in your car.

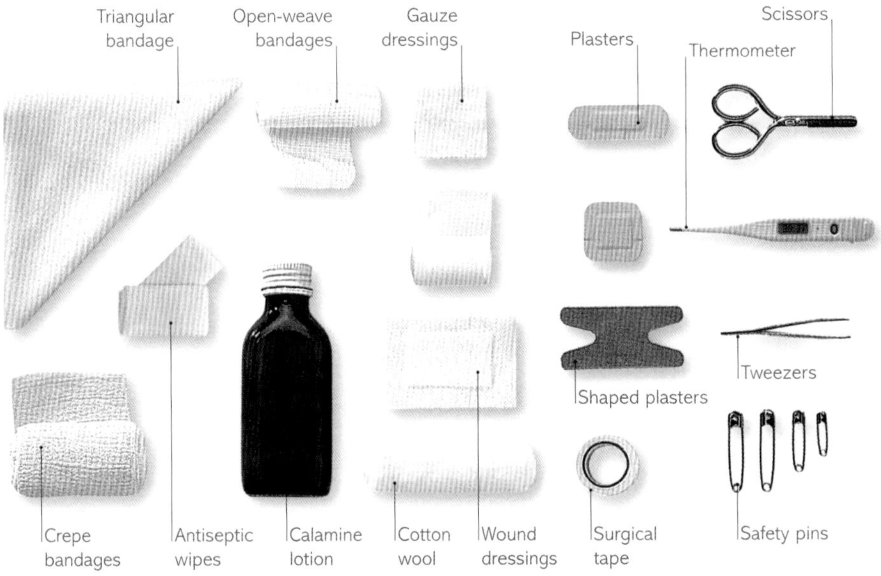

Triangular bandage

Open-weave bandages

Gauze dressings

Plasters

Scissors

Thermometer

Shaped plasters

Tweezers

Safety pins

Crepe bandages

Antiseptic wipes

Calamine lotion

Cotton wool

Wound dressings

Surgical tape

or her shoulders (NEVER shake her to see if she is conscious).

■ If she responds to you, she is conscious. Don't move her. Check her carefully and treat any injuries.

■ If there is no response, she is unconcious and you need to check to see if she is breathing.

**Is she breathing?** Open your child's airway by tilting her head back and lifting her chin. Lean close to your child's mouth to listen for breathing and feel it against your cheek. Look along her chest to check for movement, is it rising and falling? Check for no more than ten seconds.

■ If there are no signs of normal breathing, begin CPR (see pp.328–29).

■ If she is breathing normally, place her in the recovery position (see p.327) and call for emergency help if this has not been done.

## First aid training

You must learn the procedures on the following pages by heart in order to be able to make use of them in an emergency. If you have to waste time referring to this book to refresh your memory, the delay could be the difference between the life and death of a child.

This book can't make you a "First Aider". To learn first aid properly you should complete a course of instruction and pass a supervised examination. The Standard First Aid Certificate is awarded by St John Ambulance, St Andrew's Ambulance Association, and the British Red Cross (see Useful addresses, p.342). These organizations also run courses especially for parents. A first aid certificate is valid for only three years, after which you need to go on a refresher course.

## How resuscitation works

▶ **OXYGEN SUPPLY** Three factors are involved in getting oxygen to the brain. The air passage, or airway, must be open so that oxygen can enter the body; breathing must occur so that oxygen can enter the bloodstream in the lungs; and the heart must be pumping so that the blood travels around the body (circulation), taking the oxygen to all the tissues, including those of the brain.

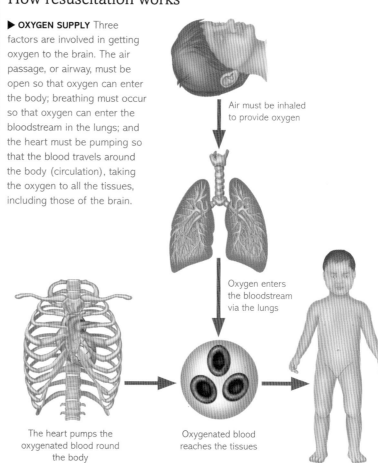

Air must be inhaled to provide oxygen

Oxygen enters the bloodstream via the lungs

The heart pumps the oxygenated blood round the body

Oxygenated blood reaches the tissues

## The ABC of resuscitation

In an emergency, if your baby or child loses consciousness, you must remember the following key points in the order given – ABC:

**A is for Airway** This must be open and clear. To open it, tilt the head, and lift the chin (see pp.326–27).

**B is for Breathing** If your baby or child shows no signs of breathing, remove any obvious obstruction from the mouth, but never sweep the back of the throat. Lift the chin again. Breathe for her with rescue breaths (see pp.328–29).

**C is for Chest compressions** If your baby or child is not breathing, her heart will stop too. You will need to give her chest compressions combined with rescue breaths (see see pp.328–29) to "pump" the oxygenated blood around her

# Unconsciousness

If your child has lost consciousness and isn't breathing, her heart will stop and she's at risk of brain damage. You need to make a fast assessment of her condition in order to know what first aid treatment to give.

If a child is unconscious, the muscles that keep the tongue off the back of the throat don't work. So the tongue falls back and blocks the air passages. If your child is unconscious, your first task is to open the airway by tilting her head back, then check breathing (it's the first question the ambulance control officer will ask you). If she is breathing, place her in the recovery position (see opposite) to keep her airways open and clear, then call for help. If she's not breathing, you'll need to give cardiopulmonary resuscitation (CPR) (see pp.328–29). If you're on your own, give CPR for one minute before you call an ambulance.

## Assessing a baby (under one year)

Tongue fallen back

Blocked airway –
head not tilted

Tongue comes forward

Unblocked airway –
head tilted

2 **OPEN THE AIRWAY** Make sure your baby is on her back on a firm surface. Put one hand on her forehead, and carefully tilt her head back then lift the chin with your fingertips. This lifts the tongue away from the back of the throat. Don't press against the soft tissues under her chin as this can block the airway again.

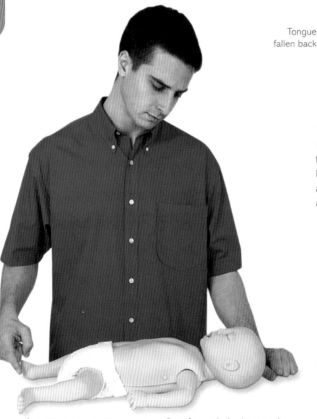

1 **CHECK FOR CONSCIOUSNESS** See if your baby is conscious by calling her name and tapping the sole of her foot. If she doesn't respond within about ten seconds, she is unconscious. Shout for help.

Look along chest for movement

3 **CHECK FOR BREATHING** Look, listen, and feel for signs of breathing. Look along your baby's chest and abdomen to see if they are moving up and down. Listen closely for sounds of breathing and feel for her breath on your cheek. If there are no signs of normal breathing after ten seconds, you'll need to give five initial rescue breaths (see p.328).

# Assessing a child

**1** **CHECK FOR CONSCIOUSNESS** See if your child is conscious by tapping his shoulder. Keep calling his name. If he doesn't respond, he's unconscious. Shout for help.

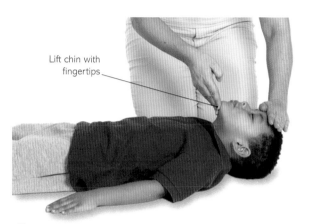

Lift chin with fingertips

Look along chest for movement

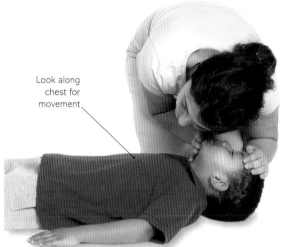

**2** **OPEN THE AIRWAY** Make sure your child is on his back on a firm surface. Put one hand on his forehead and carefully tilt his head back, then lift his chin with your fingertips. This lifts the tongue away from the back of the throat. Don't press the soft tissues under his chin as this can block the airway again.

**3** **CHECK BREATHING** Look, listen, and feel for signs of breathing. Look along your child's chest and abdomen for movements; listen for sounds of breathing; and feel for his breath on your cheek. If he is not breathing, you'll need to give five initial rescue breaths (see p.329).

# Recovery position

An unconscious child who is breathing should be placed in this position to keep the airway open and to allow liquids to drain from the mouth.

Uppermost leg should be bent at a right angle so that the hip and knee act as a "prop"

Place hand under cheek

▲ **FOR A BABY** Cradle him in your arms with his face slightly toward you and his head lower than his body in order to keep the airway open.

**1** **POSITION NEAREST ARM** If your child is lying on her back or side, kneel beside her, level with her chest. Straighten her legs and place the arm nearest to you at right angles to her body with the elbow bent.

**2** **POSITION FURTHEST ARM** Bring the other arm across her chest, toward you. Place the back of her hand against the cheek nearest you.

**3** **BEND FURTHEST LEG** Still pressing your child's hand to his cheek, grasp the thigh that is furthest away from you and pull the knee up, keeping the foot flat on the ground and placing it next to the nearer knee.

**4** **FINAL POSITION** Roll your child over into a resting position with his knee bent and his head resting on his hand.

# Cardiopulmonary resuscitation (CPR)

A unconscious baby or child who is not breathing needs cardiopulmonary resuscitation (CPR) – rescue breaths and chest compressions. You need to get air into her lungs (rescue breathing). This is possible because there is enough oxygen in your exhaled breath to keep another person alive. Then you need to "pump" the oxygenated blood around the body (chest compressions).

## CPR for babies (under one year)

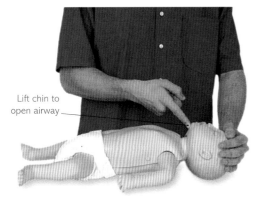

Lift chin to open airway

1 **OPEN THE AIRWAY** If your baby has stopped breathing, make sure she is on a firm surface and that her head is tilted back. Check her mouth. If you can see an obvious obstruction, pick it out with your fingers, but do not poke a finger down your baby's throat. Lift the chin with one finger.

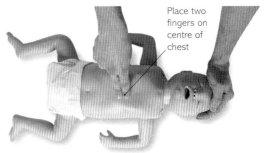

Place two fingers on centre of chest

3 **PREPARE FOR CHEST COMPRESSIONS** Place the fingertips of your first two fingers onto the centre of her chest. Take care not to press on her ribs, the lower tip of her breastbone, or the soft part of the upper abdomen.

Give five rescue breaths into mouth and nose

2 **GIVE FIVE INITIAL RESCUE BREATHS** Take a breath, put your lips over your baby's nostrils and mouth, making a complete seal, and breathe gently into her mouth and nose until you see her chest rise (about one second). Remove your lips and let the chest fall (one second). Give five initial rescue breaths at a rate of one every three seconds.

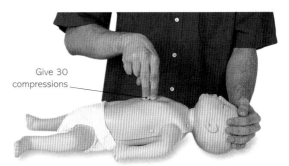

Give 30 compressions

4 **GIVE CHEST COMPRESSIONS** Press down sharply on the chest with the tips of your two fingers. Release the pressure to let the chest come back up, but don't remove your fingers from the chest. Give 30 compressions at a rate of about 100 per minute.

5 **REPEAT RESCUE BREATHS AND COMPRESSIONS** After 30 compressions, give two more rescue breaths. Then alternate 30 chest compressions with two rescue breaths for one minute. Call an ambulance (if this has not already been done); take your baby to the phone with you if necessary. Continue CPR until the ambulance arrives, your baby begins breathing normally, or you're too exhausted to continue.

# CPR for children

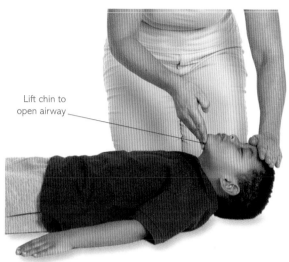

Lift chin to open airway

**1 OPEN THE AIRWAY** If your child has stopped breathing, make sure he is on a firm surface and that his head is tilted back. Check his mouth. If you can see an obvious obstruction, pick it out with your fingers, but do not poke a finger down your child's throat. Lift the chin with two fingers.

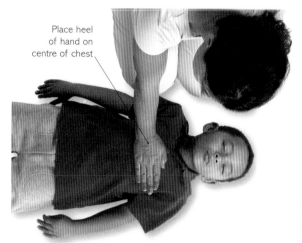

Place heel of hand on centre of chest

**3 PREPARE FOR CHEST COMPRESSIONS** Move to your child's chest. Put the heel of one hand on the centre of your child's chest. Take care not to press on his ribs, the lower tip of his breastbone, or the soft part of the upper abdomen.

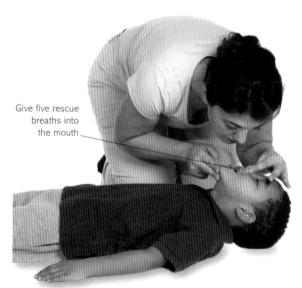

Give five rescue breaths into the mouth

**2 GIVE RESCUE BREATHS** Using your finger and thumb, pinch your child's nostrils closed. Take a breath, put your mouth over his mouth, making a complete seal, and breathe out until his chest rises (about one second). Remove your lips and let the chest fall (one second). Give five initial rescue breaths at a rate of one every three seconds.

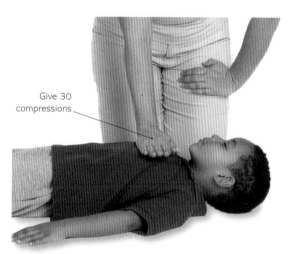

Give 30 compressions

**4 GIVE CHEST COMPRESSIONS** Press down sharply on the chest with your hand. Release the pressure to let the chest come back up, but don't remove your hand from the chest. Give 30 compressions at a rate of about 100 per minute.

**5 REPEAT RESCUE BREATHS AND COMPRESSIONS** After 30 compressions, give two more rescue breaths. Then alternate 30 chest compressions with two rescue breaths for one minute. Call an ambulance (if this has not already been done). Continue CPR until the ambulance arrives, your child begins breathing normally, or you're too exhausted to continue.

# Shock

Shock is commonly thought of as an emotional response to a distressing event, but in a medical context "shock" refers to a perilous drop in blood pressure (see below) that results in insufficient blood reaching the body tissues. If it is not dealt with quickly, the vital organs can stop functioning and the child can die.

**Symptoms** Initially, the body responds with a flow of adrenaline. This gives rise to a rapid pulse, pale, greyish-looking skin, especially around the lips, sweating, and clamminess. As shock progresses your child may be thirsty, she may feel sick, and she may even vomit. She is likely to be weak and dizzy, her breathing will be shallow and fast, and her pulse (see p.276) will be fast but irregular.

As shock progresses, the body withdraws the blood supply from the surface of the body to its core, and the oxygen supply to the brain weakens. In very severe cases, when the oxygen supply to the brain is insufficient, your child may become restless and anxious, and she may be yawning and gasping for air (known as "air hunger"). If shock is untreated eventually the child will become unconscious, and the heart will cease functioning.

**What to do** If you suspect that your child is suffering from shock call for emergency help as soon as possible.

If she's lost a lot of blood, apply direct pressure on the wound to treat the bleeding (see p.335), cool any burns (see p.336), or treat any other obvious cause of shock. Move her as little as possible, but get her to lie down with her legs raised on some pillows so that they are slightly higher than her chest. Undo any fastenings around the neck, chest, and waist. Your child will be anxious so keep

reassuring and talking to her. Fear and pain both tend to worsen shock, so keep your child as calm and as comfortable as you can. Make sure that she is warm, but not too hot. A blanket on top of her and around her head will keep her insulated. (In a very young child, wrap the blanket right round the body.) Don't warm her with a hotwater bottle.

If your child has an injury, she may need surgery when she gets to hospital, so don't give her anything to eat or drink. If she is thirsty, wet her lips with water. Keep checking her breathing and level of consciousness while waiting for help. If she becomes unconscious, see pp. 326–27.

▶ **DEALING WITH SHOCK** Lay your child down with his head on the floor and his legs higher than his chest.

Support legs in a raised position

---

# Causes of shock

Shock is due to a severe reduction in blood pressure, which can be caused in several ways.

**Severe loss of blood or body fluid** An accident may lead to profuse bleeding, either internally or externally (see p.335), resulting in a reduced volume of blood circulating in the body. The volume

of blood circulating may also be reduced by severe fluid loss, for example from serious burns or as a result of vomiting or diarrhoea.

**Allergic reaction** Your child's blood pressure will also drop rapidly if she has a severe allergic reaction to, for example a wasp or bee sting, a food, or a drug. The allergens cause blood

vessels to dilate (widen), resulting in a significant reduction in blood pressure. This type of shock is known as anaphylactic shock (see p.293).

**Other causes** Shock can also result from peritonitis (inflammation of the abdominal lining), spinal cord injury, and some types of poisoning.

# Choking

Children are very prone to choking as they have a habit of putting things in their mouths. If the airway becomes completely blocked or a child is unable to get sufficient oxygen into her lungs, she may lose consciousness. Normal breathing often returns when she loses consciousness and the muscles relax. Check her mouth for any obvious obstruction. If she doesn't begin to breathe, treat as on pp.326–27 and commence cardiopulmonary resuscitation (CPR) (pp.328–29) if necessary.

If the airway is partially blocked, the baby or child will be able to make a sound (or speak), cough, and breathe – encourage a child to cough. If her airway is completely blocked, she will be unable to speak, cough, or breathe; your child needs help and you should to act quickly. Follow the steps below.

## For a baby (under one year)

1 **GIVE BACK SLAPS** Lay your baby face down along your forearm, or on your lap, keeping her head low and supporting her head and shoulders. Slap her sharply five times between the shoulder blades.

2 **CHECK THE MOUTH** Turn your baby face up and look in her mouth. If you can see the obstruction, use a finger to hook it out, but don't put your finger down her throat.

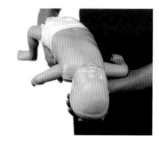

3 **GIVE CHEST THRUSTS** If back slaps haven't worked, place two fingers on the lower half of her breastbone (in the centre of her chest just below the nipples), and give five sharp downward thrusts. Check her mouth again. If the blockage hasn't cleared, repeat back slaps. mouth checks, and chest thrusts three times and then call an ambulance, taking your baby with you. Repeat steps 1–3 until help arrives.

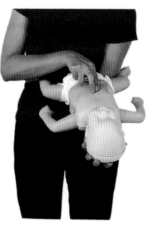

## For a child

1 **ENCOURAGE COUGHING** Reassure your child and encourage him to cough up the obstruction.

2 **GIVE BACK SLAPS** If your child can't cough, bend him forwards. Stand behind him and slap him sharply on the back between the shoulder blades using the heel of your hand. Do this up to five times.

3 **CHECK THE MOUTH** Look inside his mouth. If you can see the obstruction, pick it out, but don't put your finger down his throat.

4 **GIVE ABDOMINAL THRUSTS** If the back slaps haven't worked, place your fist between the child's navel and the bottom of his breastbone and grasp it with your other hand. Press inward and upward sharply. Repeat up to five times, then check his mouth again. Pick out any obstructions. If the child is still choking, call an ambulance and repeat back slaps, mouth checks, and abdominal thrusts until help arrives.

Place your fist thumb inward against the abdomen

# Electric shock

Your child may get an electric shock from frayed flexes or wires, light switches, or defective electrical appliances, or from touching an appliance with wet hands. It is important to warn your child about the hazards of electricity from an early age and stress that water and electricity are a dangerous combination. Replace frayed wires and put dummy plugs in any electrical sockets not in use.

**Symptoms**  In severe cases your child may lose consciousness and her heartbeat may stop. In mild cases she may have slight burns.

**What to do**  Before you go to help your child, you must break the contact between her and the source of electricity. Either switch the current off at the mains or pull the plug out. If you have to break the contact manually make sure you do it safely: push your child away using an object made of a non-conducting material, such as wood or plastic, and stand on an insulating material while you do it. If there is no alternative, drag your child away by her clothes. This can be very dangerous, however, as if you touch her skin or if her clothes are damp, you will receive an electric shock too.

Once the contact has been broken, examine your child for burns. If she has any burns, get medical advice or call an ambulance. Cool burns for ten minutes under cold water (see p.334), then cover them with a dressing.

▶ **BREAKING CONTACT** Stand on a dry insulating material and push your child's limbs away from the source (or the source from the child) with a wood or plastic object. Do not touch your child's skin with your hands.

If your child is unconscious, check breathing (see pp.326–27). Place her in the recovery position (see p.327) if she's breathing; be prepared to begin CPR if she stops (see pp.328–29).

Use a wooden object to break contact

A telephone directory makes a good insulator

# Poisoning

Common poisons include medicines; household cleaners such as bleach; weedkiller; and plants, such as berries, irises, daffodils, and fungi. You should buy medicines and chemicals in tamper-proof containers where possible, and lock them away.

**Symptoms**  A corrosive chemical often burns around the mouth and it's usual for the child to feel nauseous and vomit or have diarrhoea. With very poisonous chemicals your child may have seizures or she may even lose consciousness. There may be a poisonous substance, such as berries, pills, or a bottle containing household chemicals lying around – keep this to show to your doctor as evidence of what your child has swallowed.

**What to do**  Try to identify the poison. Call an ambulance. Keep a sample of the poison. If you can, tell the ambulance control officer how much your child took and when.

If you suspect or know that your child has swallowed a poison, don't try to induce vomiting. If the chemical is regurgitated, it will cause as much damage on the way back up as it did when it was first swallowed. Instead, give your child sips of milk or water. Traces of poison on hands or face should be washed away with water.

If your child is unconscious, open her airway and check breathing (see pp.326–27). If she is breathing, place her in the recovery position (see p.327); be prepared to begin CPR if she stops breathing (see pp.328–29).

# Drowning

A child can drown in as little as 5cm (2in) of water and so it's very important not to leave your child alone near a paddling pool, a bath, or even a bucket of water, where drowning could occur. If a drowning child is not rescued quickly, she will be asphyxiated. But make sure you don't endanger yourself in the process.

## Rescue from water

Drowning in a large body of water is a hazard to you as well as your child, so first attempt to rescue her without entering the water. Try to reach her with your hand or a pole, or throw her a lifebelt. Get into the water only if there is no alternative and it is safe for you to do so. If the water is shallow, carry your child to land by wading through the water; tow her only if she is already unconscious. While you are carrying her make sure that her head is slightly lower than her chest so that if she vomits there's less risk of her inhaling vomit.

**What to do** Take your child to the nearest warm, dry place and, without undressing her, lay her down on blankets or a coat. Check her airway and breathing (see pp.326–27), call an ambulance and, if she still breathing, put her in the recovery position (see p.327); monitor her breathing all the time. Be prepared to begin CPR if she stops breathing (see pp.328–29).

If she is conscious, replace her wet clothing and insulate her from the cold. Your child should receive medical attention as soon as possible. Call an ambulance or take her to hospital, because even if she appears to recover there is a chance that she may suffer from "secondary drowning" where the air passages swell up. Your child may also need treatment for hypothermia.

# Bleeding

Cuts and grazes (see p.340) are rarely serious and, unless infected, can be dealt with at home. Severe external bleeding or internal bleeding should be treated as emergencies as they can lead to shock and eventually loss of consciousness.

**Symptoms** External bleeding can be distressing for you and your child, and you need to act quickly to prevent shock developing. Suspect internal bleeding if your child is showing symptoms of shock (see opposite) but no obvious injury, if there is pattern bruising (bruising that follows the pattern of the object that crushed against the body), or if there's bleeding from the ears, nose, mouth, or vagina.

**What to do** Profuse bleeding should be dealt with quickly.

For internal bleeding, treat your child as for shock (see p.330).

For external bleeding, apply pressure to the wound over a clean dressing or cloth. Expose the wound if it is covered – cut away clothing if necessary. If there is an object sticking out of the wound don't remove it. Instead, apply pressure on either side of the object.

Raise the injured part above the child's heart to slow down the flow of blood to the wound, then help her to lie down, keeping the injury raised.

Cover the wound with a dressing and secure it with bandages. If blood appears through the bandage put another dressing on top. If blood comes through the second dressing, the pressure may not be in the right place, so take all the dressings off and start again. If there is an object sticking out of the wound build up padding on either side until you can bandage over the top without pushing it into the wound. Call an ambulance or take your child to hospital.

▼ **PRESS FIRMLY** Press directly on to the wound to stop the bleeding. Hold the injury up above your child's heart to help slow down the blood. Reassure her as she may be frightened.

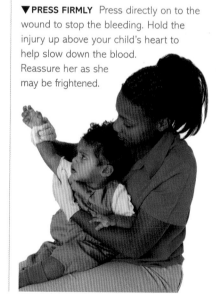

# Burns and scalds

Burns are usually described in terms of the amount of damage to the skin. Superficial burns are the least serious and can result from a minor spillage or touching a very hot surface. Partial-thickness burns are more serious and fluid-filled blisters form on the skin. Full-thickness burns are very serious since all layers of the skin are damaged, fluid loss is high due to weeping of the skin, and the nerves and muscles may be damaged. You should seek medical help for any burn on a child; either call the doctor or go to hospital.

**What to do** Hold the burn under cold running water for ten minutes. If the burn is small, you can hold it under a cold tap. If it is a large burn you can use a hose pipe or cold shower hose: lay your child down and pour water over the affected area. Unless your child's clothes are sticking to the burned area, you should gently remove them from the affected area; cut them off if necessary.

Cover the burn with a sterile dressing to protect it from bacteria. A clean plastic bag will make a good temporary dressing, if you have nothing else suitable, or you can cover it loosely with plastic kitchen film.

You may need to treat a child for shock (see p.330). If she loses consciousness, check breathing, and call an ambulance (see pp.326–27); be ready to begin CPR (see pp.328–29).

## Do not:
- Touch the affected area or attempt to burst any blisters that form.
- Apply lotion or fat to the area.
- Stick a plaster or adhesive dressing to the burn.
- Cover the burn with a "fluffy" dressing or any cloth that sheds lint.
- Remove anything that is sticking to the burn: you may cause further damage to the skin or tissue and introduce infection.
- Overcool your child if she has severe burns; this could lead to hypothermia (see p.340).

## Clothing on fire
If your child's clothing should catch fire, the first priority is to stop her moving. Any rapid movement will make the flames worse.

### What to do:
- Stop the child running around in a panic because this will fan the flames. Lie her on the floor with the burning side uppermost.
- Wrap her in a heavy woollen coat or blanket to stifle the flames. Never use nylon – it's inflammable.
- Roll her on the ground to put out the flames. Douse her with water if you have some, or with another non-flammable liquid.
- Don't try to remove clothing that's sticking to the skin.

Cool with cold running water

Cover the burned area with a clean plastic bag

▲ **COOL BURN** Stop the effect of burning by cooling the injured area. Hold the injury under cold running water for about ten miuntes.

▲ **PROTECT FROM INFECTION** Cover it with a dressing that's larger than the affected area. If you don't have a dressing, a plastic bag is ideal.

## Take care

Severe burns are dangerous: a child can rapidly go into shock (see p.330) because of the loss of body fluids. Untreated shock leads quickly to unconsciousness. The larger the area of the burn, the greater the likelihood of severe shock because of the fluid loss. If more than one-tenth of your child's body is burned she will need immediate treatment for shock; you should call an ambulance urgently.

# Head injuries

If your child bangs her head she will normally recover within minutes. If she bangs her head quite hard she may have some temporary swelling. Head injuries that should cause concern are those that cause severe bleeding or concussion. A serious condition, compression, can develop hours or days later. Watch your child for drowsiness, headaches, and nausea after a head injury.

**Symptoms** Mild symptoms resulting from a slight knock include a headache and a bump or swelling where the impact occurred. If the injury is more severe, your child may lose consciousness, possibly only for a short time (concussion). Or the symptoms of compression may follow: she may be drowsy, stunned, or dazed, and she may suffer from nausea and vomiting. Disturbances in vision and headaches are common.

If the skin of the scalp is cut, bleeding may be profuse.

**Skull fracture** Watery blood leaking from the ears or the nose may indicate a skull fracture. This must be treated as an emergency. Don't plug the ear; let any discharge drain away. Suspect a fracture if there's a depression in the scalp or the child's unconscious.

**What to do** If your child is dazed, help her to sit or lie down on the floor. Don't sit her on a chair as she could fall off. Give her a cold compress to place against the bump.

If she loses consciousness for a short time, but recovers completely, she may be concussed. Get medical advice. Monitor her level of response (for example, alert, dazed, or unresponsive) for the next few hours and note any changes.

If there is bleeding from the scalp, nose, or ears, press a clean pad firmly to the area to stop the flow. If there is a wound, don't touch it with your fingers. Once the bleeding stops, clean and dress the wound, though not if this causes the bleeding to start again. If the wound is long or jagged, take your child to the hospital to have it stitched. If the cut is small, clean it with soap

If you don't have a sterile dressing, any clean fabric pad will do

▲ SCALP WOUNDS Place a sterile dressing or clean pad on the wound and apply firm, steady pressure for ten minutes, or until the bleeding stops. The pad should be larger than the wound.

and water and place a dressing on it. If your child loses consciousness, check breathing (see pp.326–27) and call an ambulance. Place her in the recovery position if she is breathing (see p.327). Be prepared to begin CPR (see pp.328–29).

## Concussion and compression

A child who has suffered a blow to the head may show symptoms of concussion (a temporary disturbance of the brain), or of a more serious injury – compression.

**Concussion** Your child will lose consciousness for a short time and then recover completely. She may feel dizzy or nauseous and have a slight headache, and may not remember what led up to her injury. The brain is not fixed rigidly inside the skull and is free to move around a little. If there is a blow to the head, the brain can be shaken or knocked against the skull, which gives rise to the symptoms of concussion. If you suspect concussion, your child should be seen by a doctor.

**Compression** This happens when there is a build-up of pressure around the brain after an injury. It can occur several hours after a blow to the head. Monitor your child closely for 24 hours after a head injury for any deterioration in her condition. If the symptoms of concussion (above) persist or if they recur, take her to hospital.

# Seizures

The most common causes of seizures are fever (see p.281), epilepsy (see p.270), head injuries, diseases that damage the brain, and poisoning. Seizures may also occur for no apparent reason. During a seizure there's a disturbance in the normal electrical impulses in the brain, causing muscles to jerk involuntarily. It's very important not to restrain the child. Seizures usually occur on isolated occasions, but children with epilepsy have repeated attacks.

**Symptoms** Children with epilepsy may suffer from minor seizures (known as "petit mal"), which appear as a lapse of concentration or daydreaming, or from major, or tonic-clonic, seizures ("grand mal"). In a mild seizure your child may experience a tingling or twitching in some part of her body, such as her arm or leg. In a major seizure your child may cry out, then lose consciousness, and fall to the floor. Her body will become stiff and she will hold her breath. This "stiff" phase is followed by rhythmic jerking movements of the arms and legs and arching of the back. Your child has no control over her bodily functions and may empty her bladder or bowel. She may clench her teeth and bite her tongue, or froth at the mouth.

After the seizure your child's muscles will relax and she will begin to breathe normally again. When she regains consciousness she is likely to be dazed or confused and she will want to sleep. When she wakes up she won't remember the seizure.

**What to do** It's important not to intervene while your child is having a seizure. Don't hold her down. Even if you think she is at risk of biting her tongue don't try to open her mouth or put anything in it. Clear a space around your child so that she can't hurt herself, and stay with her. Call your doctor. If your child is unconscious after the seizure put her in the recovery position (see p.327). Make a note of the duration and the symptoms of your child's seizure to tell the doctor as it will help her diagnose the cause.

# Eye injuries

Any injury to the eye should be taken seriously to prevent long-term eye damage. Common injuries include a foreign object or chemical in the eye, a blow to the eye that causes bruising or a black eye, and a cut in or near the eye socket.

**Symptoms** These vary according to the type of injury, but may include bruising around the eye socket, pain, inability to open the eye fully, or spasms of the eyelid. There might be impaired vision, a bloodshot appearance, and, if the eyeball has been punctured, blood or fluid leaking from the eyeball.

**What to do** This depends on the injury, but you must act quickly. If it is a foreign object you may be able to flush it out. For anything else you may need to take your child to hospital.

■ If your child has a foreign object in her eye try to remove it using the corner of a handkerchief, or by flushing out her eye (see right). If it is embedded in the eye or is on the iris (the coloured part), tape a pad over her eye and take her to hospital.
■ For a blow to the eye place a pad soaked in cold water over the eye to minimize bruising.
■ If your child has a chemical in her eye she'll need to go to hospital, but first flush out the eye under cold running water or use a jug (see right) for about 20 minutes.

▶ **FLUSHING OUT THE EYE** Sit your child down with her head tilted in the direction of the affected eye. Pour clean water into the corner of the eye so the water flushes out the object.

■ If your child has a cut on or near her eye, tell her to try not to move her eyes. Hold a sterile pad against the wound and take her to hospital.

# Fractures and dislocations

The most common type of childhood fracture is a greenstick fracture, in which the bone bends and splits. Other types of fracture include closed fractures and open fractures (the bone breaks through the skin). A dislocation is a bone that is displaced from its joint.

**Symptoms** There is difficulty moving and a limb may look oddly shaped. There will be pain, swelling, bruising, and possibly a wound at the site of the injury. With a dislocation, your child may experience a "sickening" pain.

**What to do** Take your child to hospital or call an ambulance. Encourage your child to stay as still as possible and immobilize the joints above and below the injury by hand, or with a sling, bandages, or cushions to prevent movement. Don't let her have anything to eat or drink as she may need an anaesthetic later in hospital.

## Tying a sling

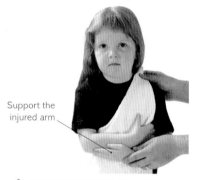

Support the injured arm

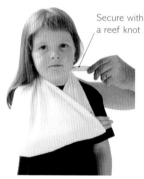

Secure with a reef knot

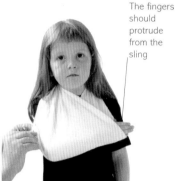

The fingers should protrude from the sling

**1 POSITION BANDAGE** Place the injured arm across the chest. Slide a triangular bandage between the injured arm and the chest. Pull one corner around the child's neck to reach the shoulder of the injured arm.

**2 TIE SLING** Bring the bottom of the bandage up over your child's forearm and tie the ends together using a reef knot. The knot should rest at the injured shoulder. Tuck in the ends of the knot to cushion it.

**3 SECURE THE CORNER** Using a safety pin, secure the loose point of the bandage at the front of the elbow. If you don't have a safety pin, tuck the point into the sling. The hand should be left exposed so you can check her fingers.

## Leg injury

Keep your child as still as possible while an ambulance is called. Don't take her to hospital yourself – she will need a stretcher. Your child could go into shock (see p.330), especially if her thigh bone is broken.

▶ **SUPPORT THE JOINTS** Sit or lie your child down, and encourage her to stay still. Hold the joints above and below the injured area. You can also support her leg with cushions or blankets. Get an adult to call an ambulance.

Support joints above and below the injury

## Back injury

If you suspect that your child has fractured her back or neck, call an ambulance. There may be damage to the delicate spinal cord carried by the vertebrae. Don't move your child – wait for the ambulance – and don't let her move her head. If the spinal cord is injured, your child may experience burning, tingling, or a loss of sensation in her limbs.

# Heatstroke

When the body overheats as a result of exposure to extreme heat the temperature control mechanism in the brain fails and the sweat glands stop working. Your child can't lower her temperature in the adult way. This is a relatively common occurrence among children who go out in hot sun before they acclimatize to it. Your child's temperature may rise above 40°C (104°F) and, in extreme cases, she may lose consciousness and stop breathing.

**Symptoms** Although the skin looks flushed and feels hot, it remains dry. Your child will develop a sudden headache, seem drowsy and lethargic, and she may have a full strong pulse rate. If untreated, she may become confused, start to lose consciousness, and eventually stop breathing.

**What to do** Take your child's clothes off and lay her down in a cool place.

Call an ambulance if your child's temperature is as high as 40°C (104°F). Sponge her with tepid water or wrap her in a cool wet sheet. Place a covered ice pack on her forehead, give her cool drinks, and direct a fan toward her body. Monitor her pulse rate and check her temperature every minute until it lowers to 37.2°C (99°F), then stop cooling, but continue to monitor her temperature (see p.278).

If she loses consciousness you should check her breathing (see p.326–27). Place her in the recovery position if she is breathing (see p.327). Be prepared to begin CPR (see pp.328–29) if necessary if she stops breathing.

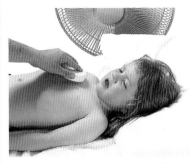

▲**LOWERING BODY TEMPERATURE** Take your child out of the sun, and sponge her with tepid water or direct a fan on to her skin.

# Hypothermia

If your child gets cold as a result of being exposed to cold, wet, and windy weather, a near-drowning, or simply being in a room that is too cold, she may suffer from hypothermia. Clinically, hypothermia is defined as a body temperature of below 35°C (95°F). Deep hypothermia occurs when the body temperature drops to below 26°C (79°F) and a child may lose consciousness. If hypothermia is not treated it can be fatal since the heart, liver, lungs, and intestines slow down and may cease functioning.

**Symptoms** Your child may be shivering and her skin will feel cold and dry. She may look pale and blue (although babies may look pink) and her breathing may be slow and shallow. She will be lethargic and there might be behavioural signs, such as apathy, confusion, and quietness. In severe cases, your child's breathing may be shallow and her pulse will be weak. She may start to lose consciousness.

**What to do** Take off any wet clothing, wrap your child in warm, dry clothes and blankets. Call a doctor. Hold a young child close to your body. Older children can be warmed up with a warm bath and warm sweet drinks.

Monitor your child's temperature constantly with a thermometer or by feeling her skin. If your attempts to warm her up are not working, or if she loses consciousness, call an ambulance.

Stay with your child until the doctor arrives or her temperature is back to normal. Never put a direct source of heat, such as a hot water bottle, on your child's skin.

Wrap your child up well

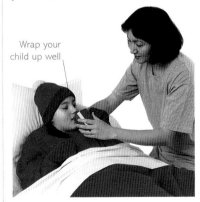

▲**REWARM GRADUALLY** Wrap your child in warm dry clothes (even gloves and a hat) and blankets. Help her to drink a warm sweet drink like hot chocolate.

# Everyday first aid

As your child grows up she will inevitably experience some commonplace accidents, such as cuts, bruises, blisters, bites, and stings. Most of the time these accidents are not serious and can be treated at home with comfort and some simple first aid measures.

## Animal bites

Animal bites can happen if your child is teasing or playing boisterously with a domestic pet, usually a dog or a cat. Although being bitten can be traumatic for your child, bites are not usually serious. The main danger is that if the animal bites deep into the flesh, bacteria will be lodged in the wound, making your child vulnerable to infection. If she is bitten by a dog or other animal while you are travelling abroad seek medical treatment at once, since anti-rabies injections may be needed.

The first thing you should do is reassure your child, as she will probably be quite frightened. If she was bitten because she was teasing the animal you should explain this to her and stress that it is an isolated incident.

**What to do** Wash the wound thoroughly with warm water and cover the bite with a dressing. If the bleeding is severe, try to control it with direct pressure over a clean pad and raise the wounded part of the body (see p.333). Cover the wound with a dressing held in place with a bandage and take your child to hospital. She may need a tetanus immunization (see p.283) if it's not up-to-date.

## Snake and spider bites

The adder is the only venomous snake in the UK and its bite is rarely fatal. Your child may be bitten by more venomous creatures while you are abroad. Depending on the snake or spider, the symptoms of a bite can include puncture marks in the skin, pain, redness, and swelling around the bite, and, in very severe cases, impaired breathing, sweating, vomiting, and impaired vision.

**What to do** Keep your child calm. Help him to lie down with his chest slightly higher than the injured area. Wash the area of the bite with water, and cover it with a dressing. Apply a broad pressure bandage to the entire length of the limb above the injury and immobilize it with more bandages. Take your child to hospital. Make a note of the snake's or spider's appearance and tell the medical team so that anti-venin can be given.

## Insect bites and stings

Stings and insect bites are not usually serious unless there is an allergic reaction (see p.293). Stings in the mouth or throat are serious, as the swelling they cause can obstruct the airway. Stinging insects include bees, wasps, and hornets; biting insects include fleas, mosquitoes, and ticks.

**Symptoms** A sting is felt as a sudden, sharp pain and appears as a raised, white area on an inflamed patch of skin. A bite is less painful and normally causes mild discomfort and inflammation. Symptoms of an allergic reaction include swelling of the face and neck, puffy eyes, impaired breathing, red blotchy skin, wheezing, and gasping.

**What to do** Apply a cold compress and, later, calamine lotion to the bite or sting to relieve discomfort. If you can see the sting sticking out of your child's flesh, scrape it off (see below). Treat an allergic reaction as an emergency; call an ambulance.

If your child is bitten by fleas, have your family pet treated and your house disinfected. Mosquito bites can be avoided with insect repellent. When abroad, always use malaria prophylaxis medicine. Tick bites are painless, but can cause infection and disease, so you should seek medical treatment.

If your child is stung in the mouth give her an ice cube to suck (if over one year old) and call an ambulance.

Gently scrape off protruding sting with the edge of a card

▶ **REMOVING A STING**
If the sting is still in the skin, remove it by scraping it off with a credit card. Then put a cold compress over the area.

## Jellyfish stings

If your child steps on a jellyfish at the beach she may experience a severe local reaction – jellyfish have stinging cells that discharge venom when touched. The severity depends on the type of jellyfish. Those in the UK are not very toxic and are unlikely to produce severe symptoms – just a rash that may itch or be slightly painful. Rare jellyfish found overseas are more poisonous, and in extreme cases can cause vomiting, shock, breathing difficulties, and unconsciousness, and can lead to death.

**What to do** The stinging cells that stick to your child's skin release their poison gradually as they burst. You can help by inactivating the cells or preventing them from bursting. Pouring alcohol or vinegar over the cells will do this, and any fine powder, like talcum powder, will make the cells stick together. If your child experiences a severe reaction to any sting or wound caused by a marine creature take her to hospital.

## Blisters

When the skin is burned or subjected to pressure or friction a blister may form as a protective cushion. Blisters are bubbles of skin with tissue fluid underneath. They are common on the heels of the feet if your child's shoes don't fit correctly or if she wears shoes without socks.

Blisters are not usually serious unless they are the result of bad sunburn (see p.291), they burst and become infected, or are very large and painful, in which case you should consult your doctor.

**What to do** Don't ever burst a blister. In a day or two new skin will form underneath the blister, the tissue fluid will be reabsorbed, and the blistered skin will dry and peel off. To aid this healing process you should cover the blister with a clean dressing (not a plaster, since this can burst the blister when you peel it off) and keep it dry. If your child's blister is very large your doctor may decide to burst it.

## Cuts and grazes

As long as a cut is superficial and is clean and not likely to become infected (this is a risk with cuts from fingernails, plants, or animals), it should not require treatment. A graze is simply an abrasion of the skin that leaves the surface raw and tender. A cut that bleeds profusely can lead to shock (see p.332) so treat it as an emergency. A very jagged cut may require stitches, and with a deep or dirty cut there is a risk of tetanus (see p.283).

**What to do** Run cold water over the wounded area. Using a gauze pad or a very soft brush, gently wash the graze with soap and water. Wipe away from the wound and use a clean piece of gauze for each wipe. Dry by patting with a clean tissue and cover with a sterile dressing or a plaster. If your child has an incision wound where the

▲ **CLEAN GRAZE** Rinse the injury to wash off any dirt. Gently pat the area dry using gauze pads. Cover with a plaster but make sure the dressing pad is larger than the graze.

cut has two straight edges you can hold them together using skin-closure tape. If the wound is dirty or deep, there is a risk of infection developing and you should take your child to hospital as she may need a tetanus injection (see p.283).

If a cut bleeds profusely you should take your child to hospital straight away, as she may need stitches. Before she gets to hospital, control the bleedng by applying direct pressure to the wound using a sterile dressing or clean pad (or your hand if you have nothing suitable) and make sure that the wounded part of the body is raised to slow the flow of blood. Cover the pad with a bandage (see p.333).

## Splinters

Small shards of wood, glass, or metal, or a thorn or spine from a plant, can easily become embedded in your child's skin, particularly if she is playing outside. Unless splinters are embedded in the flesh or they prove too painful to remove, they can be dealt with very easily at home.

**What to do** First try to find out from your child what kind of splinter it is. If it is glass, you should not try to remove it yourself as you could cut your child, or it could break. Call your doctor.

If the splinter is not glass, look for the end of the splinter. Take a pair of sterilized tweezers (you can sterilize them by holding them over a flame; then let them cool) and gently pull the protruding end of the splinter out at the same angle it entered. Squeeze the area to make it bleed a little, since this will help clean it. When you have removed the splinter, clean the skin with soap and water.

If the splinter is completely embedded in your child's skin it may

► **REMOVING A SPLINTER** If the end of the splinter is visible, use sterilized tweezers to pull it out gently. Don't try to remove a glass splinter yourself, as it could break off in the skin.

Pull the splinter out in the same direction it went in

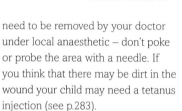

need to be removed by your doctor under local anaesthetic – don't poke or probe the area with a needle. If you think that there may be dirt in the wound your child may need a tetanus injection (see p.283).

## Bruises

Active children often get bruises from falls and knocks, and they are rarely serious; they usually take ten to 14 days to disappear completely.

**What to do** Minor bruises need no treatment, just a cuddle if your child is upset. If the bruise is large, apply a cold compress for half an hour or so to contain the bruising. Consult your doctor immediately if pain on the site of a bruise gets worse after 24 hours (this could indicate a fracture) or if your child repeatedly has bruises with no apparent cause (this could indicate a serious condition).

## Crushed fingers

This is a fairly common accident in very young children who don't understand how doors, windows, and drawers operate. A crush injury can be serious so it's vital to release the trapped hand as quickly as possible.

**What to do** If the skin is not broken, then once the finger or fingers have been released, hold your child's hand

under cold running water or hold a bag of crushed ice or frozen peas against it. When the pain has subsided a little, wrap the hand in a bandage. If the crush is severe and there is internal or external bleeding or swelling, call an ambulance. There could also be an underlying fracture.

## Foreign object in the ear

The most common objects for children to push into their ears are small beads, bits of crayon, and small components from construction toys. Occasionally an insect can fly into the ear, or cotton wool can be left behind after cleaning. A foreign object in the ear may cause temporary deafness, it may result in an ear infection, and, if left untreated, it may damage the eardrum.

**What to do** If your child has an insect in her ear canal, lay her on her side with the affected ear uppermost and pour tepid water from a jug into the ear. The insect should float out.

Any other type of foreign object needs medical treatment. If you attempt to remove it yourself you may cause more damage. Your doctor can remove it and treat any resulting infection or damage to the skin. You can reduce the risk of foreign objects in the ear by making sure your child isn't given toys with small parts, particularly if she's under three.

## Foreign object in the nose

If your child has pushed something into her nose you may not notice, though she will probably complain of pain. Occasionally it takes several days for symptoms to become apparent. Your child might develop a blood-stained discharge from the nose, she may find it difficult to breathe, and there may be swelling, inflammation, and bruising around the bridge of the nose. A foreign object in the nose is rarely serious, but there is a risk that your child could inhale the object down into her lungs, so it does require hospital treatment.

**What to do** Don't try to remove the object, as you could cause your child an injury, or push the object in further. Keep her calm, get her to breathe through her mouth, and take her straight to hospital.

At hospital a doctor will remove the foreign object using a pair of forceps; if your child is very young she may need a general anaesthetic beforehand.

## Penis caught in zip

This can happen if your child is careless when doing up his zip. The tip of the penis gets caught between the teeth of the zip, and, although there should be no long-term damage, it is very painful.

**What to do** You should not attempt to undo the zip. Instead, take your child to hospital, and relieve the pain in the meantime by placing wrapped ice cubes over the zip and penis. A doctor will undo the zip after giving your child a local anaesthetic. Aftercare includes giving paracetamol elixir to relieve pain. Your child should pour warm water over his penis as he urinates, to dilute the urine and prevent stinging.

# Useful addresses

## Postnatal support

**ASSOCIATION OF BREASTFEEDING MOTHERS**
PO Box 207
Bridgwater, Somerset
TA6 7YT
Tel: 08444 122 949
(counselling hotline)
www.abm.me.uk

**FPA (FORMERLY THE FAMILY PLANNING ASSOCIATION)**
50 Featherstone street
London EC1Y 8QU
Tel: 020 7608 5240
www.fpa.org.uk

**MAMA (MEET A MUM ASSOCIATION)**
376 Bideford Green,
Linslade,
Leighton Buzzard,
LU7 2TY
Tel: +44 0845 120 3746
(helpline)
www.mama.co.uk
*Support for new mothers and mothers to be.*

**NATIONAL CHILDBIRTH TRUST ALEXANDRA HOUSE**
Oldham Terrace
Acton, London
W3 6NH
Tel: 0870 444 8708
(Breast feeding)
www.nctpregnancyand
babycare.com

## Parents' groups

**BLISS**
68 South Lambeth Road
London
SW8 1RL
Tel: 020 7378 1122
0500 618 140 (helpline)
www.bliss.org.uk

**CRY-SIS**
BM Cry-sis
London WC1N 3XX
Helpline: 08451 228 669
www.cry-sis.org.uk
*Help for parents with special care babies.*

**FOUNDATION FOR THE STUDY OF INFANT DEATH**
Artillery House
11–19 Artillery Row
London SW1P 1RT
Tel: 020 7222 8001
020 7233 2090 (helpline)
www.fsid.org.uk

**GINGERBREAD**
255 Kentish Town Road,
London, NW5 2LX
Tel: 0800 018 5026
www.gingerbread.org.uk
*Help and advice for one-parent families.*

**MULTIPLE BIRTHS FOUNDATION**
Hammersmith House,
Level 4, Queen Charlotte's
& Chelsea Hospital,
Du Cane Road,
London W12 0HS
Tel: 020 8383 3519
www.multiplebirths.org.uk

**ONE PARENT FAMILIES**
255 Kentish Town Road
London NW5 2LX
Tel: 020 7428 5400
Helpline: 0800 018 5026
www.oneparentfamilies.org.uk

**PARENTLINE PLUS**
520 Highgate Studios
53–79 Highgate Road
London NW5 1TL
Tel: 0808 800 2222
www.parentlineplus.org.uk

**TAMBA (TWINS AND MULTIPLE BIRTHS ASSOCIATION)**
2 The Willows
Gardner Road
Guildford, Surrey
GU1 4PG
Tel: 01483 304 442
www.tamba.org.uk

**VEGETARIAN SOCIETY**
Parkdale, Dunham Road
Altrincham, Cheshire
WA14 4QG
Tel: 0161 925 2000
www.vegsoc.org

## Care and education

**BRITISH ASSOCIATION FOR EARLY CHILDHOOD EDUCATION**
136 Cavell Street,
London E1 2JA
Tel: 020 7539 5400
www.early-education.org.uk

**NATIONAL CHILDMINDING ASSOCIATION**
www.ncma.org.uk

**PRESCHOOL LEARNING ALLIANCE**
The Fitzpatrick Building
188 York Way
London
N7 9AD
Tel: 020 7697 2500
www.pre-school.org.uk

## First aid and safety

**BRITISH RED CROSS**
44 Moorfields
London
EC2Y 9AL
Tel: 0844 871 11 11
www.redcross.org.uk

**CHILD ACCIDENT PREVENTION TRUST**
4th Floor, Cloister Court
22–26 Farringdon Lane
London
EC1R 3AJ
Tel: 020 7608 3828
www.capt.org.uk

**ROYAL SOCIETY FOR THE PREVENTION OF ACCIDENTS (ROSPA)**
RoSPA House,
Edgbaston Park
353 Bristol Road,
Edgbaston,
Birmingham B5 7ST
Tel: 0121 248 2000
www.rospa.co.uk

**ST ANDREW'S AMBULANCE ASSOCIATION**
St Andrew's House
48 Milton Street
Glasgow G4 0HR
Tel: 0141 332 4031
www.firstaid.org.uk

**ST JOHN AMBULANCE**
27 St John's Lane
London
EC1M 4BU
Tel: 08700 10 49 50
www.sja.org.uk

## Special needs

**ADDISS (NATIONAL ATTENTION DEFICIT DISORDER INFORMATION AND SERVICES)**
ADDISS
PO Box 340
Edgware, Middlesex
HA8 9HL
Tel: 020 8952 2800
www.addiss.co.uk
*For information and support*

**AFASIC**
2nd Floor
50–52 Great Sutton Street
London
EC1V 0DJ
Tel: 020 7490 9410
Helpline: 0845 355 5577
www.afasic.org.uk

**ASSOCIATION FOR SPINA
BIFIDA AND HYDROCEPHALUS
(ASBAH)**
42 Park Road
Peterborough
PE1 2UQ
Tel: 0845 450 7755
www.asbah.org

**ASTHMA UK**
Summit House,
70 Wilson Street
London EC2A 2DB
Tel: 020 7786 4900
www.asthma.org.uk

**BRITISH DYSLEXIA
ASSOCIATION**
98 London Road
Reading
RG1 5AU
Tel: 0118 966 2677
Helpline: 0118 966 8271
www.bdadyslexia.org.uk

**BRITISH STAMMERING
ASSOCIATION**
15 Old Ford Road
London E2 9PJ
Tel: 020 8983 1003
www.stammering.org

**COELIAC UK**
PO Box 220
High Wycombe
Bucks HP11 2HY
Tel: 01494 437 278
Helpline: 0870 444 8804
www.coeliac.co.uk

**CONTACT A FAMILY**
209–211 City Road
London
EC1V 1JN
Tel: 020 7608 9700
www.cafamily.org.uk
*Advice and support for
parents whose children
have special needs.*

**CYSTIC FIBROSIS TRUST**
11 London Road
Bromley, Kent BR1 1BY
Tel: 020 8464 7211
www.cftrust.org.uk

**DIABETES UK**
10 Parkway
London NW1 7AA
Tel: 020 7424 1000
www.diabetes.org.uk

**DOWN'S SYNDROME
ASSOCIATION**
Langdon Down Centre
2a Langdon Park
Teddington
TW11 9PS
Tel: 0845 230 0372
www.downs-syndrome.org.uk

**DYSPRAXIA FOUNDATION**
8 West Alley
Hitchin, Hertfordshire
SG5 1EG
Tel: 01462 455016
Helpline: 01462 454 986
www.dyspraxiafoundation.
org.uk

**EPILEPSY ACTION**
New Anstey House,
Gate Way Drive
Yeadon, Leeds
LS19 7XY
Tel: 0113 210 8800
Helpline: 0808 800 5050
www.epilepsy.org.uk

**HYPERACTIVE CHILDREN'S
SUPPORT GROUP**
71 Whyke Lane,
Chichester
West Sussex PO19 7PD
Tel: 01243 539966
www.hacsg.org.uk

**I CAN**
I CAN
8 Wakley Street
London
EC1V 7QE
Tel: 0845 225 4071
www.ican.org.uk
*For children with language
difficulties.*

**MENCAP**
123 Golden Lane
London EC1Y 0RT
Tel: 020 7454 0454
www.mencap.org.uk
*For people with learning
disabilities.*

**MULTIPLE SCLEROSIS
NATIONAL THERAPY CENTRES**
PO Box 126, Whitchurch
SY14 7WL
www.ms-selfhelp.org
*Website provides information
about local advice centres.*

**MUSCULAR DYSTROPHY
CAMPAIGN**
61 Southwark Street
London SE1 0HL
Tel: 020 7803 4800
www.muscular-dystrophy.org

**NATIONAL ASSOCIATION FOR
GIFTED CHILDREN (NAGC)**
Suite 14,' Challenge House
Sherwood Drive, Bletchley
Milton Keynes MK3 6DP
Tel: 0845 450 0221
www.nagcbritain.org.uk

**NATIONAL AUTISTIC SOCIETY**
393 City Road
London EC1V 1NG
Tel: 020 7833 2299
www.nas.org.uk

**NATIONAL DEAF
CHILDREN'S SOCIETY**
15 Dufferin Street
London EC1Y 8UR
Tel: 020 7490 8656
Helpline: 0808 800 8880
www.ndcs.org.uk

**NATIONAL ECZEMA SOCIETY**
Hill House, Highgate Hill
London N19 5NA
Tel: 020 7281 3553
Helpline: 0870 241 3604
www.eczema.org

**RNIB (ROYAL NATIONAL
INSTITUTE FOR THE BLIND)**
105 Judd Street
London WC1H 9NE
Tel: 020 7388 1266
Helpline: 0845 766 9999
www.rnib.org.uk

**SCOPE**
PO Box 833
Milton Keynes MK12 5NY
Tel: 020 7619 7100
Helpline: 0808 800 3333
(Mon–Fri 9am–9pm;
Sat–Sun 2–6pm)
www.scope.org.uk

**SICKLE CELL SOCIETY**
54 Station Road
London NW10 4UA
Tel: 020 8961 7795
www.sicklecellsociety.org

# Index

# Acknowledgments

**Redsign and styling** Nicola Rodway
**Editorial assistance** Corinne Roberts
**Proofreader** Alyson Silverwood
**Index** Hilary Bird

**Models for new photography** Zebedi Casajuana, Mei Clarke,
Mia Clarke, Ryoko Clarke, Talia Cook, Liam Curran, Jeremy Davis,
Kevin Davis, Louise Graham, Maximilian Graham, Jessica Hardy,
Ben Isaacs, Jacob Lewis, Hannah Lewis, Alizée Looby, Stephen
Looby, Charlie Morgan, Elizabeth Peacock, Arya Stapleton-Dhillon
(back jacket), Raphy Timms-Hardy, Elin Wennerland

**Illustrations** Amanda Williams, David Bootle, Debbie Maizels,
Philip Wilson

**Additional photography** Ranald Mackechnie; Dave King; David
Murray; Ray Moller; Stephen Oliver; Susanna Price; Jules Selmes

**Picture library:** Romaine Werblow, Emma Sheppard

**Picture research:** Jenny Baskaya, Martin Copland

The publisher would like to thank the following for their kind
permission to reproduce their photographs:

(Key: a-above; b-below/bottom; c-centre; l-left; r-right; t-top)

**Alamy Images:** Bubbles Photolibrary 290; D. Hurst 123;
PHOTOTAKE Inc. 273, 286t; Picture Partners 101l; Stefan
Sollfors 296; **Courtesy of Avent Ltd:** 45b; **Getty Images:**
Christopher Bissell 311; Image Source Black 169; Vincent Oliver
27; Mel Yates 246; **Mother & Baby Picture Library:** 16, 64r,
135tl, 212, 239, 302l; **PunchStock:** BananaStock 240; Brand X
Pictures 278bc; **Science Photo Library:** Gustoimages 25; Petit
Format 13; Antonia Reeve 269; Saturn Stills 266l; Horacio
Sormani 48; Ron Sutherland 15b

**Jacket images:** Front and spine: **Corbis:** John Fortunato
Photography. Back: Caroline Irby for DK; Author portrait Carolyn
Djanogly for DK

All other images © Dorling Kindersley
For further information see: www.dkimages.com